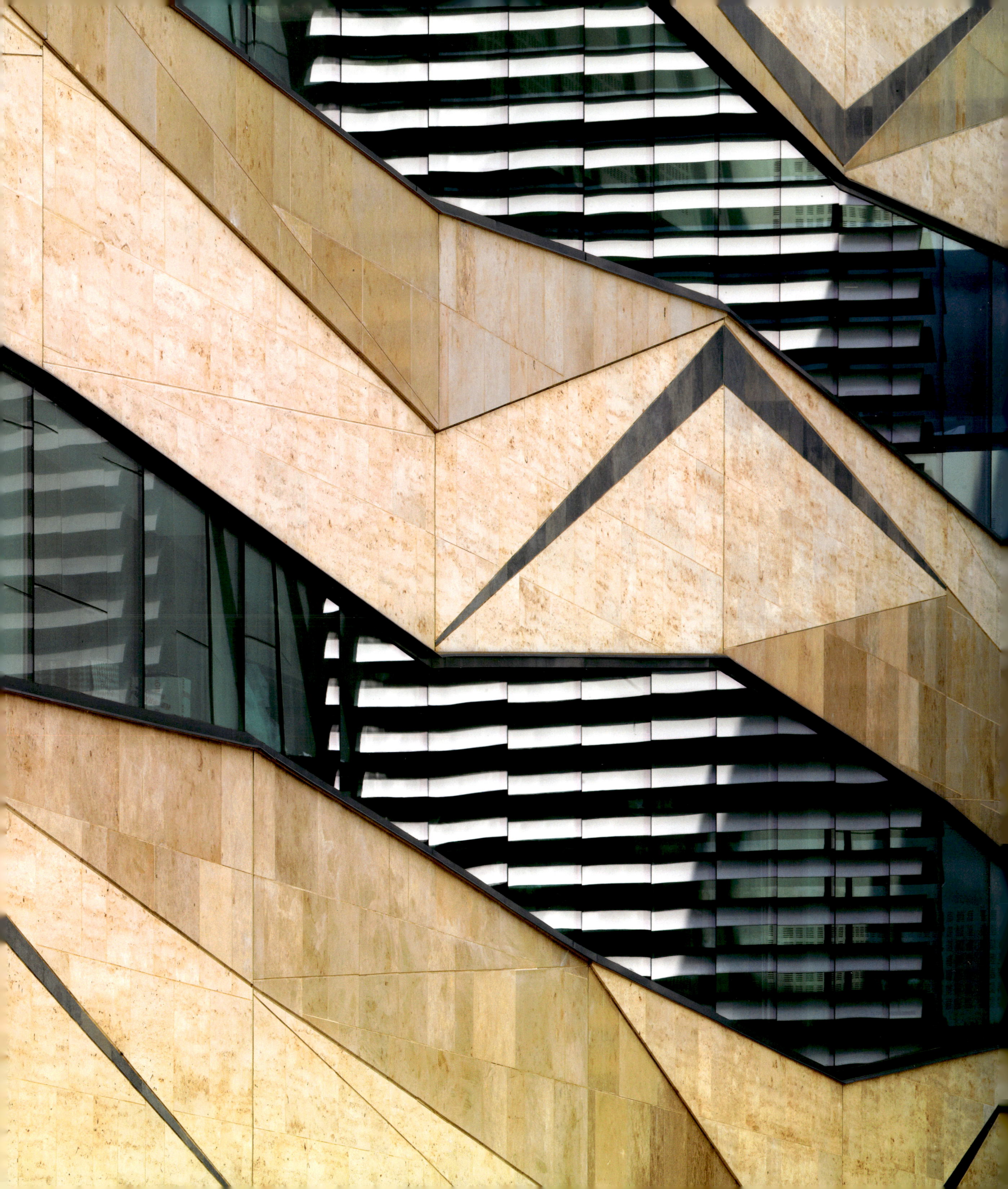

Wilkinson Eyre Architects | Works

Emma Keyte | Introduction by Jay Merrick

With 559 illustrations, 446 in colour

Pages 1–10:
Davies Alpine House, Royal Botanic Gardens, Kew, UK
(see page 51)
Liver Street Car Park, Liverpool, UK (see page 194)
Arena and Convention Centre, Liverpool, UK (see page 140)
10 Brock Street, London, UK (see page 186)
Splashpoint, Worthing, UK (see page 130)
Arts Two, Queen Mary, University of London, UK
(artwork by Jacqueline Poncelet; see page 223)
The Forum, University of Exeter, UK
(artwork by Alexander Beleschenko; see page 43)
Splashpoint, Worthing, UK (as above)
Department of Earth Sciences, University of Oxford, UK
(see page 208)
25 Great Pulteney Street, London, UK (see page 218)

Page 14:
Mathematics Building, Queen Mary, University of London, UK
(see page 223)

Pages 282, 284–5 and 287:
Guangzhou International Finance Centre, China (see page 94)
Gardens by the Bay, Singapore (see page 28)
Mary Rose Museum, Portsmouth, UK (see page 155)

First published in the United Kingdom in 2014 by
Thames & Hudson Ltd, 181A High Holborn, London WC1V 7QX

Text, design and layouts © 2014 Wilkinson Eyre Architects
Illustrations © the copyright holders; see page 283

All Rights Reserved. No part of this publication may be reproduced
or transmitted in any form or by any means, electronic or mechanical,
including photocopy, recording or any other information storage and
retrieval system, without prior permission in writing from
the publisher.

British Library Cataloguing-in-Publication Data
A catalogue record for this book is available from the British Library

ISBN 978-0-500-34298-5

Printed and bound in China by Everbest Printing Co. Ltd

To find out about all our publications, please visit
www.thamesandhudson.com. There you can subscribe to our
e-newsletter, browse or download our current catalogue, and
buy any titles that are in print.

Contents

Introduction 15
Jay Merrick

Landscape
Gardens by the Bay, Singapore 28
The Forum, University of Exeter, UK 43
Royal Botanic Gardens, Kew, UK 51
Living Bridge, University of Limerick, Ireland 59
Schools for the Future, UK 64
Maggie's Centre, Oxford, UK 77

Sky
Emirates Air Line, London, UK 84
20 Blackfriars Road, London, UK 90
Guangzhou International Finance Centre, China 94
Twin Sails Bridge, Poole, UK 107
From Landscape to Portrait, London, UK 110
London 2012 Basketball Arena, UK 113
King's Cross Gasholders, London, UK 122

Water
Splashpoint, Worthing, UK 130
Arena and Convention Centre, Liverpool, UK 140
Peace Bridge, Derry, UK 151
Media City Footbridge, Salford, UK 152
Mary Rose Museum, Portsmouth, UK 155
The Crystal, London, UK 165
Crown Hotel, Sydney, Australia 172

City
10 Brock Street, London, UK 186
Paradise Street Interchange, Liverpool, UK 194
Ceramics Galleries Bridge, London, UK 200
Museum of London, UK 203
Department of Earth Sciences, University of Oxford, UK 208
25 Great Pulteney Street, London, UK 218
Queen Mary, University of London, UK 223
New Bodleian (Weston) Library, Oxford, UK 231
Battersea Power Station, London, UK 241

Portfolio and Practice 253
Index 280
Picture credits 283
Acknowledgments 286

Introduction
Jay Merrick

This book marks Wilkinson Eyre Architects' three decades of increasingly successful practice in Britain, the Far East and Europe. Every modernist practice speaks of innovative design; very few have demonstrated it, unmistakably, from the outset; fewer still are capable of reinventing form, structure and space over and over again. As these pages went to press, Wilkinson Eyre's stream of architectural reinventions included designs for the £750 million transformation of Sir Giles Gilbert Scott's iconic Battersea Power Station in London, the organically sculpted A$1 billion Crown Hotel skyscraper in Sydney, and a cable-car system in Toulouse.

Wilkinson Eyre's style of architecture has often been referred to as High Tech, but the term straightjackets the remarkable breadth of its work. From its inception, this has been a modernist practice that truly explores design ideas, and which sees architecture as an indivisible amalgam of art, science and engineering. This dynamic braid is, as it were, hard-wired into the practice's approach to design; and it is its deeply inquisitive and artful approach to geometry, structure, space and human activity that gives its architecture its unique sense of invention.

The practice's original *mise en scène* was dryly historic, and not obviously inspiring: a rather plain room in a Victorian school building in Bowling Green Lane, London. But it was in this modest space – now the conference room at Zaha Hadid's practice – that Chris Wilkinson, Jim Eyre and a handful of young architects designed two schemes that did more than merely announce a notable arrival on the British architectural scene. Chris Wilkinson Architects' designs for Stratford Market Depot in 1991, and Stratford Regional Station three years later, immediately identified it as a genuine architectural innovator – 'a serious player', to use the American phrase.

The chronology of the practice's early development is a significant factor in its ascent to the heights of the international design elite. Chris Wilkinson set up in practice in 1983, supported by Chris Perry and Matthew Priestman. Jim Eyre joined the team in 1986. That first studio designed or project-managed such schemes as the IBM Travelling Technology Exhibition for Renzo Piano (1984), a masterplan proposal for the Royal Docks in London (1984) and an Yves Saint Laurent shop in London's Sloane Street (1986).

Then, from 1987 to 1998, the practice operated as a partnership between Chris Wilkinson and Jim Eyre, after which, in 1999, it became Wilkinson Eyre Architects. Three of Wilkinson Eyre's current directors – Paul Baker, Oliver Tyler and Stafford Critchlow – joined the practice between 1990 and 1992. Two more, Dominic Bettison and Sebastien Ricard, followed in 1994 and 1997, respectively; the newest director, Giles Martin, joined in 2004. This director-level continuity has given the practice its outstanding bedrock of experience in innovative design.

For this whole period, the two principals worked together on projects, and it is only in recent years that the rapid growth of Wilkinson Eyre to more than 150 staff has led the founders to lead and develop design schemes separately. Now, the eight directors work on projects individually, or together, sharing skills and experience to ensure quality and continuity of design. It is not enough for a practice to contain good, or even brilliant, architects; the particular synergies of talent are crucial, and Chris Wilkinson and Jim Eyre seem to sense what the mix should be. Rather, it is the ability

This page
Above: Site photograph of Battersea Power Station, London
Left: Concept sketch for Crown Hotel, Sydney

Opposite
Top: Ludwig Mies van der Rohe, *Project for Concert Hall*, 1942, The Museum of Modern Art, New York
Centre: Galerie des Machines, Paris
Bottom, left: St Pancras station, London, 1910
Bottom, right: Crystal Palace, London, 1930s

and confidence to cooperate, and work with other talented people and other disciplines, that creates truly integrated design – and there is no doubt that the practice is as comfortable exploring complex ideas with an environmental engineer as with an artist.

Debate over design concepts within the practice is often heated, but only as part of a long-established instinct to reach the most innovative solutions possible; and these might, depending on the brief, be purely solution-based, or generated by a more creative use of narrative or imagery. The Sydney tower, for example, was conceived as an inhabited artwork.

But where did the practice's design tenets originate? Predictably, Wilkinson's design DNA includes Ludwig Mies van der Rohe's concept of 'universal space'; Joseph Paxton's Crystal Palace, constructed in London's Hyde Park to house the Great Exhibition of 1851; William Barlow and Rowland Ordish's 73-metre-wide single-span roof over St Pancras station in London, completed in 1868; and Paul Cottancin and Ferdinand Dutert's even bigger Galerie des Machines, a pavilion built for the Exposition Universelle in Paris in 1889.

There is, however, a crucial extra ingredient: although wedded to the science of architecture, Wilkinson approaches his work with an artistic, perhaps even metaphysical sensibility. He believes that mankind has a psychological need to experience big, man-made spaces, and that even gigantic malls and sports stadia have the potential to impart these uplifting qualities.

Eyre's take on design raises other engrossing ideas. He reverses the most-quoted modernist dictum, for example, and says that function may follow form if the geometry of a design is sophisticated enough to determine structure and space effectively. His love of

Introduction | Jay Merrick   17

 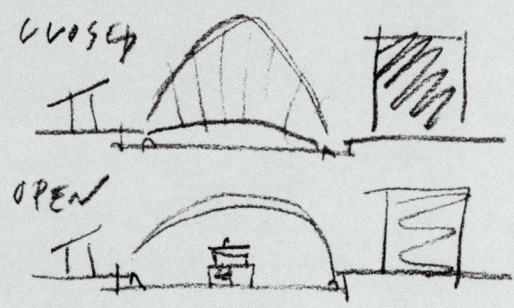

geometry reflects a profound interest in the creation of lines of visual movement in buildings and structures where there is no conceptual difference between engineering and architecture. It is hardly surprising that he speaks unashamedly about creating architecture that generates a sense of wonder.

That sense of wonder, says Wilkinson, 'requires a more instinctive approach, rather than just cleverness. We are not committed to a fixed set of ideas or materials. We are committed to the brief and context.' And, he adds, with deceptive simplicity, 'The really important thing in design is not to hold back. You have to immerse yourself in the process until the solution becomes clear.'

Most architects would say the same. But few of them actually put themselves in the risky position of attempting designs based partly on the unknown. We invariably see this confrontation between physical and conceptual adventure in the most brilliant modern architecture, in buildings as different as Auguste and Gustave Perret's *béton gracieux* Notre Dame du Raincy (1923), a church on the outskirts of Paris, and Norman Foster's darkly amoebic, environmentally advanced Willis Faber & Dumas Headquarters (1975) in the Suffolk town of Ipswich.

Wilkinson Eyre shares this instinct to identify, grasp and then reshape the apparent technical and formal cutting edge of architectural design. It is the ability to advance meaningfully the possibilities of form, structure and a sense of space and place that separates the profession's modernist leaders from its regiment of skilled copyists. In 2007 the eminent architectural commentator Peter Davey declared that the practice exhibited 'continual inventiveness, no house style, no formal tropes'.

Going for it is one thing; going for it and getting a design outstandingly right is quite another. It is significant that every time Wilkinson Eyre's designers have entered a new design territory, they have produced something architecturally special, and highly individual. This ability is the defining characteristic of much of the practice's work, and it sets them apart. 'I can go to some people in our office with the germ of an idea, go off, and it comes back better', says Jim Eyre. 'This is very precious. The mere fact that they can grasp something, and come back with something better, is wonderful.' This remark shows a self-effacement – and confidence – that is absolutely characteristic of both Eyre and Chris Wilkinson. Designs are reached through a filter of collective team inputs, and the ideas are typically pushed and refined right up to their deadlines.

'What runs through our practice is integrated design', says Eyre. 'I have always liked the idea that the structure is working with the architecture. I also like the experiential nature of architecture – what you can get from manipulating geometry. And I have gradually become more interested in juxtapositions and natural materials: the light and the delicate against massive things, or the quality of light on surfaces.' 'We see each project as an opportunity to explore new ideas', adds Wilkinson. 'We've been quite successful in competitions because of that. The Sydney tower project, in 2012, for example, was one that I was keen to win. I'd given a lecture in Sydney three or four years earlier, and I love the city. And when the tower competition came up, I said we had to go for it. We gathered a team of twelve people working on it for three months, just to compete.'

There is a greater kind of pressure: the need to invent, in a world whose zeitgeist is defined by constant

innovation in technology and communication, backlit by increasing environmental complexity. Even a truncated list of Wilkinson Eyre's major UK projects across several design sectors makes its remarkable 'first time' talents obvious: Stratford Regional Station (1999), which remains one of the most structurally and environmentally refined British transport interchanges; Explore@Bristol (2000), the practice's first cultural project, the adaptive reuse and extension of a concrete railway shed from 1906; the uniquely graceful Gateshead Millennium Bridge (2001); and the exemplar design for the Schools for the Future project (2003), the first completed school in the programme being the John Madejski Academy in Reading.

We find the same design boldness overseas, in the elegant double-taper and subtly expressed diagrid structure of the 103-storey Guangzhou International Finance Centre in China (2010). In Singapore, the ribbed biodomes of Gardens by the Bay (2012) have become the city's twenty-first-century symbol, in much the same way that Jørn Utzon's Opera House instantly became Sydney's international cultural beacon.

This seam of innovation is just as apparent in the practice's unrealized designs – the bravura toroidal span of the 1,000-metre-long Arachthos Viaduct in Greece, for example, or the shell-like form of the Newcastle Botanic Bridge. Wilkinson Eyre's less publicized buildings can be equally notable. Consider 10 Brock Street (2013), an office building in central London with diachromic panels on its main façade and an asymmetrically faceted rear elevation; or the Siemens Urban Sustainability Centre, aka the Crystal, in the London Docklands (2012), a glass building whose angular, cantilevered façades have somewhat

Opposite
Top left: Stratford Regional Station, London
Top right: Concept sketch for Gateshead Millennium Bridge
Centre: Interior view of Auguste and Gustave Perret's Notre Dame du Raincy
Bottom: Foster Associates, Willis Faber & Dumas Headquarters, Ipswich

This page
Above: Model of John Madejski Academy, Reading
Right, top: Diagrid model of Guangzhou International Finance Centre
Right: Cladding detail, 10 Brock Street, London
Far right: Façade detail, The Crystal, London

Introduction | Jay Merrick 19

unexpectedly contributed to a LEED Platinum energy-conservation rating.

A dry route march through Wilkinson Eyre's projects across the last three decades would obscure our proper quarry: the character and identity of the practice through time, what formed it, and what has kept it evolving vigorously and coherently.

The architectural historian Kurt Forster has spoken of Wilkinson Eyre's work as a kind of meditation on the paradoxical states of maximum stability and its opposite, levitation: 'Because Wilkinson Eyre really reflect on the paradox and imagine a structure that negotiates its own conflict, any echoes of Archigram and their capsules lumbering on pneumatic stilts across the territory of the city are faint indeed.' Forster's remark was triggered by Wilkinson Eyre's proposal of 2002 for a 150-metre-long glazed dirigible containing an exhibition hall, to be suspended 54 metres above the landscape of the Crystal Palace site in Sydenham, south London.

But where did the instinct to explore and express architectural or structural paradoxes begin for Chris Wilkinson and Jim Eyre, and for the cohort that has evolved securely around them since those early days in Bowling Green Lane? What has given rise to their very particular take on modern design, which is as informed by art and instinct as it is by geometry and technics?

In an essay titled 'Movement and Geometry' (2001), Jim Eyre places an image of a stealth aircraft next to the hazy velocities of J. M. W. Turner's *Rain, Steam, and Speed – The Great Western Railway* (1844). Chris Wilkinson insists that meaningful architecture always has spiritual qualities, and he is fascinated by the exquisitely tense filaments of such artworks as Naum Gabo's *Linear Construction No. 2* (1970–71), as well as the work of such abstract expressionist painters as Mark Rothko: 'That sense of passion, of everything being expressed.' We are not dealing with mere High Tech virtuosos, are we?

The origins of Wilkinson's approach to design are rooted in a handful of key domestic and academic moments. 'I remember seeing modern architecture on the back of cornflakes packets when I was a boy', he recalls. 'So this was a glimpse, even if it wasn't quite modernism. If I look further back, my great-grandfather was an artist, and my grandfather was an electrical engineer, which, at the time, was the equivalent of nuclear physics. It was the latest technology.'

But it was Regent Street Polytechnic (now part of the University of Westminster) in late 1960s London that produced the defining moment of realization. 'I liked it straight away', says Wilkinson. 'I really did believe that I could do better than what I was seeing in the architecture of the day, particularly those bad Greater London Council housing projects.

'The real enlightenment came near the end. Richard Rogers came to give a lecture to the fifth-year diploma group. He brought a box of samples for a zip-up home – extruded aluminium, rubber gaskets, aluminium panels. And I thought, what have I been doing for the last five years?' Wilkinson still has his notes from that day, 13 November 1969. One asterisked sentence reads: 'The bldg. ind. doesn't use available technology – see detailing in tube trains & refrigerated lorries.'

After finishing his degree, Wilkinson joined Denys Lasdun's office. 'It was quite a good grounding, but the architecture was rather formal and I was looking for something more. I realized that the future was with [Richard] Rogers and [Norman] Foster, who were just starting to make a mark at that time. I was lucky enough

to be offered a job at Foster Associates on Fitzroy Street in central London, which was really exciting, and I learned a lot. It was there that I started writing my first book, *Supersheds* [1991], and I went on to work for Michael Hopkins and Richard Rogers in my quest for experience of long-span, large-volume structures, before setting up on my own.'

Jim Eyre's route into architecture began when he was twelve. 'I can remember thinking, at that age, that architecture seemed an interesting thing to do. I was always interested in art and proportions, and the visual aspects of the environment.' By the time he was studying art, physics and maths in sixth form, he was subscribing to *Architectural Review*, and can recall being excited by its coverage of the new architecture emerging, such as Piano + Rogers' Centre Pompidou (1977) and Michael and Patty Hopkins's iconic metal-and-glass house in Hampstead, north London (1976).

After qualifying at the University of Liverpool – class visits to the Sainsbury Centre for Visual Arts, Norwich, and to Oxford to study townscape, 'really got me thinking' – he joined the Hopkins's young studio. 'I learned a lot about the discipline of architecture, and the need to refine designs and develop ideas further than I was used to – it's all right, but it could be better!'

The Foster–Hopkins–Rogers 'tripod' informs Wilkinson Eyre's ethos, but without blunting its originality. The design of Stratford Market Depot reflected the pared-down High Tech design of that period, yet the scheme – 'as awesome as a cathedral, and as secret as a Pharaoh's tomb', said the critic Martin Pawley – exhibited great individuality. And that originality went up several notches in the subsequent design of Stratford Regional Station, which made it

Opposite
Top: Proposal for Crystal Palace exhibition hall
Centre: Naum Gabo, *Linear Construction No. 2*, 1970–71, Tate, London
Bottom, left: J. M. W. Turner, *Rain, Steam, and Speed – The Great Western Railway*, 1844, The National Gallery, London
Bottom, right: Lockheed F-117a Nighthawk stealth fighter

This page
Above, top: Michael and Patty Hopkins, house in Hampstead, London
Top right: Piano + Rogers, Centre Pompidou, Paris
Above and right: Stratford Market Depot, London

Introduction | Jay Merrick

immediately obvious that Wilkinson Eyre was a practice that would explore design innovations in its own way.

Oliver Tyler, who has a particular interest in architectural detailing, recalls that during the design of the station, a great deal of time was invested in developing the palette of materials, and in using them appropriately. At that time, computers and computer-aided design (CAD) were relatively new to architecture, and Tyler had been recruited specifically for his skill with the new media.

'I had a lot of control over all details, and remember careful and precise consideration being given to setting out the geometry of the curve of the ribs, as well as all junctures and connections. We used many steel castings, which was unusual, having carried out a lot of research with the engineer, Neil Holloway. The ribs sit on a casting, and the trusses sit on castings on concrete columns. The nodes were shaped steel tubes bolted into the castings – very elegant, a fantastic kit of parts.' Tyler's description of one of the practice's most high-profile projects, the Emirates Air Line cable car over the River Thames (2012), yet another 'first' – exhibits the same relish for structural aesthetics.

The refinement of structure and detail at Stratford Regional Station is exceptional, and this is characteristic of the practice's architecture as a whole – not least in small-scale projects and products. We find the same concisely elegant precision of detail in the design of the steel lavatory pods at Stratford Market Depot, and in the hollow, double-curved steel CCTV camera arms for London Underground's Piccadilly line.

But it is, perhaps, the vortex-twist of the composite metal-and-timber frames forming the Bridge of Aspiration across London's Floral Street that expresses

This page
Left, top: London Underground camera arm
Above, top: WC pod, Stratford Market Depot, London
Left: Bridge of Aspiration, Royal Ballet School, London
Above: Gardens by the Bay, Singapore

Opposite
Top: Carlo Scarpa, Fondazione Querini Stampalia, Venice
Centre: Richard Rogers Partnership, Lloyd's building, London
Bottom, left: Oliver Hill, Three Lane Ends Community Primary School, Castleford
Bottom, right: Dyson Headquarters, Malmesbury

the practice's attention to detail most exquisitely. Completed in 2003, the bridge links E. M. Barry's Royal Opera House with the neoclassical façade of the Royal Ballet School, and its finesse is unmistakable, right down to the barre-like handrails. The whole structure floats above the street, as if in a balletic *battement glissé*.

The diversity of the practice's partners, in terms of their backgrounds and approaches to design, has a great deal to do with the atmosphere of architectural reinvention that pervades Wilkinson Eyre. It also produces buildings and structures whose design is wilfully anti-brand.

Paul Baker, who led the team for Singapore's Gardens by the Bay, recalls the time when the young practice was starting to grow. 'Before that, the office was very quiet – the architects wore black, and everything was drawn on tracing paper by hand, with Rotring pens.'

Baker always wanted to be an architect: 'I didn't question it, and never doubted it. Building makes me very happy. I also drew and painted and made things constantly. I think you either have an interest in aesthetics, or you don't – some people simply have an inherent visual awareness, a good eye.

'My year-out placement was with Aldington Craig + Collinge. John Craig was a tutor from college. He was a great teacher, and would explain how clever steelwork detailing told a story that expressed the structural forces. I enjoy detailing and putting things together properly – that's why I love working with good engineers. There's an intuition.'

Baker is extremely proud of Gardens by the Bay. 'Not just because of the buildings,' he explains, 'but because of the team bond that grew out of it. Working with Neil Thomas, Patrick Bellew and Andrew Grant [of Atelier One, Atelier Ten and Grant Associates respectively] was a complete joy. It's a bit like the creative dynamic that existed between Chris and Jim when they worked together – different perspectives working together, exploring ideas to see what happens. A talented and dynamic team brings out the competitiveness in you, pushing both yourself and your team to do better.'

Dominic Bettison, who pioneered Wilkinson Eyre's operations in the Far East at its offices in Hong Kong and Shanghai, traces his key design influences back to Richard Rogers's Lloyd's building, London (1986): 'I was studying industrial design at university. I went on a study trip to the Lloyd's building, and I immediately changed to study architecture. The Lloyd's building is a kind of showcase, an expression of industrial design, stripped down but with everything on display. It had that kind of clear diagram that's in our work. We don't do "blended" architecture!

'I wouldn't characterize us purely as High Tech designers, and there are still, sometimes, loose-fit and flexible spaces in our buildings – but they are very precisely designed. Maybe that's why our architecture is difficult to pigeonhole. We have strategies, but not a toolbox of design components. It's like parents creating individual sons and daughters, rather than clones.'

In the Far East, Wilkinson Eyre has a tiger by the tail. Nowhere has the practice's ability to adapt to clients, or to quantum-jumps in project scale, been more clearly demonstrated than in this market sector. 'It demands a great deal of flexibility', says Bettison. 'Clients always want to come the very next day for a meeting, not in a week or a month's time. It's not a linear process – it's a kind of fast, random series of project developments. Confucius meets Western philosophical processes!'

Introduction | Jay Merrick   23

Stafford Critchlow offers yet more proof that Wilkinson Eyre is not interested in cloned designers, or copycat architecture. His parents were architects, and he studied at Newcastle University, followed by a year in Italy with Aldo Rossi, and then a first job at Skidmore, Owings & Merrill. 'I joined Chris Wilkinson Architects at about the same time as Oliver Tyler,' he explains, 'at the time of the "Stratford shed" and the early phase of the Dyson Headquarters [1999].'

Carlo Scarpa's ideas, and Richard Meier's buildings in Frankfurt, triggered in Critchlow a profound interest in how to fit modern buildings into older contexts. 'I am less interested in pure technology, as such', he explains. 'I enjoyed the challenge of designing around the existing [François] Hennebique concrete structure for Explore@ Bristol. I was also interested in 1930s school buildings, as a precursor to subsequent school design – Oliver Hill's school in Castleford, West Yorkshire, being one example of pure modernism from someone who also designed in a Lutyens style.'

Critchlow's openness to architectural possibilities is found in all the practice's designers. It is very evident, for example, in the practice's educational projects with which he is predominantly engaged, and nowhere to more striking effect than in the design of the Forum buildings and external spaces at Exeter University. Everything about this scheme – the sloping site, the structural challenges, the Forum's environmental and socio-spatial characteristics – required a great deal of research and visualization. The design effectively rewrote the university's brief for the site, creating a brilliantly composed narrative of internal and external spaces, which have been crucial to the university becoming a member of the prestigious Russell Group.

Wilkinson Eyre's newest directors, Sebastien Ricard and Giles Martin, have added to the practice's design palette. Ricard, for example, is fascinated by the potential of the new wave of building products: 'There's a very interesting evolution in architecture at the moment. CNC [computer numerical control] robotics are making tailored components affordable, so there's a movement from standard to bespoke prefabrication. It's very exciting.' Ricard, now leading French projects, including a bridge in Paris and a cable car in Toulouse, adds: 'Good engineering is part of the justification of good architecture.' He is also immersed in the Battersea Power Station project, which takes up a great deal of his time and energy.

Martin offers yet another design perspective: 'I see buildings as planted in space, and of their time – a positive object that you react to, architecture that's confident and takes on meaning because of the quality of its design, details and materials. Making architecture appear effortless is very hard work – look at Arne Jacobsen!'

All of these contrasting strands of design thinking coalesce to form Wilkinson Eyre's distinctive approach to buildings and structures whose typological range is remarkable: the floating pavilions of the Magna Science Adventure Centre (2001), constructed inside the vast shed of the redundant Templeborough steelworks in Rotherham; the contextually sophisticated materiality and articulation of the Department of Earth Sciences in the historic centre of Oxford (2010); the 'termite mound' and furled-blind cooling system for the Davies Alpine House at Kew Gardens, London (2005); and, to mention something supposedly banal, the delightfully looping cascade of ramps at the Liver

Street car park in Liverpool (2005). In the architectural equivalent of a blind-tasting, many would assume that these projects had been designed by four different (and highly talented) practices. 'It's getting slightly easier now,' says Jim Eyre, 'because more clients believe in good design. Thirty years ago, we wouldn't talk about the concept of a design, or exactly how it would look; you'd justify the design on its functionality. You wouldn't have dared to talk about the nature of space.' The proof of his remark loomed all around us: it was October 2013, and we were standing in the central atrium of the New Bodleian Library in Oxford, crammed with scaffolding during its renovation and internal remodelling. Eyre is clearly excited by the prospect of Giles Gilbert Scott's edifice of 1940 being opened up in new ways – and he is just as expectant about the practice's proposals for the reinvention of Scott's Battersea Power Station in London.

It's an unlikely scenario, isn't it? Almost three decades after designing and delivering the stripped-down industrial structure of Stratford Market Depot, the arch-modernist practice of Wilkinson Eyre is, predictably, designing skyscrapers, yet also delivering major adaptive reuse schemes for two of Britain's most historically important mid-twentieth-century buildings.

'We are in the most interesting age, architecturally', says Chris Wilkinson. 'We are just so lucky. When I joined Foster Associates in 1974, I was at the start of this new kind of modernism in the UK. I went to the University of East Anglia recently: the Sainsbury Centre for Visual Arts is absolutely perfect. It's such a clear architectural statement. I'm always surprised by architects wanting to stick to old values. One has to embrace the new, and enjoy it. I'm more determined than ever not to do a bad building, and to search out new opportunities for something new and exciting – more so than ever, because I value my time more.'

And time, as Einstein demonstrated, bends. On a bright autumn day in 2013, Wilkinson is standing alongside the black, toroidally angled wooden boards on the façade of the practice's Mary Rose Museum in Portsmouth (2013). The *Mary Rose*, Henry VIII's favourite warship, foundered and sank into the mud of the Solent in 1545 as the British fleet massed to defeat a much larger French naval force. 'It's not an indifferent building', Wilkinson muses. 'It's like a jewellery box that houses a treasure.' Thus, history becomes re-exposed and clarified by modern architecture; there are overlaps of old and new structures, an instructive and atmospheric merging of now and then. 'When the main ship hall is completed,' says Wilkinson, 'you will be able to piece the whole thing together in your mind, and you will see and understand how the museum works.'

The remark neatly captions the essential clarity of Wilkinson Eyre's architecture. And to it we might add a thought from the astrophysicist Stephen Hawking: 'Science is not only a disciple of reason, but also one of romance and passion ... Intelligence is the ability to adapt to change.'

It is in this realm of logic, innovation and evolution that Wilkinson Eyre Architects has operated, with increasing international success, for three decades. There is no sense of pause. The practice's long-standing core of designer-directors remains intact. Its legacy, its burgeoning design confidence and its place in the twenty-first century's premier league of modernist architects seem quite secure.

Opposite
Top: Interior view of Magna Science Adventure Centre, Rotherham
Centre: Interior view of turbine hall, Battersea Power Station, London
Bottom, left: Liver Street car park, Liverpool
Bottom, right: Davies Alpine House, Royal Botanic Gardens, Kew, London

This page
Above, right: Detail of stone panels on narrative wall, Department of Earth Sciences, University of Oxford
Above: Foster Associates, Sainsbury Centre for Visual Arts, Norwich
Right: Mary Rose Museum, Portsmouth

Introduction | Jay Merrick   25

Landscape

Landscape is both design inspiration and environmental conscience. From it we take ideas of form and function, strategies for sustainability, and respite from urban chaos. Projects can be landmarks in themselves – or marks on the land – and draw from local topographies to blur the boundaries between internal and external space.

Gardens by the Bay, Singapore	28
The Forum, University of Exeter, UK	43
Royal Botanic Gardens, Kew, UK	51
Living Bridge, University of Limerick, Ireland	59
Schools for the Future, UK	64
Maggie's Centre, Oxford, UK	77

Gardens by the Bay
Singapore

Singapore's climate is typified by heat, humidity and heavy rain. Within this steamy tropical environment vegetation grows prolifically, pervading the city with a lush green ambience. There are no distinct seasons, the biannual monsoons bringing the strong winds and cloudy conditions to which the local plants have adapted – but which are completely unsuitable for many of those displayed under glass at Gardens by the Bay. Native to some of the most vulnerable climate zones on earth, these plants require cooler conditions in order to flourish. And it is these requirements that presented the central design challenge for this project: in Singapore's tropical climate, how to create cool conditions in a greenhouse, a structure more frequently used to produce a warm growing environment.

Gardens by the Bay is one of the largest landscape projects ever undertaken in Singapore, and is central to the government's visionary plan to transform the city-state into a 'City in a Garden'. This initiative aims to capture Singapore's essence as a tropical garden city, creating a sophisticated green infrastructure to balance – and enhance – future urban growth. The project, which comprises three separate gardens covering a total of 101 hectares, will help to connect a series of new cultural venues and commercial developments around Marina Bay, and will eventually be linked by bridges to form a huge, circular ribbon of green along the waterfront. Gardens by the Bay is also critical to Singapore's offering to tourists, encouraging those changing flights here en route to more distant destinations to remain an extra day, potentially contributing millions of extra dollars to the tourist economy.

At the heart of the Gardens at Bay South – at 54 hectares, the largest of the three garden sites, and the first to be completed – is the Cooled Conservatory Complex. As the focal point of the site, the complex was defined in the brief as an architectural icon, a horticultural attraction and a showcase for sustainable technology. The two main conservatory structures are among the largest climate-controlled glasshouses in the world, covering an area in excess of 20,000 square metres, and showcase the flora of those environments most likely to be affected by climate change: in the Flower Dome, the cool–dry Mediterranean zone; and in the Cloud Forest, the cool–wet tropical montane. The challenge of creating these conservatory environments under glass was a fundamental driver of the design, which was brought about through a uniquely collaborative relationship between Wilkinson Eyre and the other members of the multidisciplinary team: masterplanner Grant Associates, structural engineer Atelier One and environmental specialists Atelier Ten.

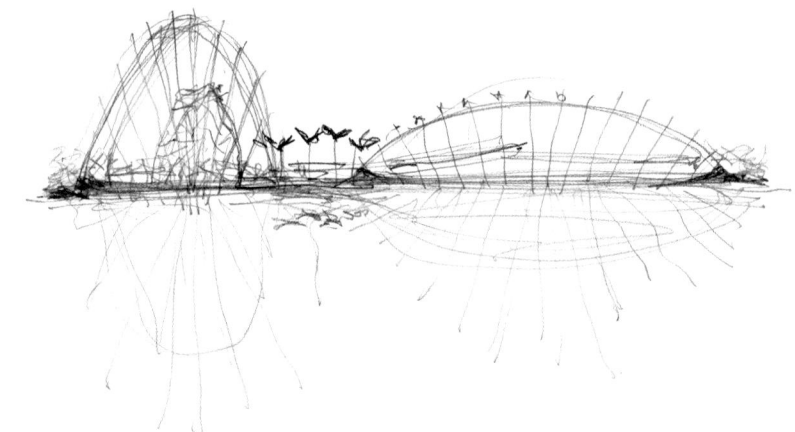

The masterplan for the site, shown here in an early sketch prepared by Grant Associates for the project design competition in 2008, takes the orchid, Singapore's national flower, as inspiration. Just as epiphytic orchids enjoy a symbiotic relationship with their host plant, so the conservatories act as positively beneficial organisms, sustaining the gardens, and vice versa, through an integrated environmental system. The bifurcated stems of the orchid are represented by routes across the site.

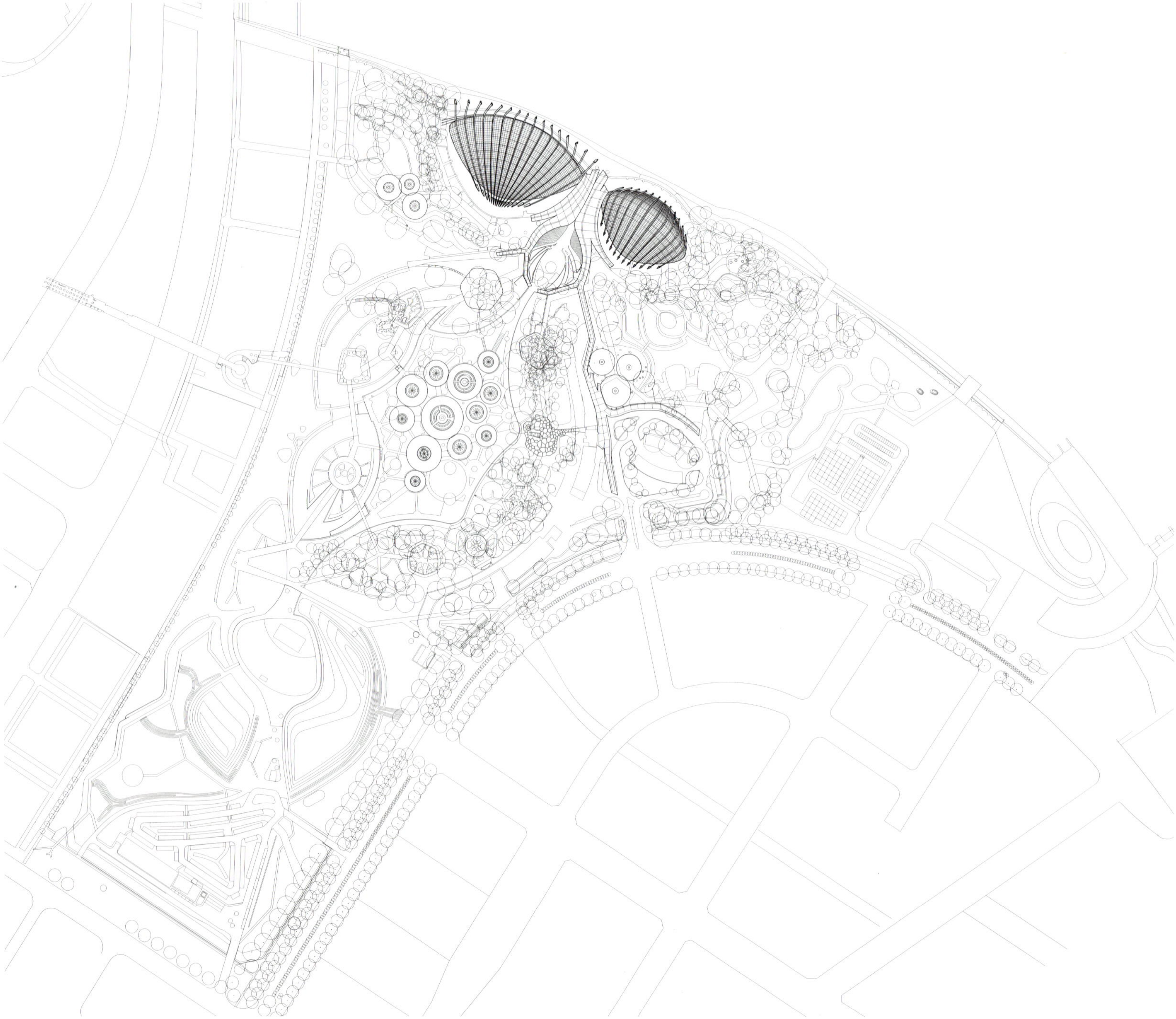

Ground plan

1 Olive Grove
2 Flower Field
3 Flower Dome group entry
4 Baobabs
5 Hub/canopy
6 Ticketing
7 Canopy cafe
8 Retail
9 Cloud Forest group entry
10 Forest Walk
11 Lost World
12 Cloud Walk
13 Treetop Walk
14 Ravine

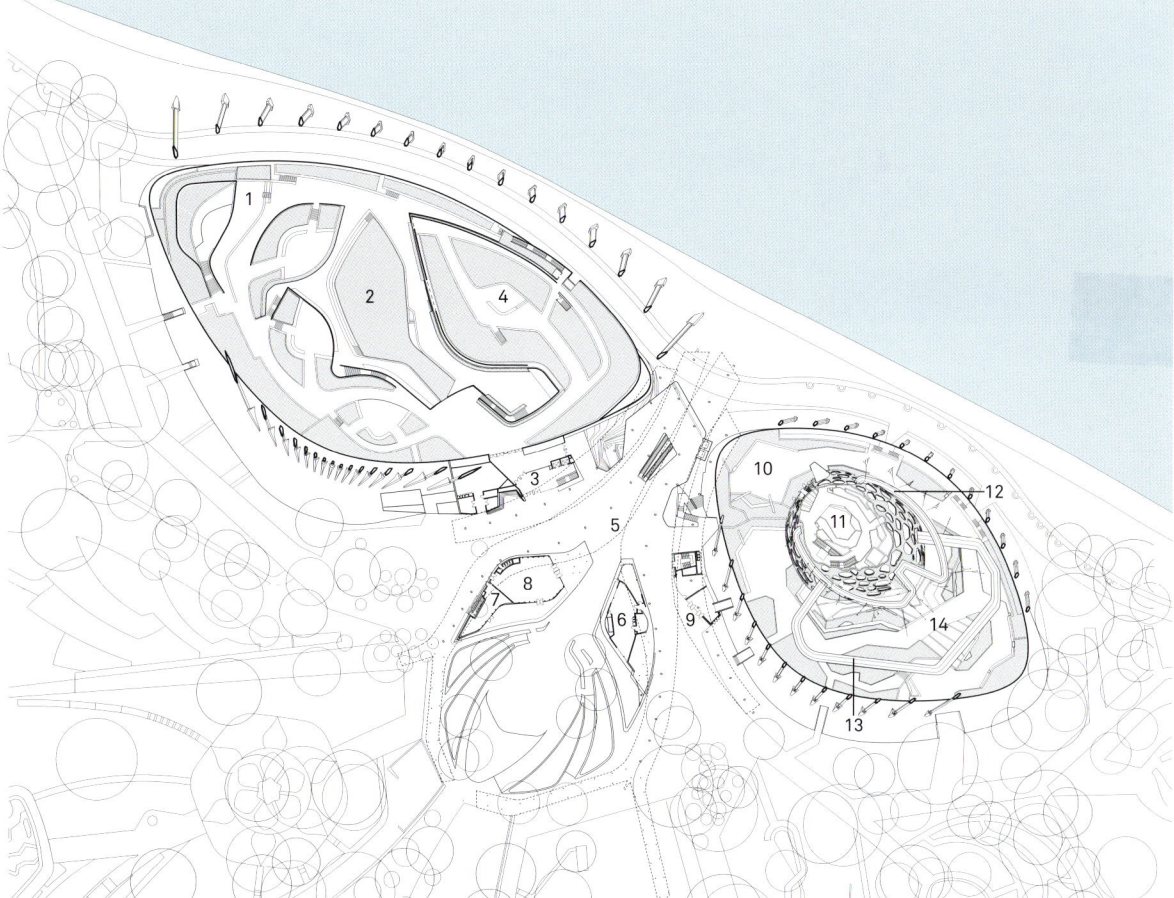

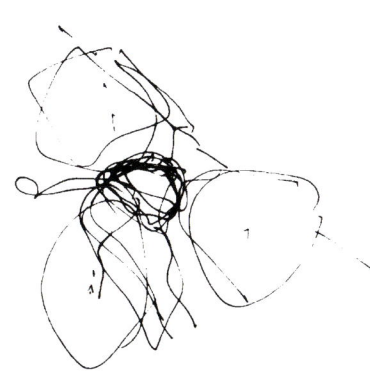

Landscape | Gardens by the Bay, Singapore   31

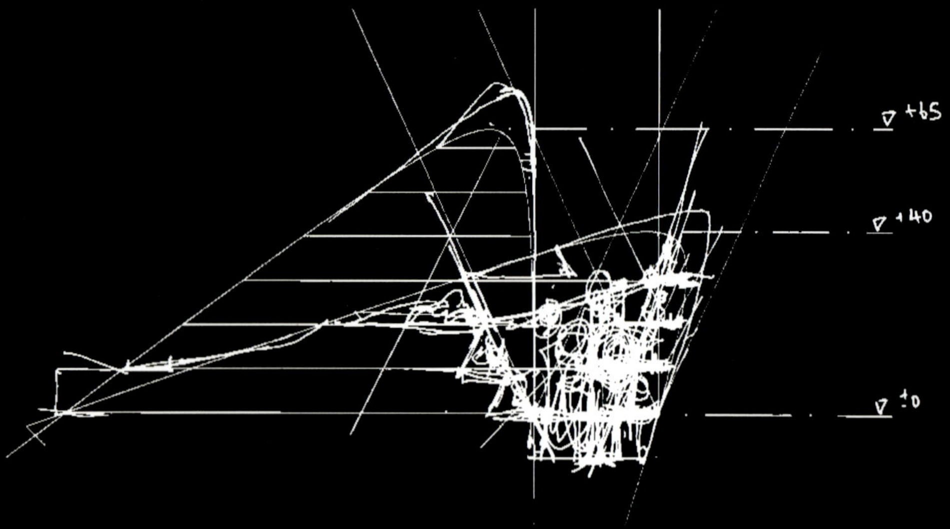

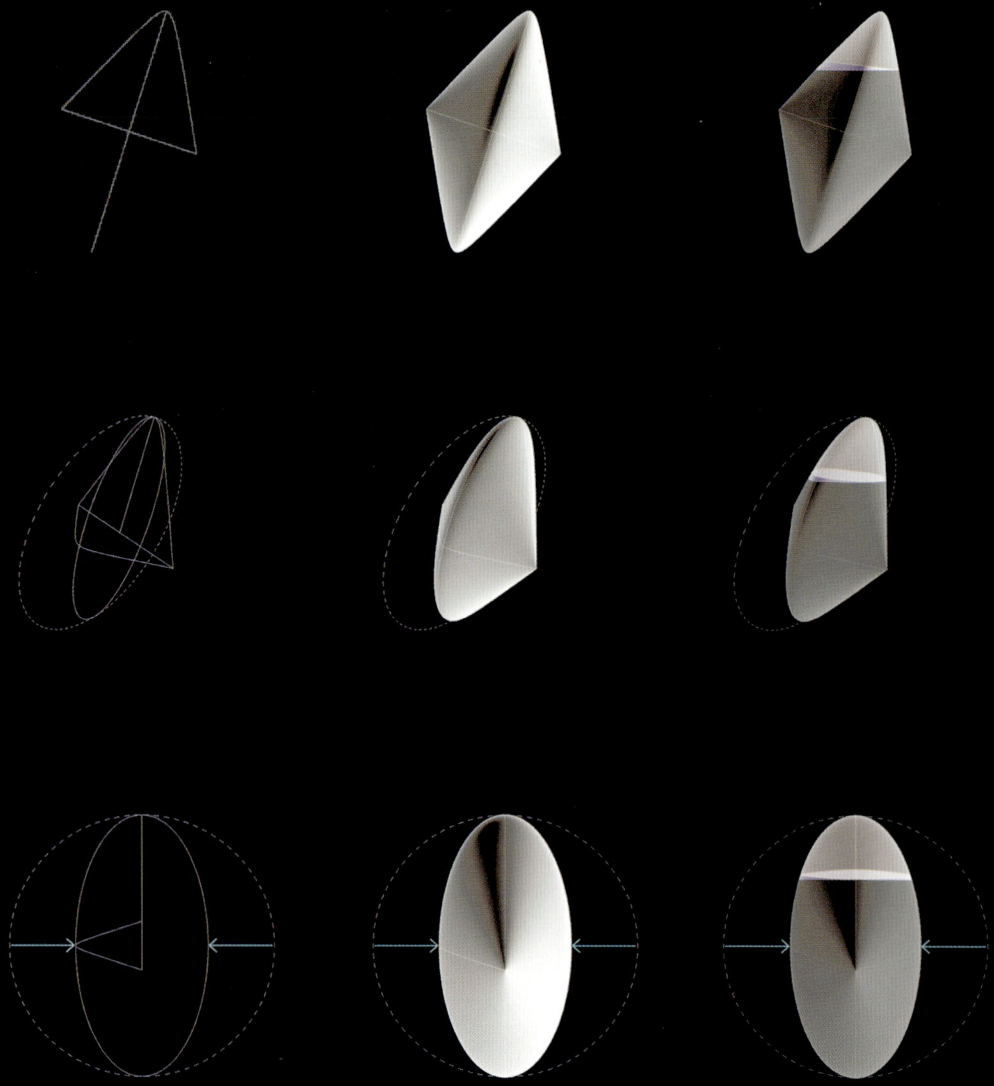

The complementary yet distinct forms of the two conservatories were generated by rotating a hyperbolic curve around an axis to create a toroid, and then making a cut through it to form the ground plane. In the case of the larger Flower Dome conservatory, the shape was then tipped over so its front façade (which faces north) did not require any additional shading. The Cloud Forest biome started with a similar geometry, but is compressed along its longer axis to create a smaller footprint in relation to its greater height.

The conservatories are an integral part of a wider environmental system developed for the gardens by Atelier Ten, in which the main structures and planting act in tandem to simulate nature at work. A biomass boiler, fuelled by green waste from across the city, provides all the energy required for cooling the two biomes – which make use of a desiccant cooling system (dried air can be cooled with less energy). The cluster of 'supertrees' act in part as giant flues for the surplus hot air from the boiler exhaust, and also gather energy via photovoltaic cells to power pumps and filtration systems for the gardens' water features.

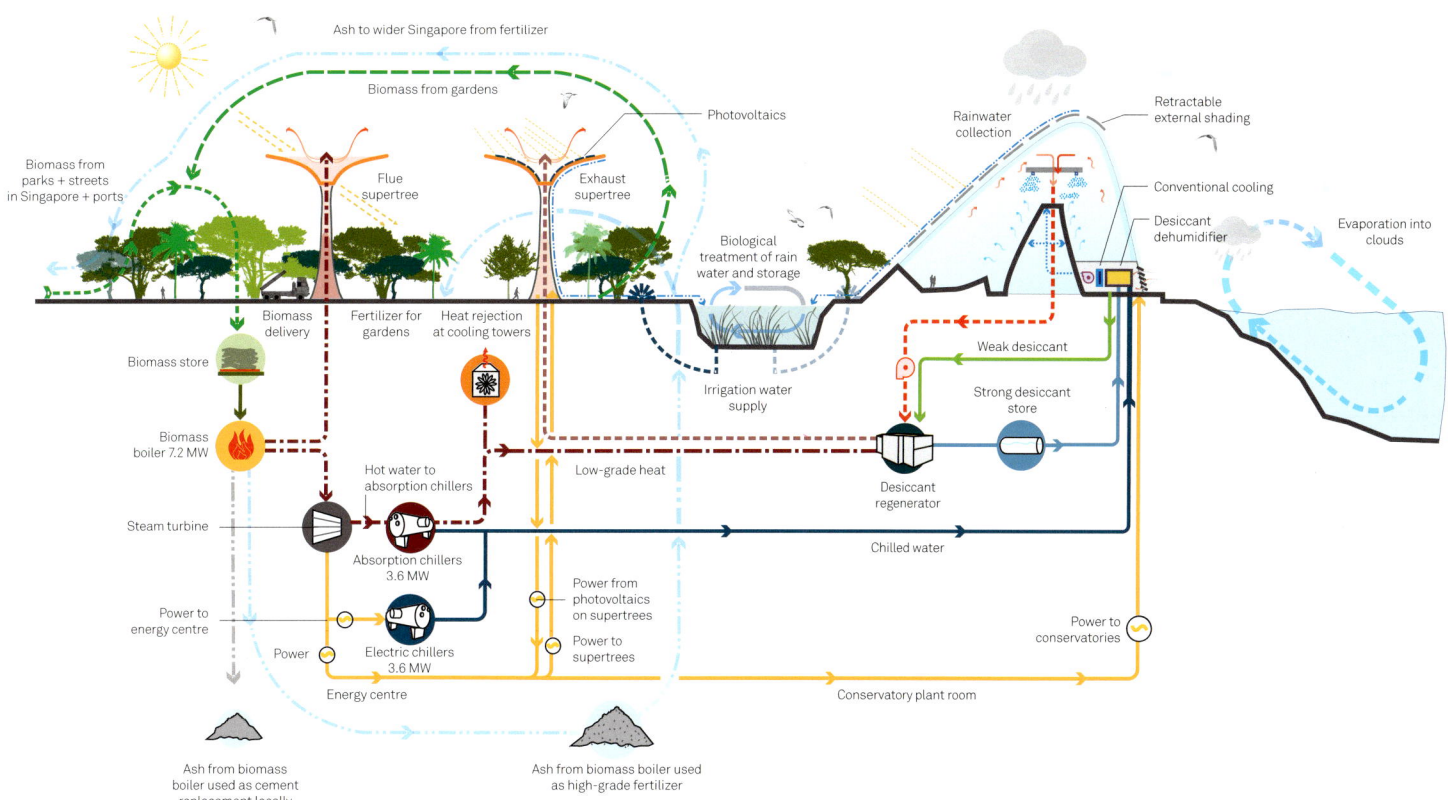

The passive environmental design of the conservatories draws on Wilkinson Eyre's collaboration with Atelier Ten on the Davies Alpine House at the Royal Botanic Gardens, Kew (left; see also page 51). Both designs represent a careful balance between light and heat: while traditional glasshouses trap the light and heat of the sun, the biomes modify this process through responsive design, letting in the necessary amount of daylight for plant growth without overheating the space within. The Alpine House achieves this using an underground labyrinth to supply cool air to the plants, while natural ventilation draws warm air out of the building by means of the stack effect.

Landscape | Gardens by the Bay, Singapore

Both biomes have a composite structure composed of a gridshell, which works in tandem with an external superstructure of radially arranged, arched steel ribs. These were introduced primarily to address the lateral loads to the gridshell, although they also give the conservatories their distinctive organic identity. This clear-span structure, coupled with the slenderness of the ribs, allows high levels of daylight to enter the building. The gridshell supports the large double-glazed units, which are key to the environmental modulation of the buildings.

The shading system is concealed in reveals within the steel ribs, its mechanism based on yacht roller-reefing. Light and temperature readings within the conservatories determine where the shade is needed, and computer-controlled motors unfurl polyester sail-fabric shades in response. The different zones within each conservatory can be shaded separately, to suit the specific requirements of the planting within.

Sunshading detail

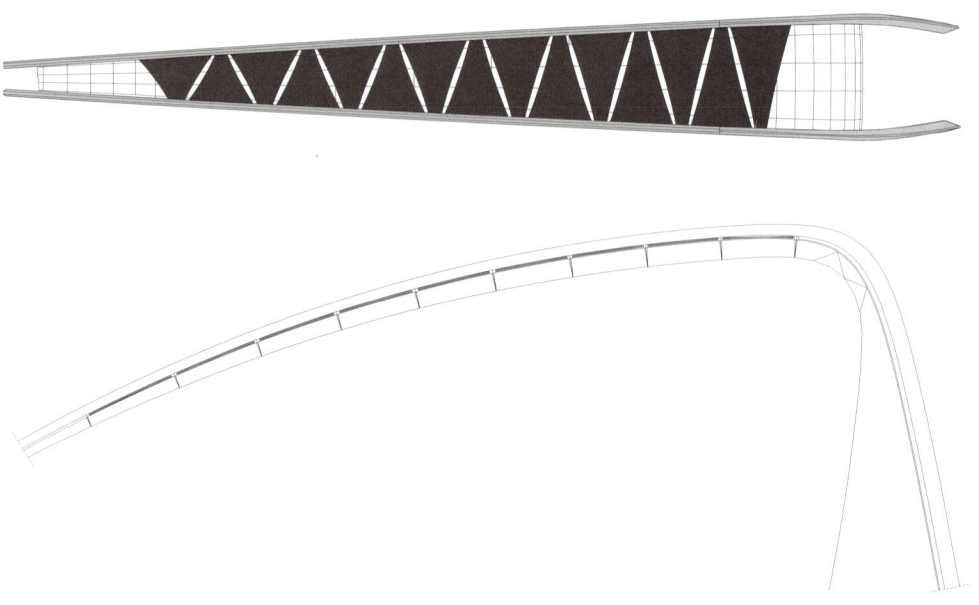
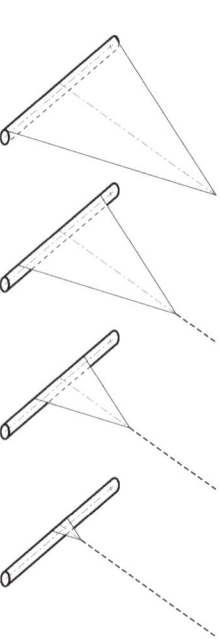

Sunshading sequence

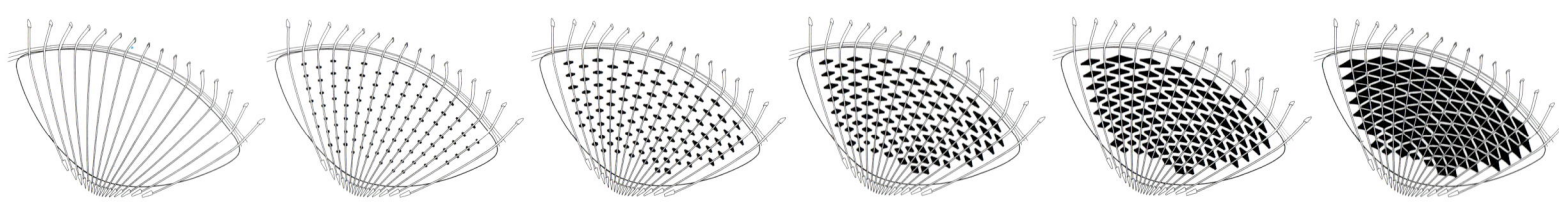

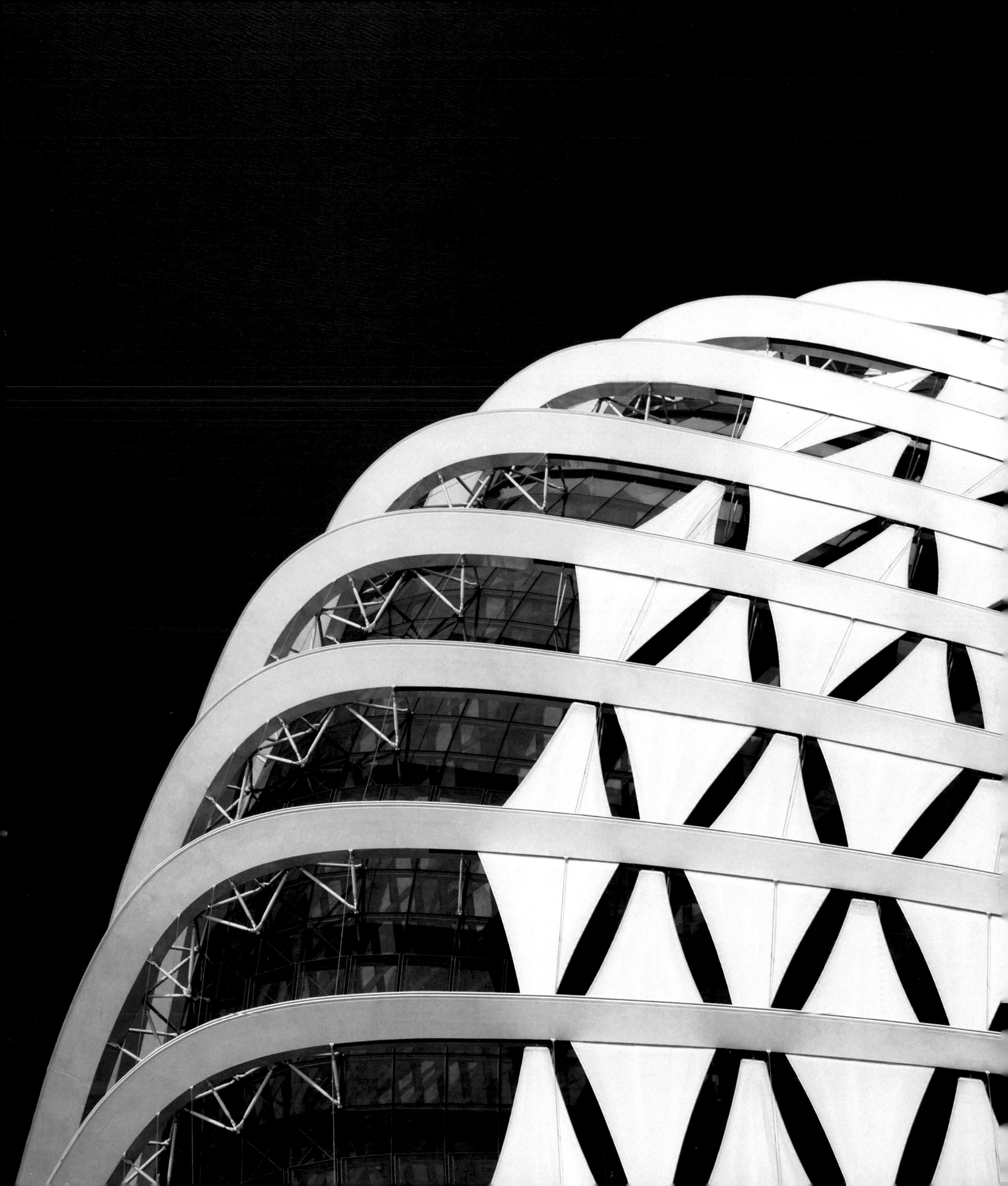

Cloud Forest cross section

1 Crystal Mountain exhibition
2 Lost World
3 Forest Walk
4 Cloud Walk
5 Treetop Walk
6 Plant room
7 Ravine
8 Marathon route

The Cloud Forest biome highlights the relationship between plants and the planet, showing how the warming of the cool tropical cloud forests threatens biodiversity. At its heart is a planted 'mountain', from which a 30-metre-high waterfall cascades. Visitors can experience the forest from walkways at several different levels, as well as exploring a series of exhibition spaces inside the mountain, which describe the impact of incremental temperature change and the sustainable technologies employed across the gardens.

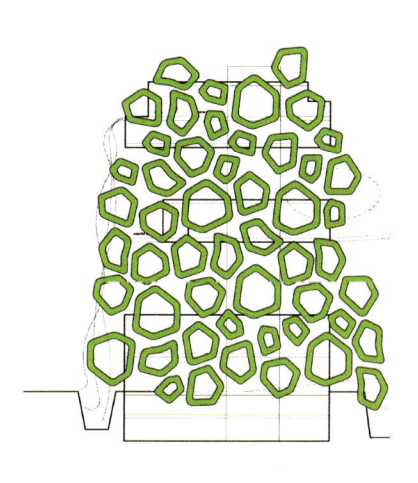

Landscape | Gardens by the Bay, Singapore

The Flower Dome tells the story of the plants and people of the Mediterranean climate zone, showing how the flora cultivated in this region will gradually become endangered as temperatures rise. It has a planted footprint of more than 10,100 square metres under glass, and brings alive the experience of seasonal change for visitors more used to Singapore's perpetually tropical climate and lush green vegetation. The landform of the biome draws inspiration from Mediterranean landscapes, with planted terraces overlooking the central Flower Field – a vast carpet of flowers in bloom, which is curated to reflect the changing of the seasons.

Flower Dome cross section

1 Australian garden
2 Pollen restaurant
3 Olive Grove
4 Flower Field
5 Event space
6 Baobabs
7 Marathon route
8 Plant room

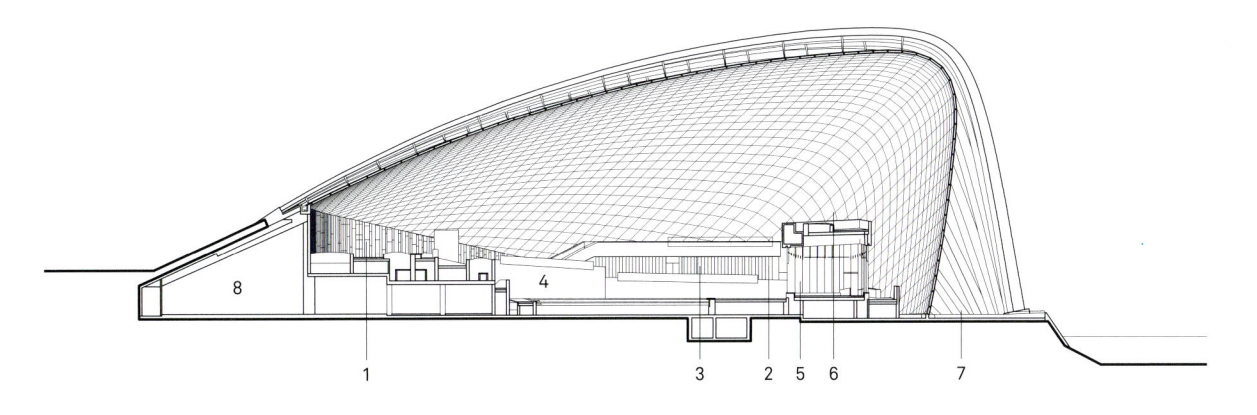

Landscape | Gardens by the Bay, Singapore   39

Already one of Singapore's most popular visitor attractions, the conservatories provide a backdrop to major sporting and cultural events on the bay – and a new picture-postcard view of the city.

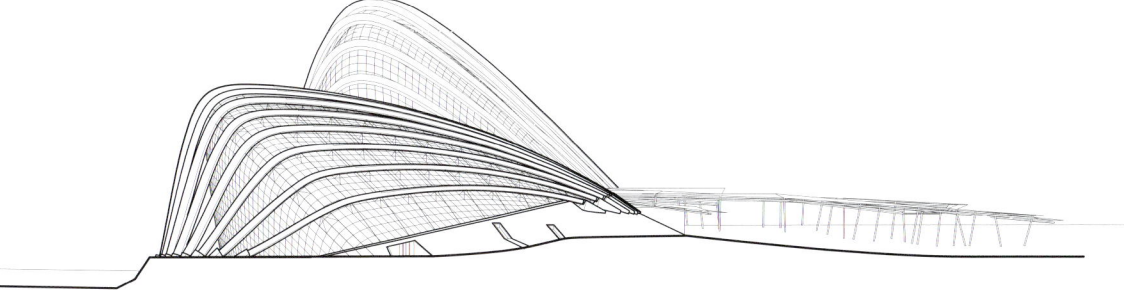

Landscape | Gardens by the Bay, Singapore

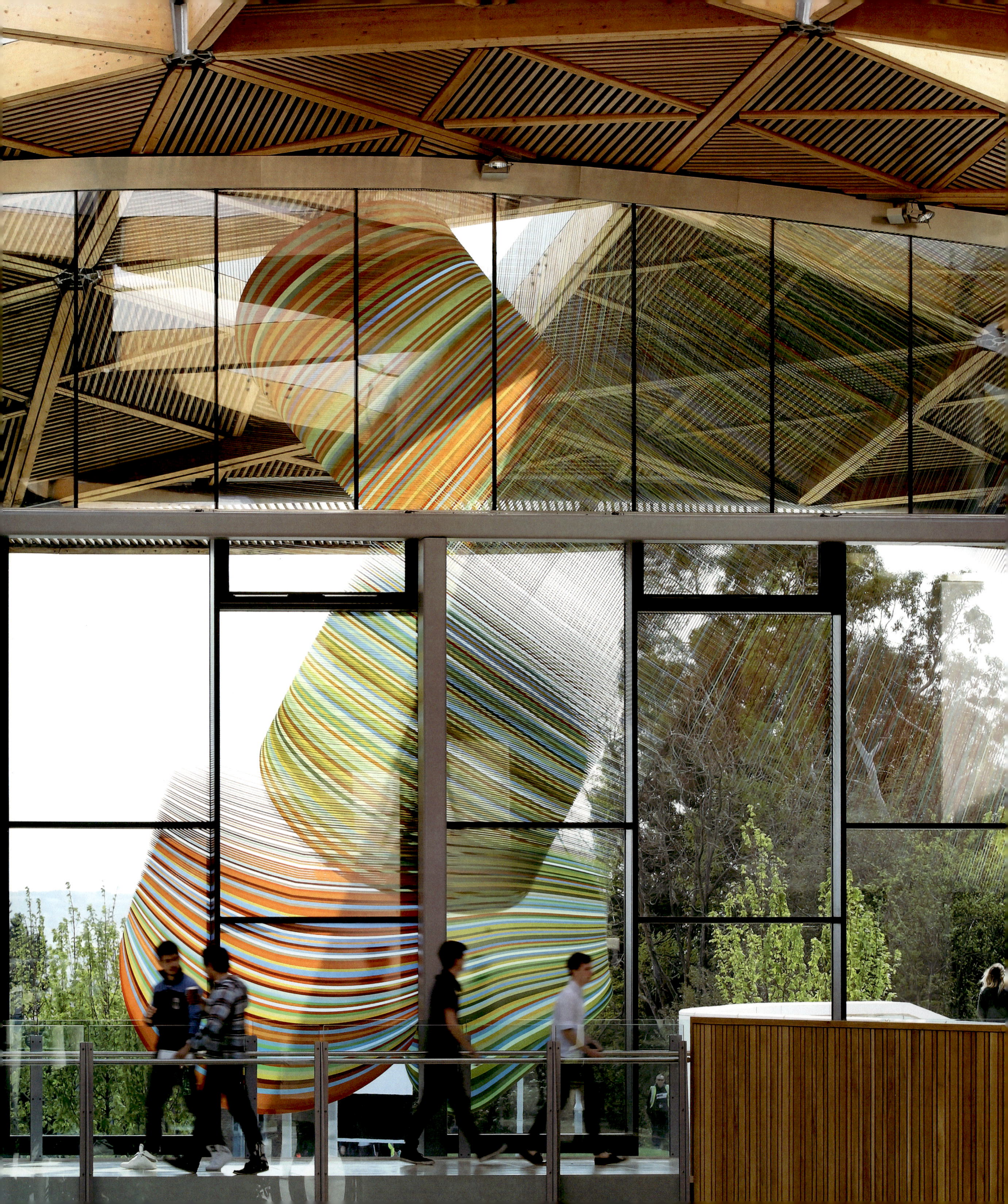

The Forum
University of Exeter, UK

The University of Exeter's membership of the select Russell Group of universities, together with a changing fee structure in higher education, forms the background to the Forum project. Considering the improvement of its facilities to be a crucial element in elevating its status, as well as in attracting and retaining students now paying up to £9,000 in fees, the institution viewed the Forum as a key means of propelling Exeter into the list of top ten British universities.

Exeter's main Streatham campus occupies a commanding position on hills to the north-west of the city centre. The lush, green, maturely planted site – originally the gardens of Reed Hall – is one of the university's most distinctive features, with 1950s buildings set across the undulating landscape in a manner reminiscent of some of the Ivy League universities in the United States. In contrast to the many UK campuses designed and developed from scratch to a coherent masterplan during the twentieth century, the Streatham site has been developed incrementally over the last 100 years. A rather formal masterplan proposed by Vincent Harris in 1928 was abandoned, owing to the impossibility of implementing it across the steep sections of the site, in favour of a more informal layout by Sir William Holford, informed by the rich topography, and with winding roads linking scattered groups of buildings.

Inspired by the landscape of this beautiful campus, Wilkinson Eyre's new Forum – the victor in a closely fought design competition – extends this conversation between buildings and nature, the organic shape of its undulating timber gridshell roof reflecting the contours of the site. The winning concept was for a 'non-building', a landscape-inspired response that allows activity to flow from the outside spaces into the Forum, which contrasts with and connects the existing rectilinear brick buildings. It provides a new centre of gravity for students and staff, and an identifiable heart for the campus, on which both existing and more recent buildings can now focus. The sheltering roof links such older buildings as the main library with newer spaces to create a hub with many functions: it is, in essence, a snapshot of university life. As well as the main reception, the Forum includes flexible teaching spaces – designed to accommodate innovative ways of learning and study – for use by all academic departments, a student services centre, refurbished library spaces, a 400-seat auditorium and a food court. The generous, street-like foyer between these individual 'rooms' acts as a new meeting place, with space for art, performance and informal learning.

The university has an important art collection, much of it accessible as an outdoor sculpture trail across the Streatham campus, and a strong heritage of imaginative art commissioning. The artistic centrepiece of the Forum is a commissioned work in glass by the internationally renowned artist Alexander Beleschenko. Conceived and developed in close collaboration with Wilkinson Eyre, this piece is inspired by the colours of the university gardens, and has a ceramic frit on two surfaces to give it a subtle shimmer.

With the Forum acting as a focal point for the campus, student life has been reinvigorated, and in 2012 Exeter was named Sunday Times University of the Year for 2013.

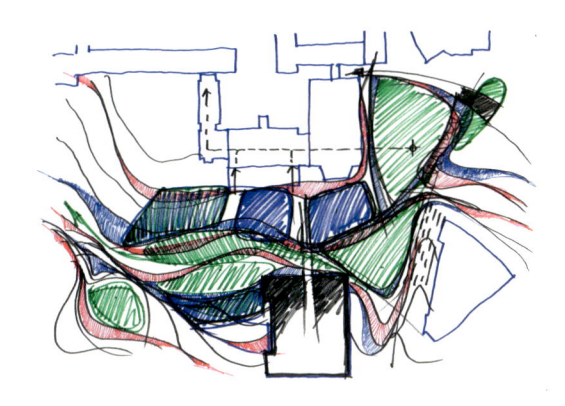

An important strand of thinking behind the design was the desire to make a 'mark on the land', rather than a landmark. The Forum's sequence of buildings and spaces is related closely to the topography of the campus, establishing an architectural language that is less about placing objects in the landscape and more about an organic response to it. The structure – and its adjacent landscaped piazzas – is oriented according to the contours of the hillside, with a newly added green corridor serving as the main pedestrian route through the scheme. Within, the hilly topography has been rationalized into two circulation levels, which connect the library and the Great Hall, thereby unifying two significant centres of academic life that were once separated by a steep slope.

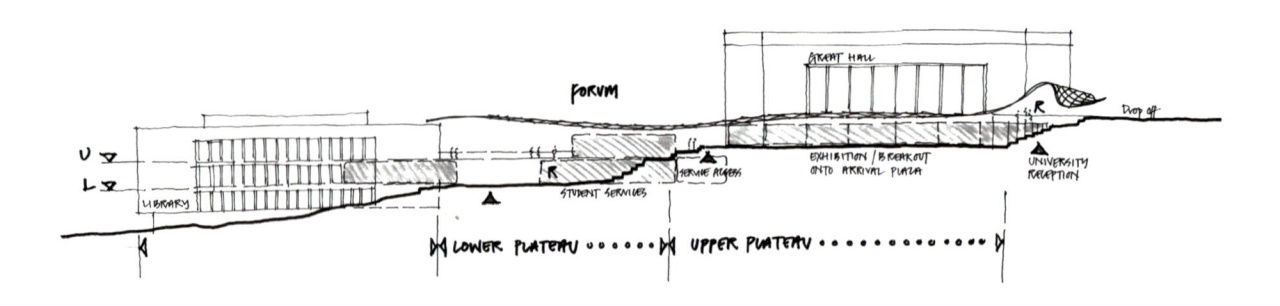

Landscape | The Forum, University of Exeter, UK

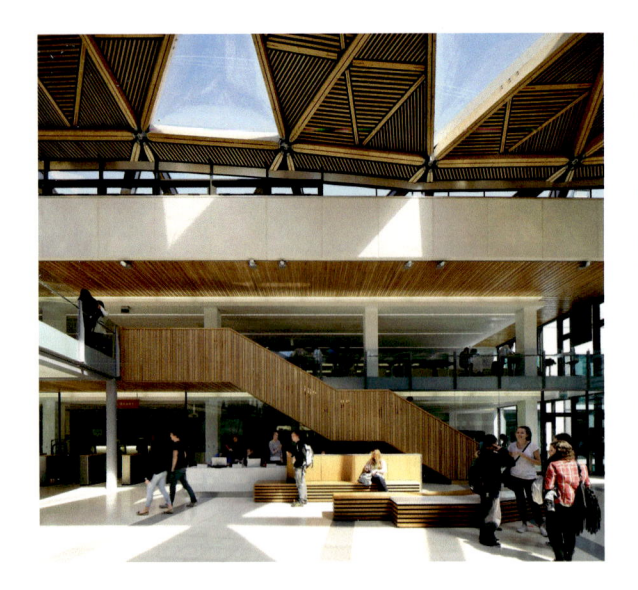

Fundamental to the Forum brief was a need for study spaces that could accommodate more informal, collaborative and networked learning. Much of the main street – the central circulation space within the Forum – and its associated breakout areas is covered by high-speed Wi-Fi, while wired power and data points allow students to recharge laptops and tablets, and connect directly to the network.

The Forum also shelters two sixty-seat exploration labs. The first has tablet PCs and video-conferencing facilities, while the second is designed for Harvard-style group learning with multi-touch 'surface tables' – among the first of their type to be found in a British university.

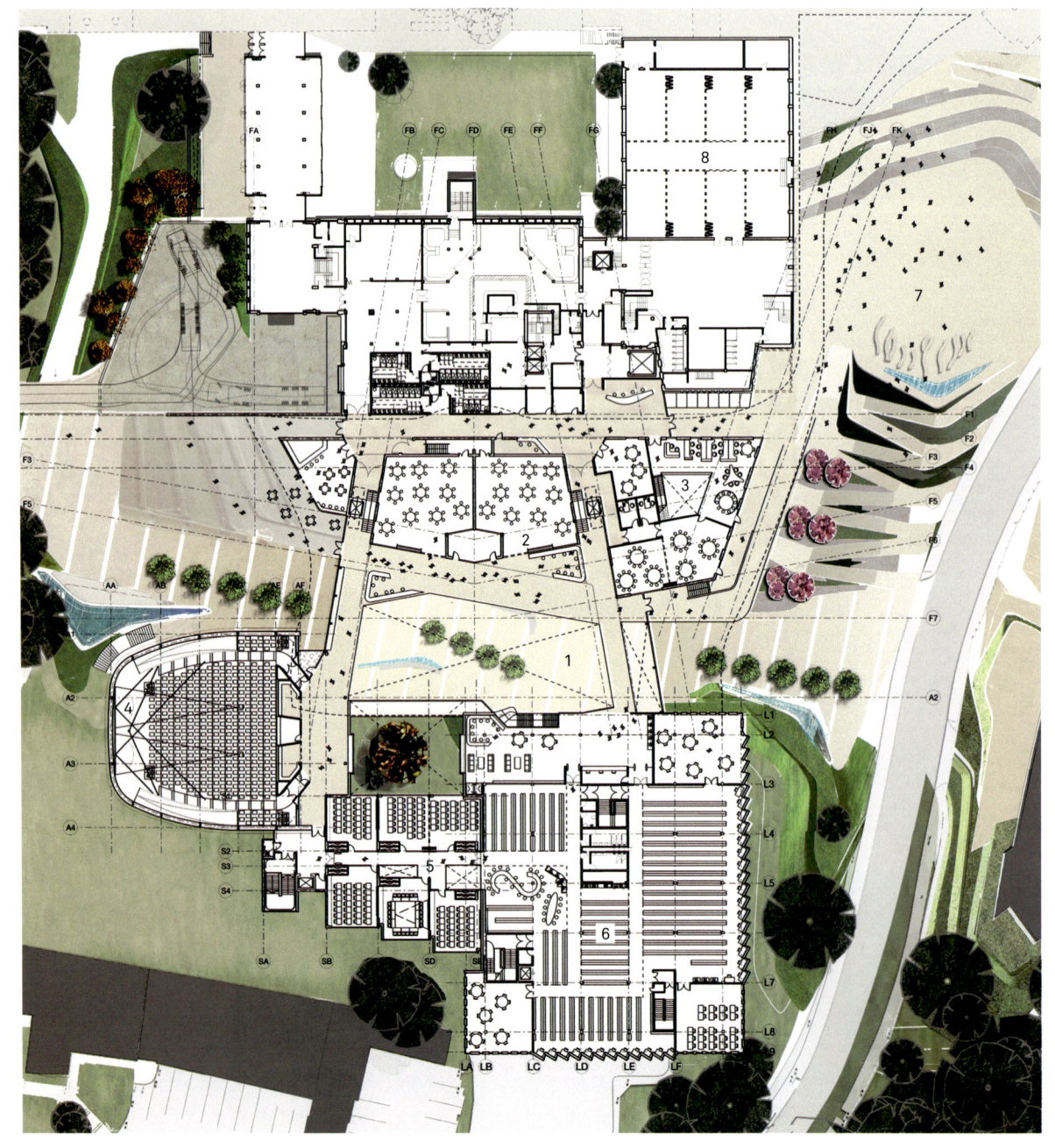

Site plan

1 Forum street
2 Exploration labs
3 Student services centre
4 Auditorium
5 Seminar rooms
6 Existing library
7 New piazza
8 Existing Great Hall

To the north-west, the Forum opens on to a sweeping entrance piazza. Here, its most distinctive feature – the gently undulating gridshell roof – merges with a curving timber canopy, supported by delicate steel pylons propped off the precast concrete walls. The canopy shelters a new reception space before rising a single storey to skirt the northern elevation of the Great Hall as a covered walkway.

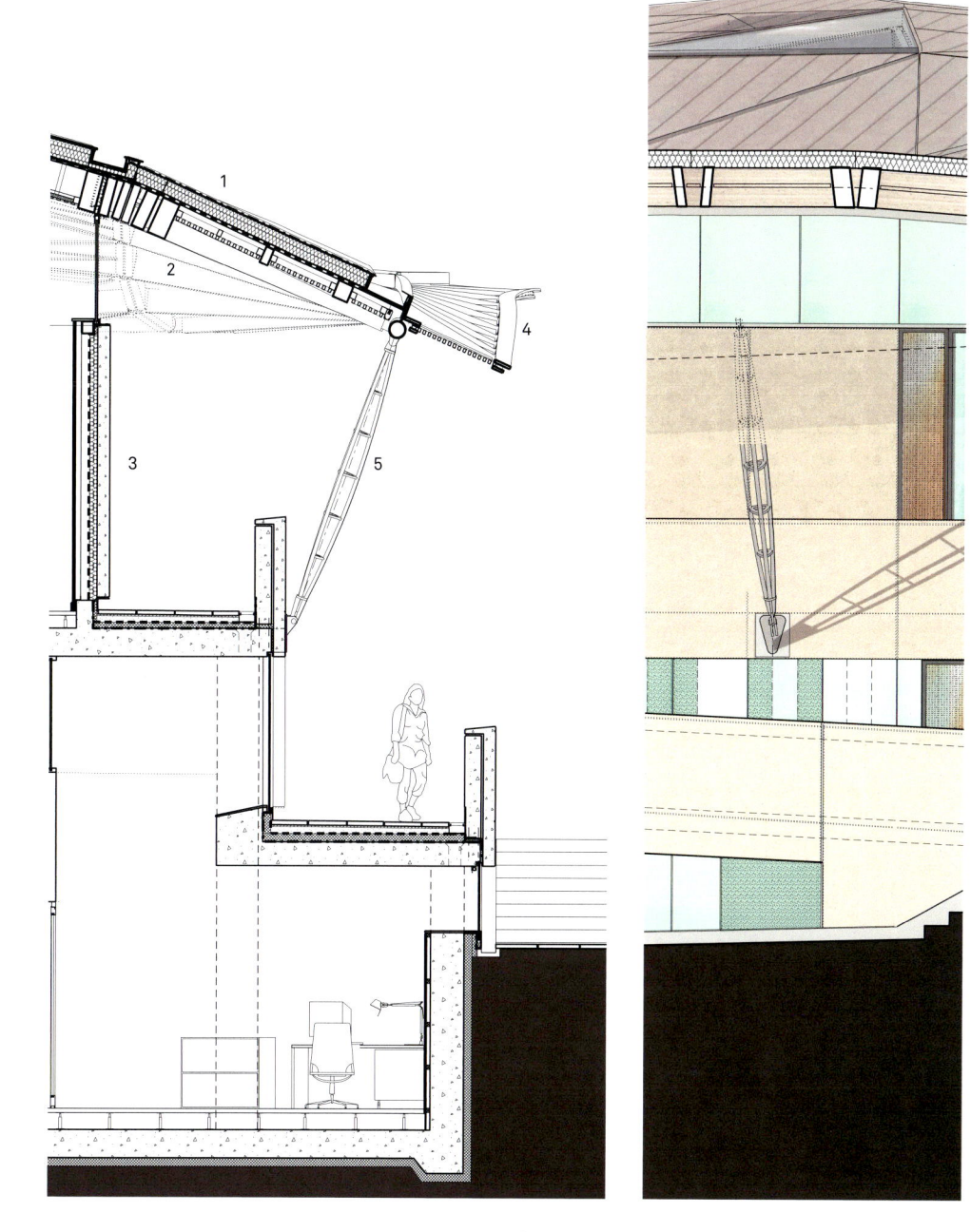

Canopy detail

1. Copper roof
2. Clerestory shuffle glazing
3. Precast cladding panel
4. Green-oak roof edge
5. Pylon column

Landscape | The Forum, University of Exeter, UK

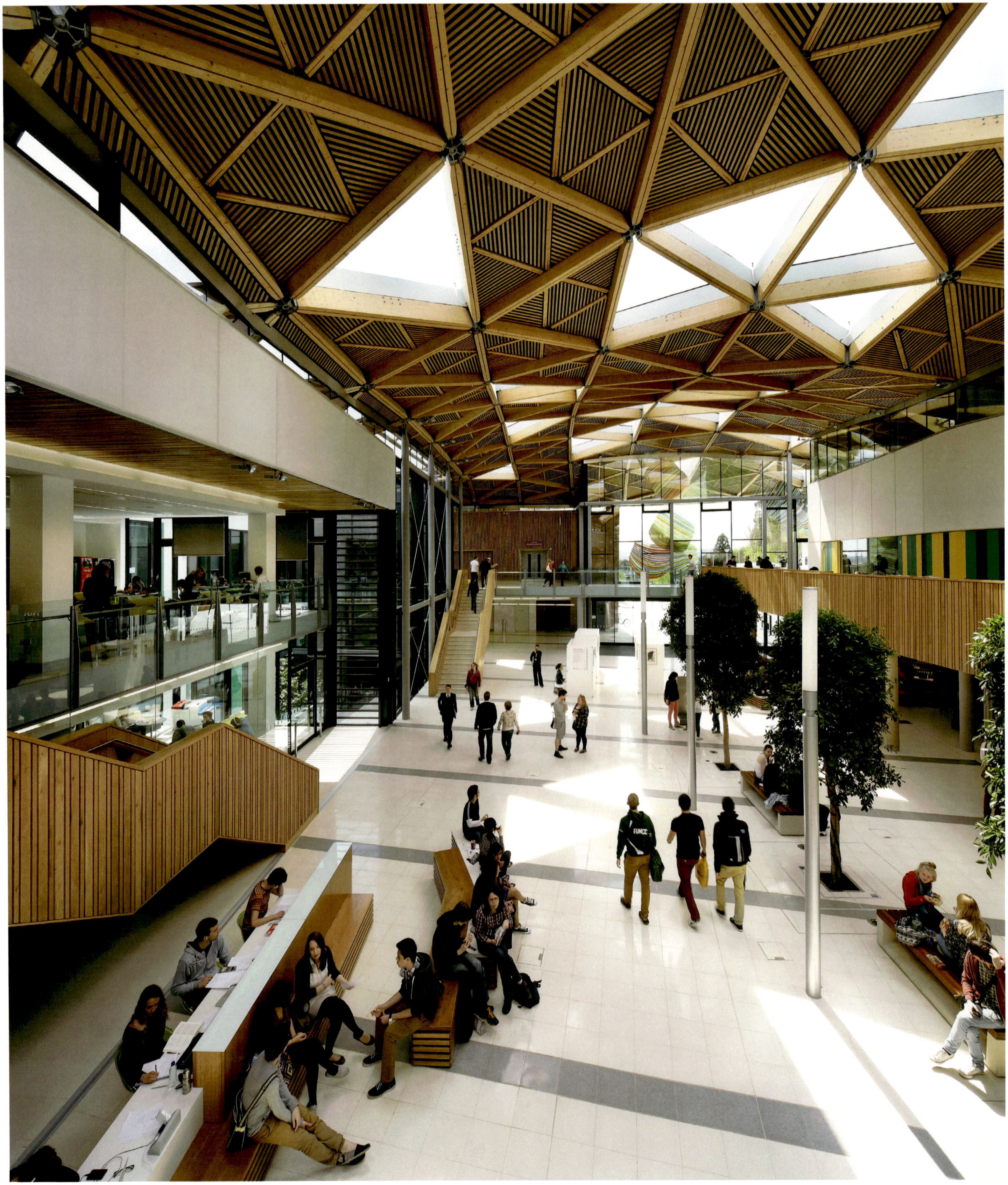

With an area of more than 3,200 square metres, the Forum's roof is the largest freeform timber gridshell in the UK, and stands in distinct contrast to the orthogonal brick façades of the buildings it connects. Designed in collaboration with engineers Buro Happold, the matrix of spruce members – joined at steel nodes, and with oak slats and black acoustic quilt filling each triangle – weaves fluidly between the existing buildings. The team developed software in-house to enable the standardization of parts for the technically ambitious, geometrically complex roof, minimizing variants and therefore cost.

The triangular timber cells are either clad with copper, which will develop a verdigris finish over time, or glazed – the smaller ones over the teaching areas with glass, the larger ones with ETFE (ethylene tetrafluoroethylene) – to flood the internal spaces with natural light.

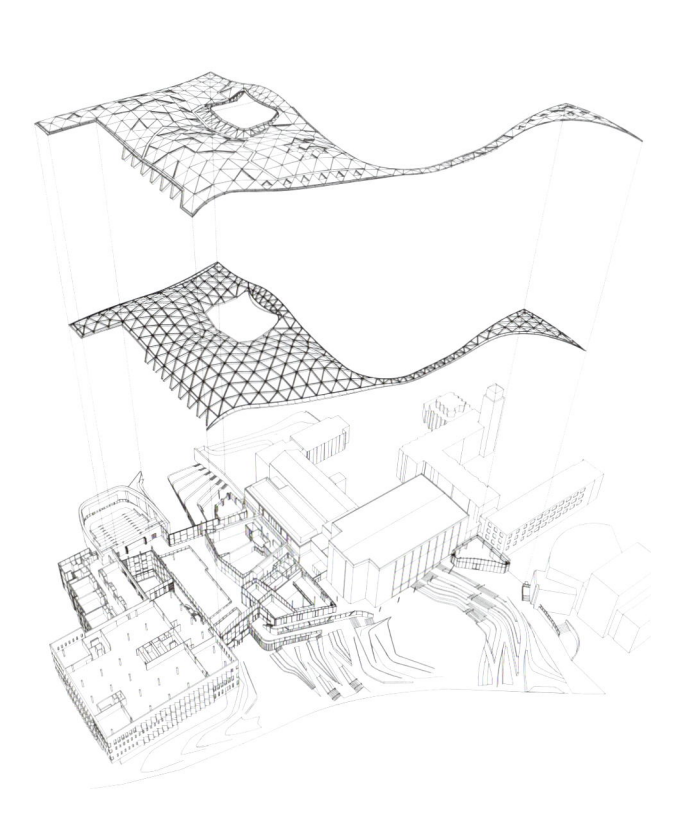

Landscape | The Forum, University of Exeter, UK

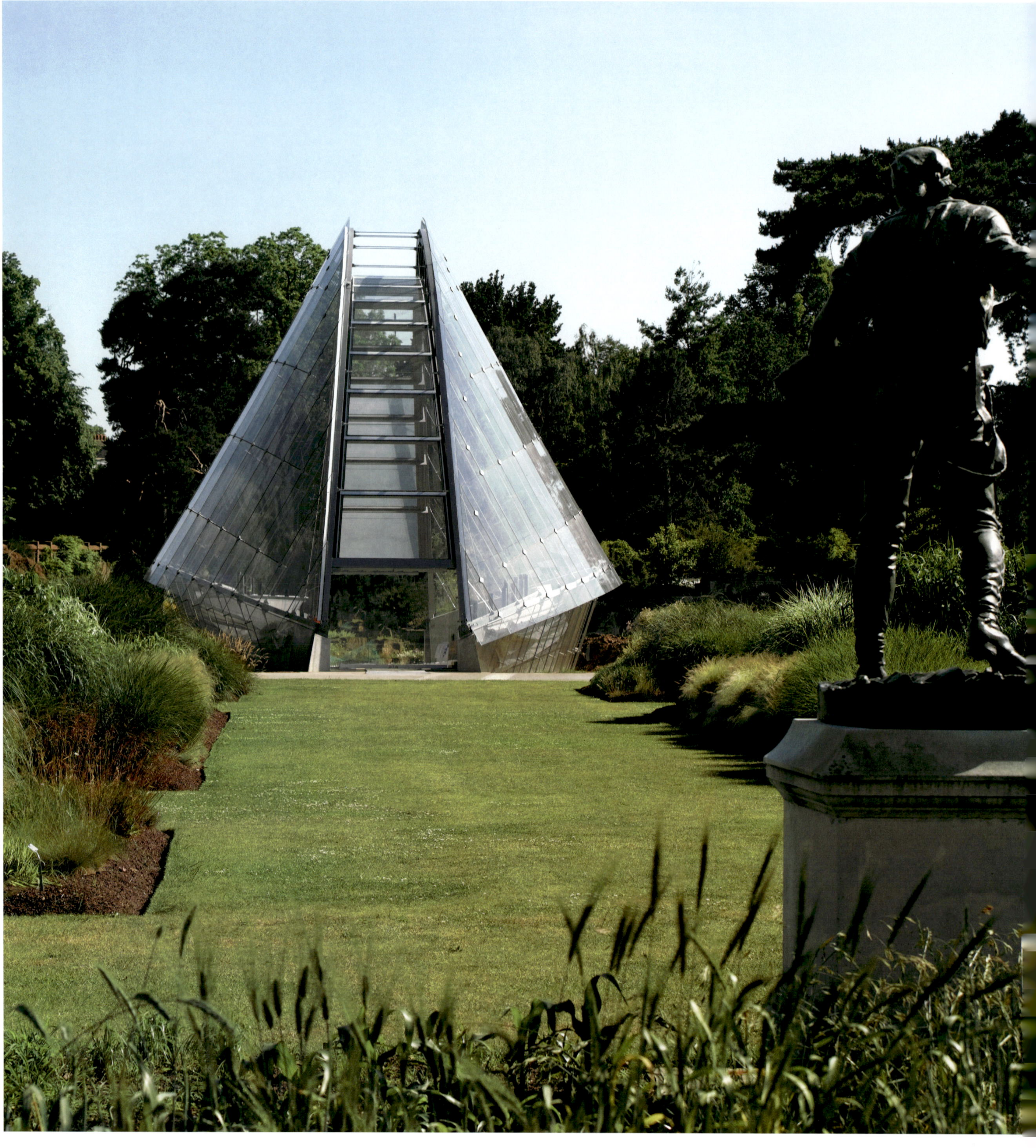

Royal Botanic Gardens
Kew, UK

The Royal Botanic Gardens at Kew is one of the world's great landscapes, a complex tapestry of innovative buildings and structures, formal landscape features and more naturalistic settings. Kew's strategic, far-sighted approach to planning and design has enabled the gardens to continue to evolve, rather than remaining frozen in time since they received World Heritage status in 2003. The armature that has supported this continuing evolution is the site-development plan prepared by Wilkinson Eyre shortly before the UNESCO announcement. Central to the project was the question of how a botanic garden should look in the twenty-first century: while developing as a tourist destination, how could Kew maintain its reputation – and increase its public profile – as a leading centre for scientific research? And how could the gardens' unique character – William Nesfield's formal vistas and Decimus Burton's glasshouses overlaid on to two adjoining gardens by William Chambers and Lancelot 'Capability' Brown – be retained and celebrated? The development plan, in response to these challenges, is therefore less a masterplan and more a series of programmes and initiatives designed to reveal Kew afresh to the visitor while allowing the organization to build much-needed new facilities for display and the rationalization of its archipelago of behind-the-scenes accommodation.

The plan defined a sweeping arc across the site to draw visitors away from the central 'honeypot' around the Palm House, punctuated by a series of architectural events. Many of these – such as Marks Barfield's Treetop Walkway and John Pawson's Sackler Crossing – have now been built. Among them is the Wilkinson Eyre-designed Davies Alpine House, formally opened in 2006, the same year in which the Royal Botanic Gardens was named Client of the Year by the Royal Institute of British Architects (RIBA). It was the first new glasshouse to be constructed at Kew for more than twenty years, and the 'clients' – the collection of tiny alpine plants that had long been considered one of Kew's lost gems – were particularly demanding in their need for plenty of light and cool, constantly moving air. Their new home demonstrates the same spirit of innovation and quality of design that are seen in Kew's other famous glasshouses, achieving much within its tiny footprint. To attain the necessary environmental conditions within, fresh air is delivered to the plants, via displacement nozzles and pipes, from a labyrinth below, where it is cooled by the thermal mass of the concrete foundation slab. The twin parabolic arches that lend the glasshouse its distinctive form provide sufficient height to induce a stack effect, drawing the air up and out of the building as it warms. Sunshades, developed in collaboration with sailmakers and based on a fan-like form similar to a peacock's tail, help keep the house cool in direct sunlight.

In 2006 Wilkinson Eyre also completed the Wolfson Wing extension to the Jodrell Laboratory, a base for interdisciplinary research across the plant sciences. This project in particular continues Kew's long-term strategy of rationalizing the built elements of the site and reinforcing their connection to the landscape. The extension also enabled Kew's renowned Mycology Section to be consolidated with the molecular laboratories, providing the former with additional research space and extra storage for its important collections. Further improvements by Wilkinson Eyre to the gardens' research and study facilities include a new Quarantine House.

INITIATIVE 4
Arc in the Landscape

INITIATIVE 3
Riverside Terrace

INITIATIVE 2
Northern Destination

INITIATIVE 1
Main Entrance and Plant Information Centre

INITIATIVE 5
Temperate House Area

INITIATIVE 6
Victoria Gate and Palm House Area

INITIATIVE 7
Jodrell Facilities

William Nesfield's drawing of 1845 illustrates the original geometry on which Wilkinson Eyre's masterplan is based. Strong vistas from the Palm House radiate out into the gardens, and are linked by an 'arc of opportunity'. This is now marked by a series of new structures designed to draw visitors out into the landscape, raising awareness of Kew's scientific mission and demonstrating mankind's interdependence with nature.

52

The Davies Alpine House (below) sits at the entrance to Kew's existing rock garden, on a strong north–south axis established by the nearby Grass Garden and Sir Hamo Thornycroft's famous statue *The Sower* (1886; see pages 50–51). The ground floor of the house follows a natural incline down into the rock garden, creating a smooth transition through the landscape. Close by, the Wolfson Wing extends the Jodrell Laboratory (right) to create a new three-sided 'quadrangle' around the Aquatic Garden, giving a collegiate feel to the complex, and establishing a stronger relationship between the gardens and the scientific activity within. The most distinctive external feature of the Wolfson Wing is its horizontal cedarboard cladding, which is mellowing with age to imitate the trunks of the eucalyptus trees outside.

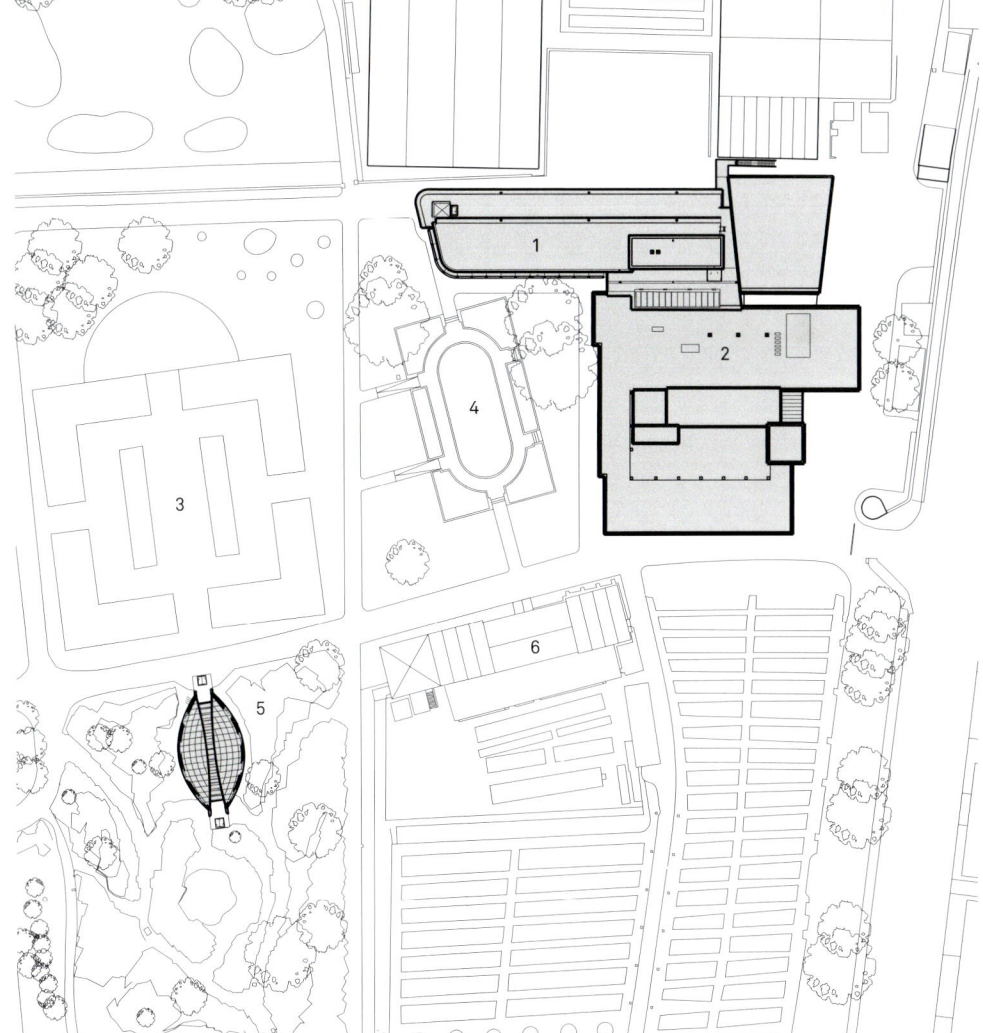

Site plan

1. Wolfson Wing extension
2. Jodrell Laboratory
3. Grass Garden and *The Sower*
4. Aquatic Garden
5. Davies Alpine House
6. School of Horticulture

Highly tensioned stainless-steel rods tie the Alpine House's twin arches together, anchoring them down and transferring loads to the concrete retaining wall and the foundations below. A central glazed spine has automated air vents. To maximize the transmission of light into the interior, a structural glass system was used – obviating the need for a framing support – together with low-iron glass, which has a visible-light transmission rating of more than 90 per cent. The internal shading system of blinds protects the plants by reducing solar gain and accelerating the stack effect.

Environmental diagram

1. Labyrinth: daytime purge
2. Labyrinth: daytime high load
3. Labyrinth: night purge
4. Underground concrete labyrinth
5. Perimeter air inlet
6. Air supplied at floor level displaces warmer air upwards
7. Heat gain from sun reflected and absorbed by blind
8. Automated roof vents allow warm air to escape

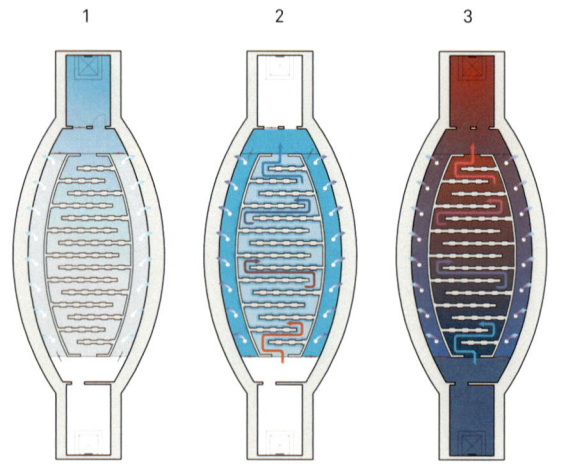

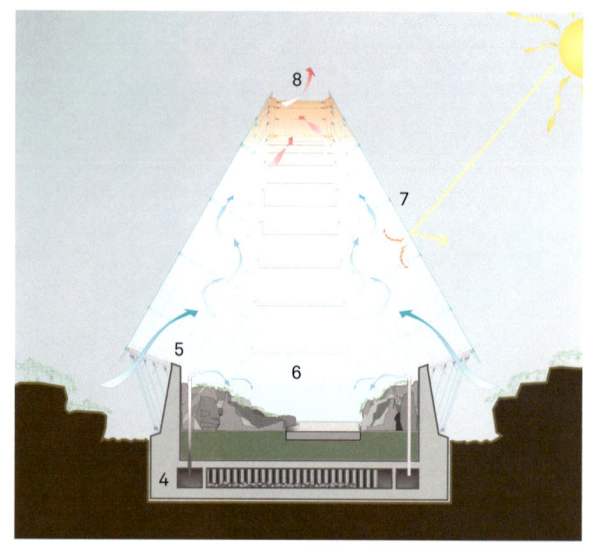

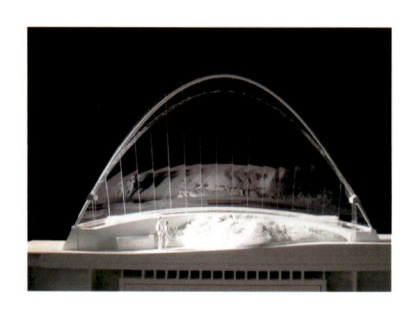

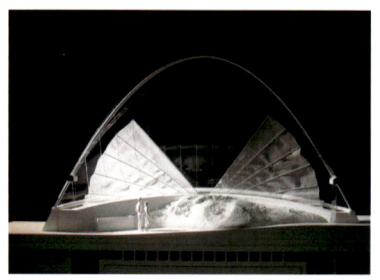

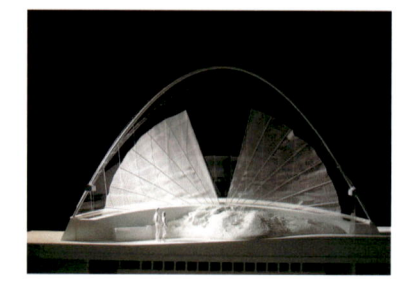

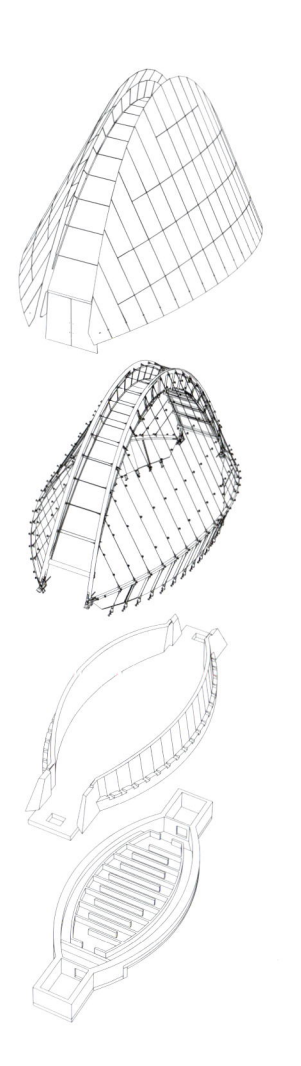

The environmental system for the Alpine House was developed in collaboration with engineers Atelier Ten. It is based on the natural cooling strategy used in termite nests, where the insects open or block tunnels to control the flow of fresh air into the nest, while hot air is drawn out through flues in the structure as the wind blows. The underground tunnels of the nest are replaced here with a concrete labyrinth below ground, which cools air before it is delivered into the glasshouse through displacement nozzles and pipes.

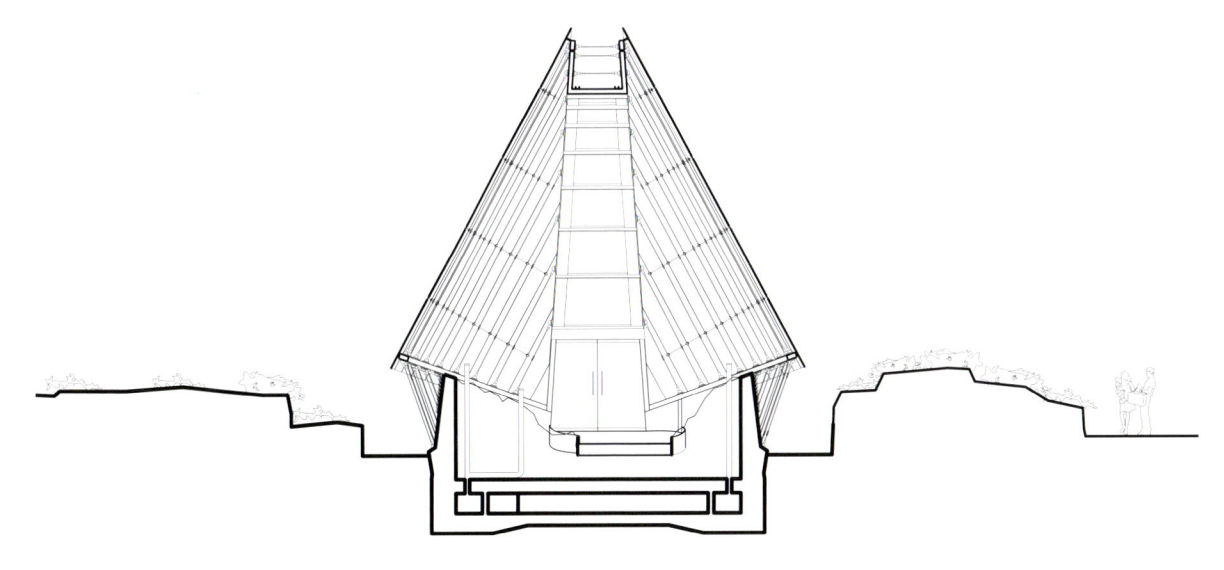

Landscape | Royal Botanic Gardens, Kew, UK

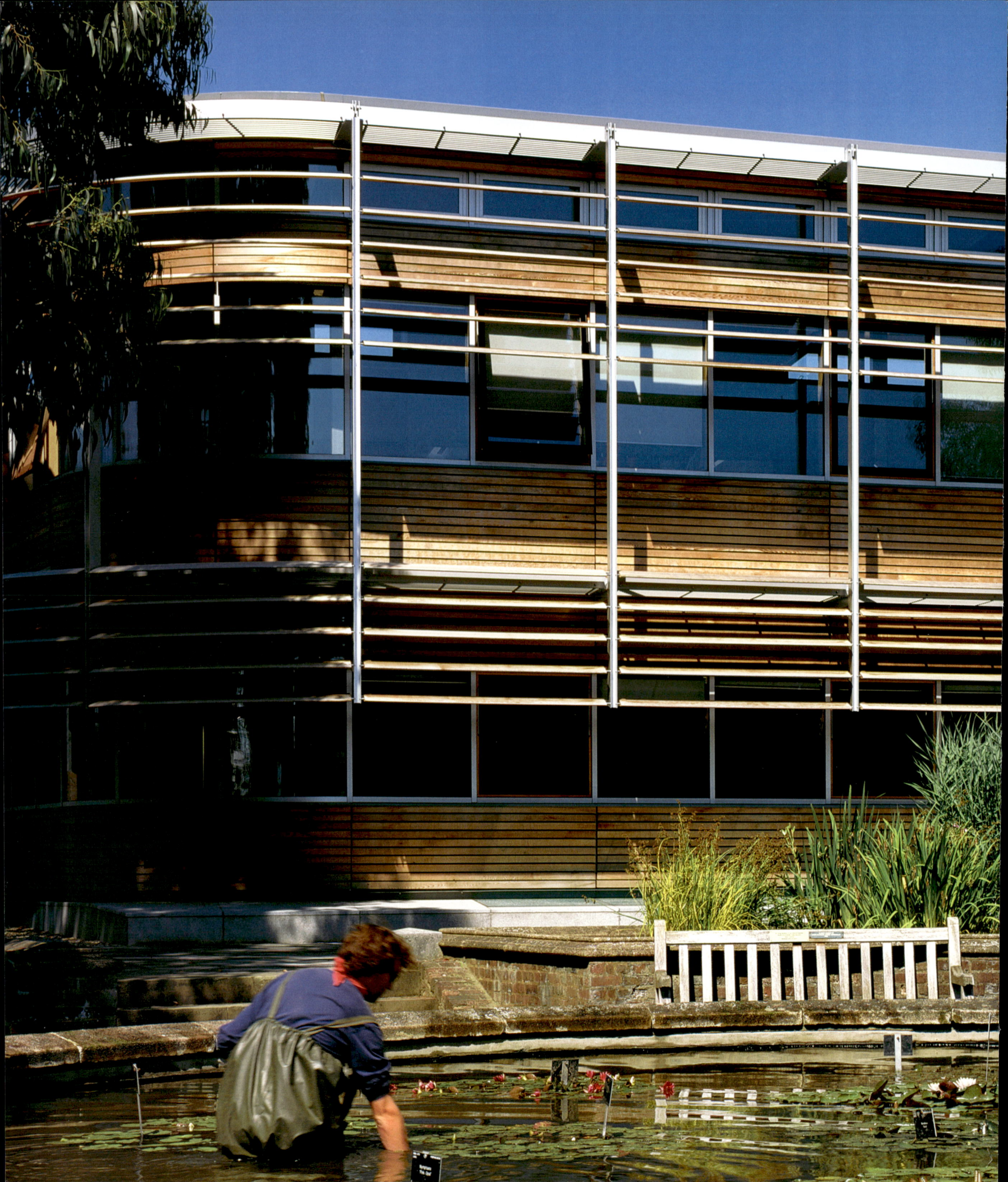

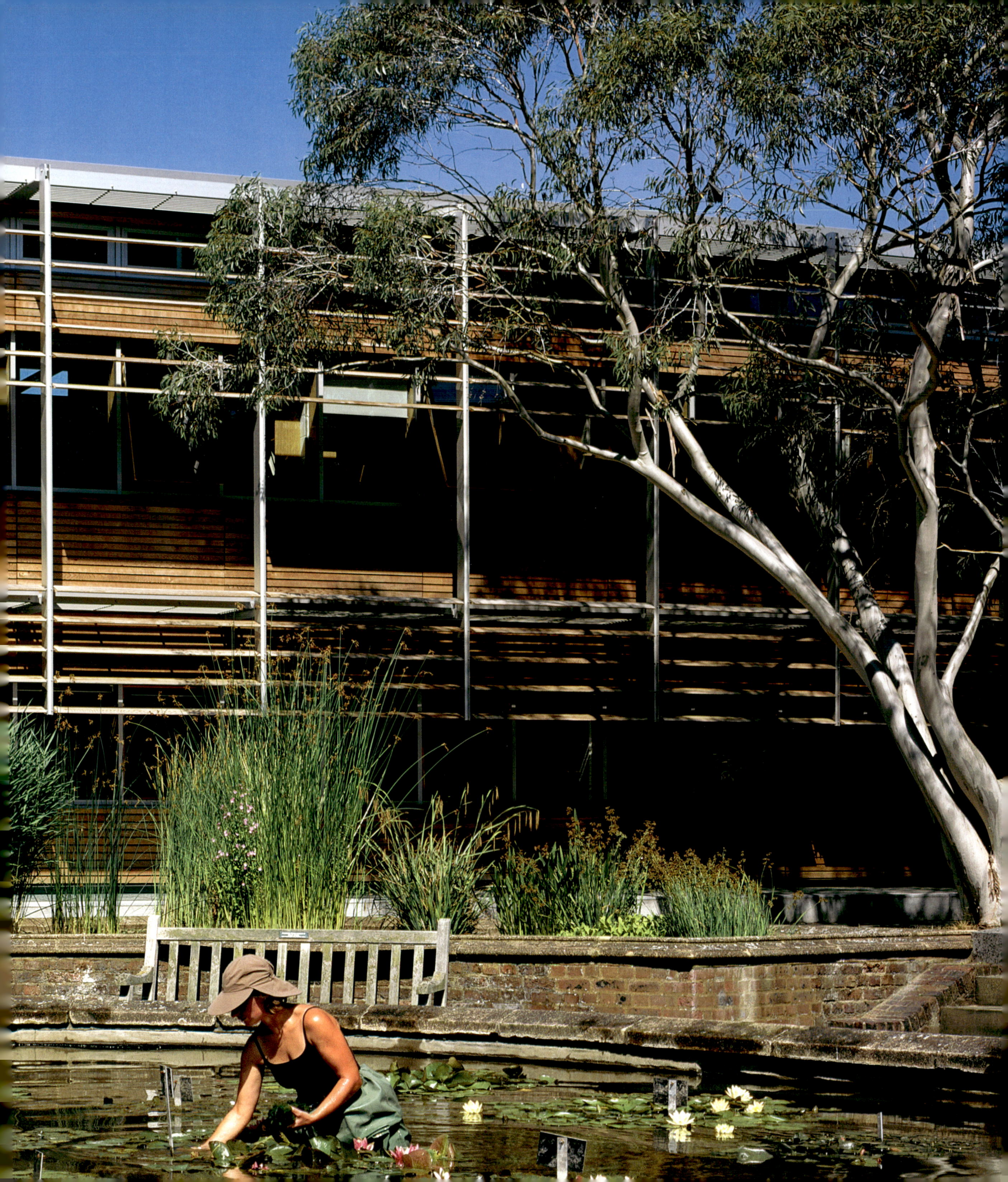

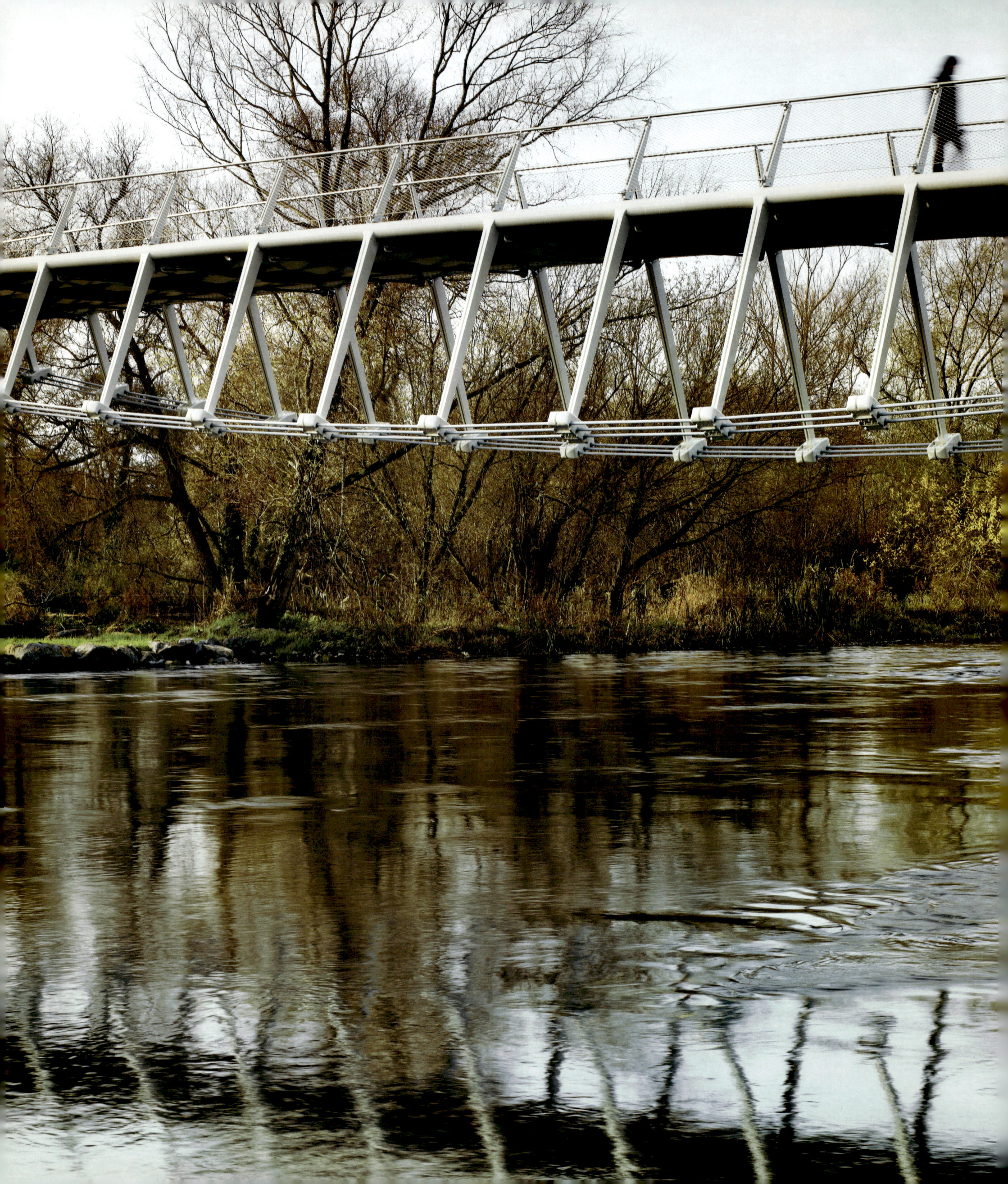

Living Bridge
University of Limerick, Ireland

The River Shannon is the defining natural feature of the University of Limerick's 133-hectare rural campus. Despite the fact that the site had no existing infrastructure, it was selected from a number of possible locations for the university, which was founded in the early 1970s, simply on account of its beautiful riverbank landscape. The river valley now forms the quiet heart of a busy student community, nestling between the established, southern part of the campus and a newer annexe to the north. A road bridge upstream, completed in 2004, opened up this northern bank for development, but an increase in the number of both students and buildings, including new student residences and a large performing-arts centre, subsequently accelerated the need for greater connectivity between the two halves of the campus.

The gentle riparian landscape of the river corridor has been identified as one of international environmental importance. At this point the Shannon flows wide and shallow, fragmented by wooded islands, which effectively form stepping stones across the meandering waters, and enclosed by stands of low trees on either bank. Entering this secret world is a real delight, and the intention behind the design of the Living Bridge was to celebrate its essential quality with a structure that threaded through the landscape and invited users to linger and engage with their surroundings.

The bridge is a deliberately modest visual statement, spanning at low level and with minimum impact to create an organic relationship between nature, bridge and user. It skips across the river in six equal spans, arranged on a continuous sweeping arc a little like the trajectory of a skimming stone. The landing points are coincident with the islands in a manner reminiscent of an ancient clapper crossing. The spans are supported by tetrapod pier footings, which act as cutwaters to prevent the erosion and movement of the islands. From each end, the curving deck seems to disappear into the landscape, inviting users to become temporarily enclosed in the natural environment of river and trees during their crossing, as views of their destination gradually unfold. To further extend the journey, and to encourage students to occupy and inhabit their bridge, the 4-metre-wide deck broadens to 7 metres at each pier to provide a small refuge for informal gatherings or contemplation against the backdrop of the tree canopy.

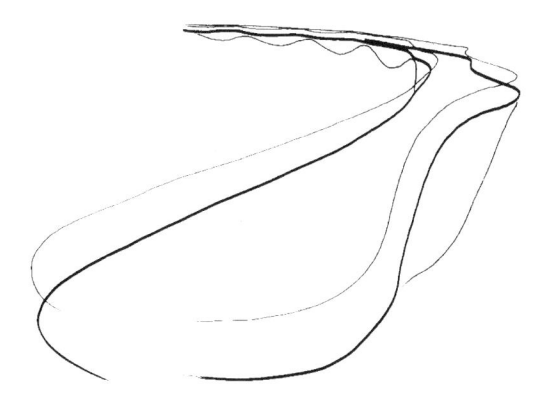

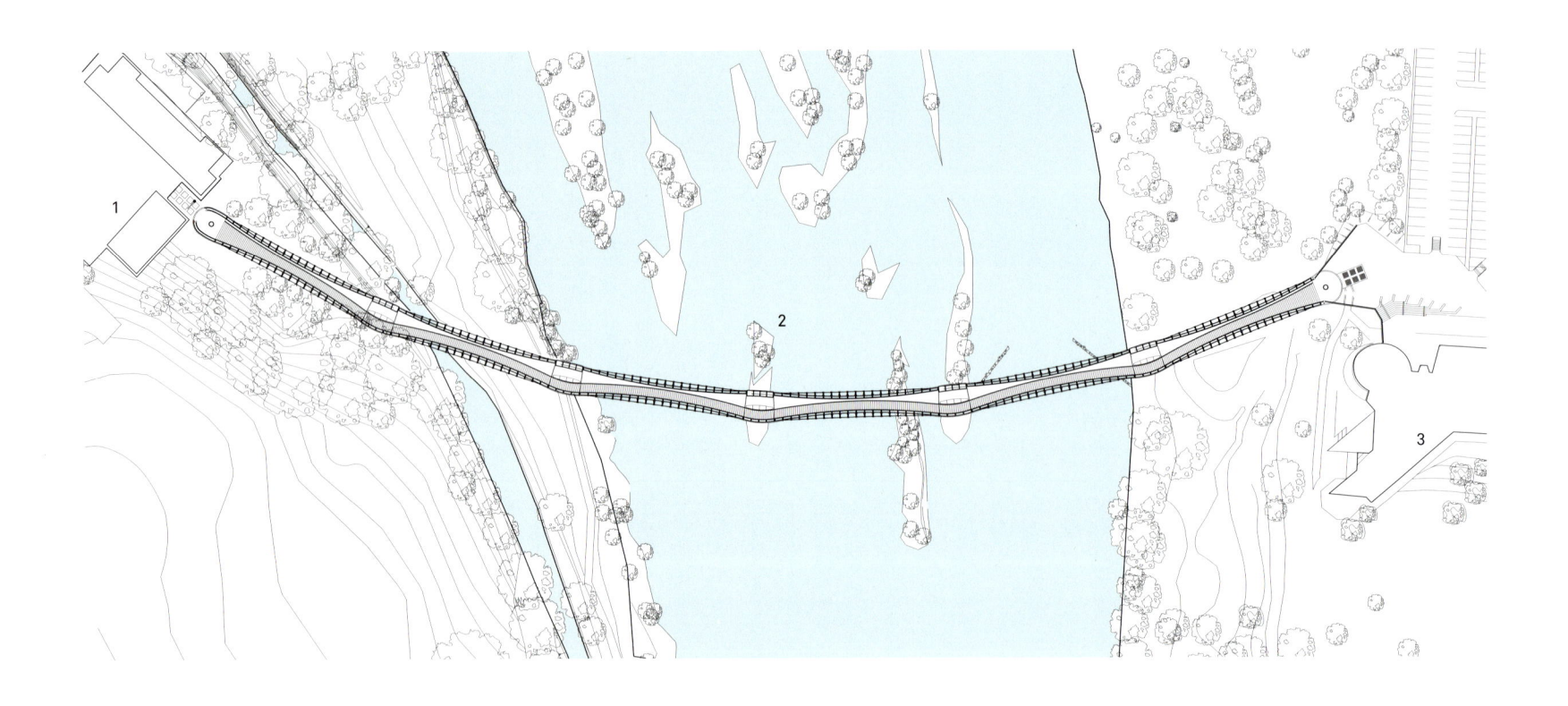

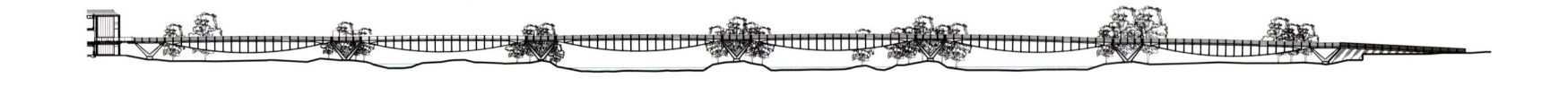

The bridge, 350 metres long in total, curves on a 300-metre radius in six equal spans between table-like pier sections. The deck pulses from a width of 7 metres at the piers to just 4 metres at centre-span, defining each separate span while providing a continuum across the whole structure.

Site plan

1. Main campus
2. River Shannon
3. North campus

To avoid the tall pylons typical of a suspension bridge, a more restrained structural approach was adopted, with the deeper-spanning structure of the bridge located below deck level. The tetrapod piers are connected by steel bridge sections supported from below by a pair of cable trusses, each of which consists of three parallel steel catenary cables suspended between the pier locations. Steel compression members rise from the cables to support the deck, and extend further to form the parapet posts and handrail supports. The curving lines of cable, deck and handrail are continuous across the pier construction, giving the bridge an overlying sense of unity.

The bridge is intended to be inhabited, a place for social interaction, and so each pier supports a small refuge, protected by a vertically cantilevered glass screen. These screens frame the tree canopy beyond and shield an integral timber bench facing into the bridge deck. A second bench acts as a 'cutwater' for pedestrians, and allows for face-to-face gatherings.

As this is a 24-hour crossing, essential to the campus infrastructure, the lighting strategy was developed to ensure safety and visibility, but also to enhance the experience of the user and reinforce the geometry of the bridge. A variety of light sources has been employed, incorporated into the superstructure and deck furniture as discreetly as possible. On the approaches to the bridge, glass-lens pavement lights are lit from beneath with strong colour, while the bridge spans are washed at low level by softer light from linear fluorescent luminaries. Floodlights behind the bench assemblies light up the glass panels, illuminating the fritted pattern on the glazing and casting a glow on to the adjacent trees.

Landscape | Living Bridge, University of Limerick, Ireland

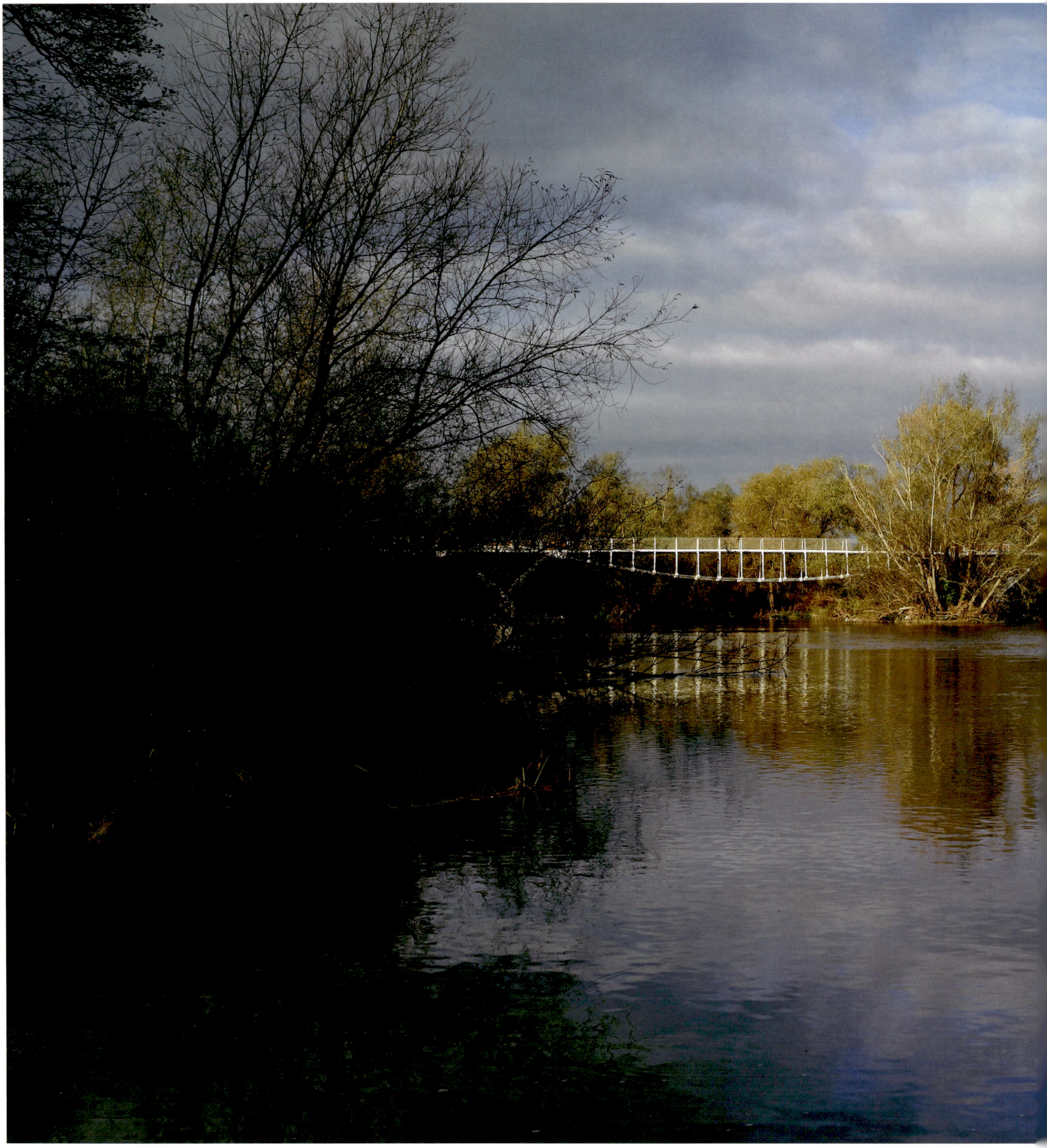

Landscape | Living Bridge, University of Limerick, Ireland

Schools for the Future
UK

In 2003 the Department for Education and Skills (now the Department for Education) commissioned a number of design practices to develop 'exemplar designs' for primary, secondary and all-through schools in anticipation of the then-government's Building Schools for the Future (BSF) programme. Begun in earnest in 2005, the BSF programme committed £45 billion to the rebuilding or refurbishment of every secondary school in England. The exemplar schemes, although designed for real sites, were not necessarily intended to be built, but instead demonstrated what could be done in architectural terms to support both the BSF programme and a rapidly changing learning landscape.

Wilkinson Eyre's exemplar secondary-school scheme was based around a kit of parts – a series of components that could be configured according to a wide variety of different sites and learning scenarios, and which, where possible, blurred the thresholds between indoor and outdoor space. The basic building block was a distinctive, two-storey learning cluster, which could be allocated to a specific house or year group, subject area or educational need, providing a 'school within a school' for up to 300 students. Several of these clusters were arranged – together with simple, orthogonal support buildings – around a central agora space. Environmental performance drove the design of the learning clusters, an acoustic labyrinth to the external façades allowing natural ventilation at low level without external noise. A stack effect drew warm air up through the central void of each, to be vented out through a distinctive perforated-steel roof cowl.

The Wilkinson Eyre kit of parts was the first of the exemplar schemes to be adopted by a real client: the John Madejski Academy in Reading, which opened in 2007. The sponsor, John Madejski, chairman of Reading Football Club, had won plaudits for his youth-training programme, and sport was chosen as the academy's specialism. The new building replaced an undersubscribed school in one of the most deprived wards in the country, offering an improved learning environment for both local students and others admitted on the basis of their aptitude for sport. Having already worked on the exemplar scheme, the team was able to test the flexibility of the kit of parts, tailoring it to suit the needs of the site and delivering the academy a year sooner than others commissioned at the same time. Three learning clusters are arranged either side of a curving agora space, connected by bridges at first-floor level. Using a non-departmental arrangement, each of the three clusters has a pair of science studios and design and technology/art rooms, as well as standard classrooms. The central space within each cluster is used for small 'house' assemblies, social study and display, and has an adjacent staff base for passive supervision. A fourth cluster has a more adult feel, containing the learning resource centre, sixth-form area and staff development space. The central amenities (for dining, assembly, central administration and sport) are contained in rectilinear buildings, with the sports facilities designed to accommodate a quarter of the school population at any one time. They are also large enough to host regional tournaments.

The kit of parts was subsequently adopted for a number of schools in Bristol, as part of the city-wide BSF programme. It was employed at the Bristol Metropolitan Academy, where three two-storey learning clusters, arranged by academic department, are located along the straight side of an internal street, facing flexible spaces that house specialist areas and a sports hall. At a second school in the city, the Bridge Learning Campus, three learning clusters form part of one of the UK's very few all-through schools. Here, a nursery, primary and secondary school are combined with a severe learning difficulties unit and a student support centre for the rehabilitation of excluded pupils. Wilkinson Eyre was also involved in the design of two further schools in Bristol: Bristol Brunel Academy, the first secondary school in the UK to be delivered under the BSF programme, configured as a linear building over four floors around a central atrium; and, in collaboration with architects FLACQ, Brislington Enterprise College.

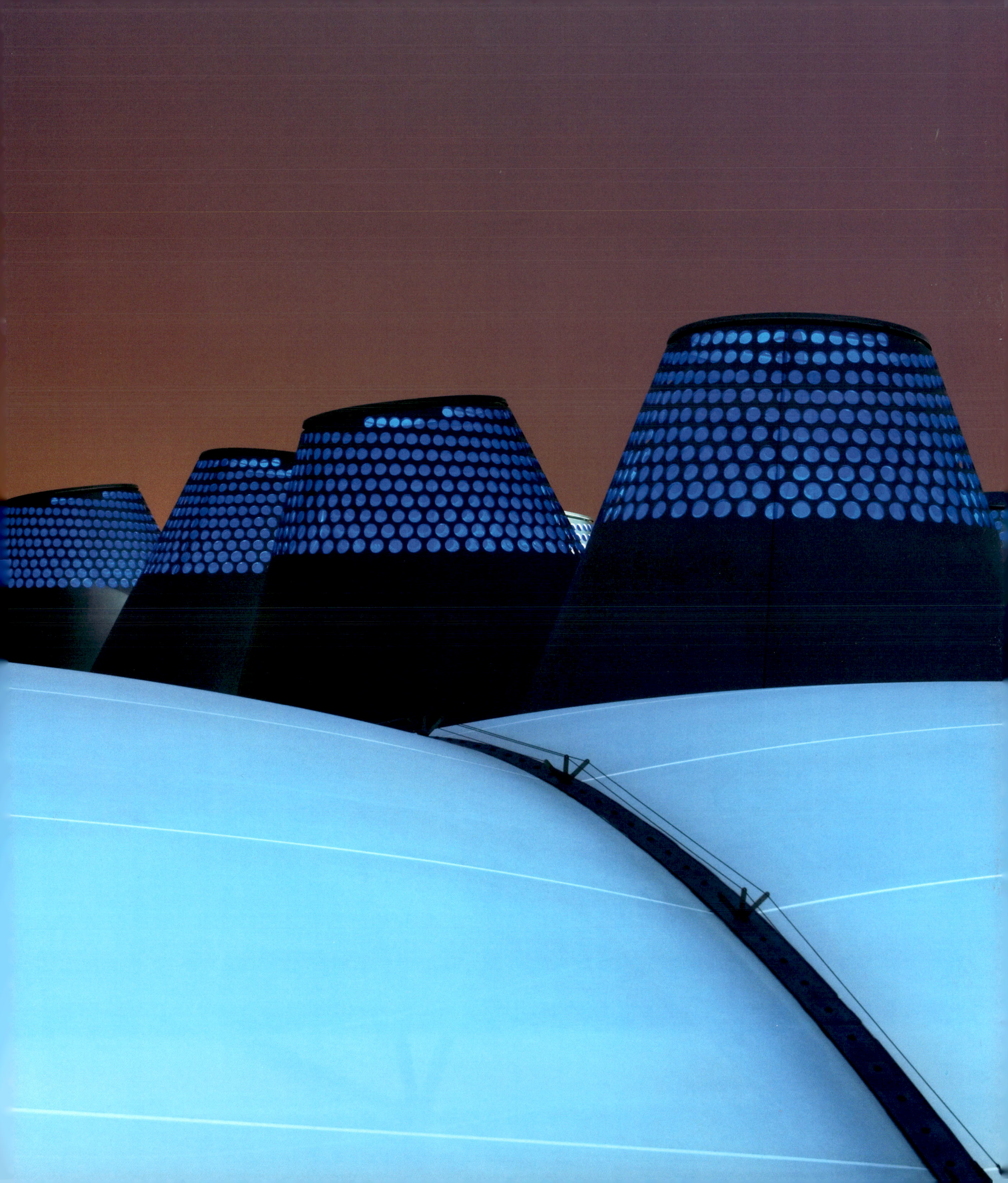

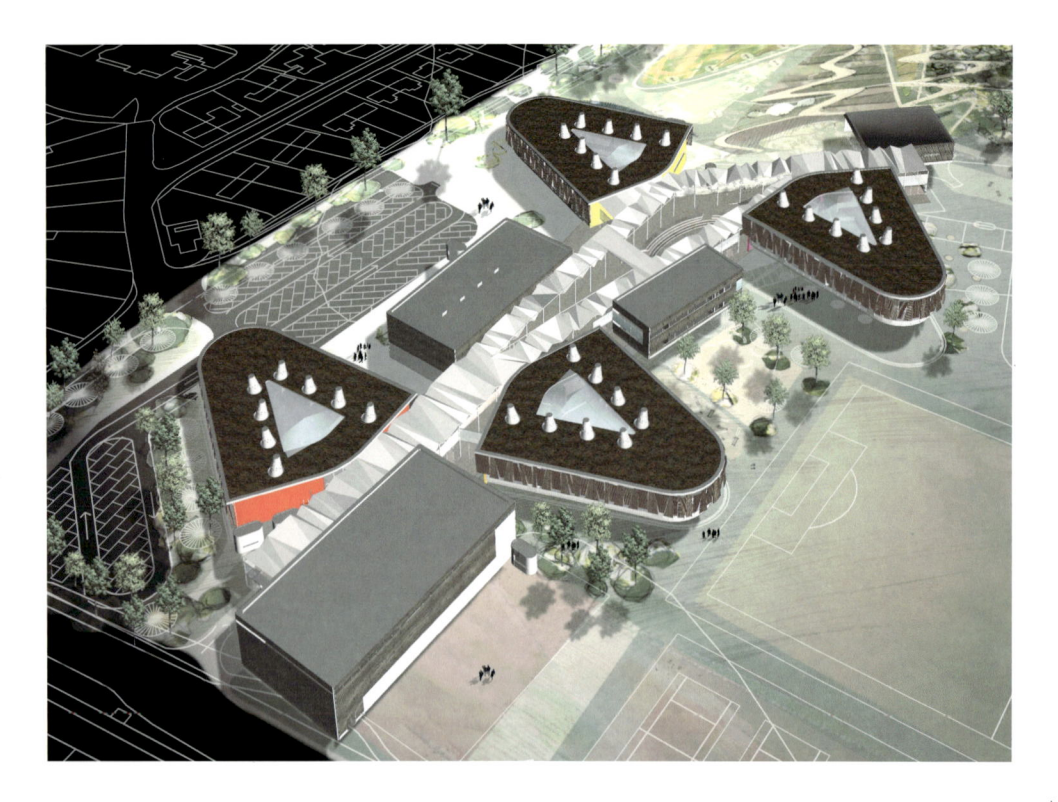

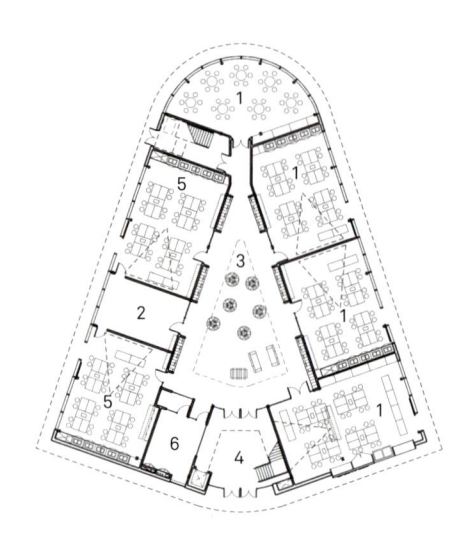

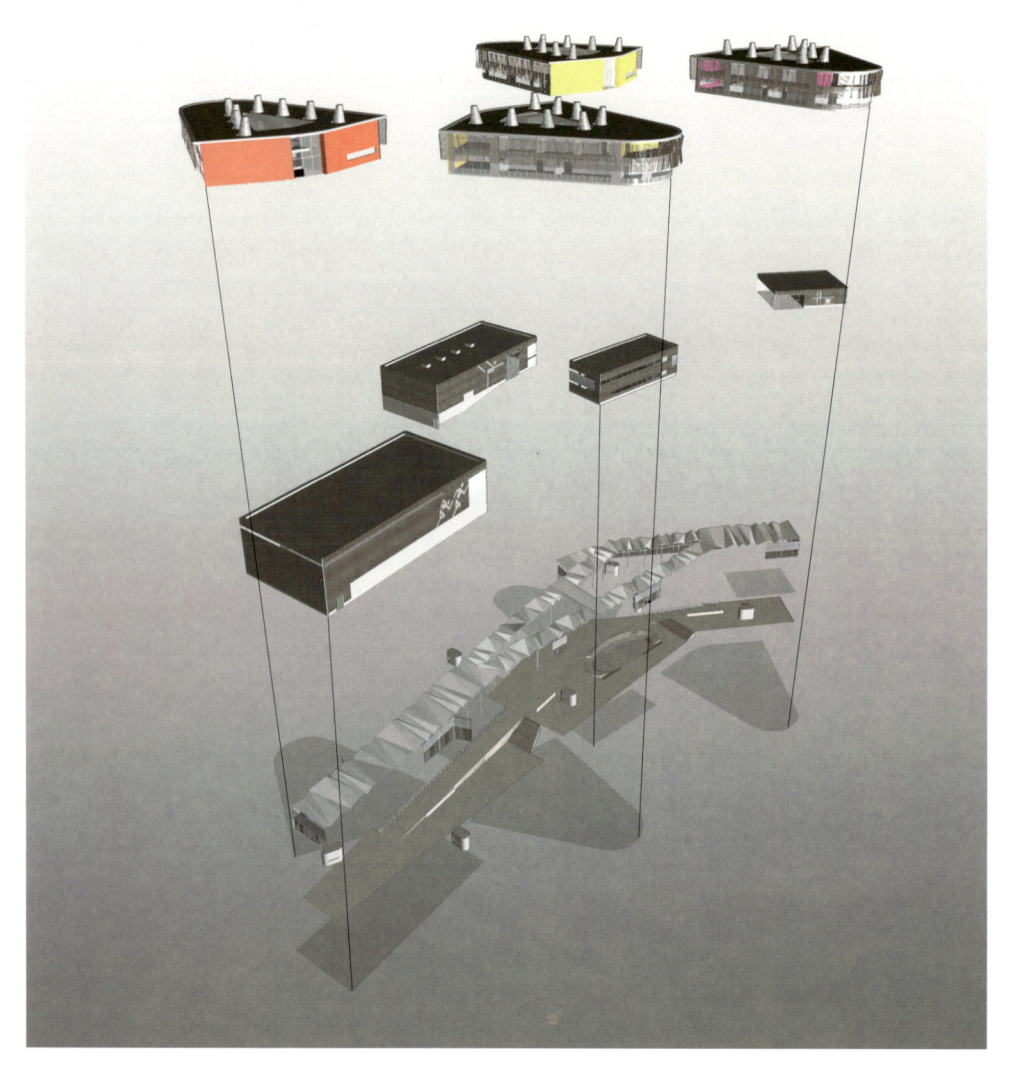

Learning cluster ground-floor plan

1. Specialized teaching space
2. Prep room
3. Learning resources
4. Lobby
5. Science studio
6. Staff base

The kit of parts developed for the exemplar scheme included the wedge-shaped learning clusters, which subsequently became affectionately known as 'strawberries', together with orthogonal support buildings.

The central space around which these elements are arranged was inspired by the agora – a public open space in ancient Greece used for gatherings and markets – and effectively eliminates the need for a traditional school corridor by offering a large space for interaction, assemblies and events.

The learning clusters enable an otherwise overwhelming building scale to be broken down into 'houses', each of which can operate as a school within a school. The clusters also significantly reduce the need for pupil movement around the school because 'half-day' working can be timetabled into a single building.

Landscape | Schools for the Future, UK

Site plan

> Entrance
1 Multipurpose hall
2 Cluster A (sixth form, learning resource centre, vocational study, special educational needs and staff development)
3 Agora
4 Cluster B
5 Cluster C
6 Cluster D
7 Dining hall
8 Sports hall

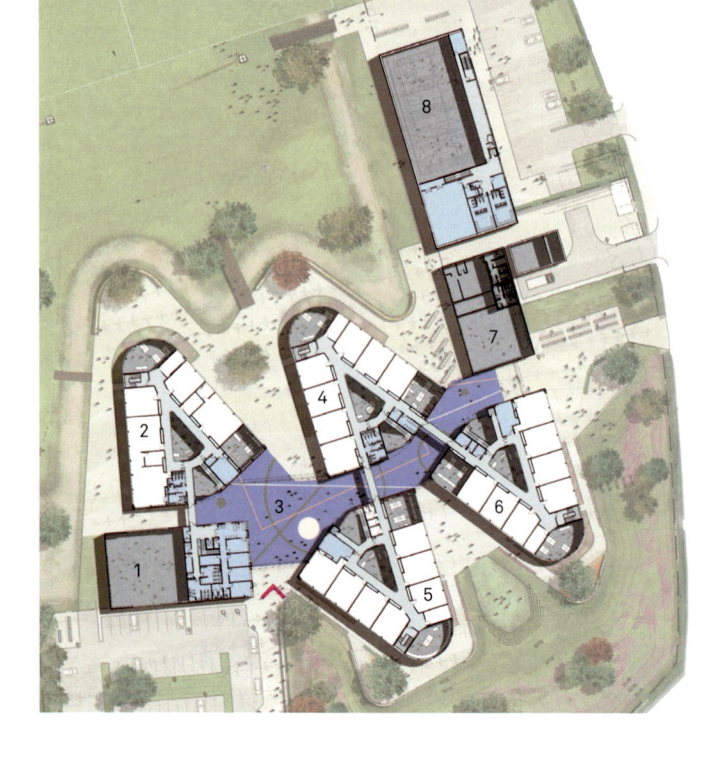

At the John Madejski Academy, three learning clusters are configured on a non-departmental basis; for example, there is a pair of science studios in each. A fourth cluster is more open-plan, and is designed for older students, staff development and vocational study. Each floor in the learning clusters is planned around 8-metre-deep spaces for daylight and ventilation, with room modules of 60, 90 and 120 square metres to suit different specialisms. Rooms with specific servicing requirements, such as science labs and design and technology/art rooms, are generally located on the ground floor, with more generic classrooms above.

The agora canopy is made of single-foil ETFE pillows supported by steel trusses and cables that span between the learning clusters, giving the academy a column-free central circulation space. The agora is unheated, while the rubber crumb floor deadens noise like a giant carpet.

Environmental section

1. Acoustically separated ventilation shafts
2. Acoustic plasterboard with shaped-ash capping piece
3. Clerestory glazing
4. GRP (glass-reinforced plastic) cowls
5. High-level vent for purge ventilation
6. Low-level vent allowing air to pass through a SonaVent acoustic labyrinth and across the top of a radiator
7. ICT resource/social area
8. Classroom

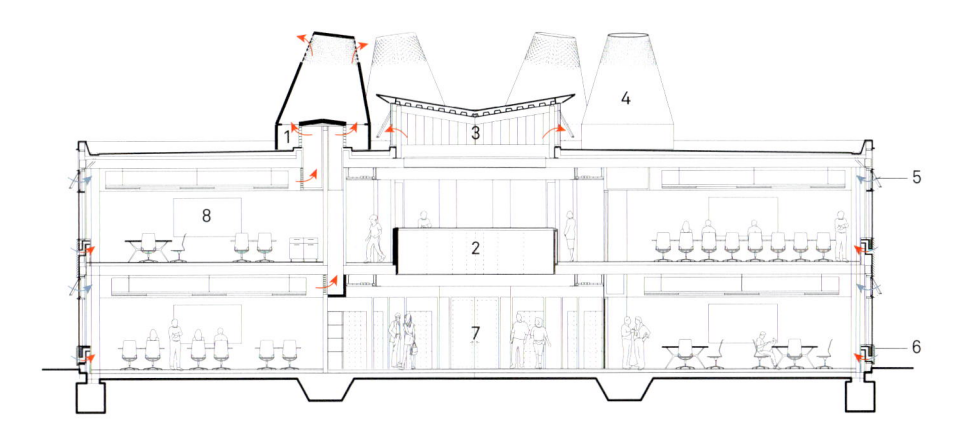

Landscape | Schools for the Future, UK

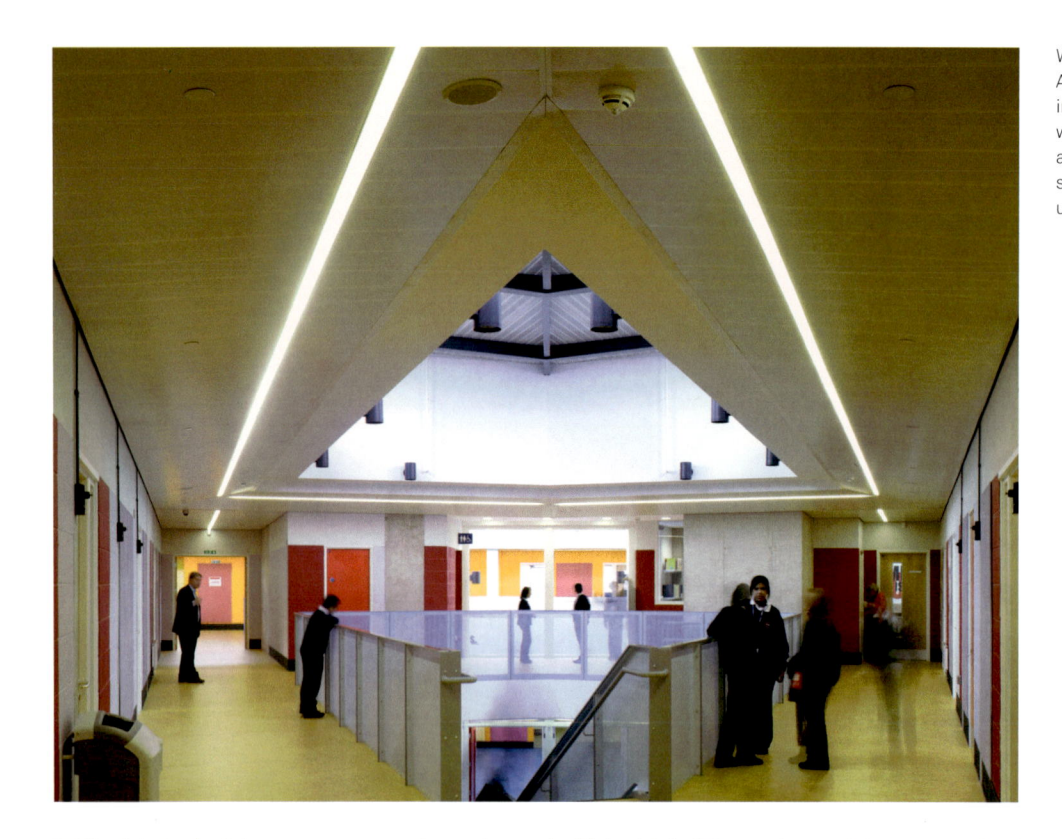

While students at Bristol Metropolitan Academy tend to spend extended periods in their 'home' cluster, the street is filled with activity at lunchtimes, when the dining areas spill out to occupy the central space, sheltered by a tessellated roof plan that undulates along its length.

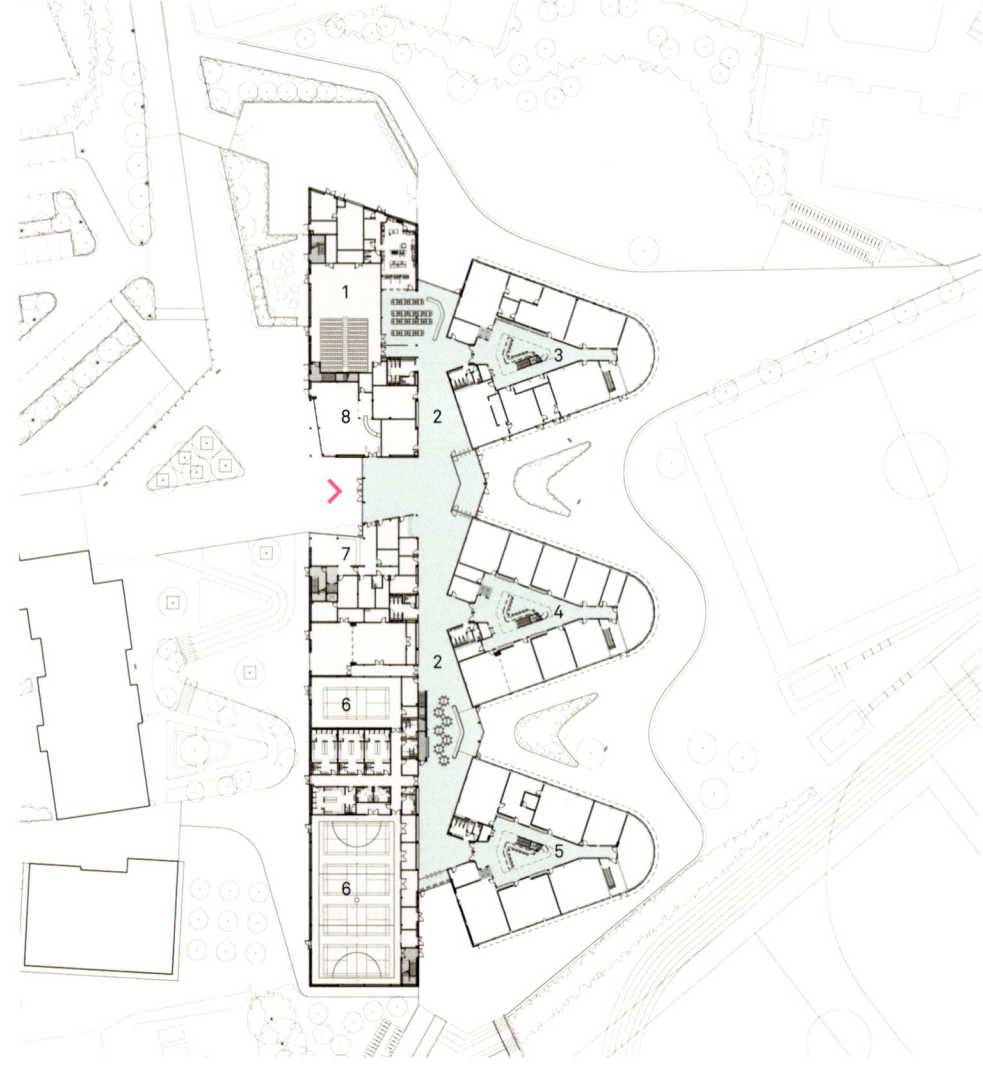

Bristol Metropolitan Academy site plan

> Entrance
1 Assembly/dining area
2 Agora
3 Technology and art
4 Languages and business
5 Science
6 Sports hall
7 Administration
8 Learning support and resources

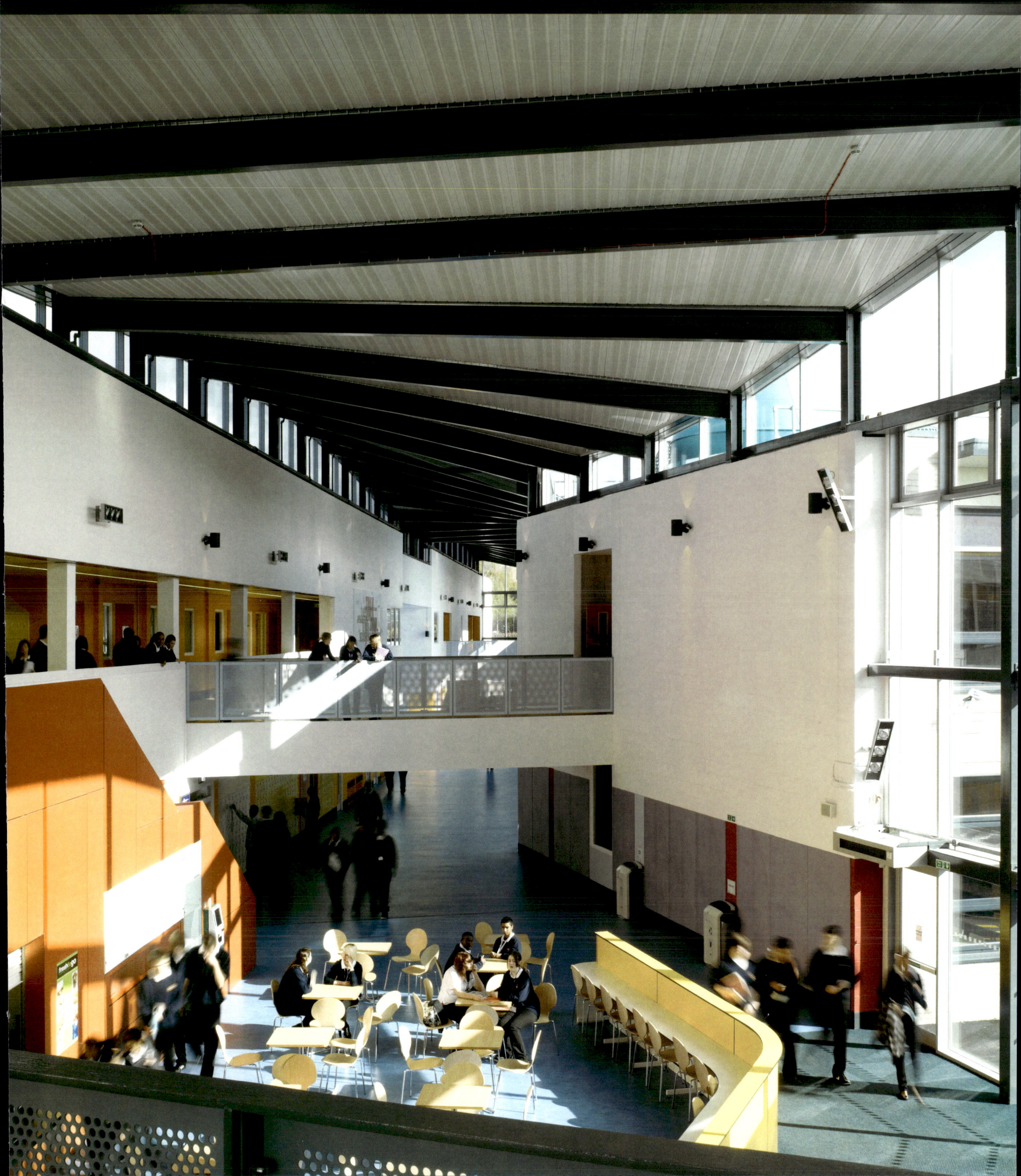

72

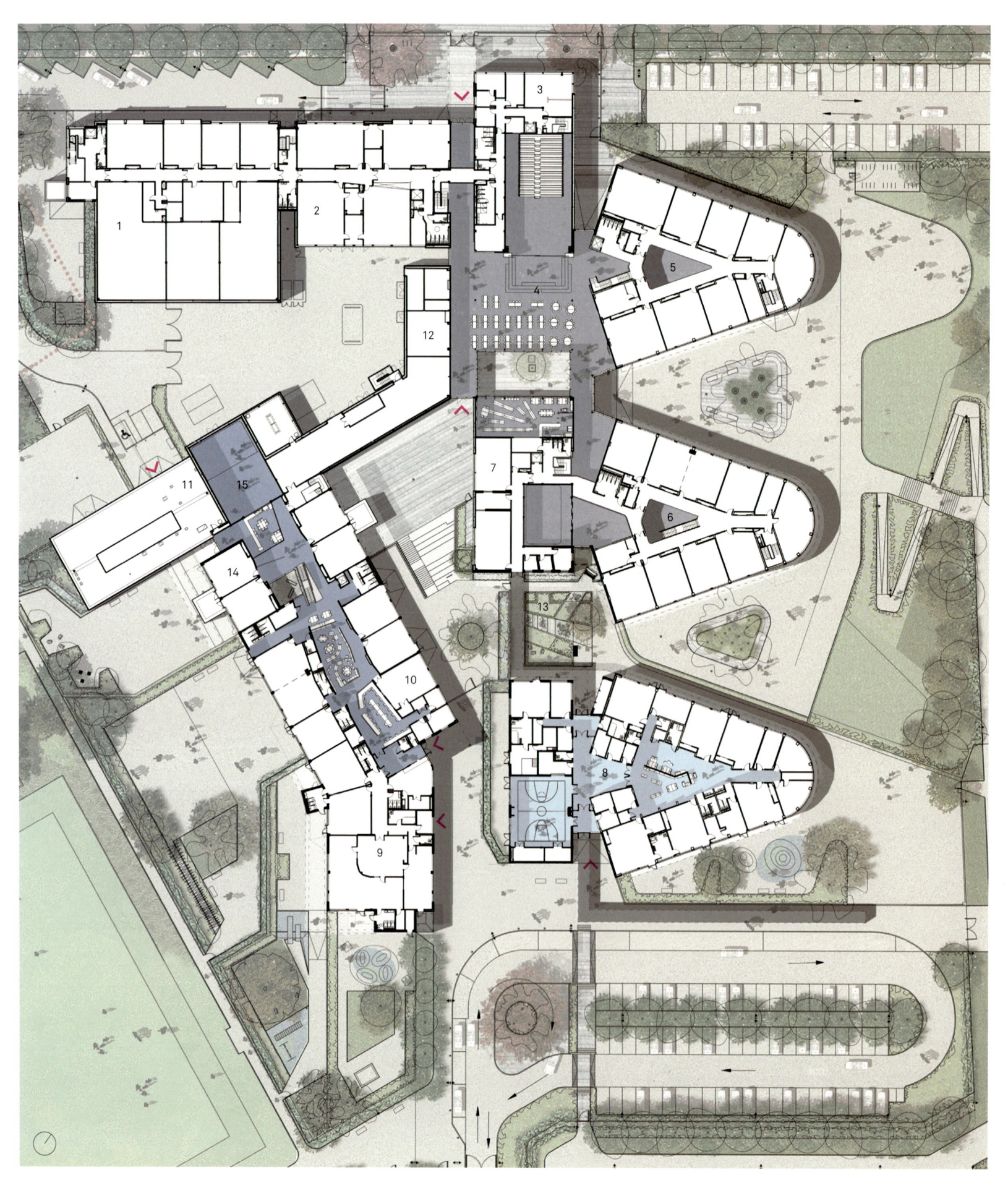

The Bridge Learning Campus combines five educational centres, from nursery school through to further education college. The learning clusters built here comprise science and humanities bases for secondary-age students, as well as a single-storey version for students with severe learning difficulties. The topography of the sloping site reinforces the progression of students in this all-through school, with toddlers entering small-scale buildings at the top of the site and gradually moving towards the more civic-scaled buildings lower down as they grow older.

Bridge Learning Campus site plan

> Entrance
1. Vocational college
2. Secondary (Technology)
3. Administration/secretariat
4. Central dining, assembly and performance space
5. Secondary (Science)
6. Secondary (Humanities)
7. Learning resource centre/ music and drama
8. Profound and Multiple Learning Difficulties unit
9. Nursery
10. Primary (Key Stage 1)
11. Student support centre
12. Central catering
13. Sensory garden
14. Primary (Key Stage 2)
15. Primary hall

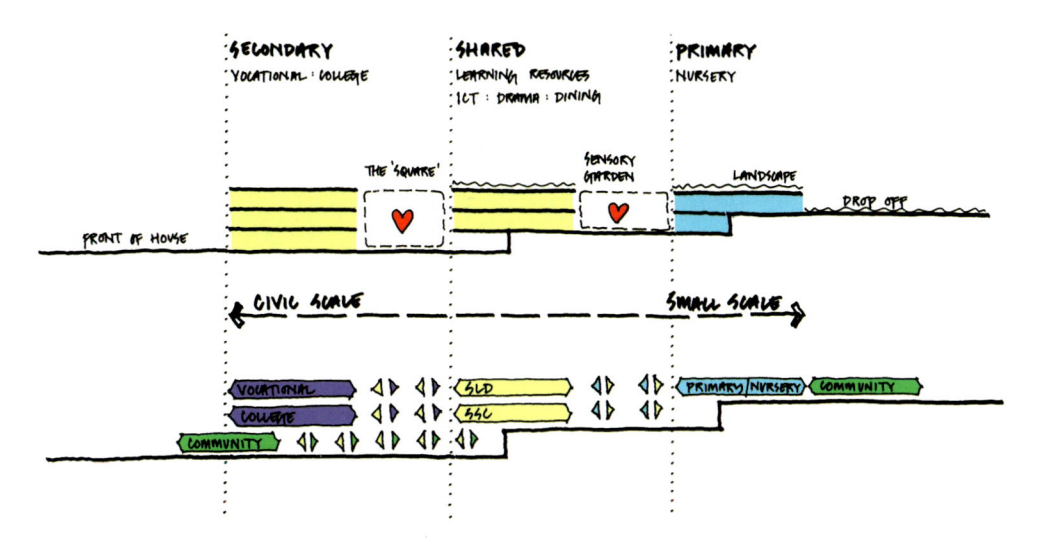

Landscape | Schools for the Future, UK

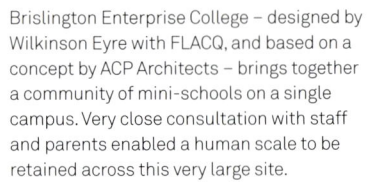

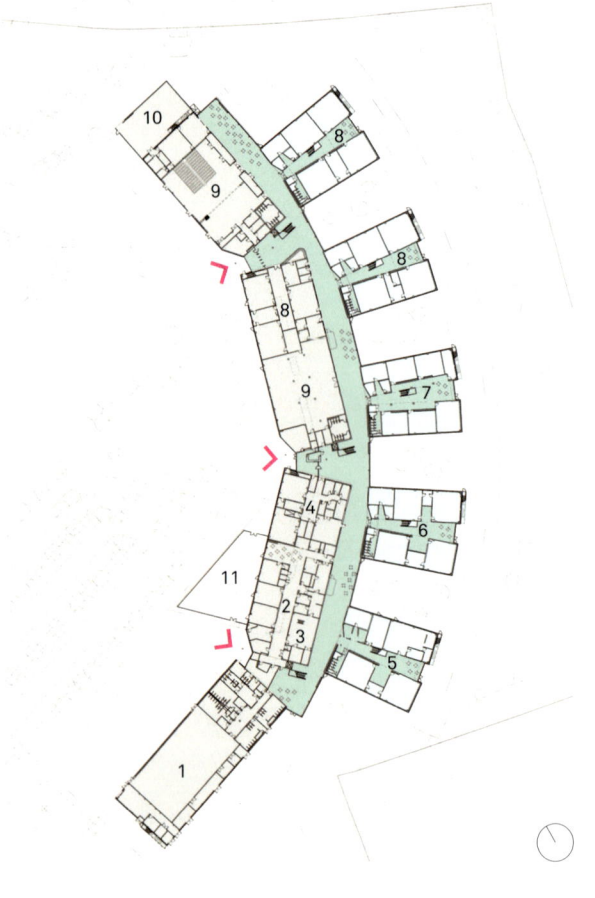

Brislington Enterprise College site plan

> Entrance
1 Sports hall
2 Severe Learning Difficulties unit
3 Hydrotherapy pool
4 Music department
5 Design and technology
6 Electronics
7 General teaching
8 Science
9 Drama/assembly hall/dining area
10 Service yard
11 Sensory garden

Brislington Enterprise College – designed by Wilkinson Eyre with FLACQ, and based on a concept by ACP Architects – brings together a community of mini-schools on a single campus. Very close consultation with staff and parents enabled a human scale to be retained across this very large site.

At Bristol Brunel Academy, the kit-of-parts design approach was not feasible, so the school is based on a very simple, orthogonal plan, with a three-storey, linear block of accommodation anchored by the sports hall and dining hall at either end, and split lengthways to create a central atrium. Two banks of classrooms are connected by a series of internal footbridges and perimeter walkways. A cranked wing of leisure accommodation at ground-floor level effectively faces the local community, welcoming its members on to the site to use the academy's sports facilities.

The close engagement between design team and school community during the project is demonstrated in a series of artworks throughout the school, including one in which staff and students share their aspirations on a 'wall of wishes'.

Bristol Brunel Academy site plan

> Entrance
1 Community leisure facility
2 Student services
3 Learning support and resources
4 Language and business
5 Technology and art
6 Kitchen
7 Assembly/dining area
8 Performing arts
9 Sports hall

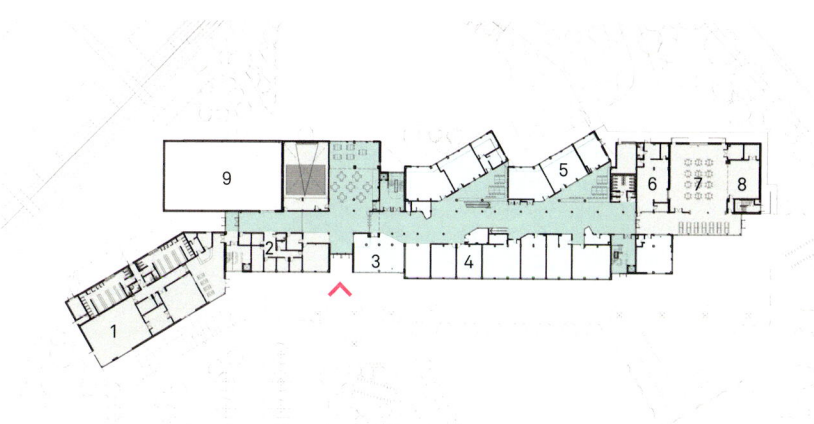

Landscape | Schools for the Future, UK 75

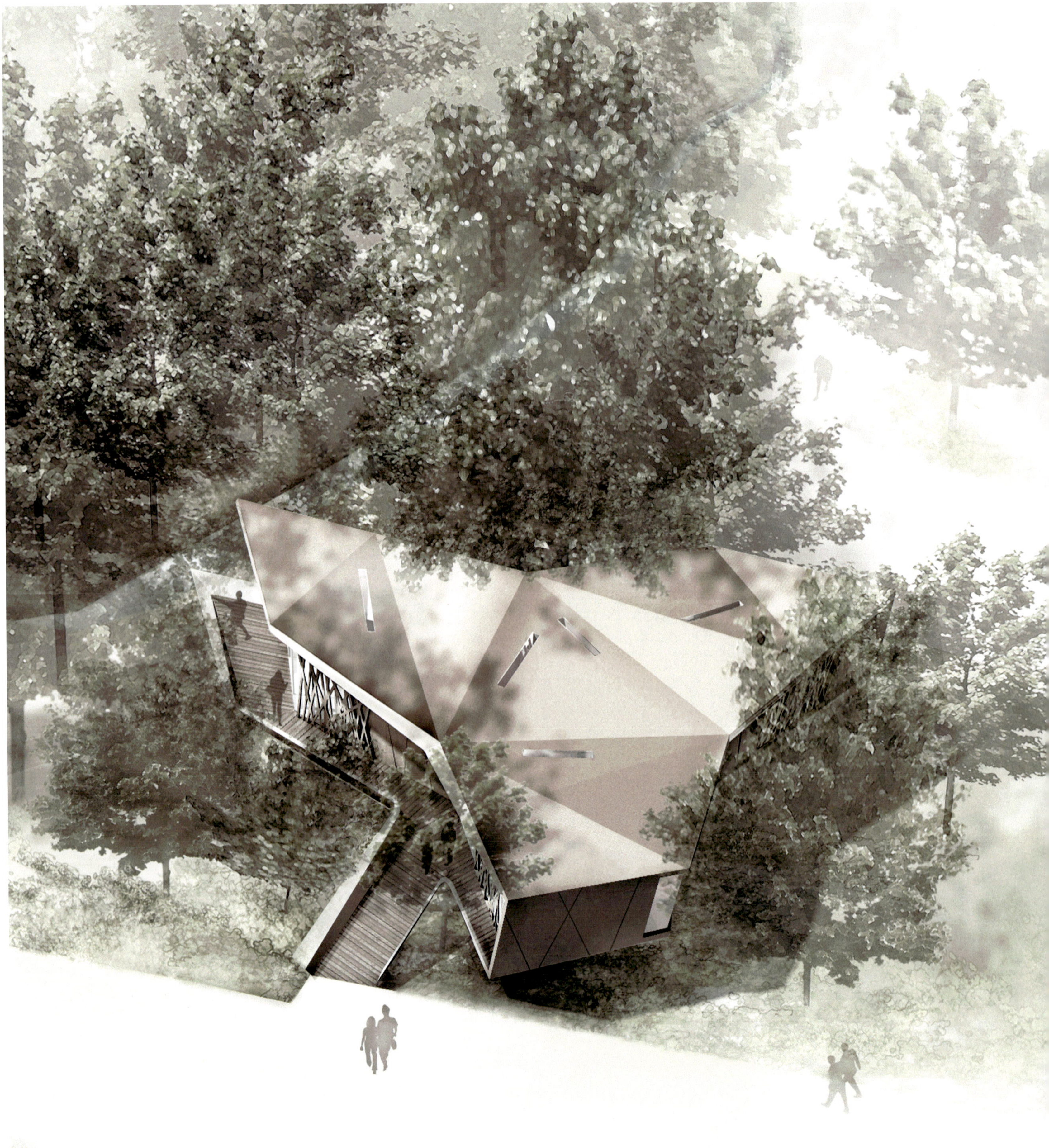

Maggie's Centre
Oxford, UK

The Maggie's Cancer Caring Centres are the legacy of Maggie Keswick Jencks, who formulated an idea for a caring centre that would enable those living with cancer to take a more active and informed role in their treatment. The article in which she first expressed her idea, 'A View from the Front Line', has served as the blueprint for the Maggie's Centres that are now either open or planned for more than twenty sites across the UK. Although attached to more conventional hospitals, all the centres are connected by their relaxed and non-clinical atmosphere, their domestic scale, and the visionary commissioning of their architecture – which is seen as a significant influence on the users' sense of well-being.

Wilkinson Eyre was invited to create a new centre for Maggie's in Oxford in 2006. The building sits on the densely wooded boundary of the Churchill Hospital, and, so as to tread lightly in this sensitive environment, has been designed as a tree house, raised above the landscape. It is formed from a series of fragmented planes, which fold and wrap into one another around a tripartite plan that allows the structure to fit among the existing trees – and users to escape visually into the landscape. The floor and roof planes rotate on top of each other so that the folds of the roof, walls and floor inform the internal space planning. The building is supported on informal clusters of columns, some tilted, which evoke a thicket of tree trunks in the woods. Taking advantage of the steep slope across the site, the floor of the building projects into the trees, poised 4 metres above the ground on one side while remaining accessible by a flat bridge from pavement level on the other. The woodland below is also accessible, and can be glimpsed through windows set within the floor.

In keeping with the woodland context, the centre is constructed out of lightweight timber. With the help of engineers Alan Baxter, a construction methodology was developed to allow the cross-ply laminate components to be prefabricated off site – thereby minimizing disruption during the building process. Using such advanced technologies as CNC cutting machines, a set of bespoke components with limited repetition was produced to fit the precisely defined geometry of the building. Its perimeter walls are a mixture of solid, perforated or fully glazed panels, according to the function of the internal space and the external aspect. The solid panels are clad in insulated timber and treated with a protective grey Solignum stain, while the perforated screens will act as shading devices, filtering light through a trellis designed to evoke interweaving tree boughs. The undulating roof, part of which oversails the building, is clad in traditional copper sheeting, which will patinate with age.

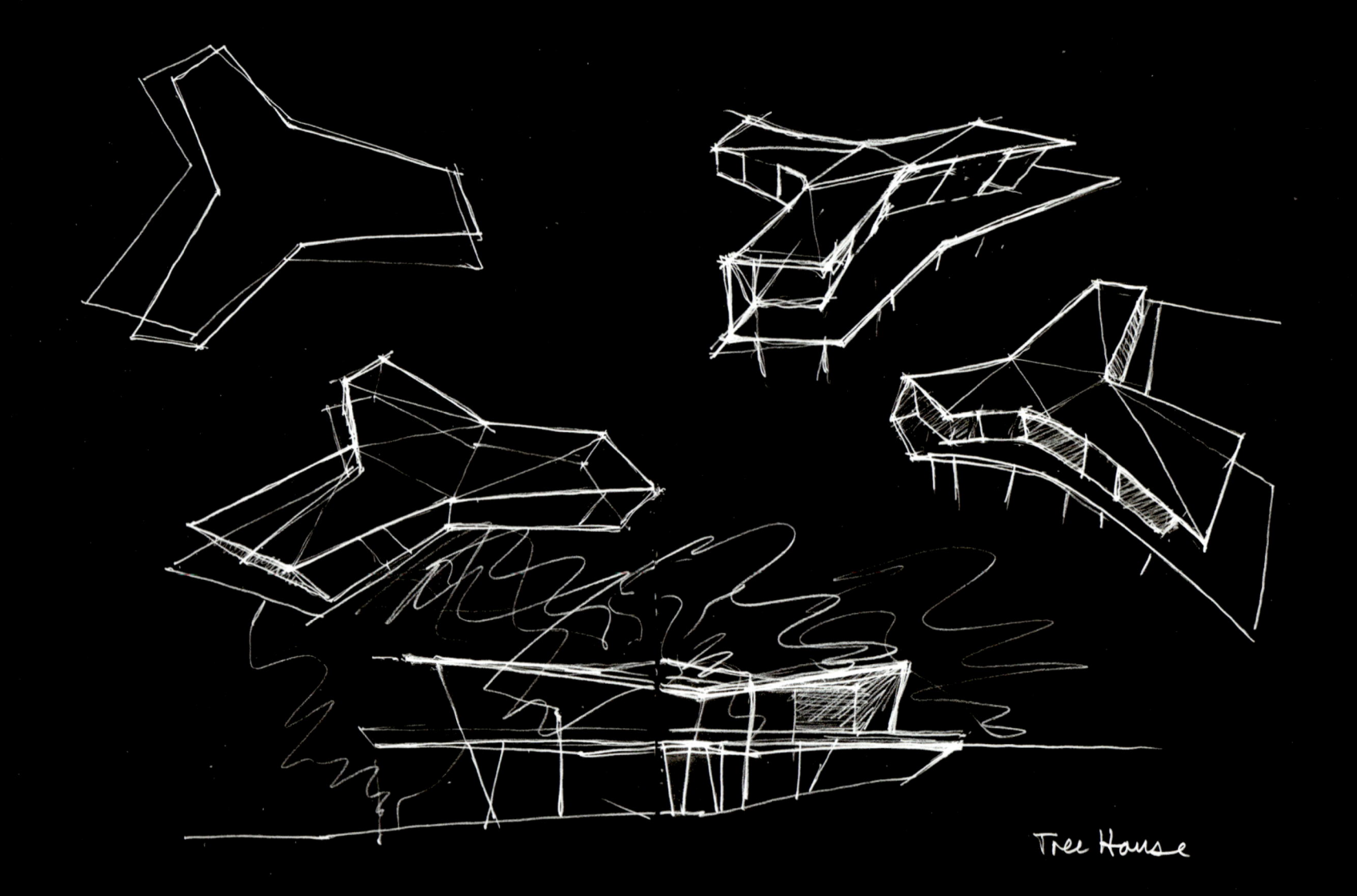

Tree House

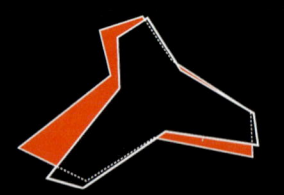

| Terraces | Movable partitions – adaptable space | Roof lights | Enclosures and orientation |

| Form follows function | Offset | Twist |

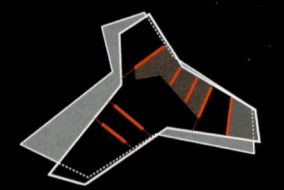

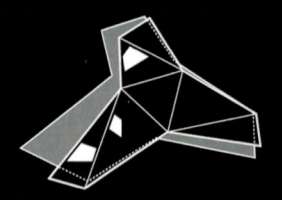

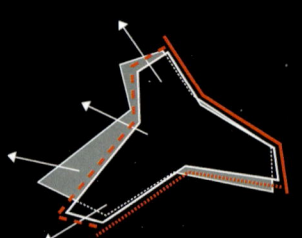

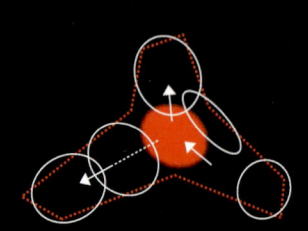

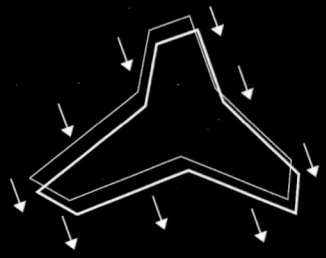

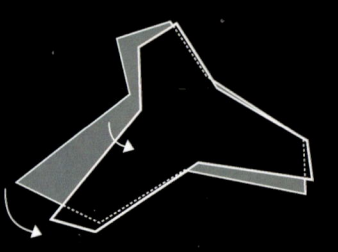

The plan is organized as a set of informal spaces all directly related to one another, eliminating the need for corridors and minimizing the number of enclosed rooms. These spaces provide areas for relaxation, emotional support and more practical information-sharing. At the centre of the plan is a triangular 'hearth' space for sitting, cooking and eating, a roof light directly above the main table illuminating this focal point. The hearth is an integral part of every Maggie's Centre, an inviting place where all the building's users can meet and relax. Leading off this is a wing of smaller, more intimate consultation spaces, while the western wing is a more open-plan, flexible lounge area, with large windows and direct access to the balcony that skirts the building.

Ground-floor plan

> Entrance
1 External stair
2 External timber deck
3 Sitting/group activity
4 Kitchen and dining
5 Group consulting room
6 Consulting room
7 Library
8 Office
9 Access bridge

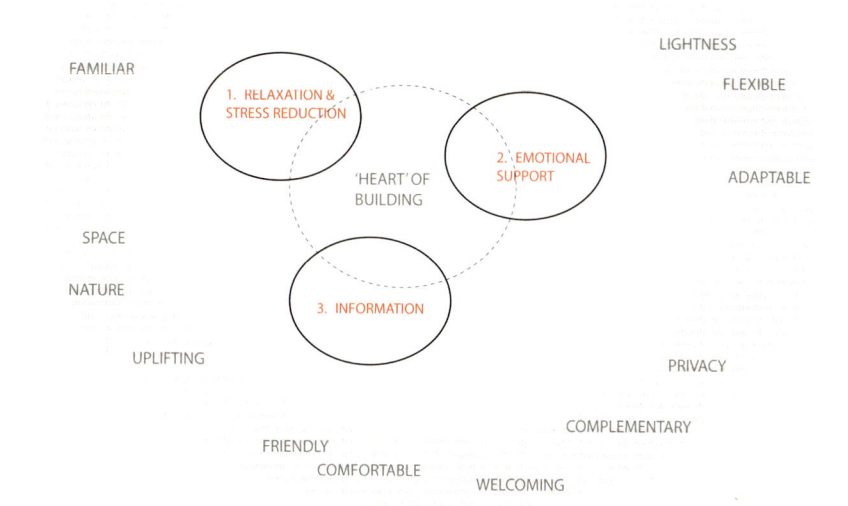

Landscape | Maggie's Centre, Oxford, UK

On the east side of the building, the floor plane folds up to become the wall, which then becomes the roof; on the west side, the dominant feature is the elegant roof, which here oversails a generous balcony.

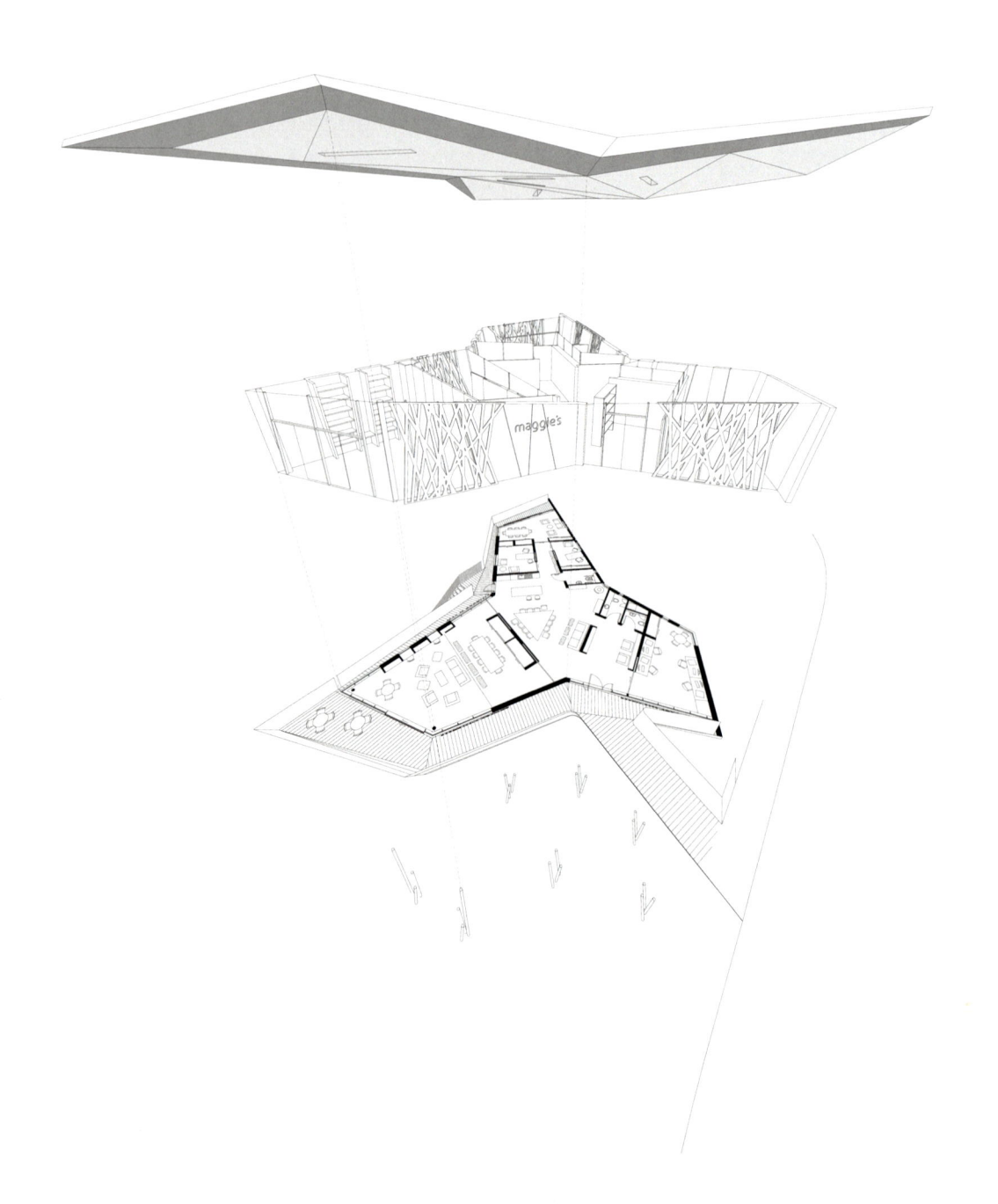

Landscape | Maggie's Centre, Oxford, UK　　81

Sky

The idea of building into the blue suggests lightness, transparency, airiness, wide spans, an elegant aerodynamic quality. These projects develop this trajectory of thinking, building high or spanning wide to frame, capture, punctuate and inhabit the sky.

Emirates Air Line, London, UK	84
20 Blackfriars Road, London, UK	90
Guangzhou International Finance Centre, China	94
Twin Sails Bridge, Poole, UK	107
From Landscape to Portrait, London, UK	110
London 2012 Basketball Arena, UK	113
King's Cross Gasholders, London, UK	122

Emirates Air Line
London, UK

Wilkinson Eyre's first involvement with the redevelopment of London's Royal Docks was in 1984, when the practice drew up masterplan proposals for a new retail and residential district. Although the docks, owing to their lack of infrastructure and distance from London's cultural and commercial centres, have regenerated relatively slowly since then compared to Canary Wharf and the Isle of Dogs, the focus has gradually shifted, and they are now home to the University of East London, the ExCel exhibition centre and London City Airport, as well as a number of large residential developments. The expansive docks have been retained – water and all – rather than filled in, leaving a neighbourhood of big skies and a strong connection to the river estuary and, beyond it, the sea.

The ExCel centre and the O2 Arena, at the tip of the Greenwich Peninsula across the river to the south, were major venues during the London 2012 Olympic Games, and have continued to be anchors for local regeneration. The Emirates Air Line connects the two, supporting this regeneration and also providing the only above-ground link across the Thames between Tower Bridge and the Queen Elizabeth II road bridge, 24 kilometres to the east. It is the first urban cable car in the UK, and the brief for its design included numerous constraints relating to the proximity of City Airport, multiple landholdings, clearance for tall ships on the Thames, and existing and future infrastructure. The resulting crossing, a series of slender, spiralling towers, lifts passengers up to 90 metres above the river. As the cabins begin their 1.1-kilometre transit between each of the waterside terminals, incredible panoramas open up across the docks and then to the broader urban landscape beyond – clustered towers to the west, and estuary to the east.

Each tower is formed from a series of steel ribbons, arranged as a tapering spiral that separates out into a 'fork' to pick up the cable-car running gear at the top. The ribbons are held in place by a helical tie, which corkscrews up the inside of the structure. The effect is one of lightness and movement, with the loose curves of the central helix providing the necessary stiffness with the minimum amount of steel. The gaps in the structure add to this feeling of lightness, and help to shed wind loading. The terminal buildings are pragmatic and functional, with a rounded form derived from the movement of cable-car cabins through the station. Passengers access the cabins from a cantilevered upper deck with glazed cladding that glows at night, dynamic with movement. Contained accommodation blocks are situated centrally at ground- and first-floor level to minimize heating requirements – the power for which is supplemented by photovoltaic panels.

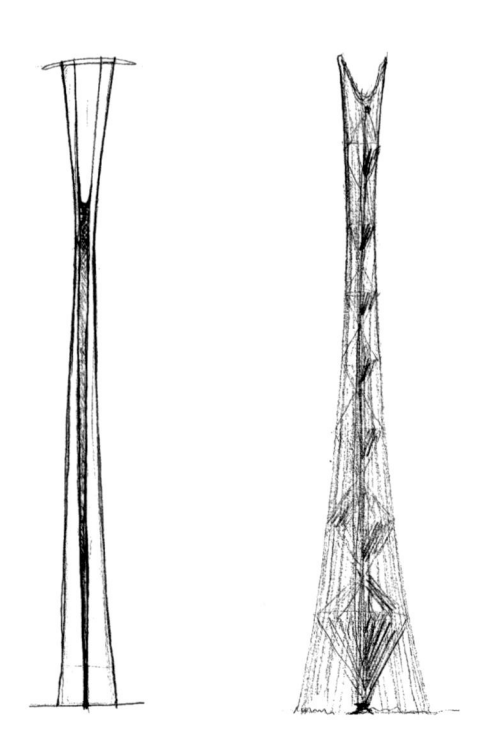

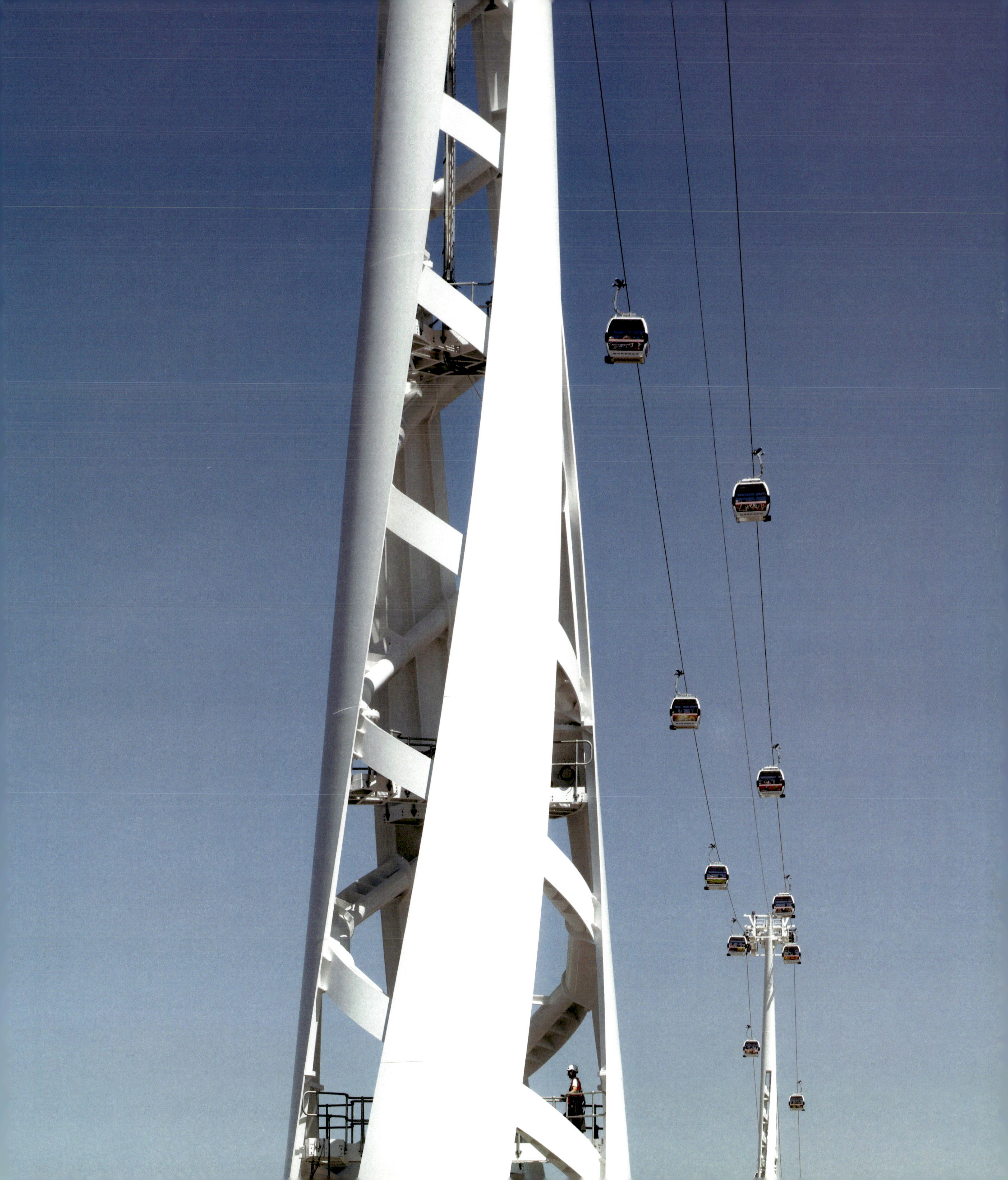

Site plan

1 River Thames
2 O2 Arena
3 The Crystal
4 Royal Victoria Dock
5 Emirates Air Line

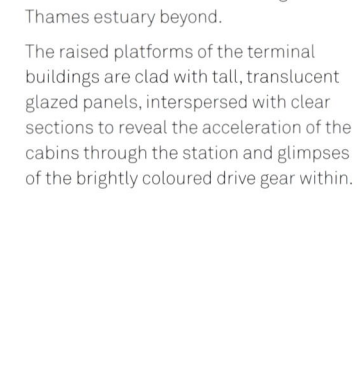

The cable-car crossing links the Greenwich Peninsula and the south bank of the River Thames with the Royal Docks to the north. Some distance downstream from the heart of the city, this is the only above-ground crossing point for miles, and offers a spectacular vantage point. Views to the west take in the growing clusters of towers at Canary Wharf and in the City of London, while to the east there are long vistas across the regenerated Royal Docks and City Airport to the Queen Elizabeth II road bridge and the Thames estuary beyond.

The raised platforms of the terminal buildings are clad with tall, translucent glazed panels, interspersed with clear sections to reveal the acceleration of the cabins through the station and glimpses of the brightly coloured drive gear within.

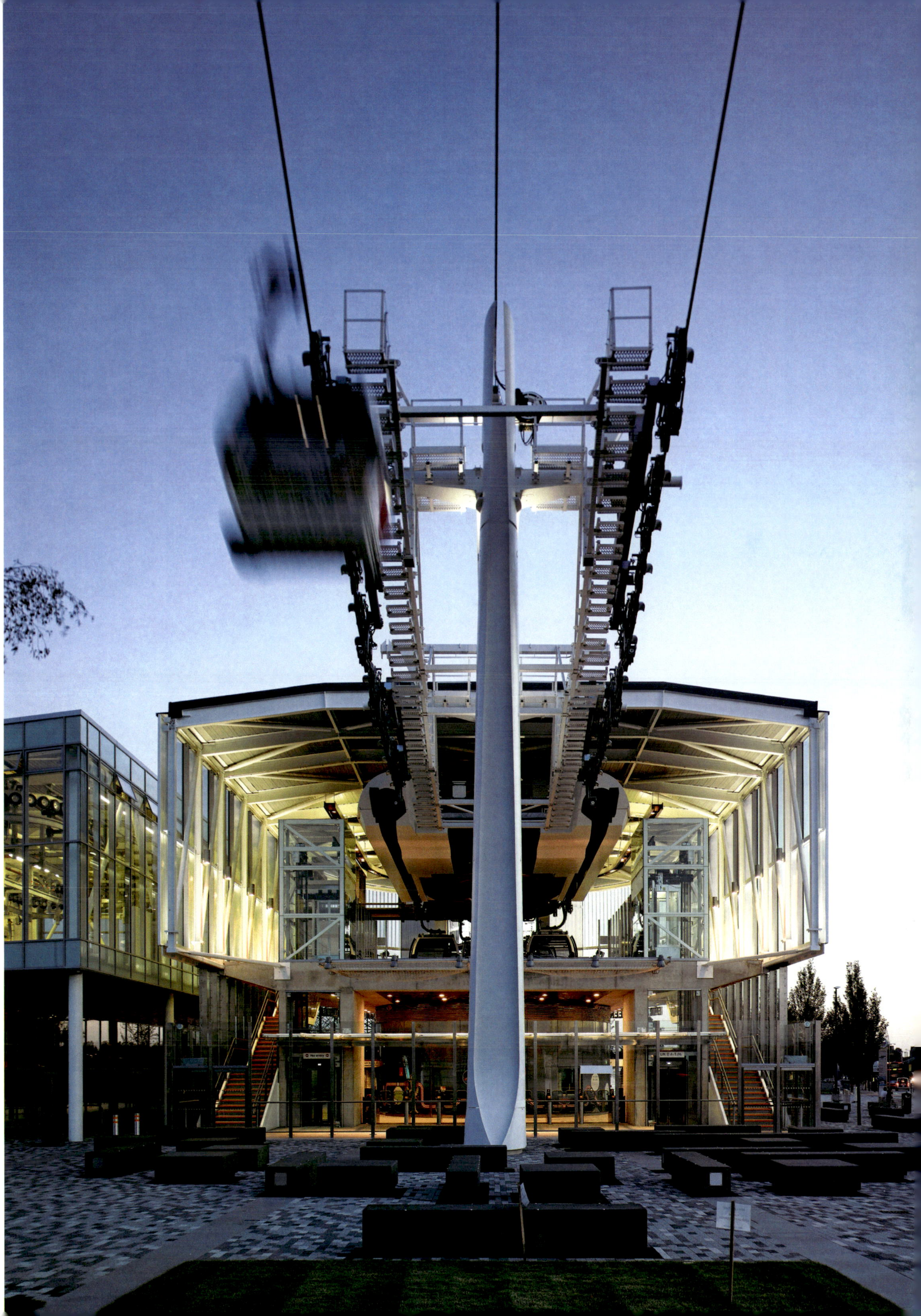

Tower sections and elevations

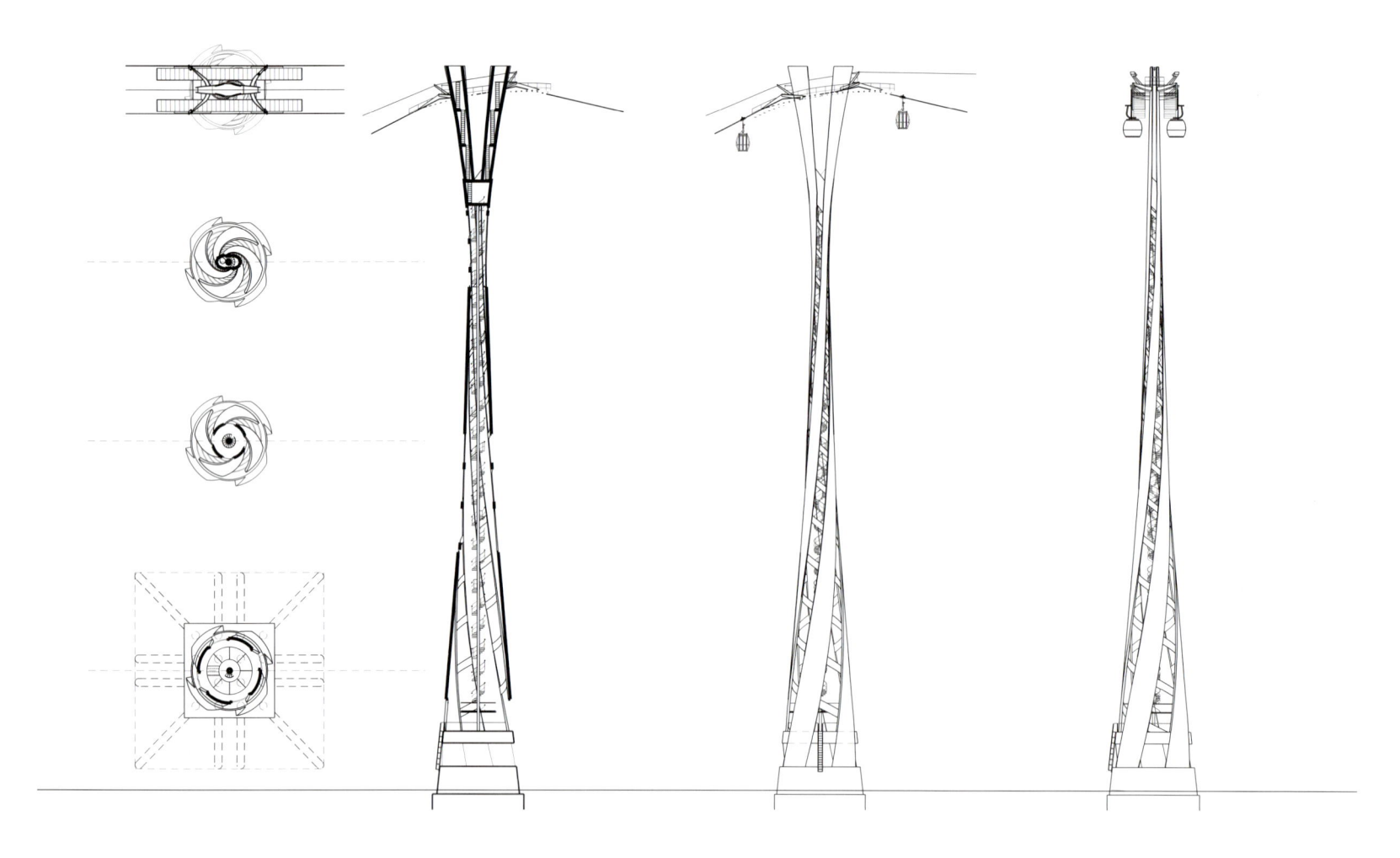

The towers were designed to have a minimal impact on their respective sites. The south tower, located in the Thames, stands on a concrete support structure, sculpted after extensive hydrodynamic modelling to minimize scour and disruption to the river bed.

Sections taken through the towers at various points demonstrate the balance between aesthetics and performance in the structural design, which was developed in collaboration with Expedition Engineering. The towers are made up of a series of steel ribbons, which spiral around a central, helical tie. Wind testing and tuning were undertaken as part of the design process to mitigate whistling.

88

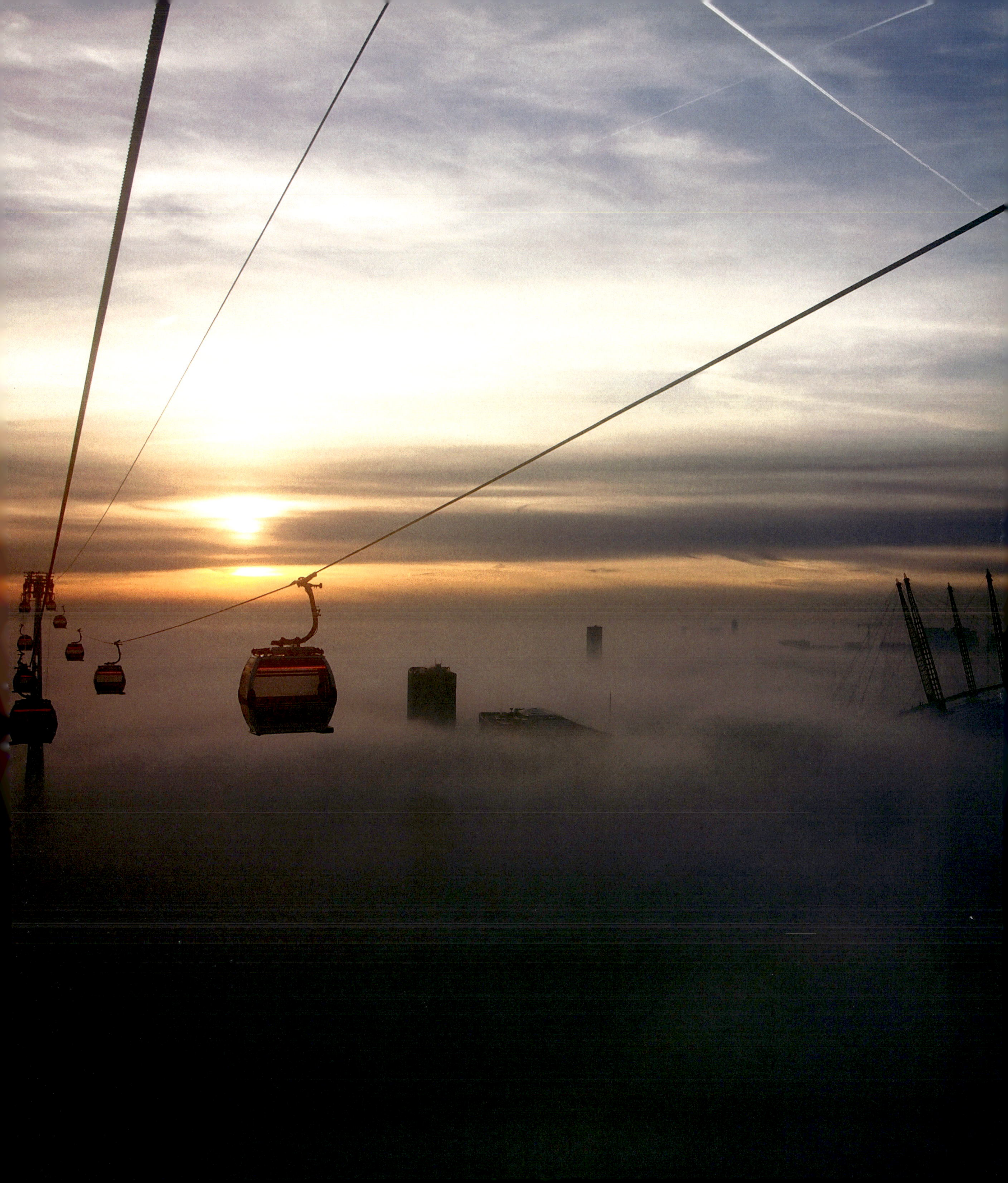

20 Blackfriars Road
London, UK

Facing the City of London from the south bank of the Thames, Southwark has historically been a far more permissive quarter than its heavily regulated neighbour to the north. But in recent years the area has taken on increased strategic importance for London's commercial growth, with a series of significant schemes appearing along the riverfront, and clusters of taller buildings being developed around Tate Modern and the Shard. Blackfriars Road leads to London's only north–south bridge, spanning the Thames at the apex of the river's huge curve up into the heart of the city, and so any address along this important route is remarkably central to London's major historic, cultural and financial landmarks – and to protected views across the city. Wilkinson Eyre's six-year involvement with the site at 20 Blackfriars Road reflects the changing aspirations of developers and planners, and the considerable scrutiny under which any tall building in central London is placed.

In 2002 the practice was appointed by J Sainsbury Developments to investigate the redevelopment potential of two buildings on Stamford Street. When this land, and an adjoining plot fronting on to Blackfriars Road, was acquired by Land Securities in 2003, Wilkinson Eyre was retained as architect and briefed to develop a commercial office tower. With a number of tall buildings planned for the neighbourhood, the resulting design achieved the necessary commercial yield and met the requirement for large floor plates, as well as creating a humanly scaled environment at street level. The developer's brief was further amended in 2006 to favour a scheme with a richer mix of uses. One tower became two, with residential and commercial accommodation assigned to each respective volume, all connected at ground level by retail and community spaces.

The complex topographic façades of the residential tower were derived by mapping the relationships between the site and various landmarks across London, the wider cityscape in essence defining its form. Each facet faces a landmark either distant or local, and is inclined down towards parks and green spaces or up towards taller landmarks in a mediation between earth and sky. These tilted vertical planes form a textured surface of transparency and reflection, responding continuously to the shifting light, and are constructed from triple-glazed shingles, which protect balconies and winter gardens. Each of the towers is further oriented to ensure its environmental efficiency: northern façades are clear to maximize views towards the City and to take full advantage of the natural light, while the east and west façades incorporate angled louvres to shade the interior from the sun. The southern façades have metal screens to control heat gain.

The design became the subject of a planning inquiry in 2008, at which it was praised by the inspectors and successfully gained approval.

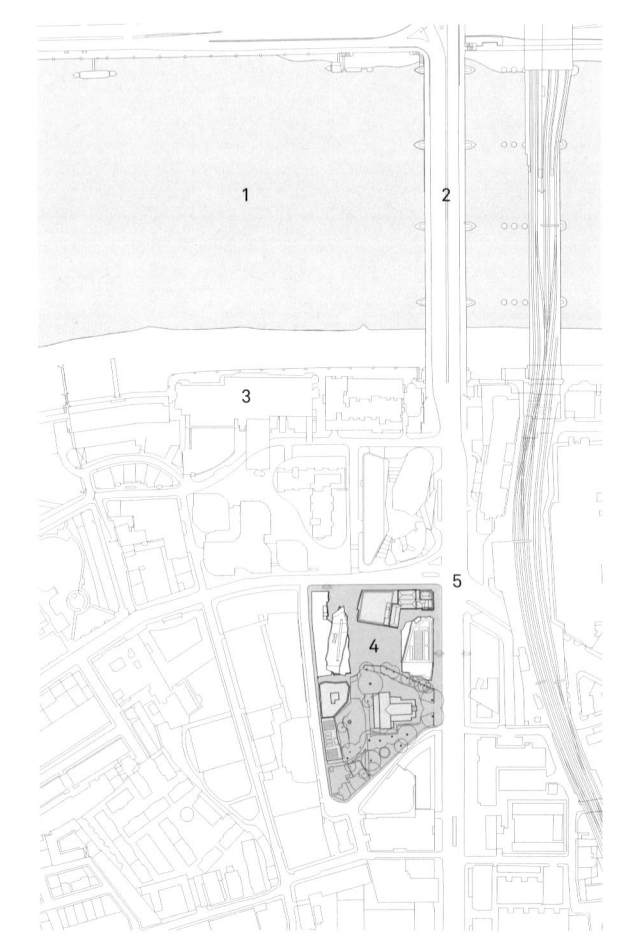

Location plan
1 River Thames
2 Blackfriars Bridge
3 Sea Containers House
4 20 Blackfriars Road site
5 Blackfriars Road

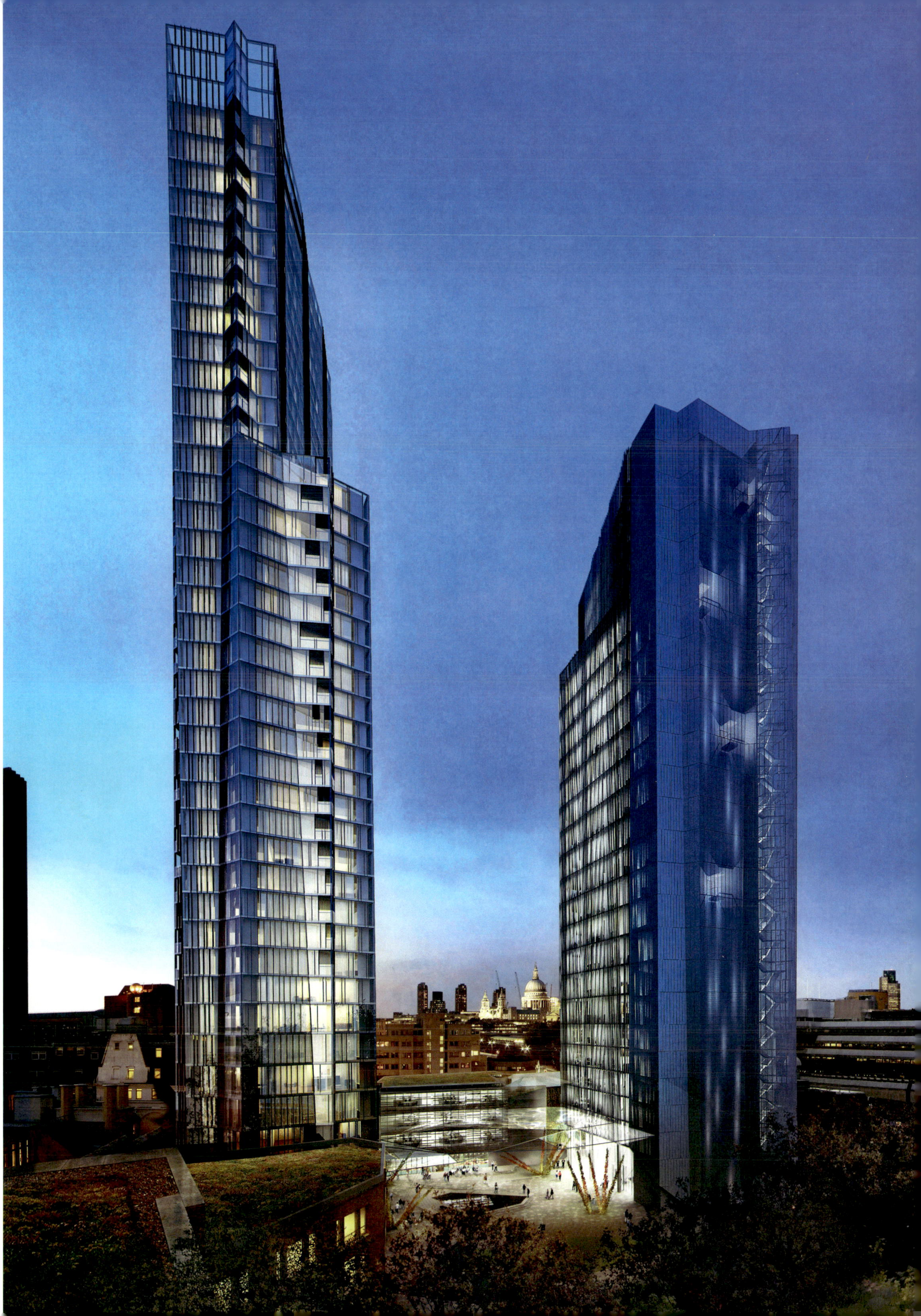

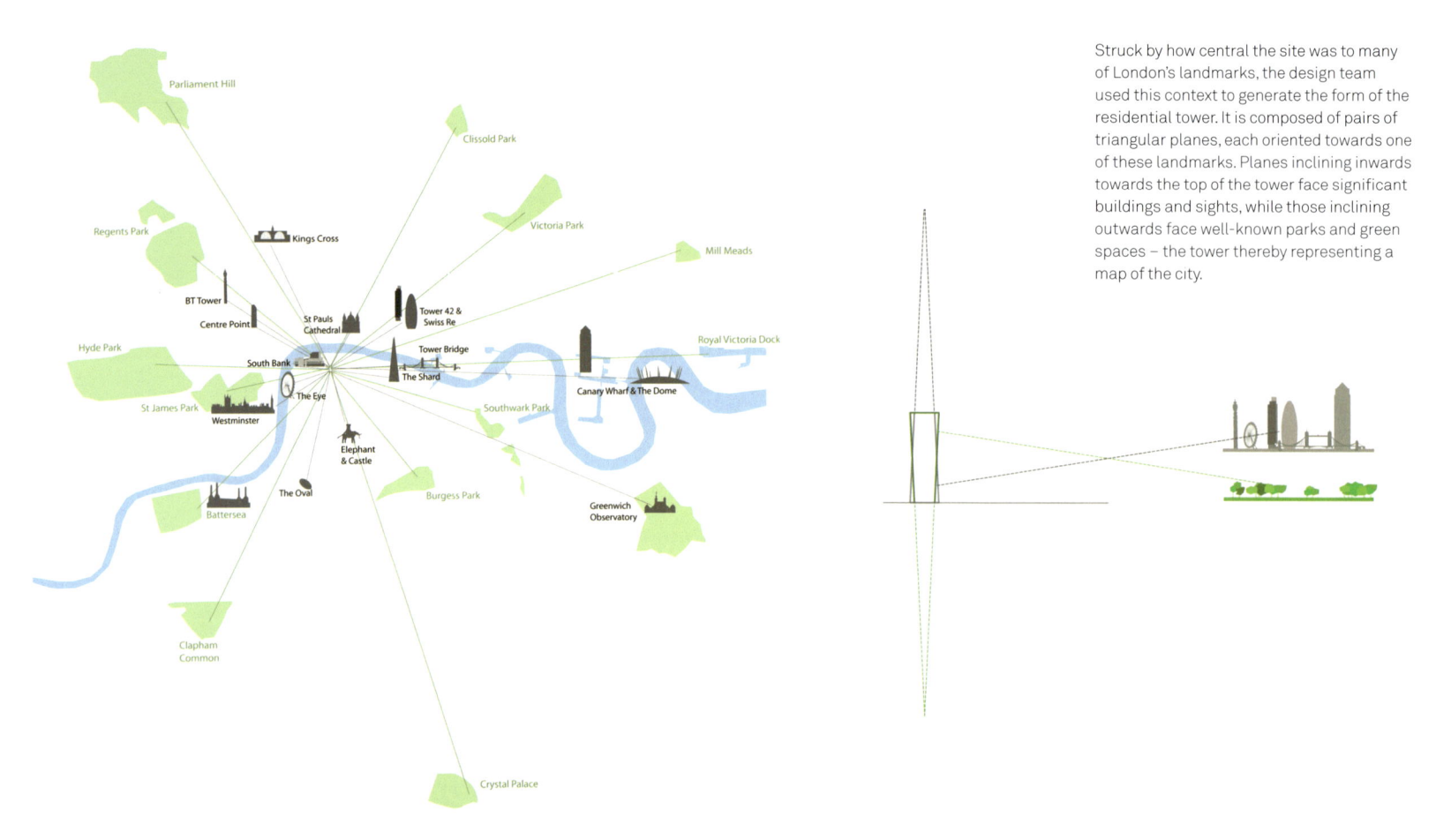

Struck by how central the site was to many of London's landmarks, the design team used this context to generate the form of the residential tower. It is composed of pairs of triangular planes, each oriented towards one of these landmarks. Planes inclining inwards towards the top of the tower face significant buildings and sights, while those inclining outwards face well-known parks and green spaces – the tower thereby representing a map of the city.

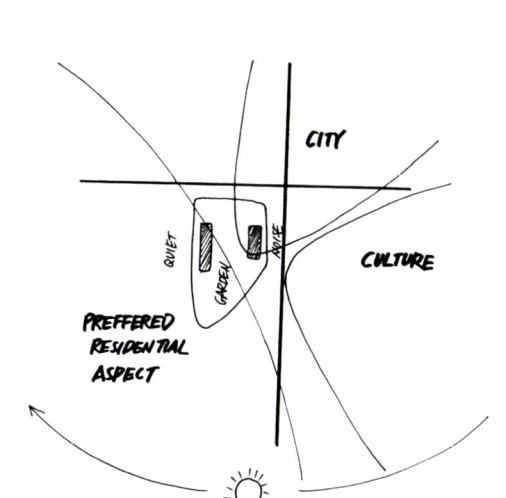

Site plan

1. Residential tower
2. Office tower
3. Public realm
4. Christ Church Southwark
5. Sports and community centre

Thoughtfully designed public-realm space was an important aspect of the project, helping to negotiate between the height of the towers and lower-level listed buildings nearby, and has been conceived as a series of 'urban rooms'. Occupiers and public move from the street into a semi-formal entry space bounded on two sides by enveloping green walls, and on into a more informal central piazza. This is surrounded by retail frontages, and is partially covered by a glass canopy, the structure of which forms a support for creepers and vines.

Sky | 20 Blackfriars Road, London, UK

Guangzhou International Finance Centre
China

With a population of 14 million, Guangzhou (formerly Canton) is China's third largest city; it is also one of the country's oldest. Owing to its explosive growth in recent years, many of the city's districts have been re-planned around dramatic urban set pieces – processional routes and formally arranged parks – which lend structure to their ongoing development. Guangzhou's new central business district, Zhujiang New Town, is no exception: its spine is a broad landscaped park, reinforced by metro lines, which runs south from the city's main eastern railway station to terminate in the television tower on the far shore of the Pearl River. The Guangzhou International Finance Centre, envisaged as one of a pair of towers creating a spectacular gateway to the business district on this central boulevard, lies at the point of transition between the city's financial hub and the lower-lying cultural quarter to the south, home to Guangzhou's opera house, museum and library. The west tower (its partner to the east is currently under construction) is accompanied by an extensive podium. Together, they have a total floor area of more than 450,000 square metres, and contain conference, retail, office and luxury hotel accommodation. Rising to 440 metres, with 103 floors above ground and a helipad, the 235,000-square-metre tower is now the eleventh tallest building in the world.

The Guangzhou International Finance Centre differs from many other tall buildings in the purity and elegance of its aerodynamic shape. A desire to achieve such clarity of form, free from distractions and informed by technology rather than symbolism, was the guiding thought behind the design, the simplicity of which belies the refined geometry from which it is generated. The tower utilizes the world's tallest constructed diagrid structure, which is clearly expressed through the building's transparent envelope. Each diamond in the grid is 54 metres high, while the structural members – formed of steel tubes filled with concrete – are up to 2 metres in diameter. Glimpsed either through the glazed façades or from within, where it frames the views from the hotel floors, the diagrid lends the tower a distinctive visual character.

The rounded triangular plan of the tower, informed by the need for efficient floor plans, is rotated 15 degrees anticlockwise from north to minimize wind loads and solar gain, and to take advantage of views out to the Pearl River. At ground level, the tower is ringed by a triple-height entrance lobby, which provides access to the building's lift core; this includes double-decker shuttles to the higher levels. Offices occupy levels 2 to 67, the perimeter diagrid structure leaving the floor plates free for a variety of workplace layouts. Described as 'an icon of style in the sky', the Four Seasons Hotel occupies floors 67 to 103, its 374 rooms ranked around a 33-storey internal atrium, faceted and enclosed on the upper storeys to create a kaleidoscopic effect. All the hotel rooms have panoramic views of the city, but those on the upper floors (up to the ninety-eighth) are the highest in the world, sitting just below the helipad, restaurant and sky bar, which occupy the topmost levels of the building.

In 2012 the tower was awarded the RIBA Lubetkin Prize for the best building by a British architect outside the European Union.

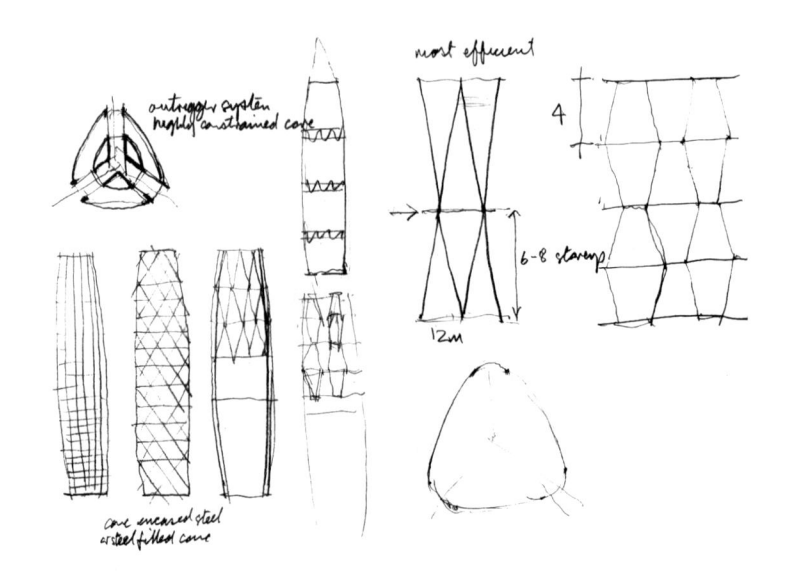

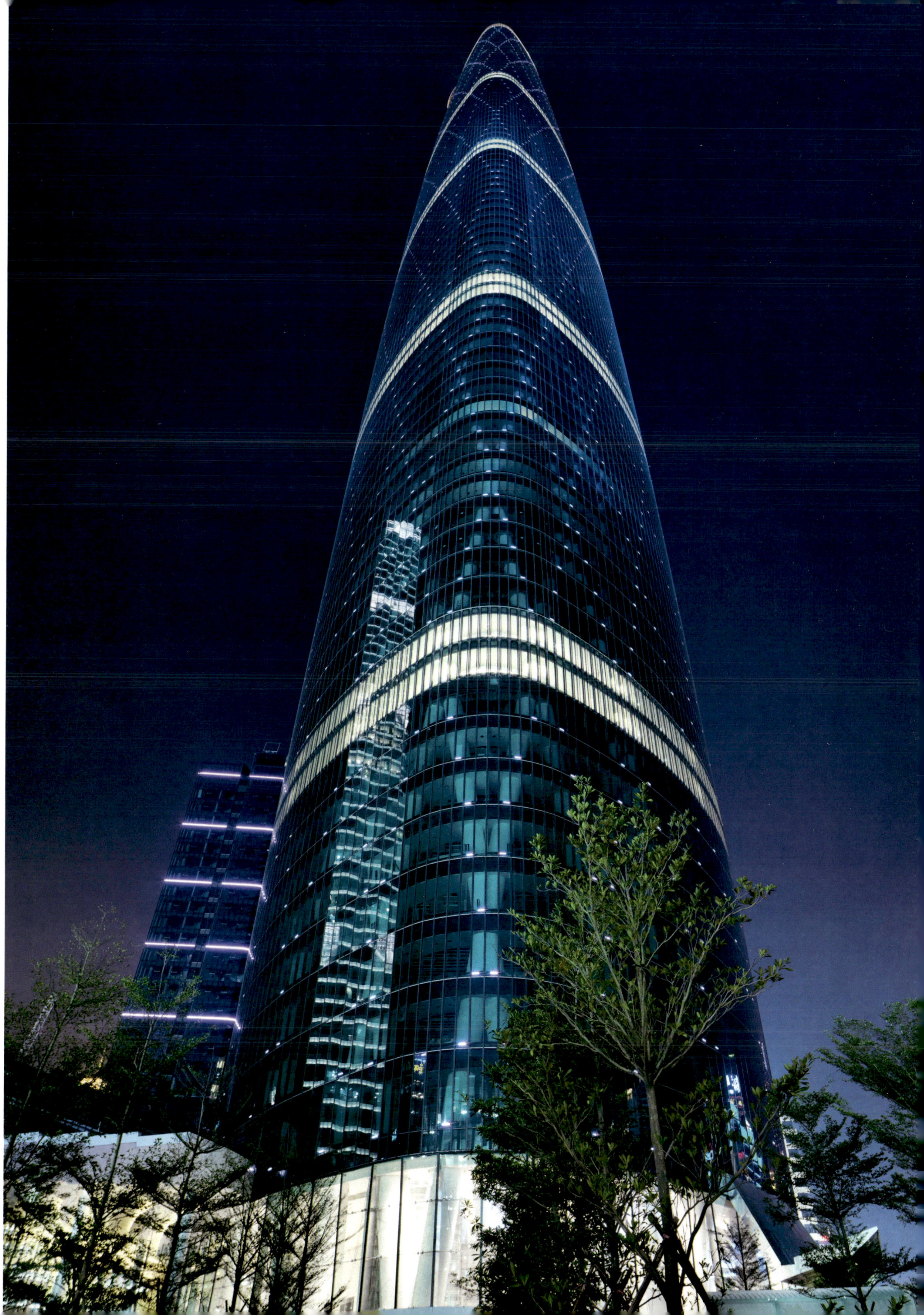

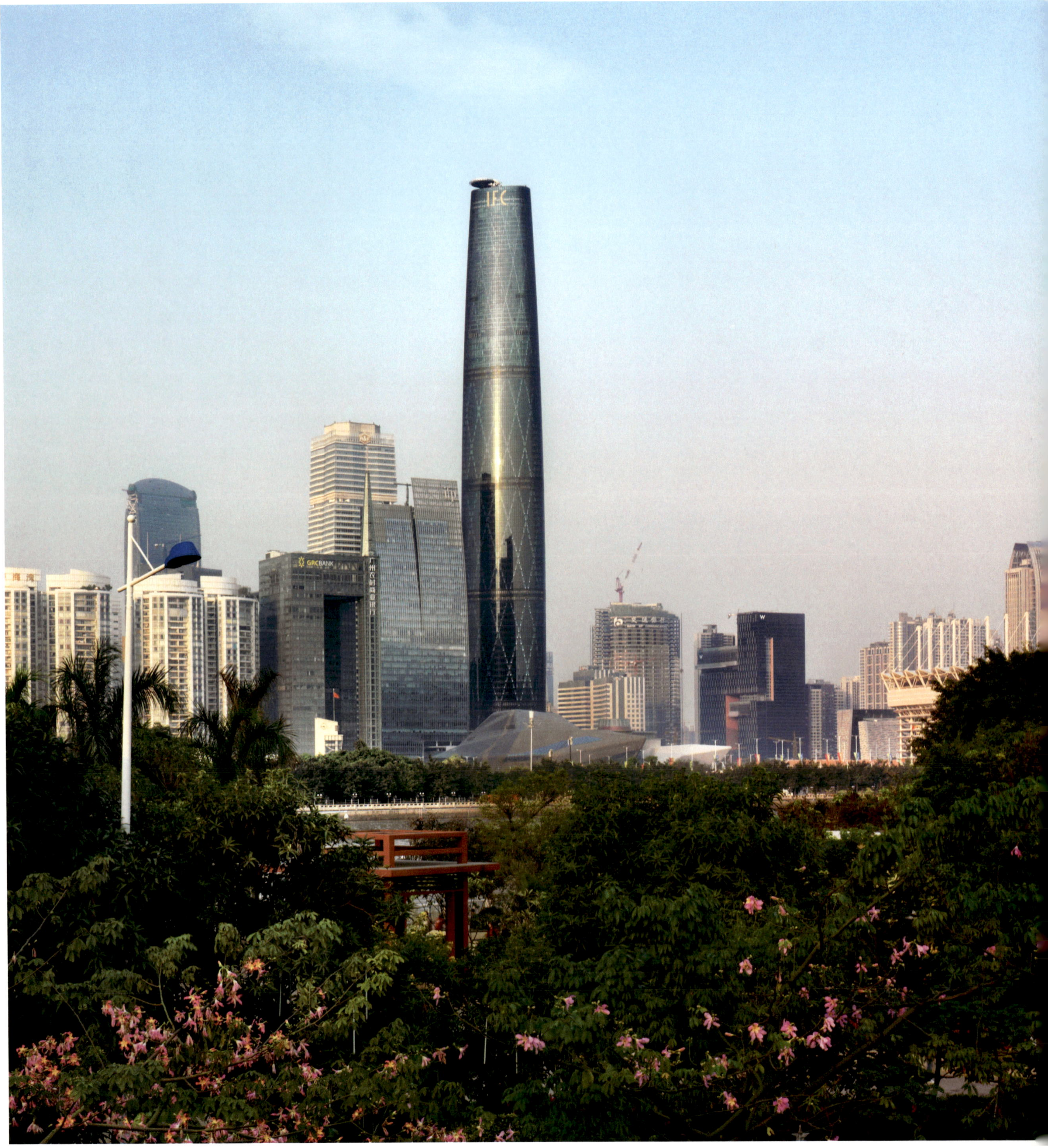
IFC
GRCBANK

The tower was part of a strategic masterplan intended to consolidate a grand central park and a new civic and financial centre ahead of the 2010 Asian Games. At ground level, it connects with a substantial podium complex containing a retail mall (itself 100 metres high), a conference centre and exhibition hall, and serviced apartments. The tower and podium connect to a large retail mall and transport hub below ground, with a retail loop encouraging connections beneath the landscaped central axis.

Site plan (roof level)
1 Retail mall (below)
2 Exhibition hall and conference centre (below)
3 Guangzhou International Finance Centre
4 Zhujiang Boulevard West

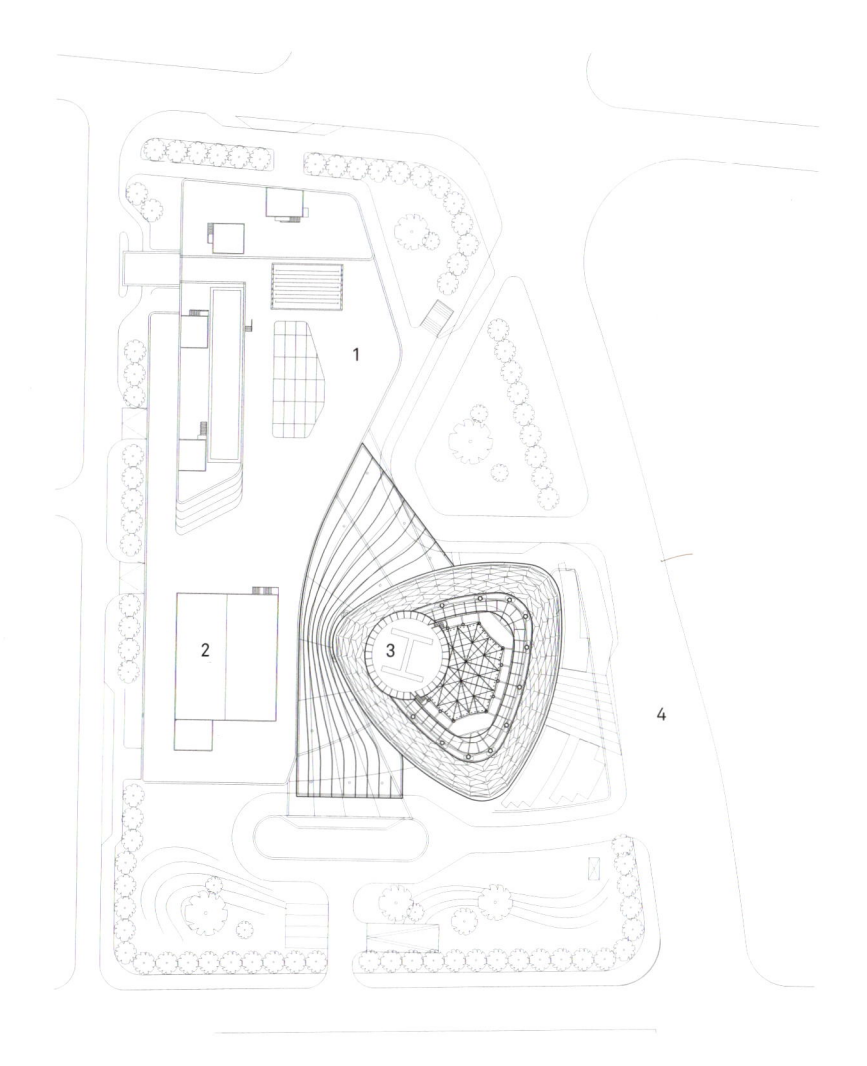

Wind-testing models

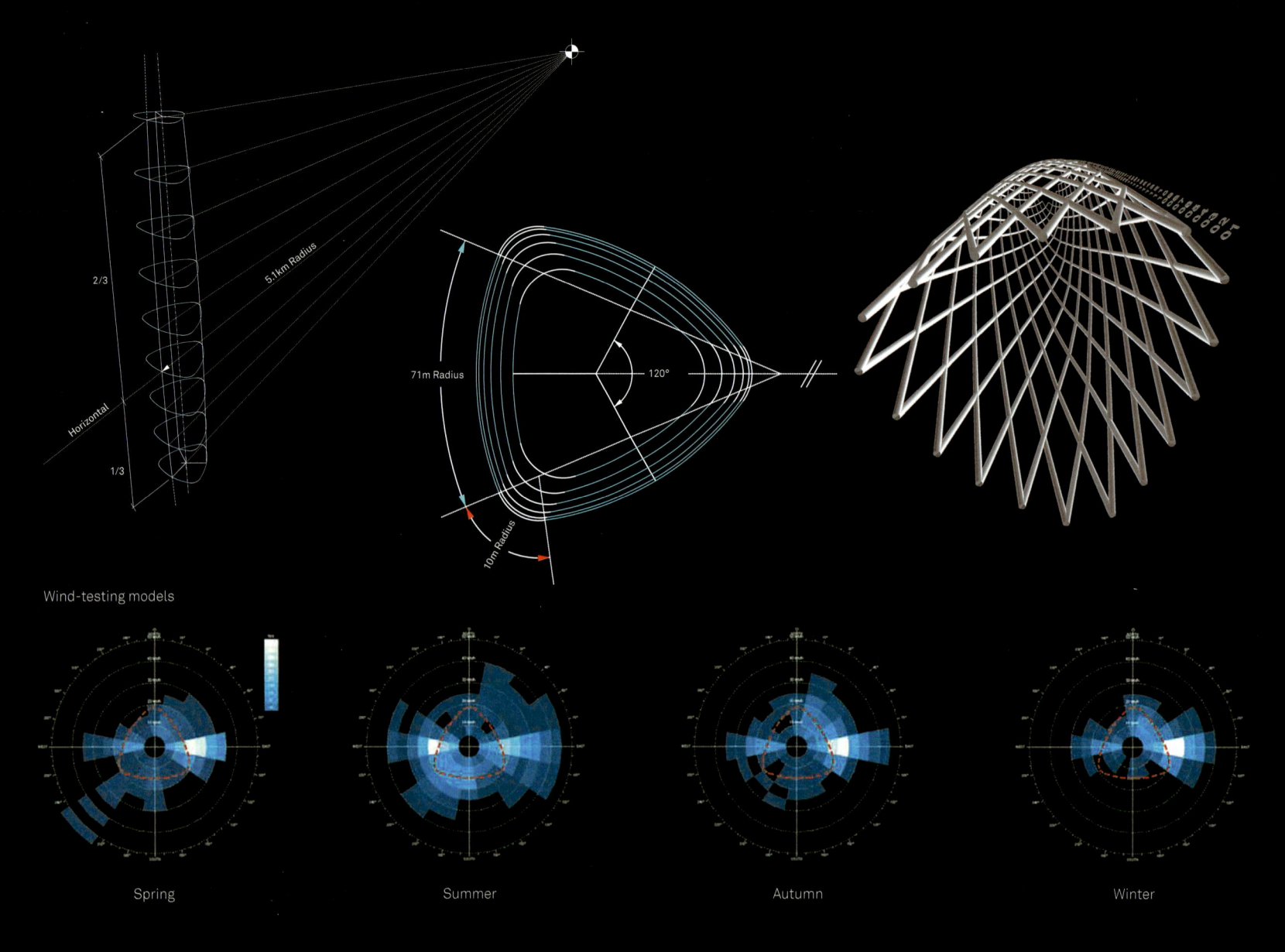

Spring　　　Summer　　　Autumn　　　Winter

The curves that form the three vertical faces of the tower are set out as arcs of a huge circle with a radius of 5.1 kilometres. The centre of the circle is offset so that the resulting tower form is at its widest a third of the way up; from here, it gradually narrows towards its upper floors. The plan is generated by three arcs, each with a 71-metre radius, joined at each corner by further arcs of 10 metres radius.

Analysis from detailed wind testing enabled the building form to be refined, a process that, in turn, reduced the size and weight of the structure.

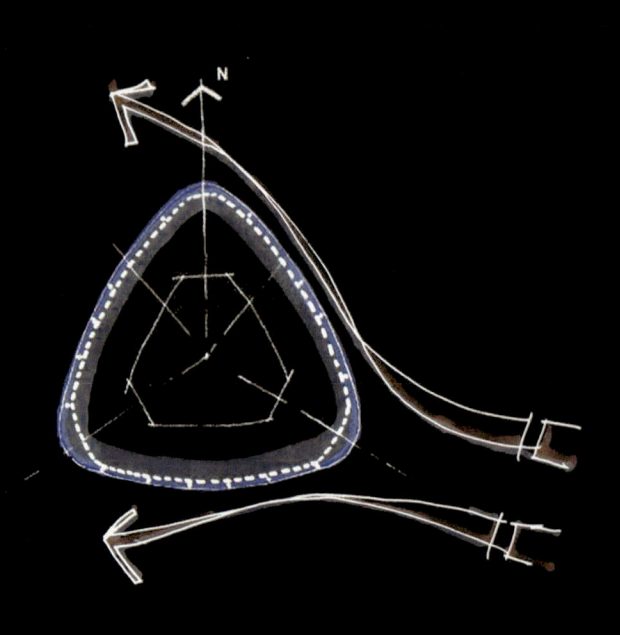

The diamond-shaped diagrid structure provides a strong visual contrast to the smooth, curved form of the glazing. Each diagrid member is formed from concrete-filled steel tubes to provide both good stiffness and fire protection. The tubular diagrid meets at a nodal point every 12 storeys, thereby forming 54-metre-high steel diamonds. At the base of the tower the structural members are 2 metres in diameter, reducing in breadth to just 900 millimetres at the top of the building.

The structural core takes much of the gravity load of the building's floors, and is linked back to the diagrid structure at the perimeter via floor beams, which create a stiff 'tube within a tube' structural system. The inherent rigidity of the structure minimizes steel tonnage while providing resistance to acceleration and sway, thereby maintaining high comfort levels for the buildings' occupants. It also means that no damping of the structure is required.

Sky | Guangzhou International Finance Centre, China

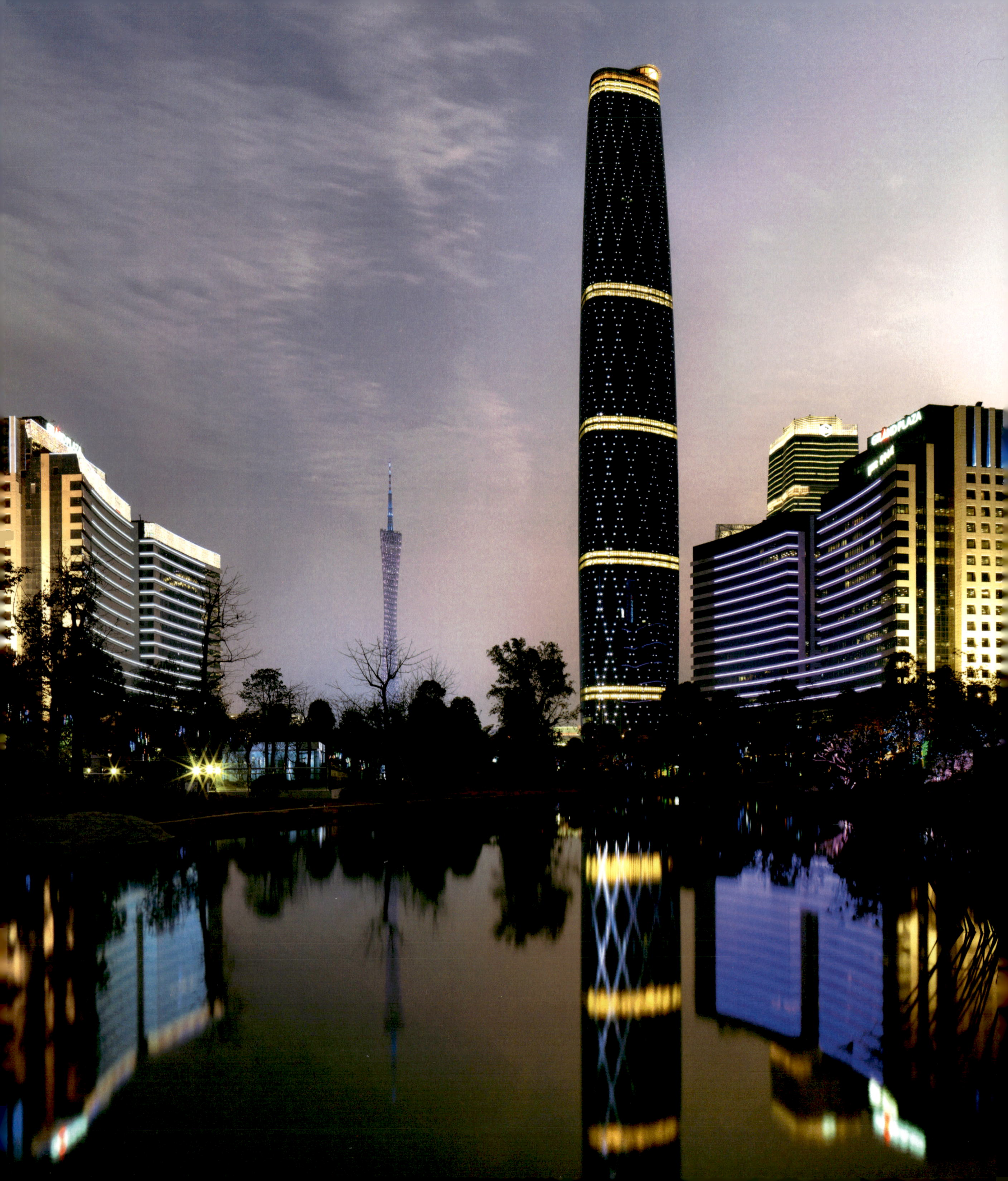
GRAND PLAZA

The plan for the office floors shows a flexible 'doughnut' of space around the central core – with the structural diagrid at its perimeter – adaptable to a wide variety of configurations. Through the careful planning of the core, an average usable floor space figure of 70 per cent has been achieved for the office floors, and 68.9 per cent overall.

The hotel rooms, all with breathtaking views across this rapidly growing city, are arranged around the perimeter of a soaring central atrium space.

Typical hotel floor

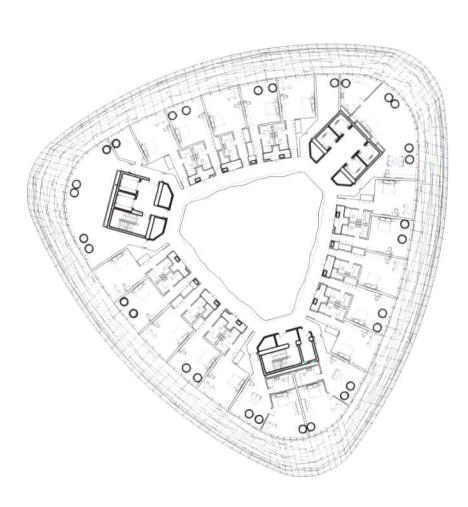

Typical office floor

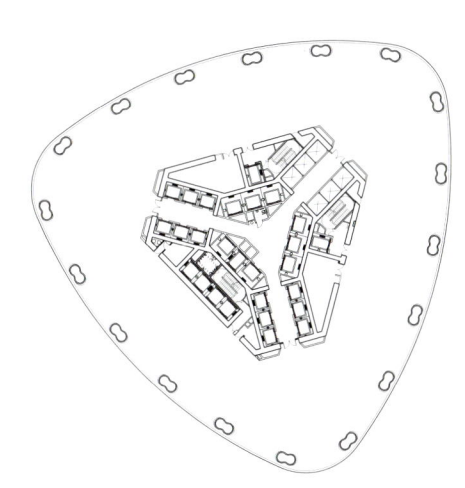

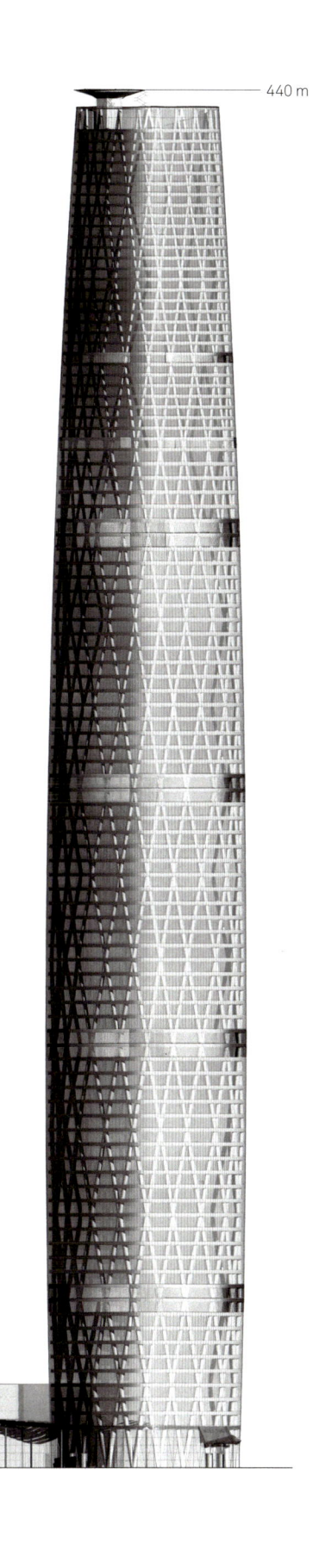

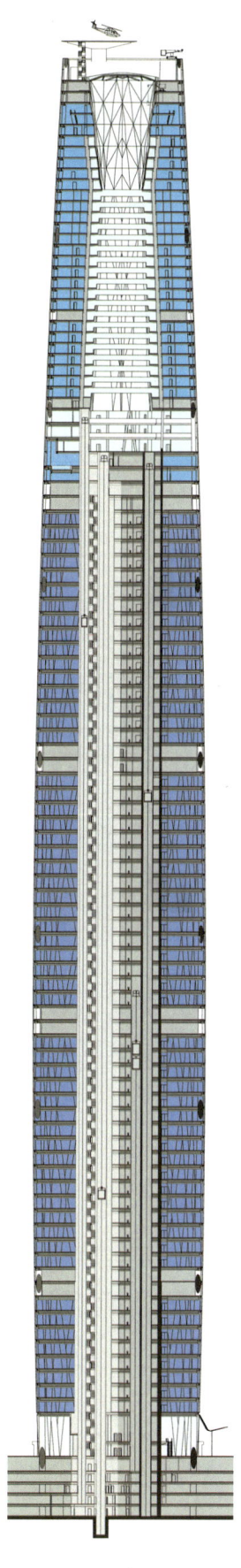

440 m

Sky | Guangzhou International Finance Centre, China

As a global luxury brand, Four Seasons demanded spectacular accommodation of the highest quality. Nowhere is this more apparent than in the dramatic 33-storey hotel atrium, clad in sparkling glass, which is tall enough to house London's St Paul's Cathedral.

Sky | Guangzhou International Finance Centre, China

The tower, with its shimmering façades, is a calm presence amid the frenetic Guangzhou cityscape. The cladding was designed as a ventilated double skin with interstitial louvres for energy efficiency, but this was omitted during construction for cost reasons. It was replaced by a unitary system of high-performance glass, with care taken to ensure that it was sufficiently transparent for the structural diagrid to be clearly seen through it.

A distinguishing feature of the tower's curtain wall is the series of double-floor horizontal bands that mark the refuge and intermediate plant floors. These have a different glazing module to allow ventilation.

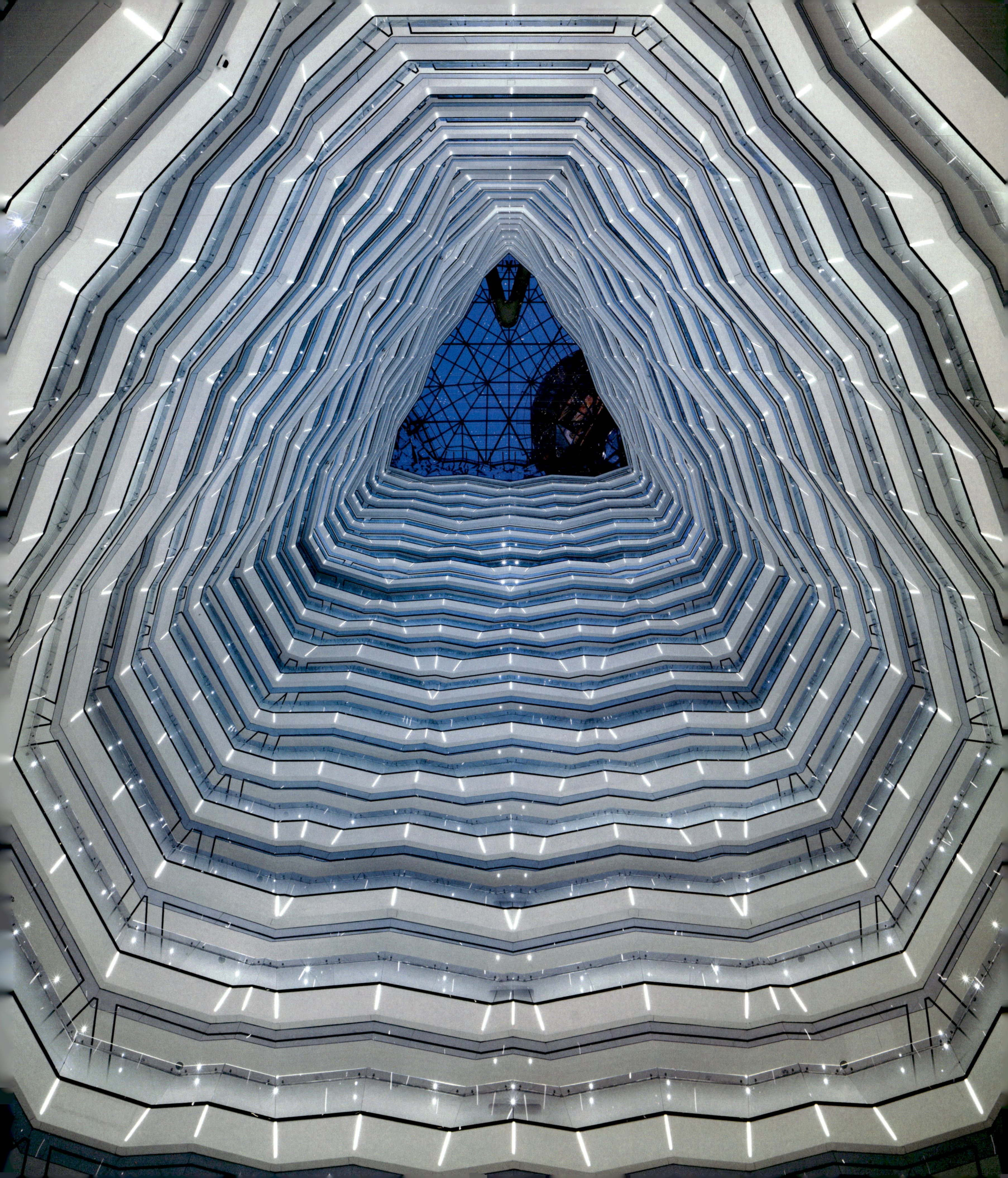

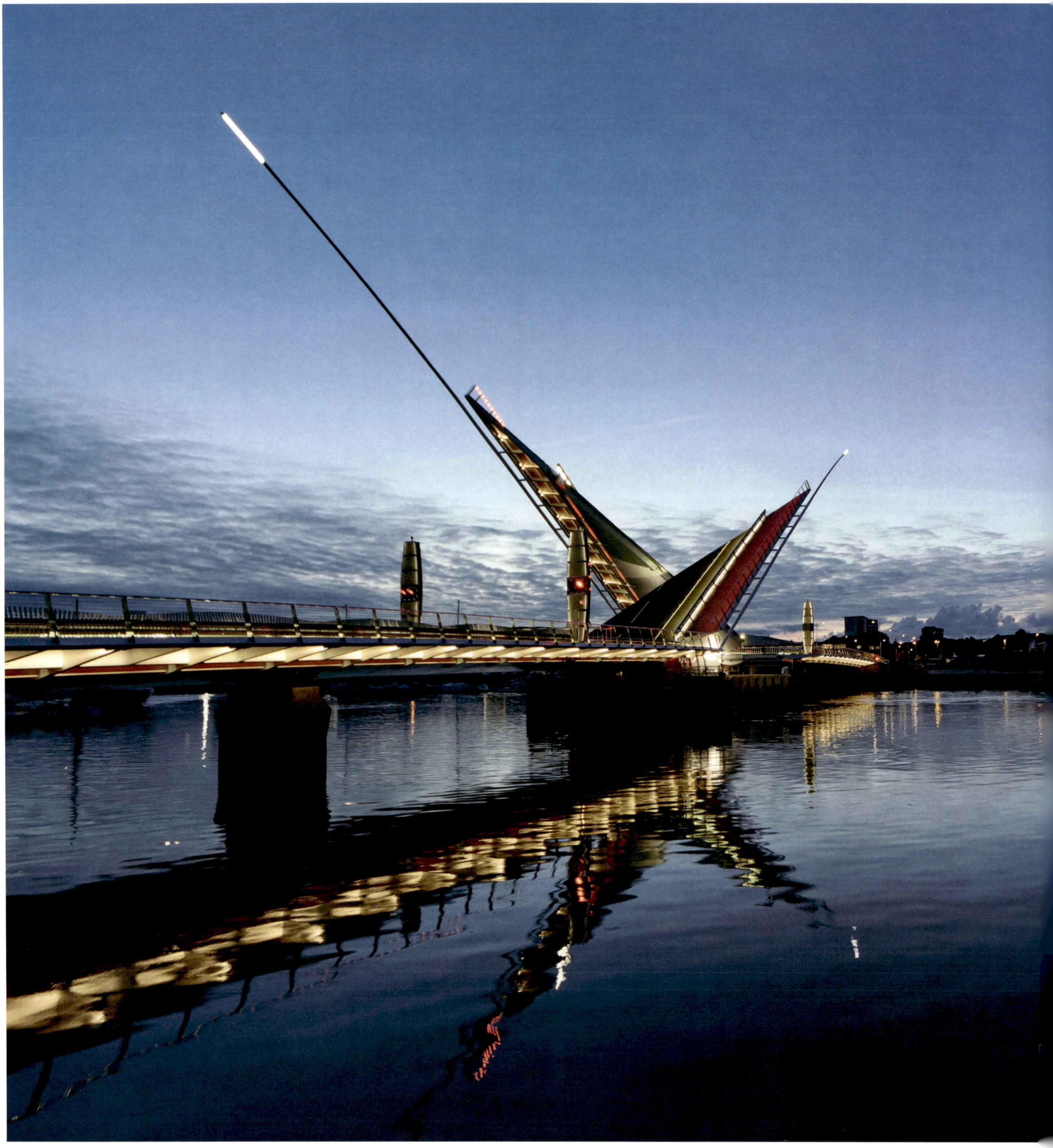

Twin Sails Bridge
Poole, UK

The ancient harbourside town of Poole is separated from its ferry port and the newer suburb of Hamworthy by the narrow Backwater Channel, which leads into the sheltered waters of Holes Bay – the pool that gives the town its name, and home to a popular yacht marina. The existing lifting bridge across the channel is the third on the same site, and has been serving the town since 1927; however, with increasing traffic loads and up to 6,000 lifts per year, it was causing significant delays. Although locals had campaigned for decades for a new crossing to alleviate the congestion, proposals to create a high-level, fixed-bridge bypass right across Holes Bay stalled in 1998. With the development of a 26-hectare brownfield site in Hamworthy promising to create 2,000 new homes, the bridge site was relocated to the northern end of Backwater Channel, and the brief reworked to call for an opening bridge across this shorter and more direct route closer to the centre of town.

The design of the bridge, which is required to open thousands of times a year in coordination with the Poole Lifting Bridge downstream, is in essence two simple, hydraulically operated bascule leaves. The short span meant that no above-deck structure was required, so in order to dramatize the opening of the bridge and distinguish it from others of this type, the two leaves are connected along a diagonal joint, rather than the usual lateral, orthogonal one. In its closed position, the bridge exists as a natural extension of this low-lying environment of marshes and mudflats, but as it opens the two triangular bascules rotate into the vertical position, temporarily lancing the sky to give the impression of a pair of yachts tacking under sail.

The bridge superstructure is steel, with cantilevered armatures supporting lightweight decking. To reinforce this light touch, a stainless-steel post-and-wire parapet at the edge of the pedestrian walkway allows views out across the water and to the nearby yacht marinas. Separating walkway and road is a steel screen inspired by a repeating wave pattern. A series of highly polished slats incrementally rotate back and forth to create a warping surface, and a functional piece of contextual art.

Owing to the frequent openings of the bridge, absolute reliability was essential. As a consequence, the basic solution is entirely standard: two bascule leaves, hydraulically operated in the same way as London's Tower Bridge. In expression, these two leaves are anything but standard, being connected along a diagonal joint, rather than a lateral one. As they rise they reference the maritime heritage of Poole, the world's largest natural harbour, their form an abstract of passing yacht sails.

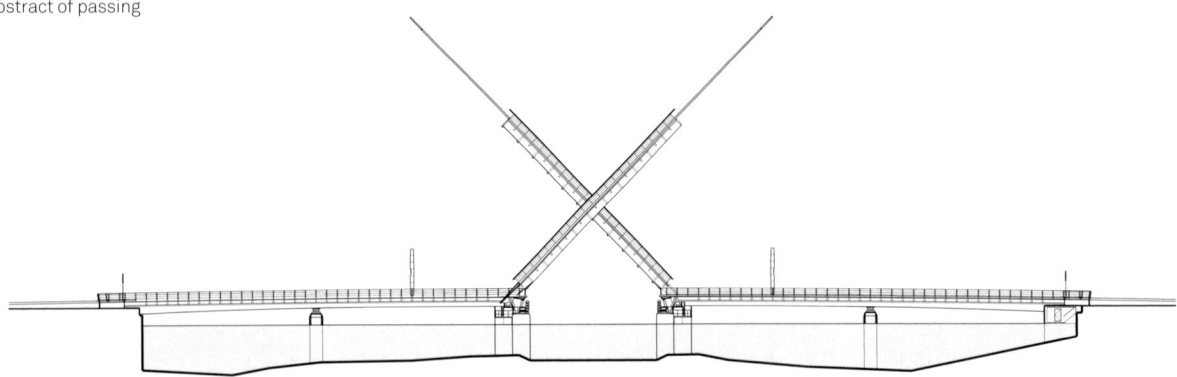

Elevation in partially raised position

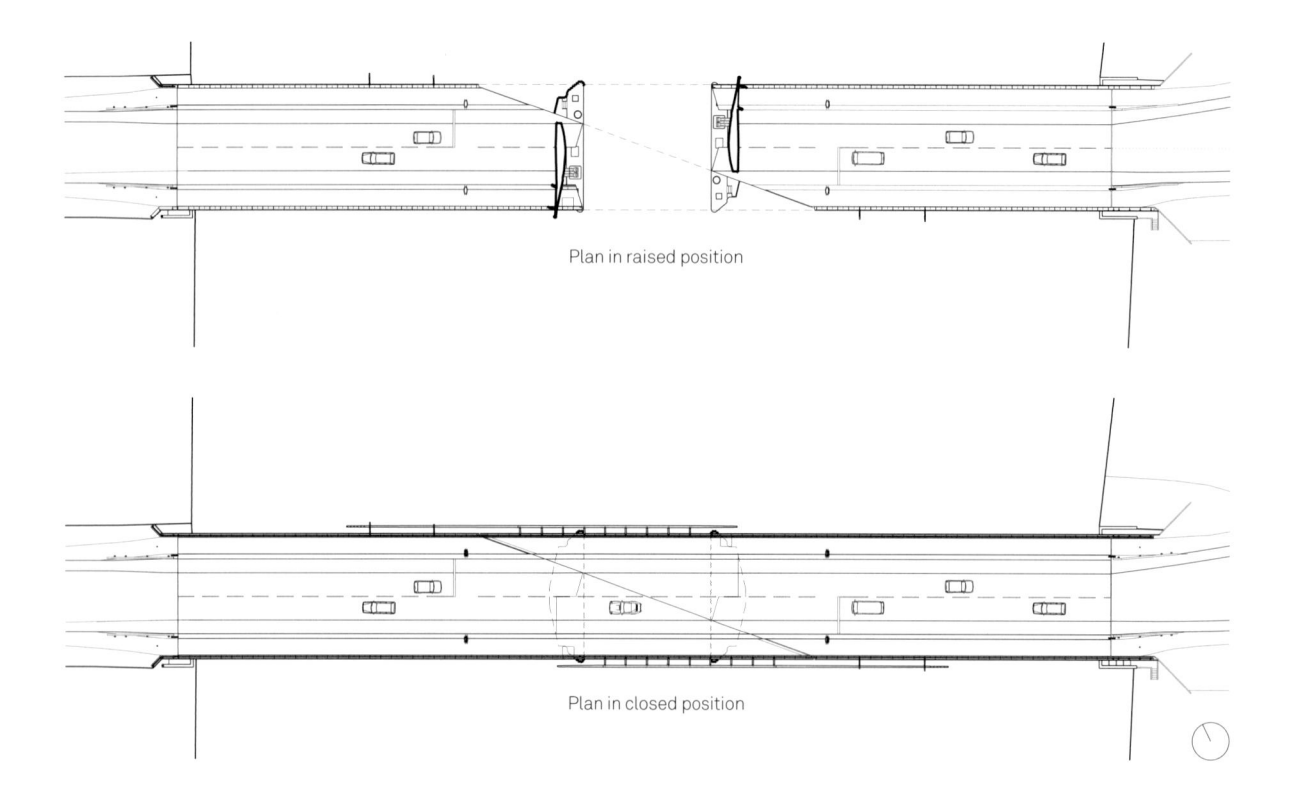

Plan in raised position

Plan in closed position

Sky | Twin Sails Bridge, Poole, UK

From Landscape to Portrait
London, UK

The Royal Academy of Arts was founded in 1768 and promotes an appreciation of the visual arts through a wide-ranging programme of exhibitions and educational activities. Many of the UK's most distinguished artists belong to the academy, allowing for much interdisciplinary debate and collaboration, and so Chris Wilkinson's appointment as an academician in 2006 has reinforced his interest in working across traditional artistic boundaries. This interdisciplinary approach is exemplified in *From Landscape to Portrait*, a site-specific installation designed for the academy's 244th Summer Exhibition in 2012. The annual Summer Exhibition is the largest open-submission exhibition in the world, attracting work from professional artists, academicians and amateurs, much of it available for sale to the public. With architect Eva Jiricna, Chris Wilkinson co-curated the architecture gallery of the 244th exhibition, and therefore wanted to create a piece that would help celebrate and shape visitors' initial experience of the show, as well as illustrating a dialogue between art and architecture.

Located in the Annenberg Courtyard – the imposing outdoor entrance space to the academy's home at Burlington House on Piccadilly – the 12-metre-long sculpture took as its narrative a series of picture frames, a familiar motif to all academicians. The eleven wooden frames were supported on a timber structure clad in polished stainless steel, and made a sequential twist through 90 degrees, from a landscape format facing the Piccadilly entrance to a portrait one in front of the academy's doors. In plan, they were set out on a sine curve, which accentuated the powerful sense of movement. As they pirouetted, the frames captured sections of the London sky high above the open courtyard – and the classical buildings surrounding it – in dynamic sequence, while the mirrored base reflected both the sky and people interacting with the piece.

As part of the London Festival of Architecture in June 2012, choreographer Katie Green was commissioned to create a dance piece in response to the geometry and rhythm of the installation, while the simple graphic motif of the rotating frame was adopted as the visual identity for the Summer Exhibition's promotional campaign, appearing on posters on the London Underground and at other prominent sites. At the end of the exhibition, the piece was dismantled and re-erected in Montgomery Square at Canary Wharf.

Sky | From Landscape to Portrait, London, UK

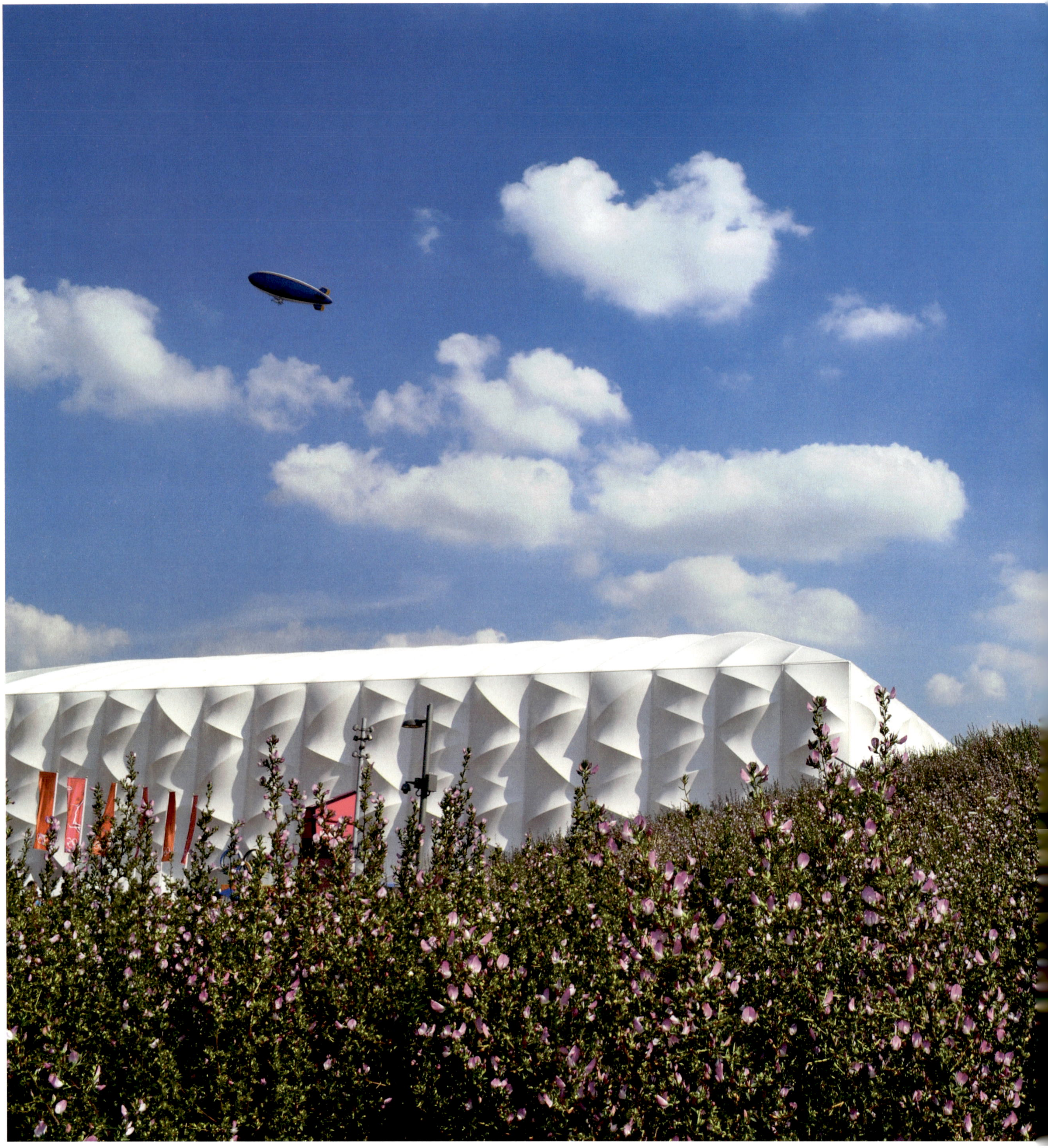

London 2012 Basketball Arena
UK

The London 2012 Olympic Games were widely billed as the most sustainable ever, and the first for which there had been a thorough consideration of economic and environmental sustainability, both for the duration of the event and beyond. While huge villages of temporary structures have long been essential to the staging of the Olympics, London 2012 was certainly one of the most ambitious in terms of the scale of the venues to be removed once the Games were over. The 12,000-seat basketball arena, designed by Wilkinson Eyre in collaboration with SKM and sports consultants KSS, was the third-largest venue in the Olympic Park – and the largest temporary venue ever built for an Olympic Games.

The early stages of the project involved detailed explorations of the best strategy for delivering a building that was simple to erect and flexible enough to be reconfigured for a variety of uses elsewhere. As a multi-use venue, it was used for basketball, handball, wheelchair rugby and wheelchair basketball (the last two events during the Paralympic Games), and therefore had to provide a field of play, spectator seating and media facilities suitable for each of these events. Perhaps more importantly, it had to create a sense of occasion and celebration for both spectators and athletes during the Games. The final strategy combined hired-in and reusable elements (seating system, accommodation modules, seating-bowl steelwork and precast concrete elements) with recyclable materials (fabric cladding, roof steelwork, reinforced concrete foundations and slabs).

The arena was located on a prominent site on high ground towards the north end of Olympic Park, justifying a distinctive architectural language for the building that celebrated its transitory nature, rather than attempting to hide it. The structure of the 30-metre-high, rectangular volume (equivalent to a seven-storey building) was composed of a series of portal frames, connected by a dramatic matrix of lightweight steel members. This structure was wrapped in 20,000 square metres of translucent PVC, stretched across arched-steel framing modules that pushed the fabric out to create an undulating, three-dimensional texture across the façades. The simple building diagram had the field of play as its focus, with spectators accessing the stands from a spectacular concourse between the enclosing structure and the underside of the seating bowl. Spectator facilities were located within the main volume, while back-of-house media and warm-up areas were located in modular units immediately outside the building footprint.

Despite the simplicity of the design strategy, the building's exterior was highly expressive, with sunlight playing over the crisply sculptural white membrane during the day. During evening sessions, the venue was transformed into a theatrical light installation, with dynamic colour-changing effects across the surface skin developed in collaboration with United Visual Artists.

The architectural language of the basketball arena differed from that of the surrounding permanent venues, the design being expressive of its temporary nature. After exploring a series of strategies for creating a structure with reusable and recyclable elements, the team opted for a lightweight steel frame and fabric cladding, allowing the arena to be constructed in just six weeks.

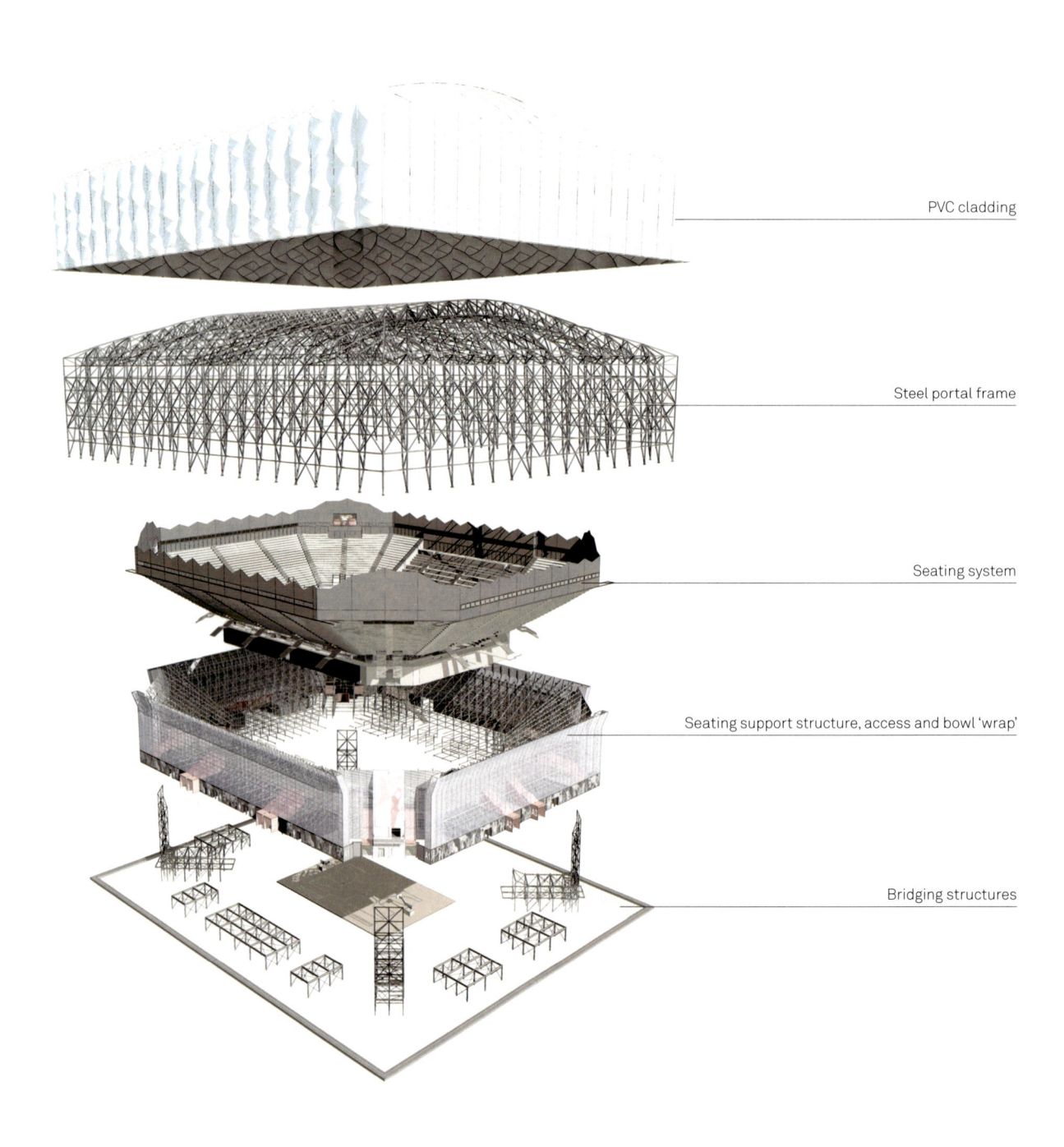

- PVC cladding
- Steel portal frame
- Seating system
- Seating support structure, access and bowl 'wrap'
- Bridging structures

Cross section

1. Field of play
2. General seating
3. PVC cladding
4. Steel portal frame
5. Spectator WCs
6. Scoreboard
7. Olympic Family seating
8. Press tribune
9. Commentator control room
10. Public concourse
11. Back-of-house accommodation

The cloud-like outer skin of the basketball arena was designed to provide visual interest both close up and from a distance. During the Games, it faced the velodrome across a public plaza, which acted as a collecting space for the vast numbers of people attending events within both venues, but could be seen from most parts of the wider park – primarily from the huge bridge that connected the arena with the main pedestrian thoroughfare on the other side of the River Lea.

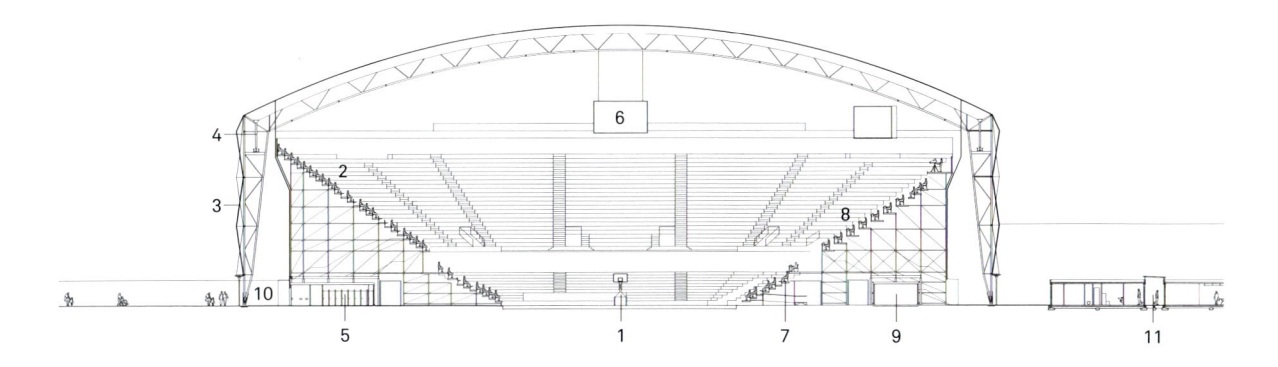

Sky | London 2012 Basketball Arena, UK

Ground-floor plan

1 Public concourse
2 Spectator WCs
3 Field of play
4 Commentator control room
5 Olympic Family seating

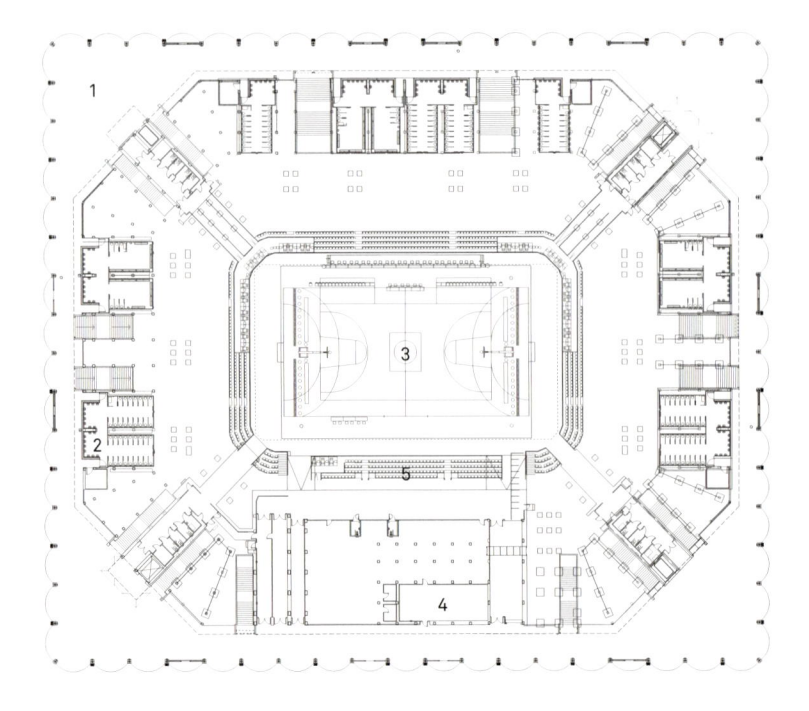

Seating-bowl plan

1 General seating
2 Field of play
3 Press tribune

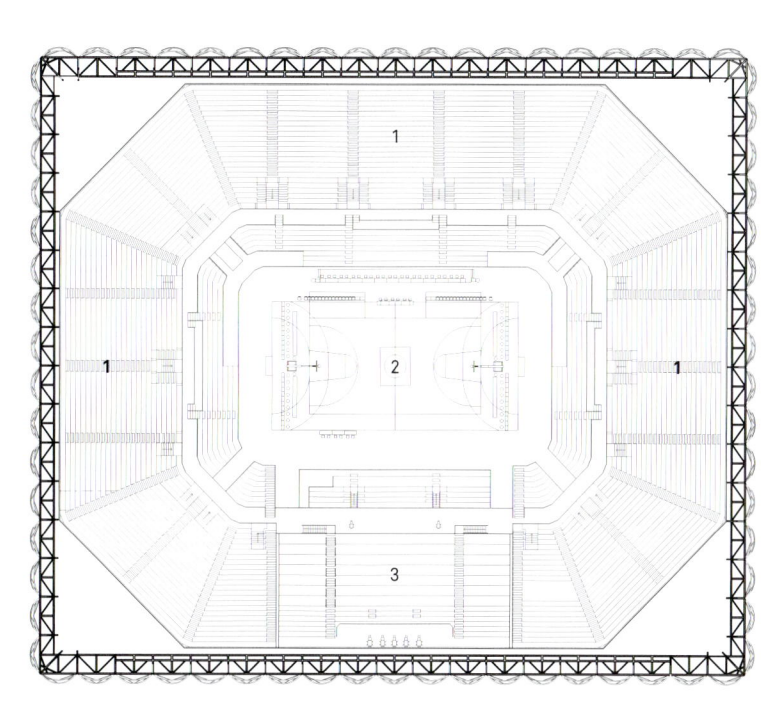

Sky | London 2012 Basketball Arena, UK

The layers of structure and cladding were clearly visible in the public concourse that circumscribed the building, the steel members creating a complex lattice to support the external skin. This envelope enclosed an interwoven blackout layer, which blocked out sunlight during daytime game sessions so that the artificial lighting within could be optimized for both players and media.

The concourse also provided access to WCs and other spectator facilities, all hidden beneath the slope of the seating bowl.

Sectional detail

1 Blackout PVC membrane
2 PVC cladding
3 Primary steel superstructure
4 Secondary steel fabric tensioners
5 Blackout fabric to rear of seating
6 Seating system

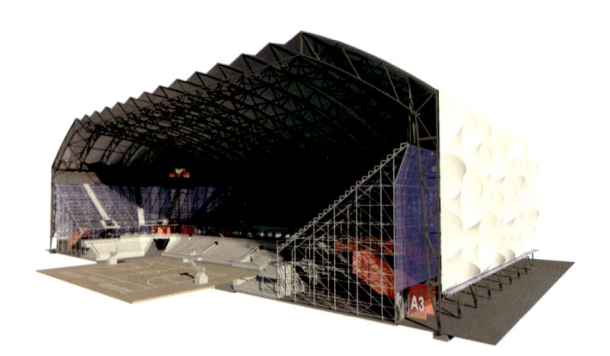

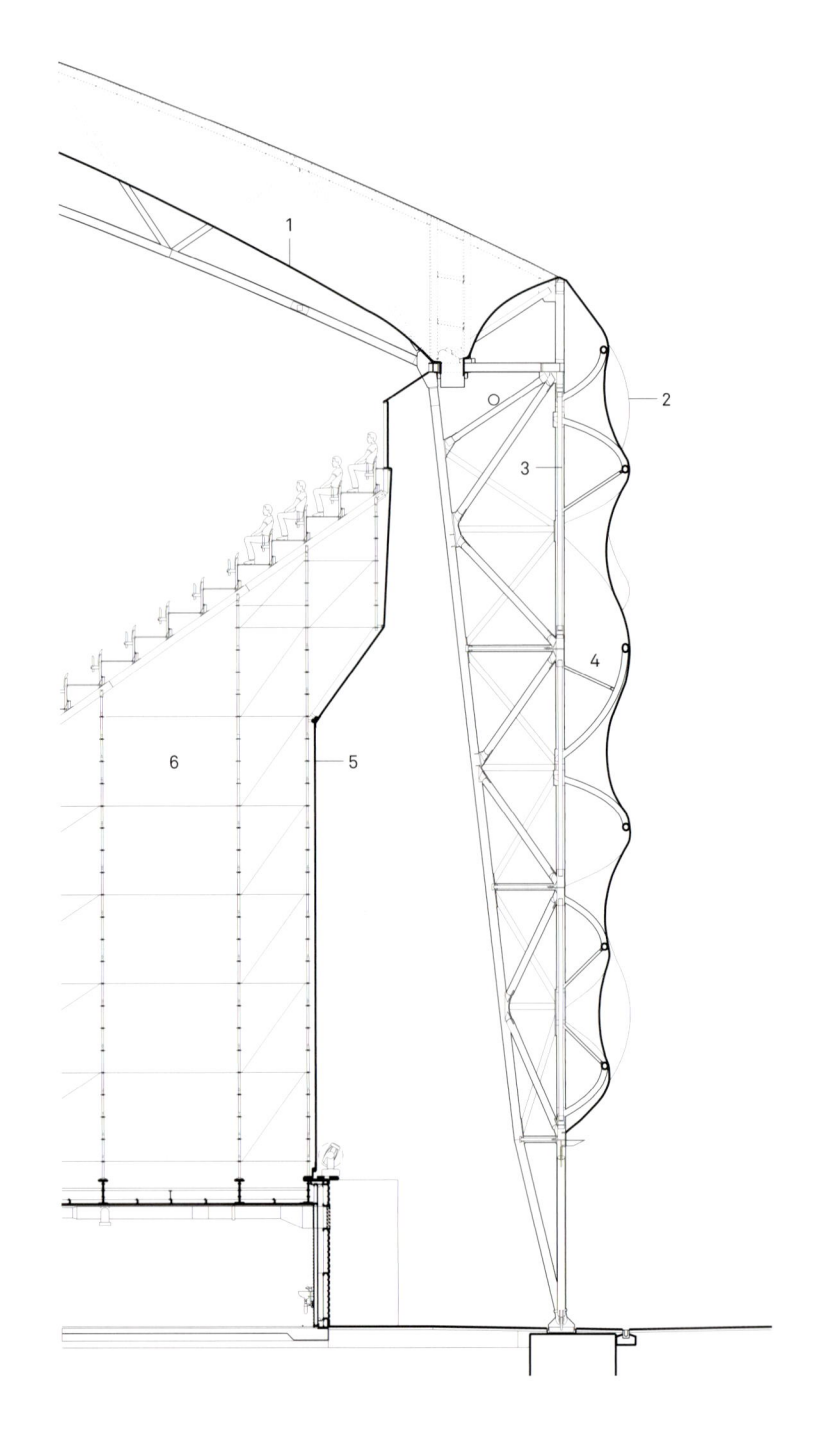

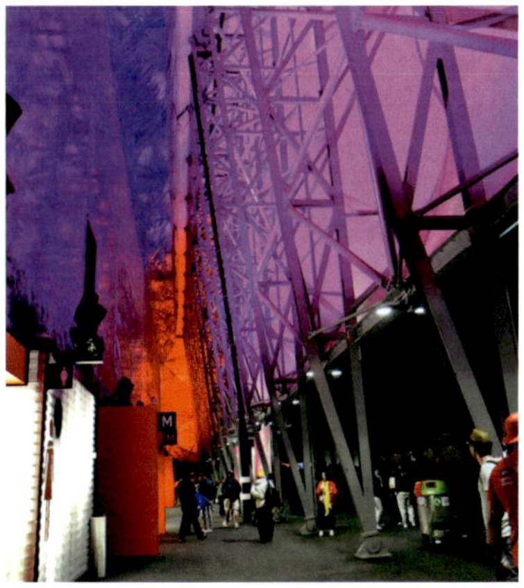

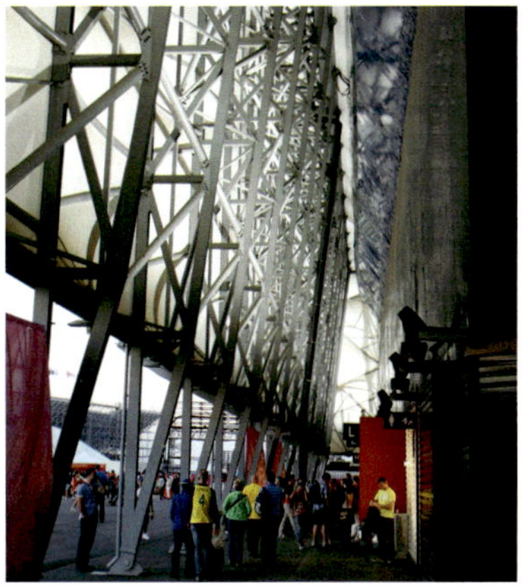

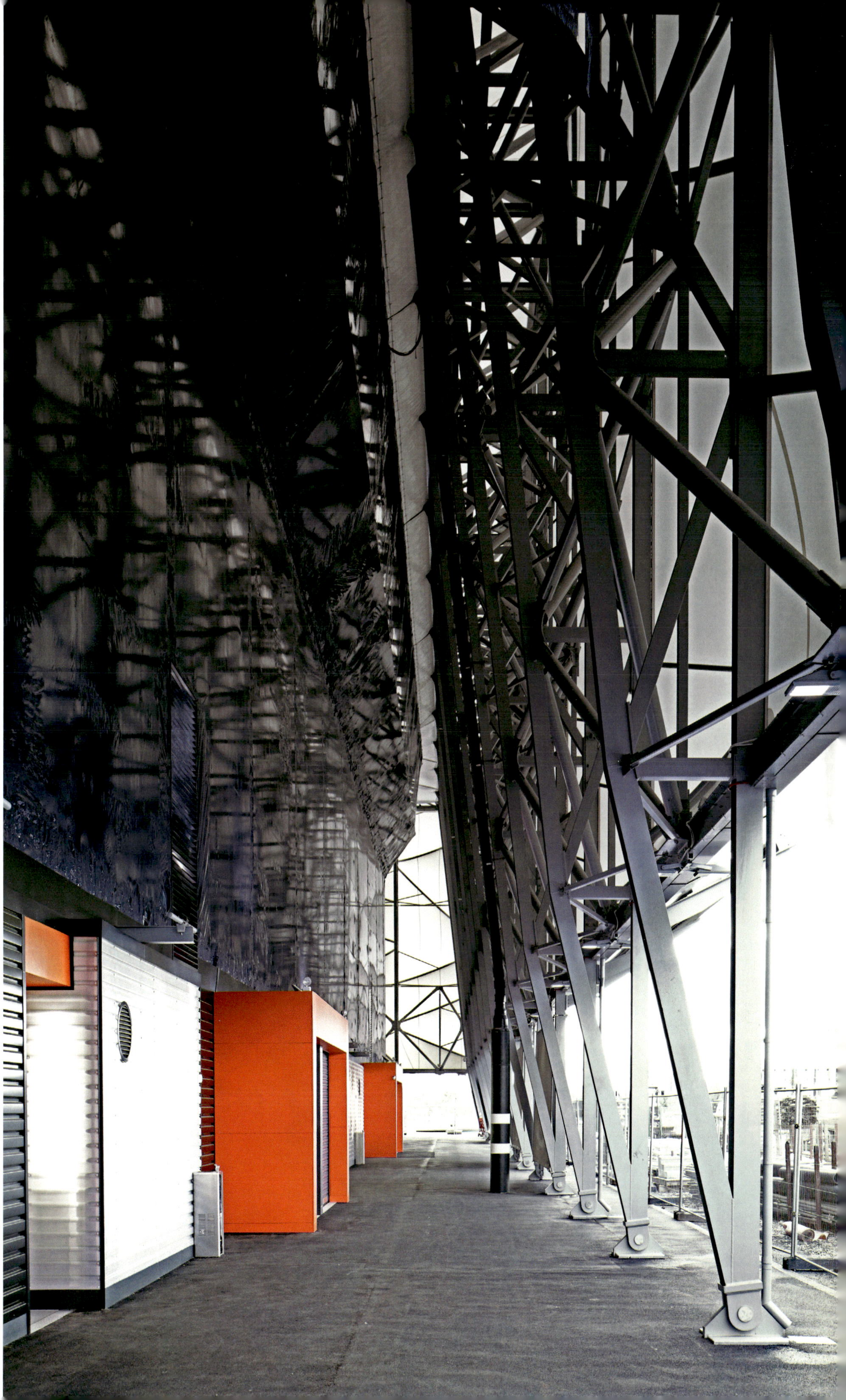

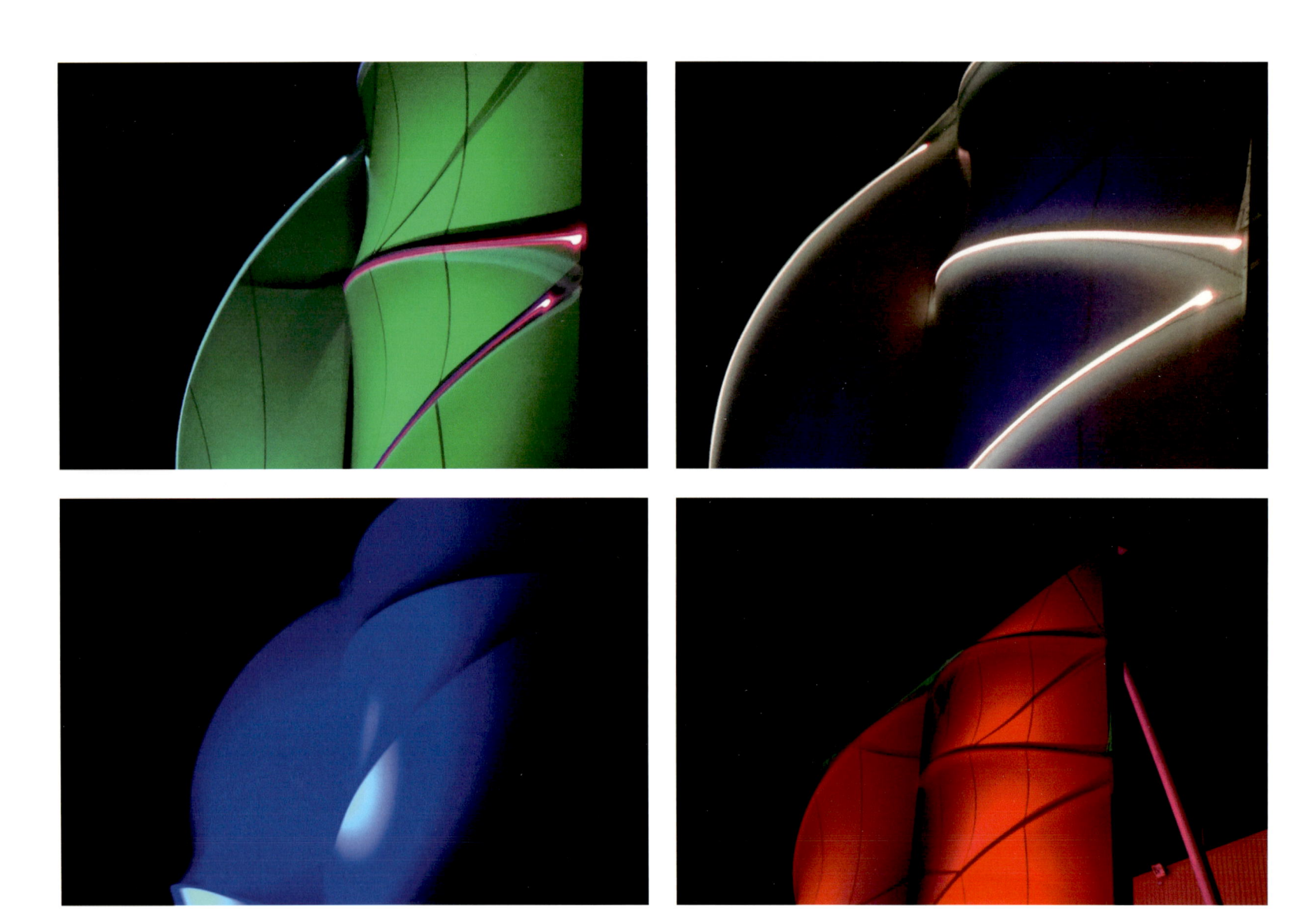

Wilkinson Eyre worked with United Visual Artists, specialists in concert lighting and installations, to create light effects across the surface of the arena for evening sessions of the Games. After extensive testing on a full-scale mock-up, a dynamic colour-changing sequence was chosen to transform the entire building into a giant light installation, visible from far across the Olympic Park.

Sky | London 2012 Basketball Arena, UK

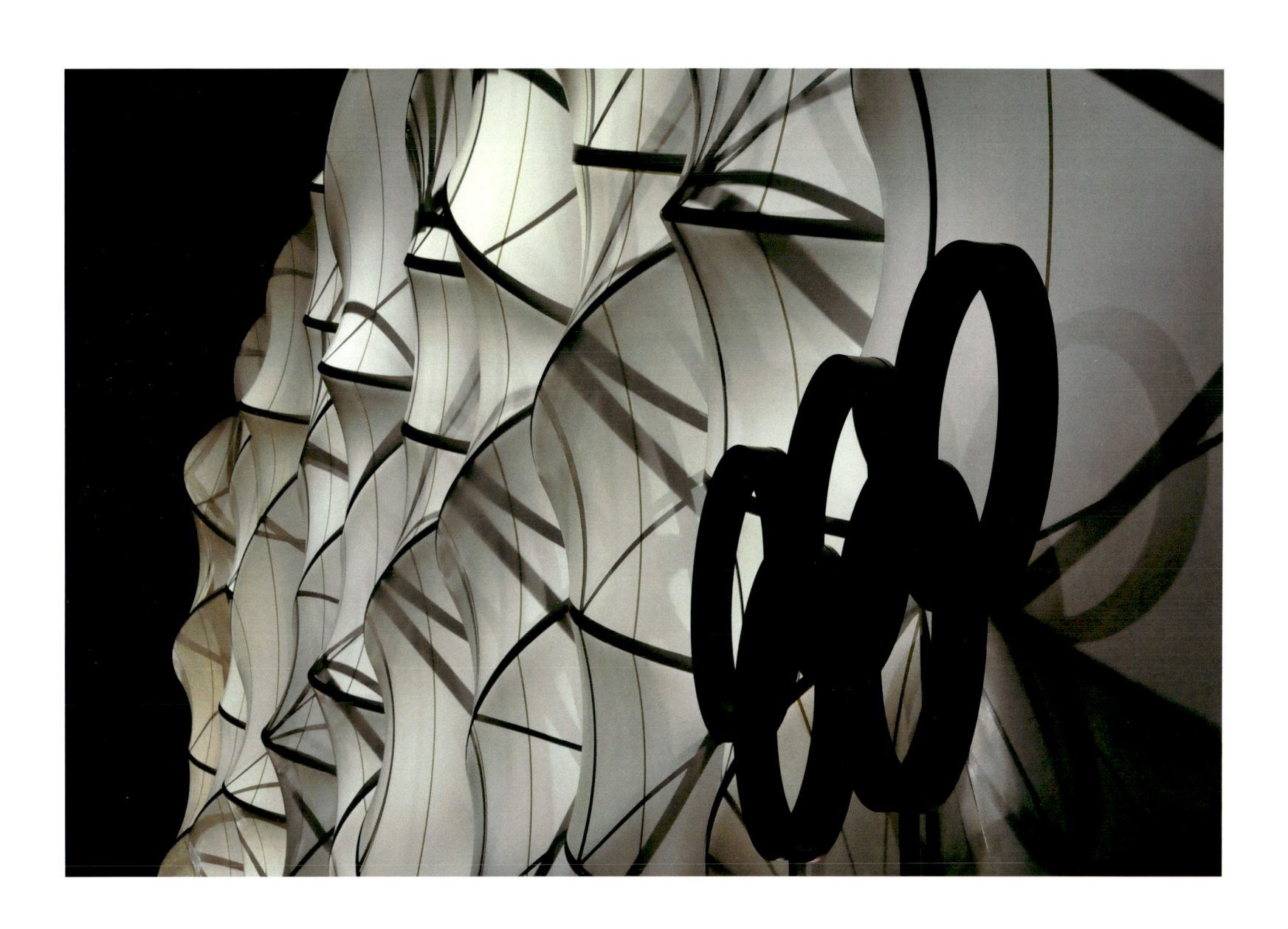

King's Cross Gasholders
London, UK

King's Cross is the largest urban redevelopment scheme in Europe, a 27-hectare post-industrial landscape to the north of the recently refurbished railway station. The rich industrial heritage of the site has been embraced by the developer, Argent, which has respected the physical remnants of the past, incorporating them into the new scheme. This strategy has ensured that, as part of its dramatic renaissance, King's Cross has retained – and evolved – a real sense of place. Among the most distinctive and beautiful features to be retained is a triplet of gasholder guide frames, constructed in 1867 and now Grade II-listed, which has long been a prominent landmark for anyone arriving at King's Cross by train from the north. The triplet was dismantled in 2001 to allow the construction of the Channel Tunnel Rail Link, and this offered an ideal opportunity to comprehensively refurbish the gasholders and relocate them to better suit the wider masterplan for the site.

Wilkinson Eyre won a design competition in 2005 with a concept for three residential buildings to be housed within the elegant cast-iron frames. The concept proposed three drums of accommodation at differing heights to suggest the movement of the original gasholders, which would have risen up or down depending on the pressure of the gas within. A fourth, 'virtual' drum, located at the centre of the frames, formed an open courtyard, celebrating the convergence of the cast-iron structures at their point of intersection.

The design, which was put on hold to suit the phasing of the development, has now been progressed, and construction will begin in late 2014. With the opportunity to revisit this unique brief, the concept has been developed to create a dynamic contrast between new and old. The heavy industrial aesthetic and raw physical materiality of the guide structures provide a counterpoint to the lightness and intricacy of the interior spaces, which draw inspiration from the delicate refinement of a traditional watch movement. Each drum of accommodation is independently supported, and is set back from the guide structures. The cladding is composed of upright modular panels of steel and glass, textured with a veil of shutters, which can be adjusted to provide shade and privacy as necessary. Designed for the busy urbanite, the apartments within incorporate innovative technologies that will allow residents to alter, control and environmentally fine-tune the living spaces to suit their individual needs. All systems will close down when not in use, coming alive again at the touch of a smartphone.

The apartments are accessed via the private central courtyard, each drum volume having its own atrium and core. These are linked by a series of circular walkways that garland the courtyard, where light is reflected in a central water feature. In another play of contrasts, the roofs are planted as gardens to bring nature to this re-inhabited urban landscape.

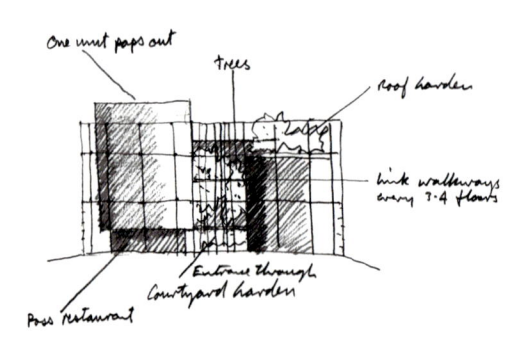

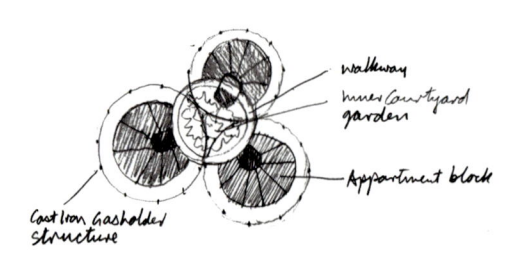

Sky | King's Cross Gasholders, London, UK

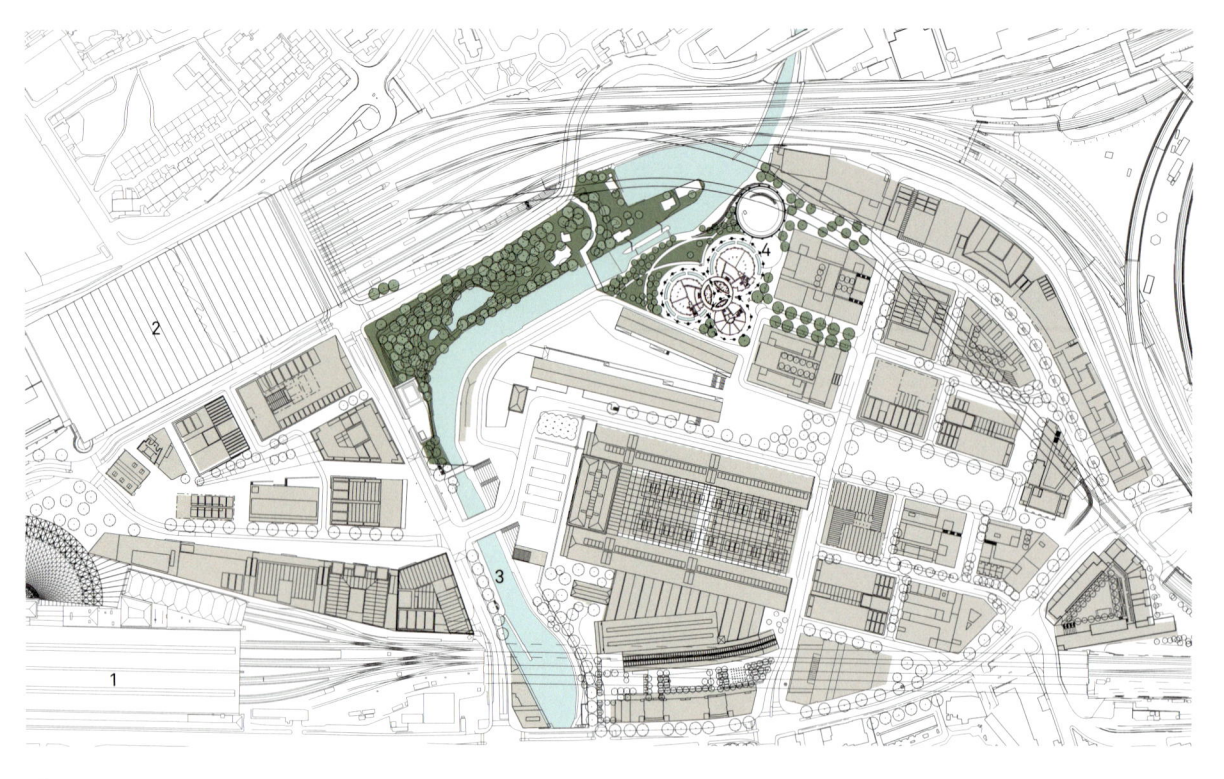

The gasholder guide frames were originally constructed in 1867 as part of the Imperial Gas Works, and were enlarged a decade later. With their wrought- and cast-iron frames sharing a central spine, gasholders 10, 11 and 12 became known as the 'siamese triplet'. The triplet was an immediately identifiable landmark during the neighbourhood's industrial heyday, but was abandoned as heavy industry moved to the outskirts of London. It remained abandoned in the middle of the wasteland behind King's Cross station until 2001, when it was dismantled and taken to Yorkshire for storage and a comprehensive refurbishment ahead of its restoration to a new home on the northern bank of the Regent's Canal.

These historic references have been used to develop an industrial aesthetic for the exterior of the accommodation volumes that are to be built within each of the guide frames. It is expressed in a veil of metal and structural elements that form operable and static panels for the control of the environmental conditions within. The dark steel cladding contrasts with elements of brass and bronze.

Location plan
1 King's Cross station
2 St Pancras station
3 Regent's Canal
4 Gasholders site

124

The trefoil-shaped cluster has an intricate web of wrought-iron columns and tiers at the point where the three volumes intersect. Inspired by the delicately layered, interconnected discs and cogs of a traditional watch movement or astrolabe, this central space has been widened into a large circular courtyard by biting into each of the surrounding volumes, allowing the complex engineering at the heart of the structure to be better celebrated.

The structural grid is set out according to the diameter of each gasholder frame, with a variety of apartment types located around the perimeter of each volume. The structural columns and shear walls are arranged radially, giving every unit a sense of the original curved structure.

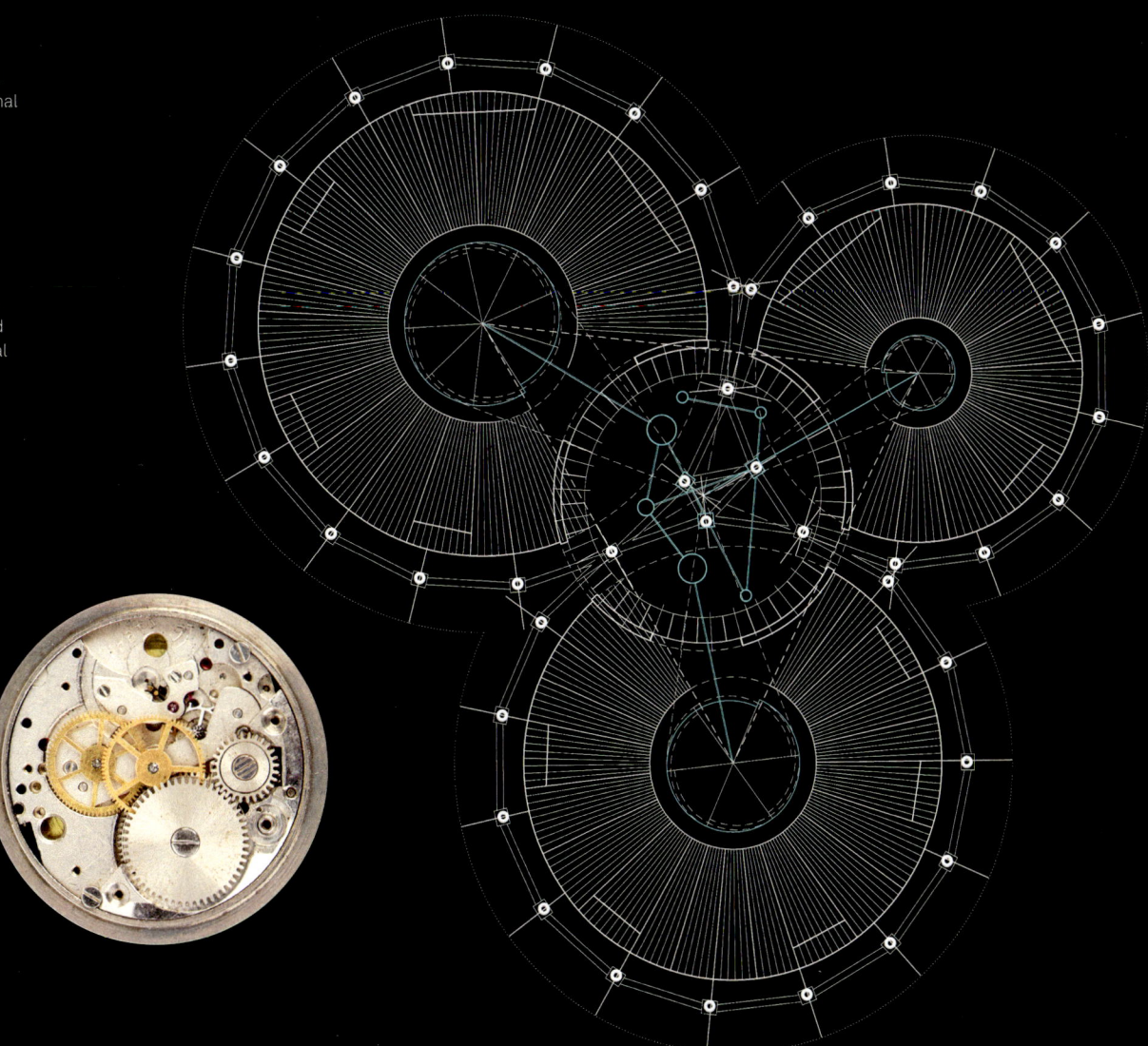

Typical floor plan

1 Courtyard
2 Atrium
3 Studio
4 Three-bedroom duplex
5 Two-bedroom apartment
6 Three-bedroom apartment
7 One-bedroom apartment
8 Two-bedroom duplex

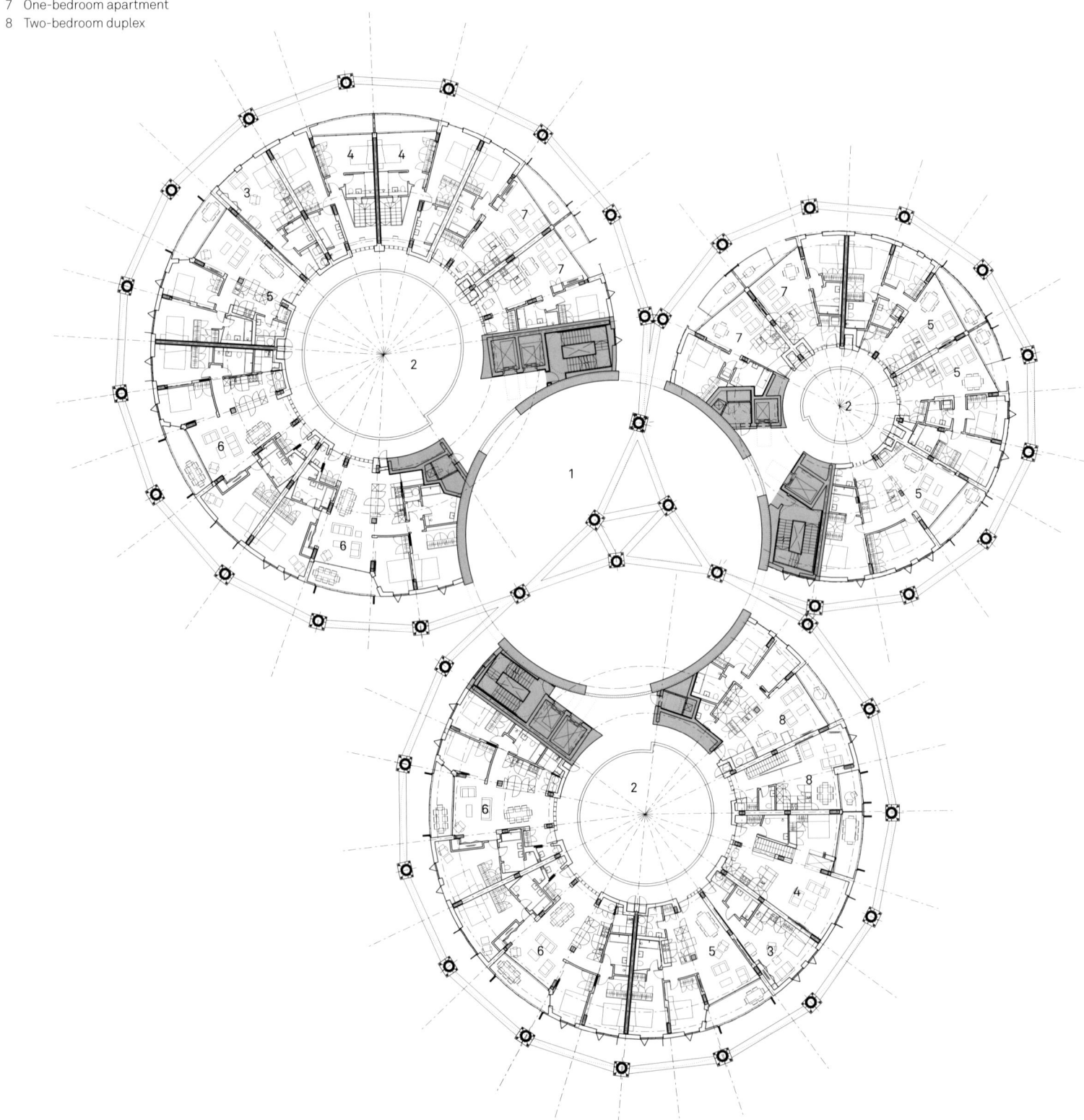

The height and dimensions of the three primary building forms are dictated by their relationship to the framing guide structures, and by the maximum permitted building heights set out by the planning parameters. Each guide frame has a different diameter, number of columns and lattice-beam length, and these dimensions have informed those of the built elements within. While the accommodation peeps over the top of the guide frame at gasholder 11, the built volumes sit well below the frame in the case of its fellow structures.

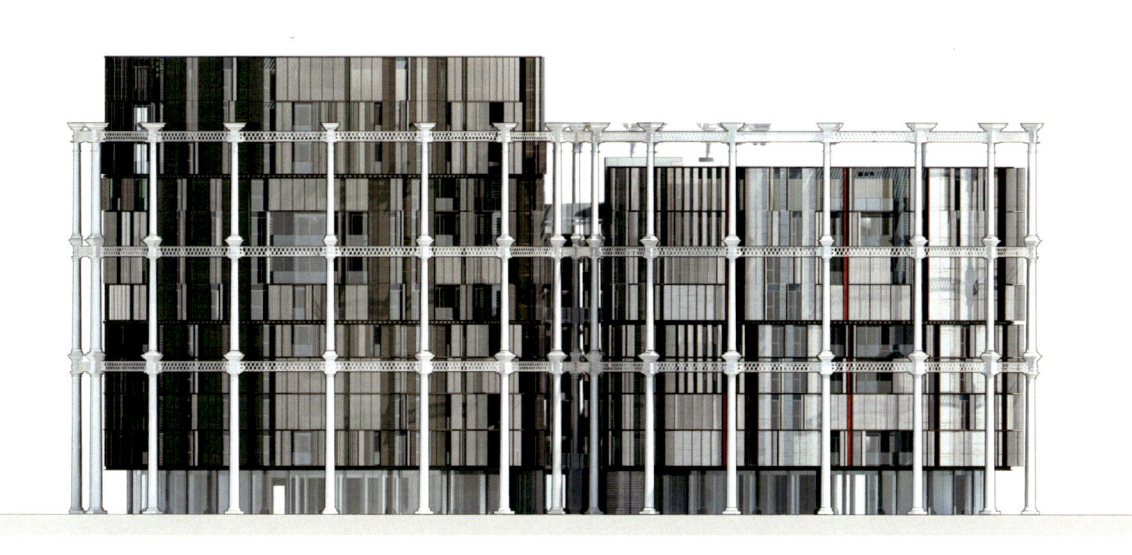

Sky | King's Cross Gasholders, London, UK

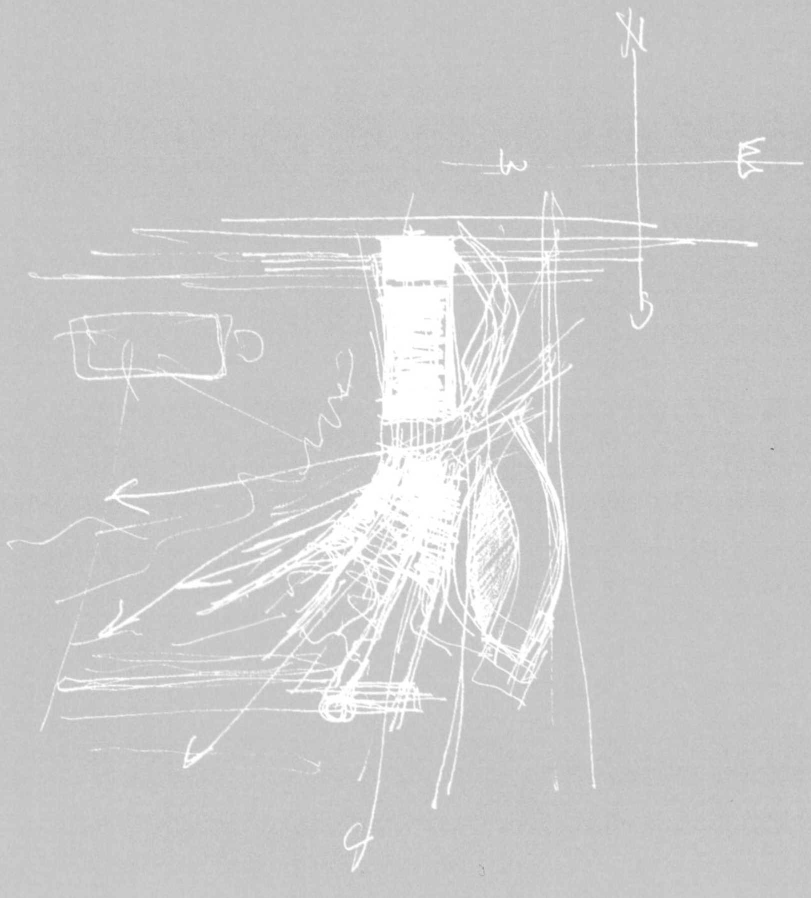
N
E

Water

Designing by the water demands ingenuity and robust techniques, but the challenges are compensated by the opportunity to work with an incredible palette of reflected light. Water suggests adventure, exploration, new possibilities, grand harbour vistas and the rich texture of inner-city docks.

Splashpoint, Worthing, UK	130
Arena and Convention Centre, Liverpool, UK	140
Peace Bridge, Derry, UK	151
Media City Footbridge, Salford, UK	152
Mary Rose Museum, Portsmouth, UK	155
The Crystal, London, UK	165
Crown Hotel, Sydney, Australia	172

Splashpoint
Worthing, UK

The architectural ambition behind this leisure centre on Worthing's seafront was to connect town and beach. Worthing is a traditional English seaside resort, which, although it has struggled in recent decades against global recession and more localized poverty, has a charming human scale in its street patterns and architecture that has not been spoilt by wholesale redevelopment. The new Splashpoint leisure centre has a prominent location overlooking the beach – the natural focus of activity in the town – occupying as it does a narrow site between Brighton Road and the seafront. The diagram of the building is deceptively simple: a series of fluid extrusions that act as viewfinders to connect road and beach, continually channelling the user's gaze towards the sea.

The building form follows this diagram, and is composed of a cluster of undulating linear volumes. These echo the repeated form of the protective groynes on the beach below, as well as picking up on the scale of nearby terraced houses. They take informal, organic lines, with the roof pitching at different angles to reduce the visual mass of the building, folding and twisting southwards to terminate in a series of large portals that frame views of the beach and sea.

Splashpoint sits adjacent to the ornamental gardens of the Regency Beach House, and within this genteel context suggests a new kind of architectural language for seafront buildings based on a palette of raw, natural materials, rather than stucco and whitewash. The volumes are clad in materials chosen to withstand, and weather gracefully amid, the brisk, salty conditions of the seafront. The fluid, curving forms of the main swimming-pool hall are wrapped in copper, and, to their northern end, are defined by the rectilinear arrangement of the diving and competition pools. These forms gradually become more disobedient as they approach the beach, widening and splaying to house a large leisure pool. The health and fitness wing, in contrast, is clad in red cedar, and mediates between the straight site boundary and the curving geometry of the pool volume.

Large areas of glazing to the sectional façades welcome visitors on their approach from the town, the internal arrangement of the building immediately setting up a strong visual connection with the sea. To reinforce this, the building has been raised to create the impression of an infinity pool in the main hall, the surrounding portal framing views of the distant horizon.

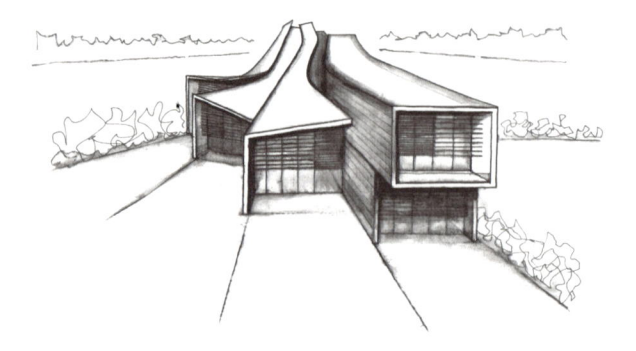

Water | Splashpoint, Worthing, UK

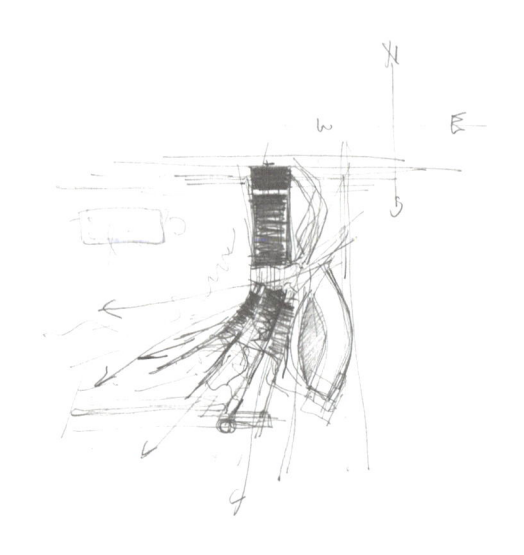

Reminiscent of a series of dunes, the dynamic, fragmented form of the leisure centre acts as a link between the domestic scale of nearby suburban homes and the more expansive landscape of sea and shore.

Site plan
1. Beach House
2. Beach House grounds
3. Beach
4. Splashpoint
5. Existing Aquarena

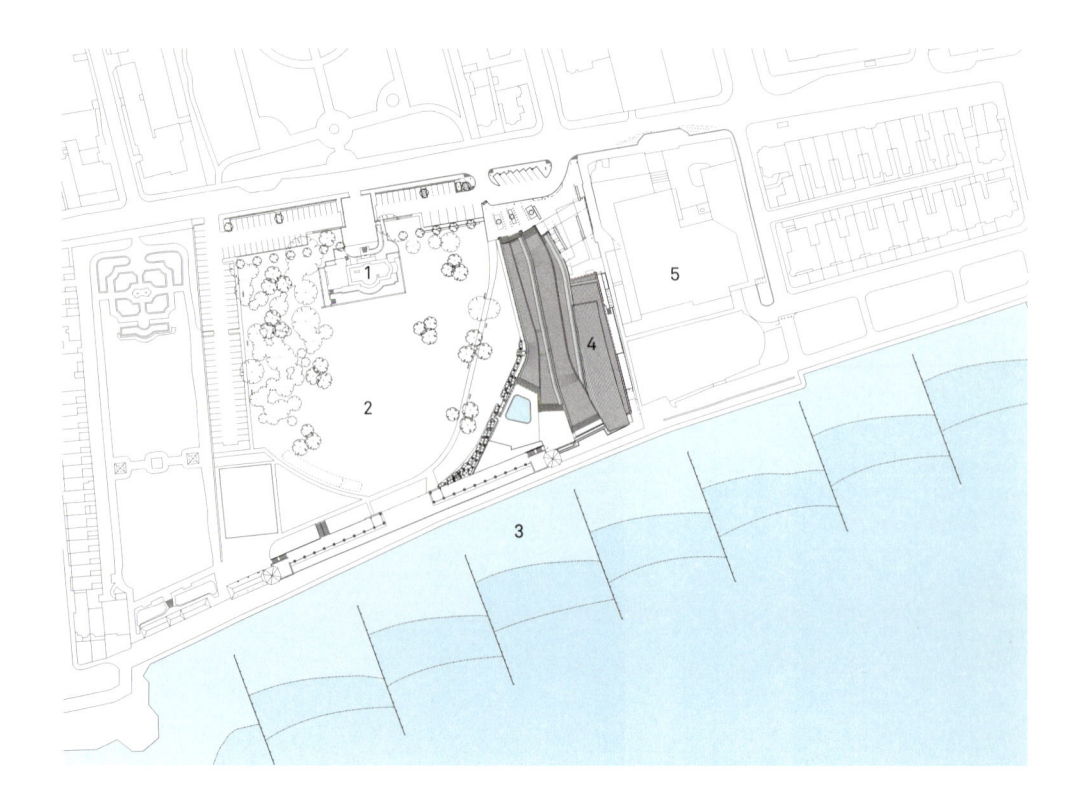

The main pool hall acts as a viewfinder, connecting the street with the seafront, where the building terminates in a series of glazed façades overlooking the water. This device creates a spectacular internal space, drenched with natural daylight, and establishes Splashpoint as both amenity and destination within the town.

Water | Splashpoint, Worthing, UK

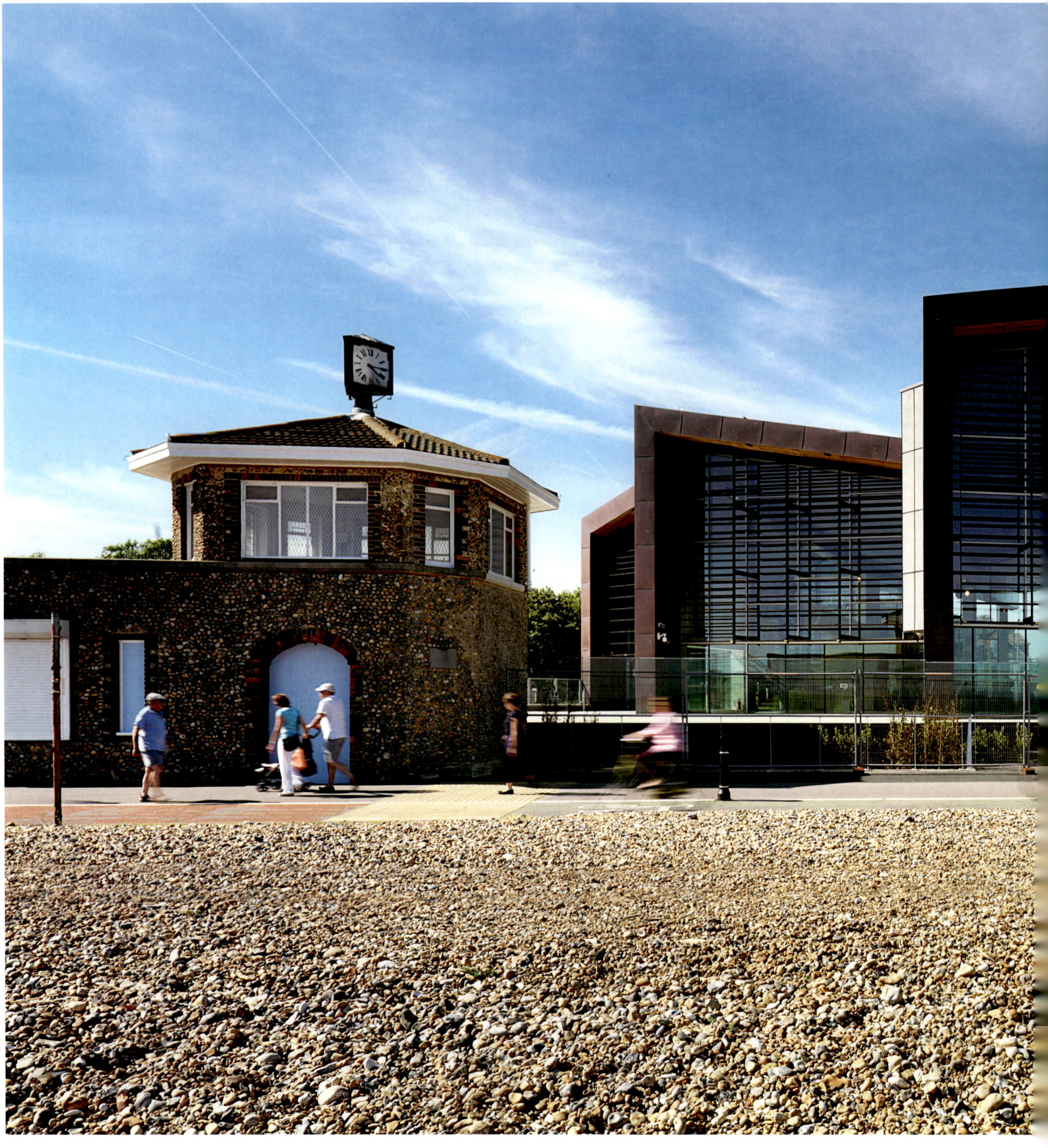

Water | Splashpoint, Worthing, UK

136

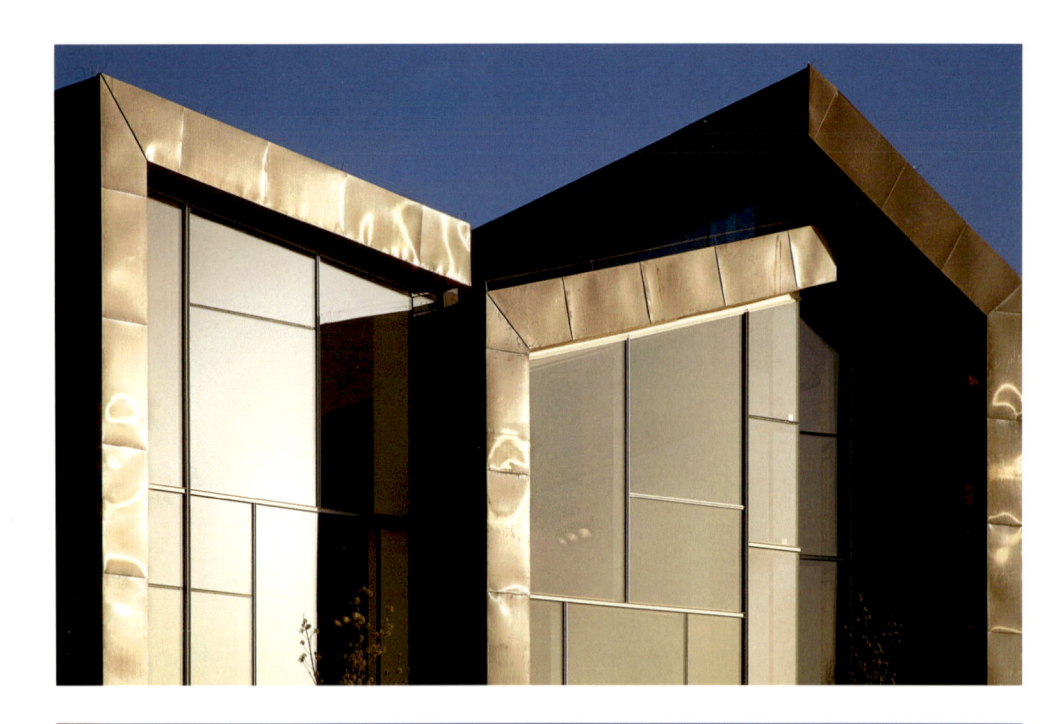

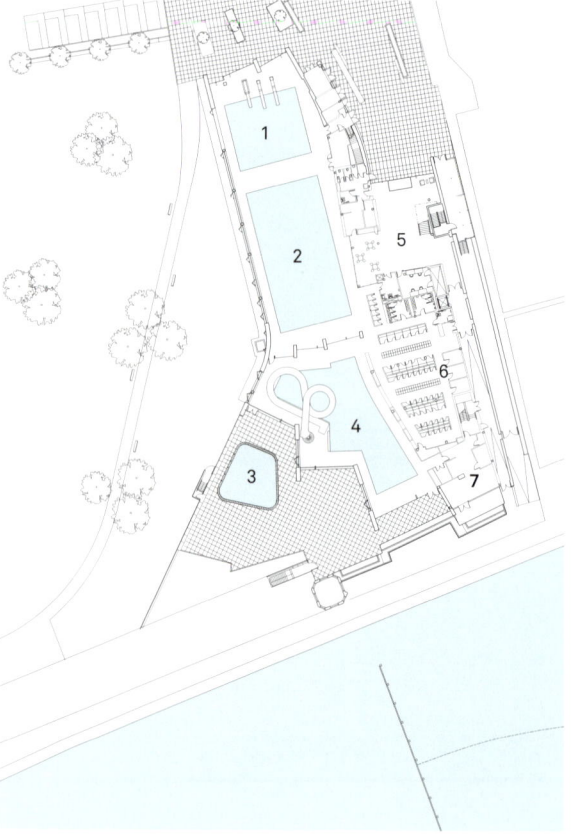

The saline conditions of the seafront, coupled with the chlorine-rich pool areas, make for a harsh environmental context. The copper and timber cladding will provide the structure with a robust envelope, and will gradually weather as the building settles into its surroundings.

Splashpoint was designed with the close involvement of a number of user groups and other community stakeholders; in fact, its name was chosen after a local newspaper ran a competition inviting schoolchildren to suggest a moniker for the new complex. In its first month, May 2013, Splashpoint welcomed an unprecedented number of visitors, with more than 54,000 people passing through its doors.

Ground-floor plan

1. Learner/diving pool
2. Competition pool
3. 'Lazy River' pool (outdoor)
4. Leisure pool
5. Entrance lobby and cafe
6. Changing rooms
7. Sauna and steam rooms

Long section

1. Learner/diving pool
2. Competition pool
3. Leisure pool
4. Gym
5. Terrace

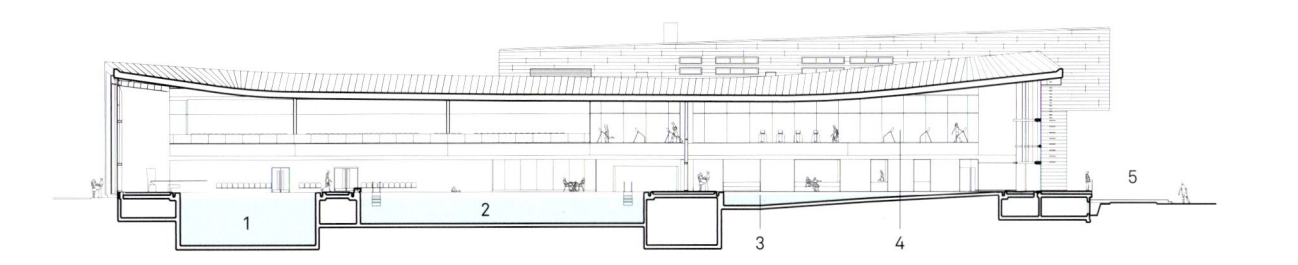

Water | Splashpoint, Worthing, UK

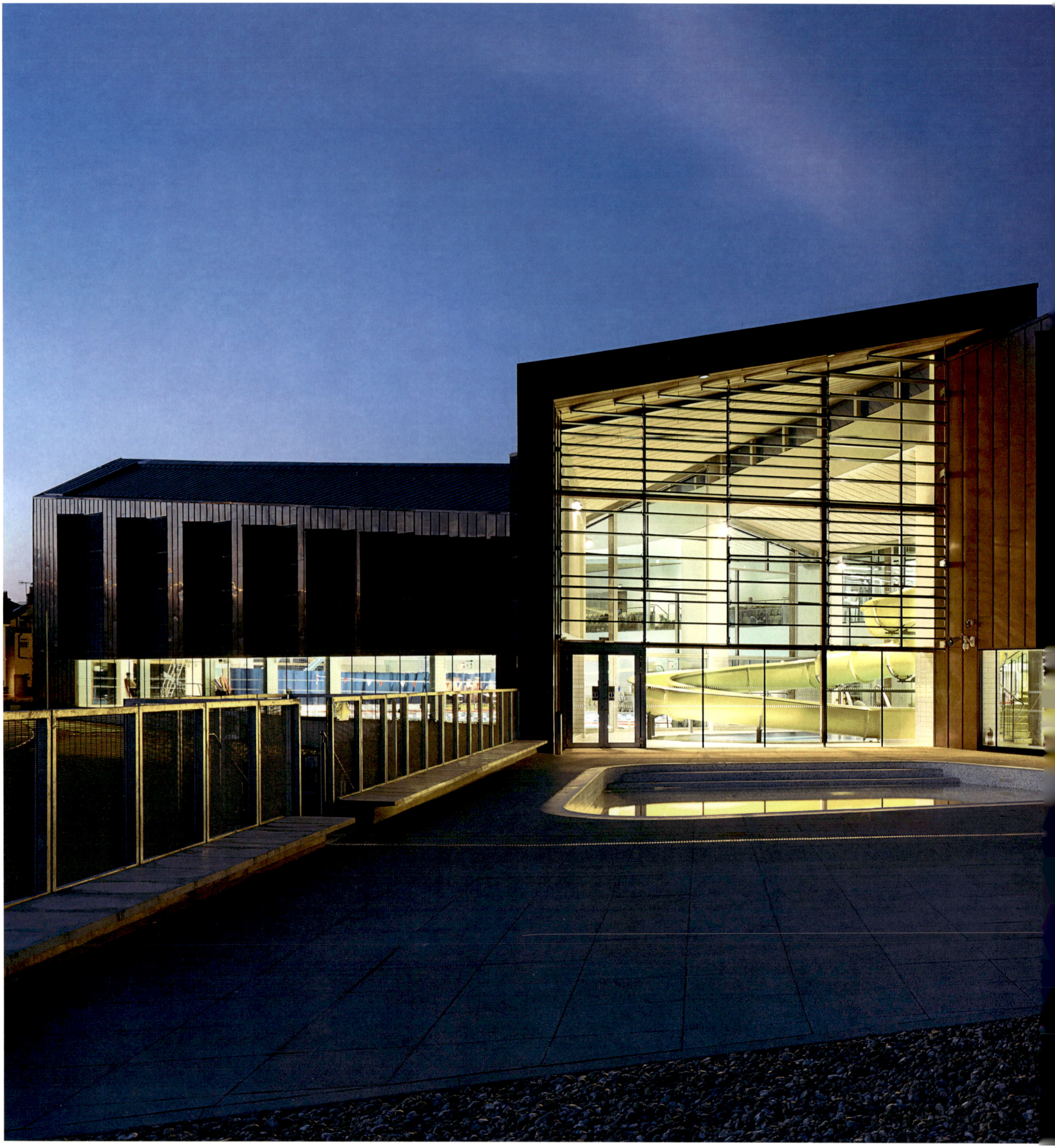

Water | Splashpoint, Worthing, UK

Arena and Convention Centre
Liverpool, UK

The Liverpool Arena and Convention Centre was the focal point of the city's year as European Capital of Culture in 2008, taking its place in a string of culturally significant buildings along the famous Mersey riverfront. The fluidly curved architectural form is a direct response to the river, mediating between water and city, and contrasting emphatically with the orthogonal ranks of warehouses around the Albert Dock. The original masterplan for Kings Waterfront, developed by Liverpool Vision, imagined a major leisure venue but with the arena, conference centre and exhibition space as discrete elements. Wilkinson Eyre's design combines all of these functions to create a single complex, wrapped in a unifying skin and stretching low along the river as two sculptural forms on either side of a central galleria. This innovative strategy not only allows activities to overlap and share spaces within the building, but also has a multiplying effect, drawing in new audiences and bringing vitality and activity to the waterfront.

This is a civic building in every sense, and the site diagram helps to make the building welcoming for all, reinforcing routes between the city and the river. The last part of this journey is through the galleria, which provides the pivot point for the two main 'wings' of the building, as well as acting as a viewfinder, delivering visitors to the Mersey through an airy, double-height space. The Echo Arena is situated to the north of the galleria, and is accessed via a dramatic glazed concourse beneath the exposed-concrete underside of the bowl. Inside, the horseshoe configuration is flexible enough to be adapted for a wide range of sporting and cultural events. To the south, the conference centre houses a large auditorium, a multipurpose exhibition hall for trade events, and a suite of support spaces. The auditorium features two revolving seating volumes, which allow it to be reconfigured into three small spaces in just a few minutes.

Viewed from the river, the structure appears to span the gap between Liverpool's Anglican and Roman Catholic cathedrals on the skyline beyond. This elevation is broken down into layers to reduce its mass, with the cladding arranged in three horizontal bands of varying transparency: clear glass at the base, an intermediate layer of patterned translucent glazing, and an overhanging, metal-panelled rainscreen, which defines the roof edge. This palette of robust yet delicate design treatments is inspired (and necessitated) by the Mersey, with its strong tides, blustery winds and powerful reflected light.

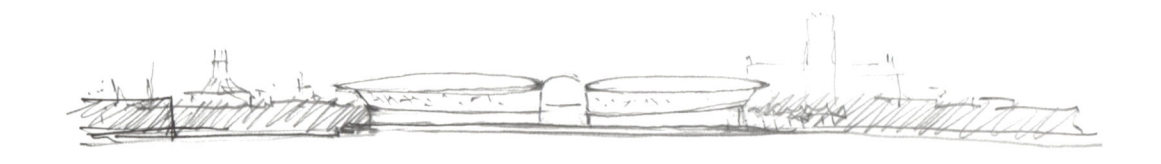

140

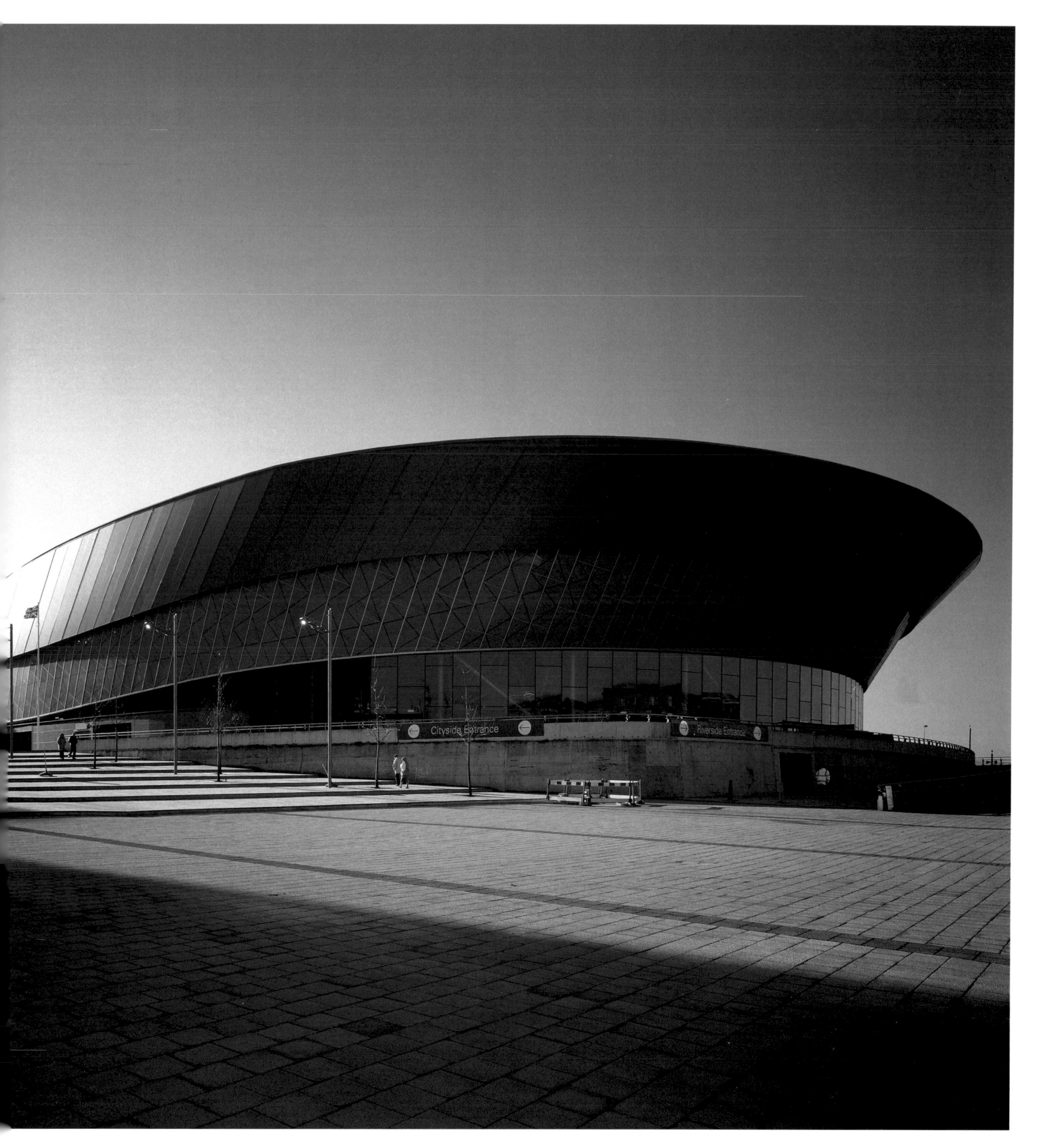

Water | Arena and Convention Centre, Liverpool, UK

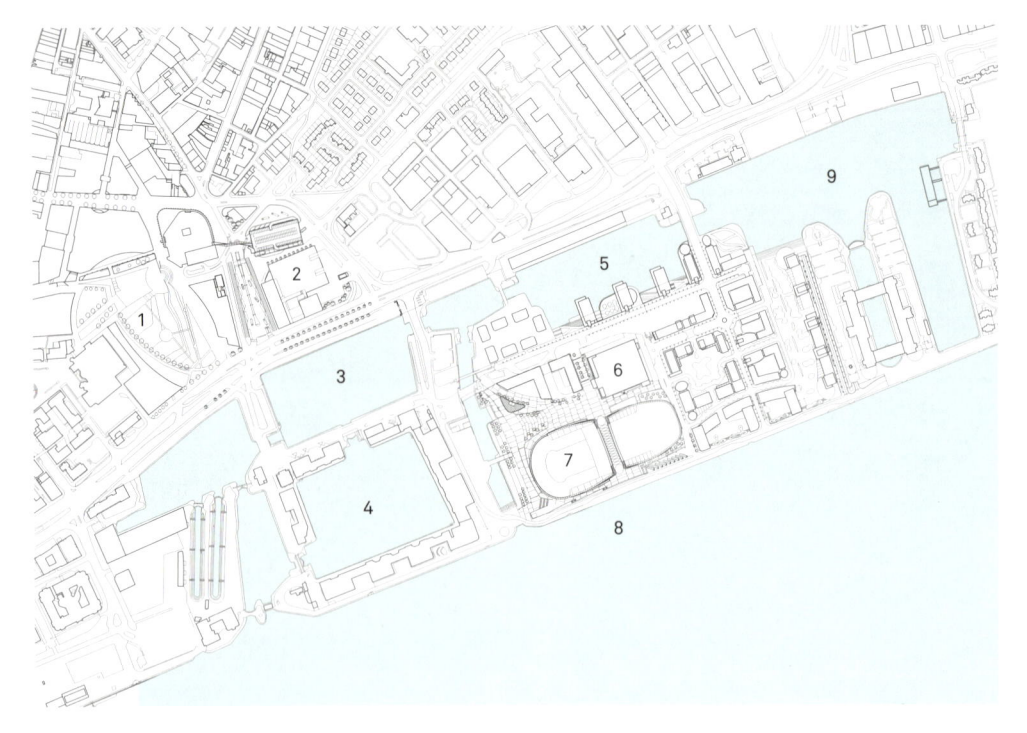

Wilkinson Eyre's design brings together in a single structure the discrete elements identified in Liverpool Vision's Kings Waterfront masterplan. The building relates closely to a new public piazza, which, enclosed to the north by a hotel and car park, provides a civic setting for a wide range of artistic and cultural events. Although such large structures as this can seem very imposing amid smaller-scale spaces, its façades have been enlivened by exposing the circulation areas within the arena (through transparent glazing), and by sizing and positioning the entrances appropriately.

Location plan
1 Chavasse Park
2 Liverpool One
3 Salthouse Dock
4 Albert Dock
5 Wapping Dock
6 Car park
7 Arena and Convention Centre
8 River Mersey
9 Queen's Dock

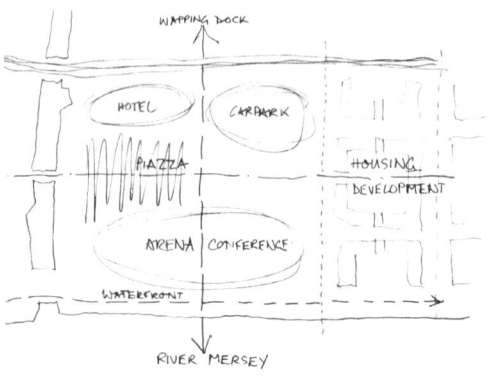

Water | Arena and Convention Centre, Liverpool, UK

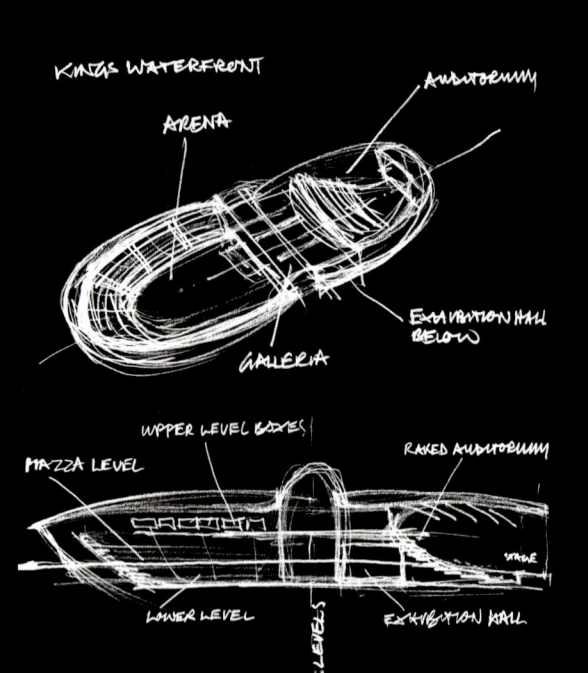

This is a building that could not have been built a decade earlier owing to the technology required to develop its form. The distinctive curves of the arena were shaped using 3D technologies in an approach akin to product design, the form developed as a virtual model from a very early stage in the design process.

The most distinctive aspect of the building envelope is the steel-framed, glazed curtain wall, which has varying levels of transparency and complex geometric patterning. The galleria roof, meanwhile, is spanned by sculpted steel ribs 'glazed' with air-filled ETFE pillows.

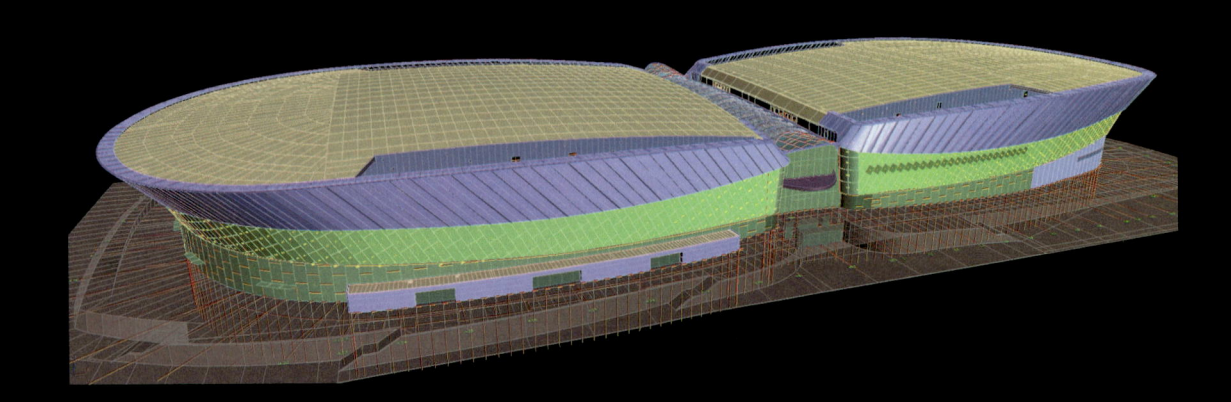

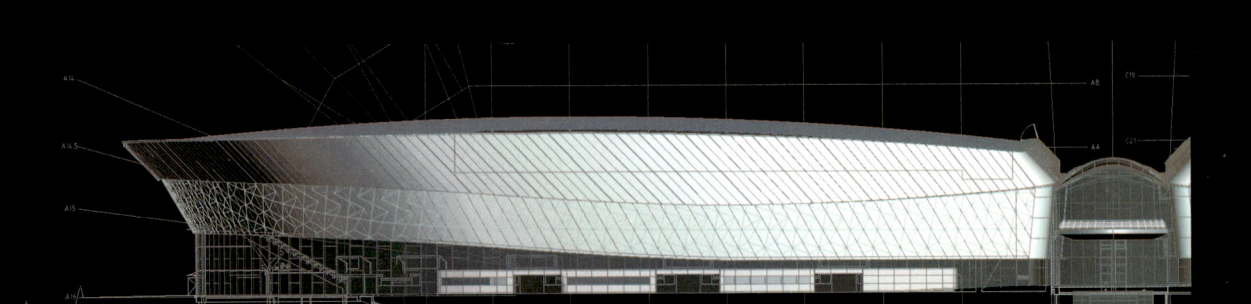

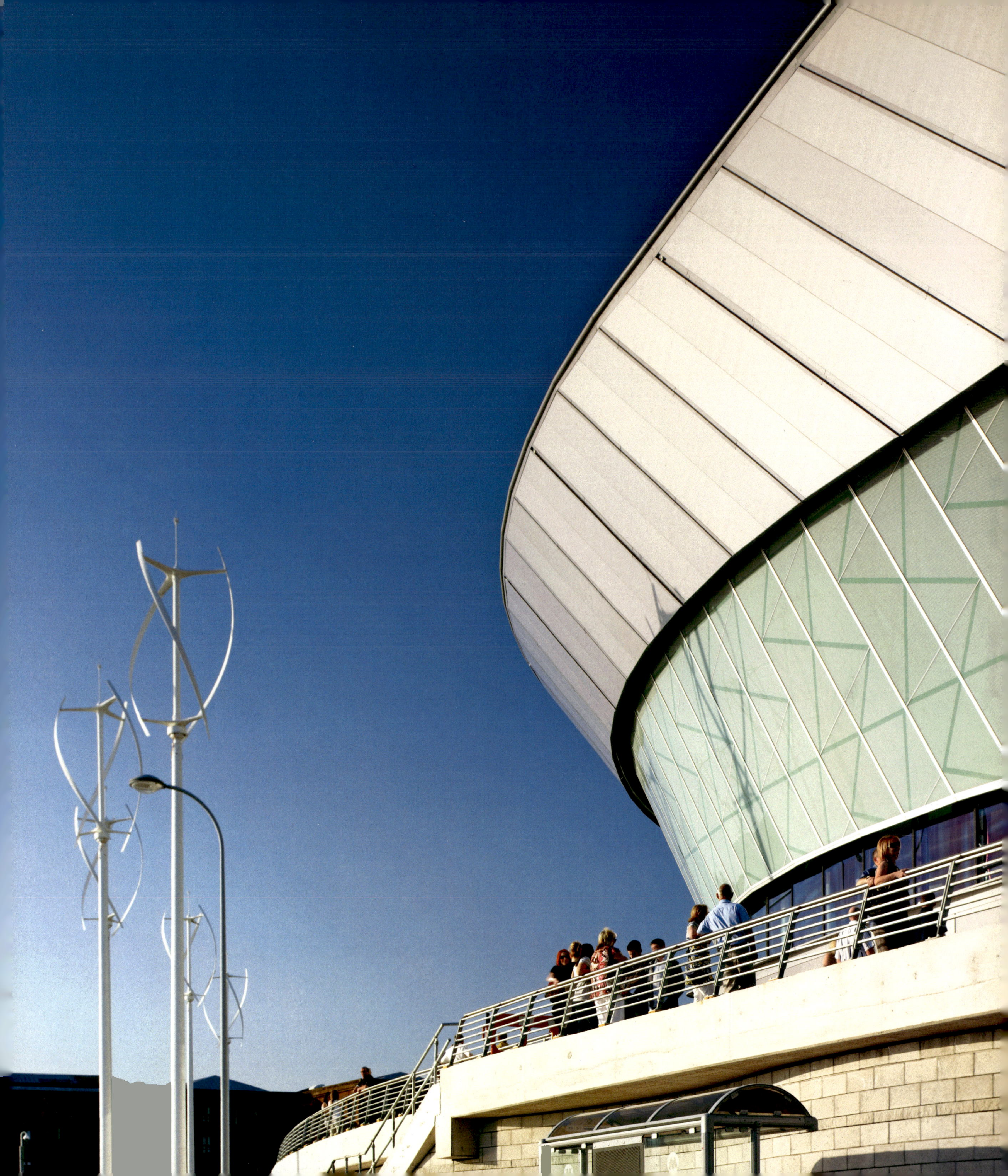

ACC Liverpool, as the building has come to be known, has made an important economic contribution to the city's recent growth – more than £200 million during its first year of trading – and has secured a reputation as one of the UK's leading venues. During that first year, it hosted more than 200 events and welcomed 665,000 visitors. It continues to provide the setting for a huge range of conferences and events, and a performance venue for some of the world's leading artists.

Site plan
1 Jurys Inn Hotel
2 Piazza
3 Echo Arena
4 Galleria
5 BT Convention Centre
6 Car park
7 River Mersey

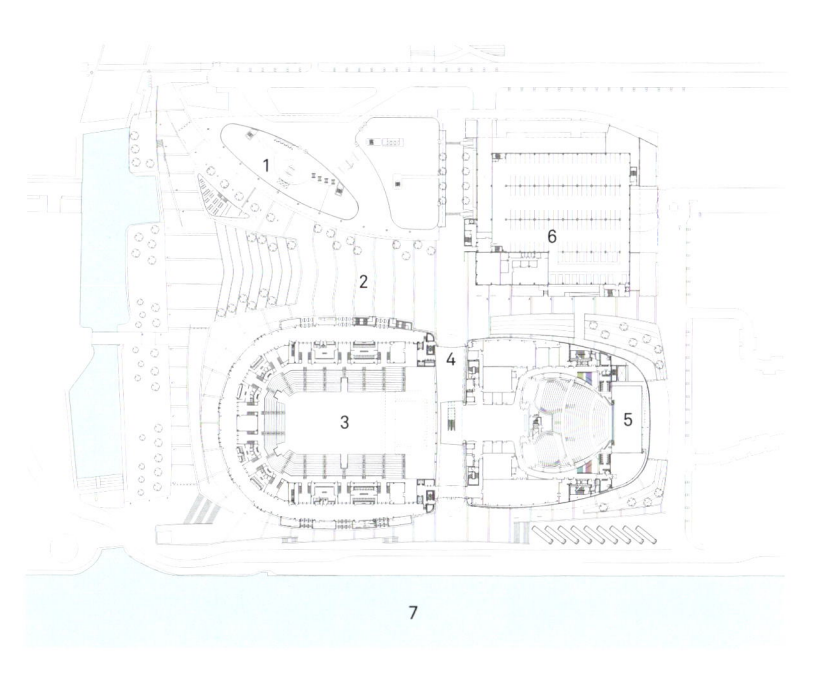

Water | Arena and Convention Centre, Liverpool, UK   147

Liverpool's Maritime Mercantile City was designated a UNESCO World Heritage Site in 2004, its main focus being the kilometre-long stretch of riverfront between Pier Head, home of the Three Graces, and the Albert Dock. ACC Liverpool lies just beyond the southern edge of the UNESCO site, but the design was subject to extensive consultation with English Heritage to ensure it did not detract from the protected buildings.

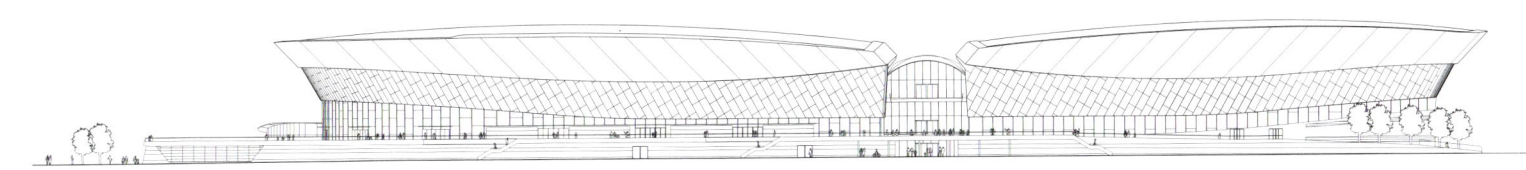

Water | Arena and Convention Centre, Liverpool, UK

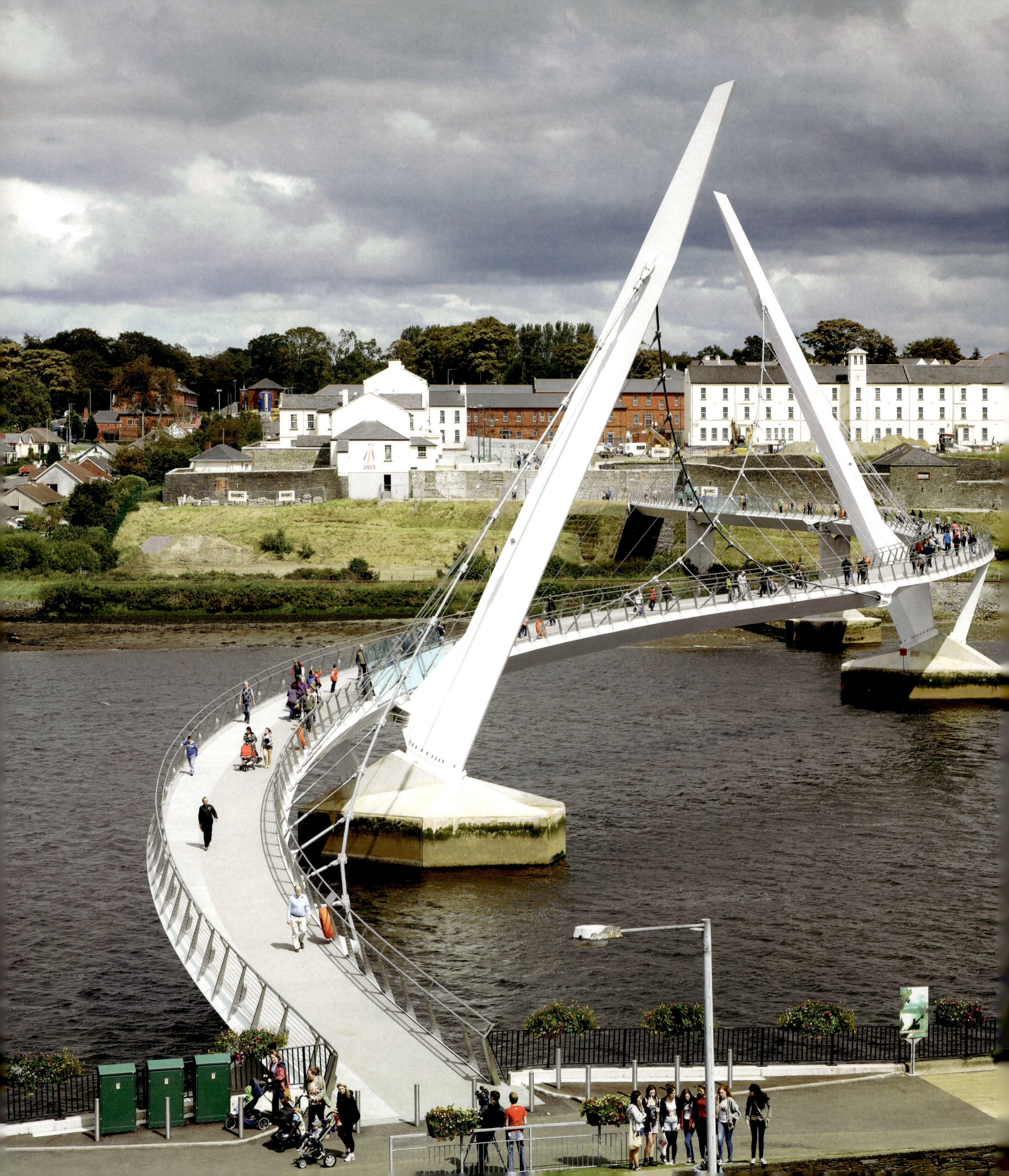

Peace Bridge
Derry, UK

The city of Derry-Londonderry in Northern Ireland is central to the country's turbulent political history, which is manifest even in the evolution of the city's name. As the inaugural UK City of Culture in 2013, it has undergone an ambitious programme of economic, physical and social regeneration. As part of this initiative, a bridge was proposed to link a new mixed-use development at the disused Ebrington Barracks on the east bank of the River Foyle with the historic city centre to the west – a connection whose real significance lies in the fact that it would reunite two communities who, until recently, have been in a state of conflict. The resulting structure is a flagship of the European Union's PEACE III Programme, which aims to create new, genuinely shared spaces in which to tackle the problems of separated communities in Northern Ireland and the Border Region.

As a device intended to heal spatially the historic divide in the city, it was important that the bridge should not be visually allied to either bank of the river, and that it be seen to serve both in unison. It was designed as two separate halves, each suspended from a single, inclined steel pylon, which overlap at the centre of the river to form a 'structural handshake' – a powerful metaphor for reconciliation, and a form first adopted by Wilkinson Eyre for the South Quay footbridge in London's Docklands in 1997. The sinuous, 96-metre-long deck curves to resolve two strong – but unaligned – axes on either bank: an existing route past the Guildhall into the walled city centre, and the main circulation spine of the Ebrington redevelopment. The portion of the bridge supported from the western pylon bows out to the north, giving long views towards Lough Foyle, unimpeded by the cable-stays that support the bridge on the southern edge of its deck. Towards the eastern bank, the cables switch to the northern edge, inviting pedestrians to look south towards the Craigavon Bridge. At the midway point, the catenary cables on either side overlap to form a valley, creating a sense of enclosure and protection.

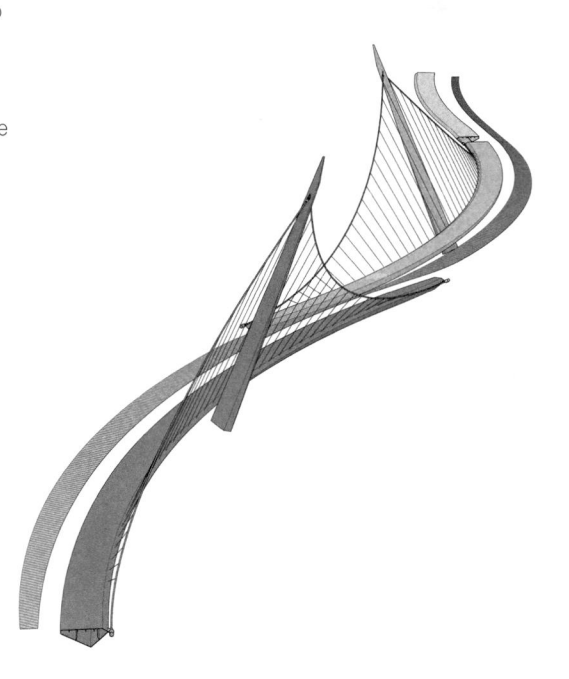

Media City Footbridge
Salford, UK

Salford Quays has long been a centre for transaction; the docks here were among the busiest in the UK during the early part of the twentieth century, handling millions of tonnes of cargo every year. In 1985, following the gradual decline of the docks, the area finally became the subject of an innovative regeneration plan, which brought to the waterside such attractions as the Lowry theatre and gallery complex and the Imperial War Museum North. The latest stage in this transformation has brought a new trade – in ideas and creativity – to the docks. The BBC's decision to move a number of its production departments north provided the anchor for Media City, a new community of digital and media businesses, which, having reached a critical mass, are now attracting leisure, residential and academic tenants.

Wilkinson Eyre's footbridge signals – and underpins – the renaissance of the docks, forming a visual landmark and sculptural gateway to the Media City site, and connecting it with satellite developments and attractions on the southern side of the Manchester Ship Canal. It is a key element in the weaving together of the new urban grain, establishing links that were not there before, and helping to bring about a new sense of place.

The curved, 100-metre deck of the bridge responds to the radial masterplan of the site, and reinforces an orbital pedestrian route around the canal basin. Rather than being a stationary element in the network of infrastructure, the bridge has been designed as a piece of active sculpture, swinging open when needed to allow vessels to continue their journeys along the canal. The choice of a cable-stayed structure was pragmatic: to keep the bridge deck as low as possible over the water, and to minimize the gradient and length of the approach ramps, the curved deck is supported from one edge by tensile stays. This solution has also allowed the structure below the deck to be kept minimal, giving the bridge a lightweight elegance.

The flamboyant cable arrangement provides an effective marker for the bridge when viewed from a distance. The centrepiece is the distinctive mast configuration – reaching up to 30 metres – formed from a fanned array of the pylons that support the stay cables. The bases of the masts converge on a steel pedestal above the pivot point of the bridge, which rotates with the bridge as it opens to form a counterbalance to the main span. Although the masts are a direct functional response to the forces flowing through them from the stays above, they work as part of a wider architectural composition in this part of the quays, reflecting in particular the interlocking curves of Daniel Libeskind's Imperial War Museum.

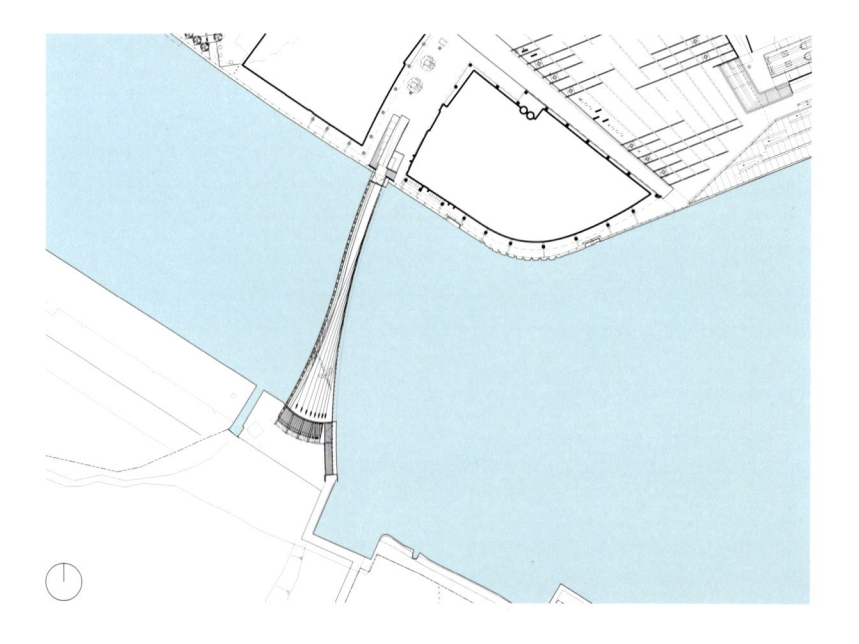

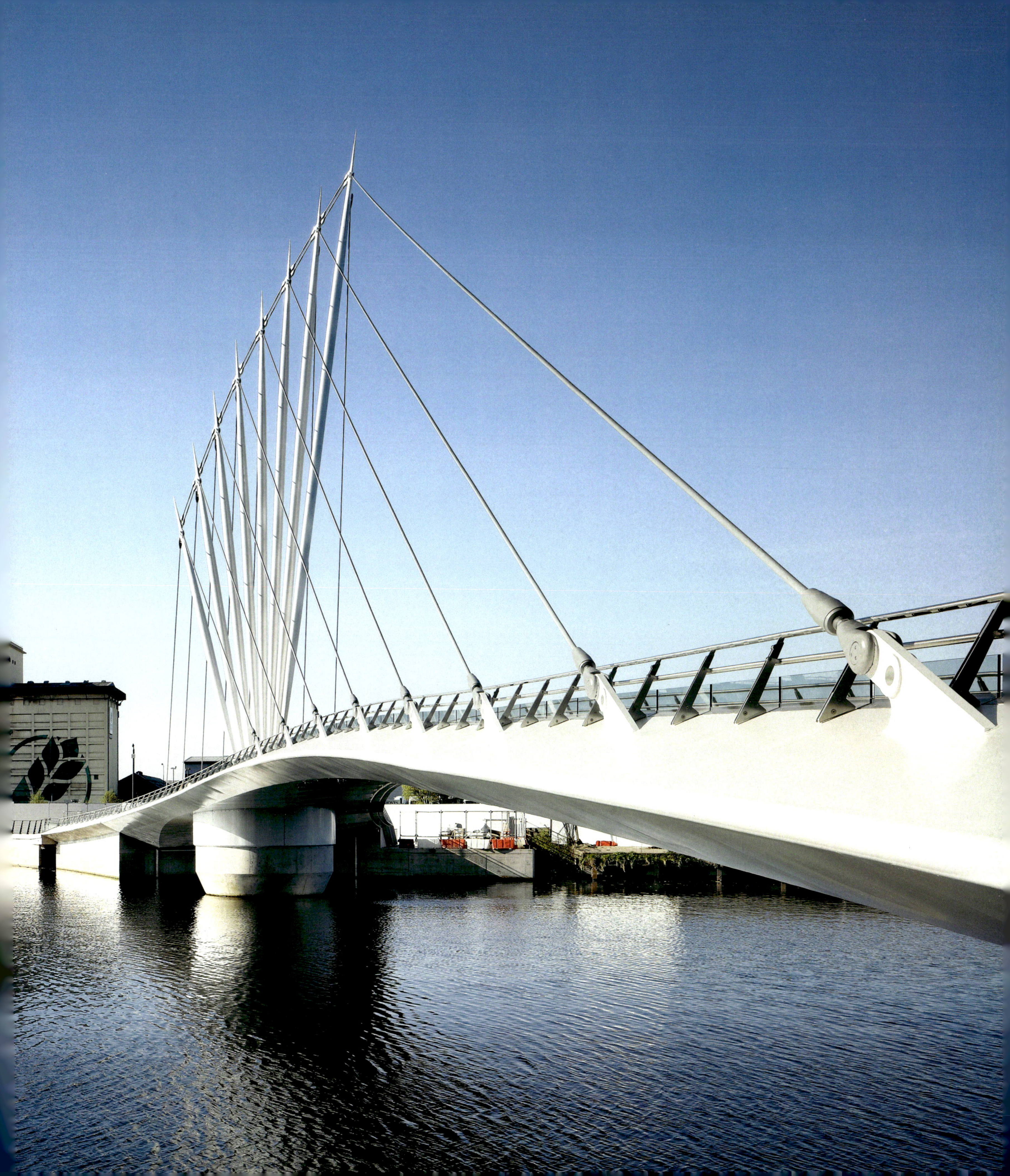

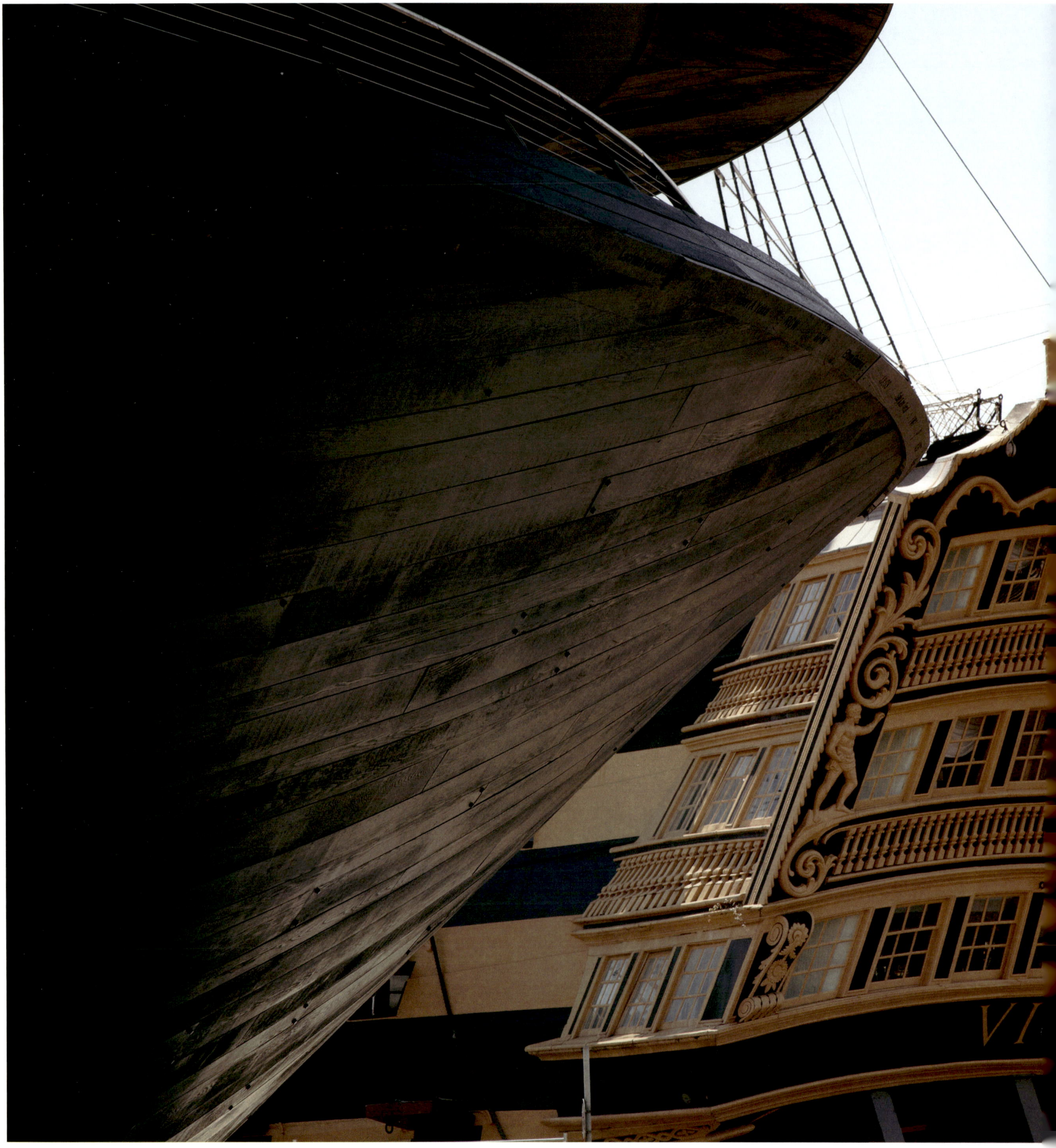
VI

Mary Rose Museum
Portsmouth, UK

Henry VIII's favourite warship, the *Mary Rose*, sank during a battle with the French in 1545 with 500 men on board. It was preserved in the mud at the bottom of the Solent, along with 19,000 objects – a unique and extraordinary snapshot of a moment in Tudor history – until it was raised in 1982, when it was immediately placed in the temporary enclosure of a dry dock at Portsmouth to begin a lengthy period of conservation.

Designing a museum for the *Mary Rose* and its artefacts was a challenge of many layers, one of which was the need to find an architectural language appropriate to the ship and its unusual context among the listed admiralty buildings of Portsmouth Historic Dockyard, and adjacent to HMS *Victory*, Nelson's flagship at the Battle of Trafalgar; another was the curatorial and conservation requirements of its very special contents. Wilkinson Eyre won the competition to design the new museum in 2005, working with Pringle Brandon Perkins + Will as interior architects, with the concept of designing from the inside out.

The remaining timbers of the ship appear centre stage in a ship hall; alongside, a 'virtual' hull has been built to house the retrieved objects in their original positions. Vast numbers of artefacts – cannon, shot, personal items, weaponry – are laid out in context, providing a vivid representation of the port side of the ship, most of which was lost as the ship lay submerged. Between them, three context galleries run the full length of the ship, mirroring the original deck levels to show how each was configured. Dipping gently between bow and stern, intentionally darkened, and filled with the noise of creaking timbers and the rushing of wind and sea, these galleries strongly evoke the claustrophobia of being below deck. At either end of the elliptical plan, interpretation galleries describe in more depth aspects of life on board, exploring the context of the ship's sinking, and showing in detail the objects and belongings of the crew members – and through them their everyday routines.

The exterior of the museum is a discreet enclosure that protects and hides the sparkle of its contents in the manner of a jewel box. Low, minimal and humanely scaled, the building had to be constructed over the top of the preserved hull, still temporarily sealed in its 'hot box' tent structure. Its design references both the *Mary Rose* itself and its more flamboyant neighbour, HMS *Victory*, without mimicking either ship, the toroidal geometry of its curvilinear form derived from the shape of the hull and the dry dock beneath – which is itself listed as a Scheduled Ancient Monument. The timber cladding refers back to the carvel-built hull of the *Mary Rose*, highly innovative for its time, while the roof maintains a low profile in order to reduce the volume of environmentally controlled space within the building. Two pavilions flank the building, serving to reduce its mass and housing the entrance, shop and cafe on one side, and the education centre and plant on the other.

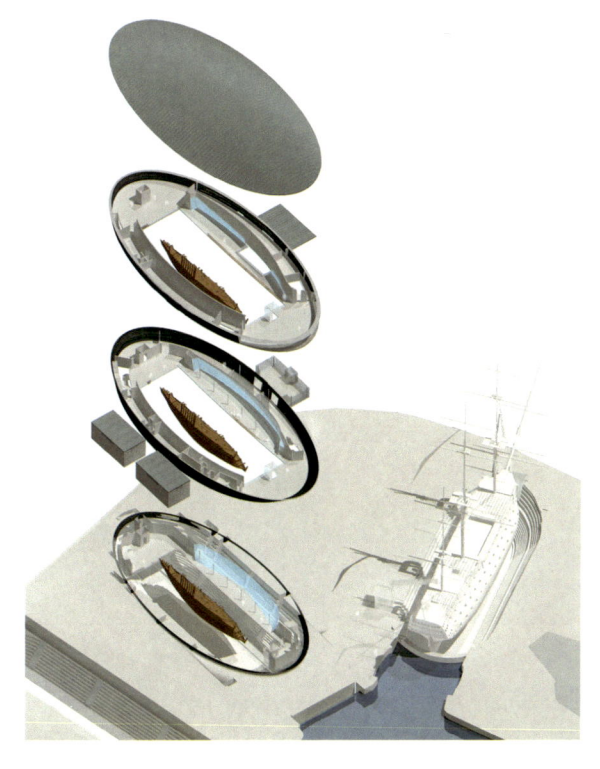

The remains of the hull, still sealed in an environmental 'hot box' more than thirty years after their salvage, were the inspiration for the inside-out design concept. Protected like a jewel in a wooden casket, the timbers are now supplemented by a 'virtual' hull, which gives a powerful impression of the space inside the original ship.

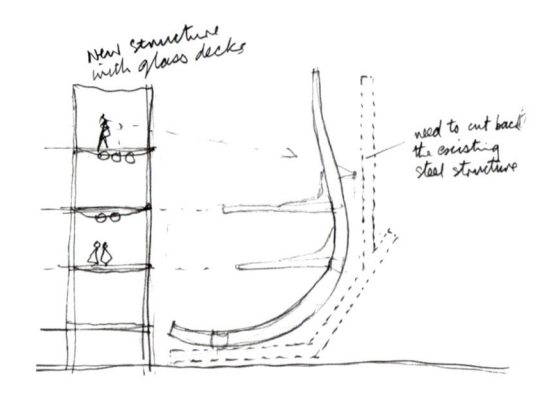

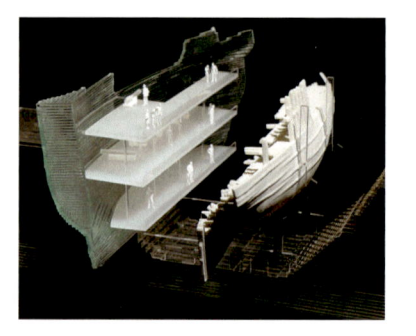

Site plan
1 No. 1 Basin
2 Dock No. 1
3 HMS *Victory* (Dock No. 2)
4 Mary Rose Museum
5 Dock No. 4

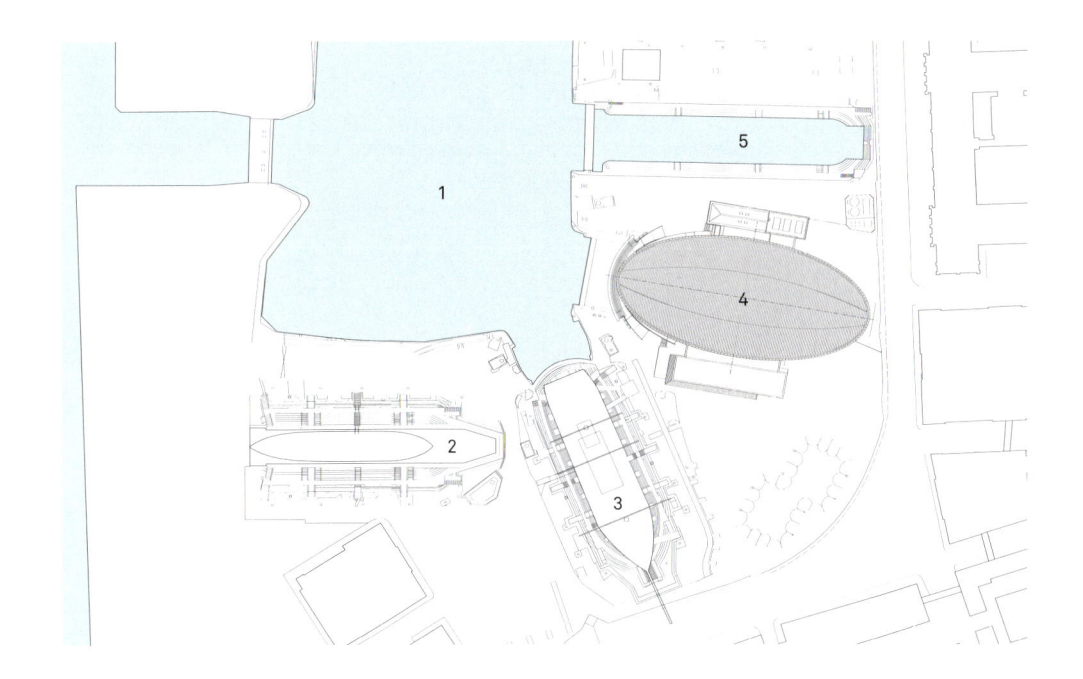

Water | Mary Rose Museum, Portsmouth, UK

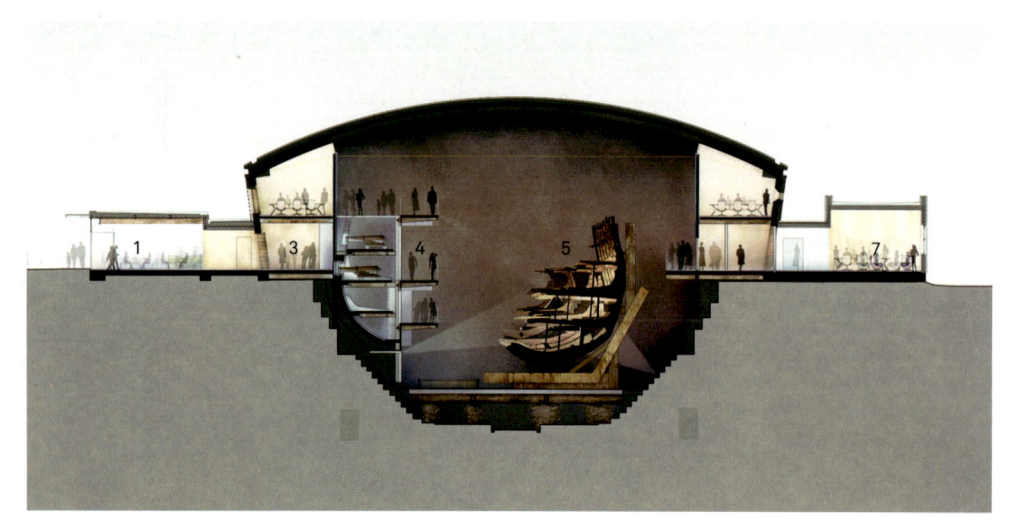

The elliptical plan reflects the curved, raked steps of the historic dry dock in which the *Mary Rose* sits. Context galleries, echoing the original deck levels of the ship, connect interpretation galleries at either end of the oval. These explore in detail the many characters among the crew, and investigate some of the questions that still surround the ship's sinking.

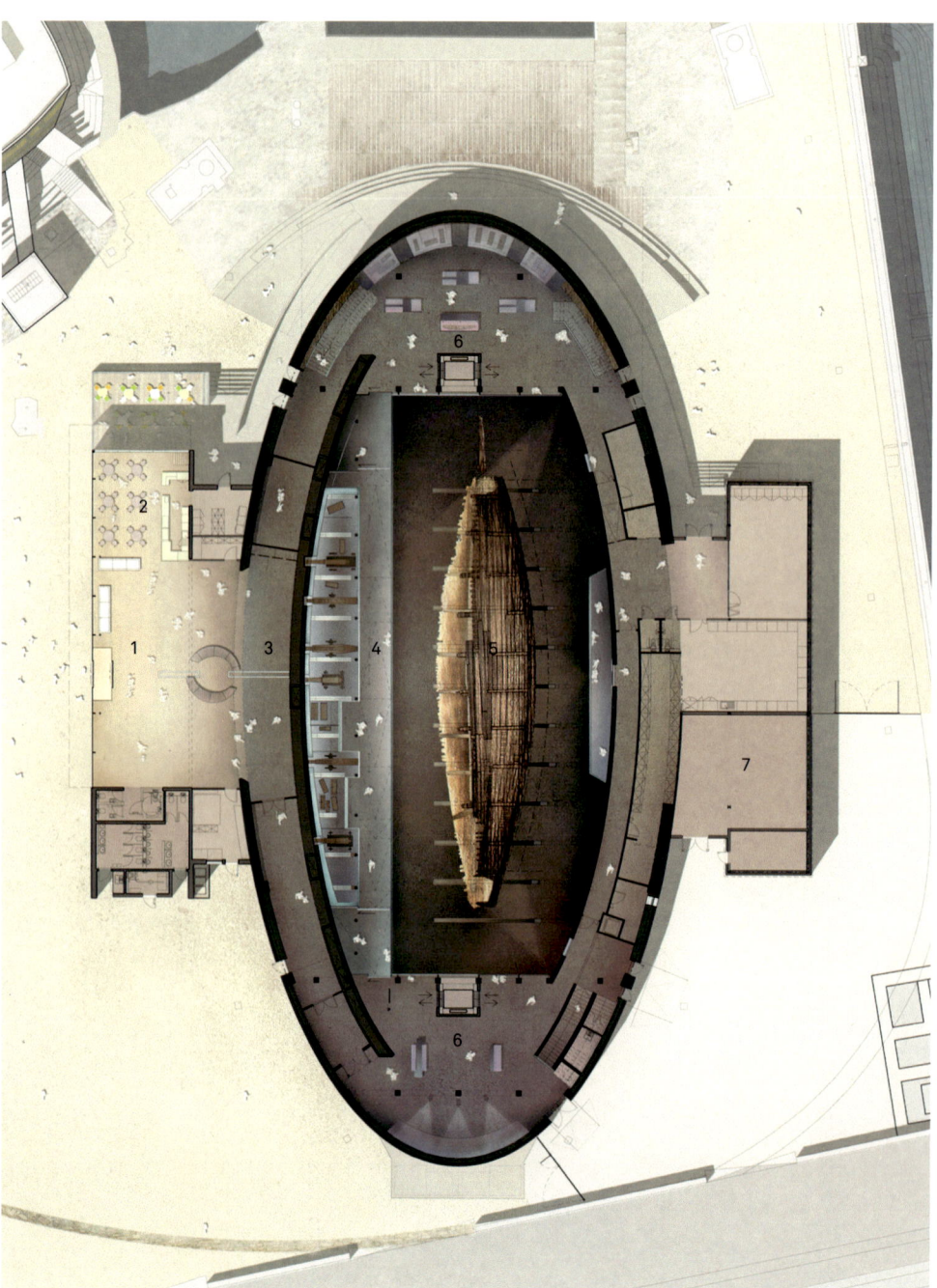

Cross section and ground-floor plan
1. Entrance foyer
2. Cafe
3. Orientation gallery
4. Context galleries
5. Ship hall
6. Interpretation galleries
7. Classroom

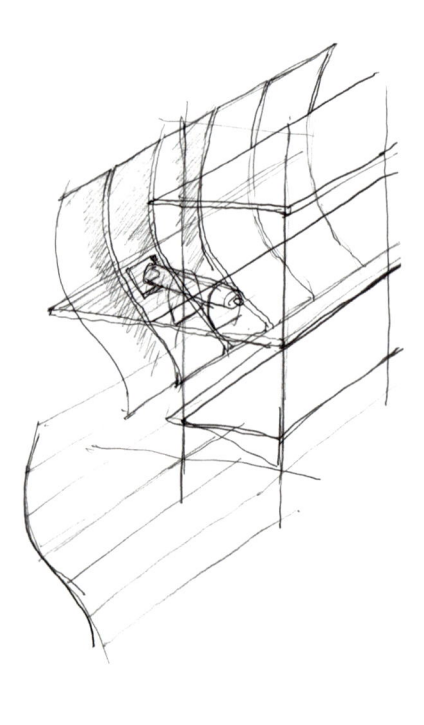

158

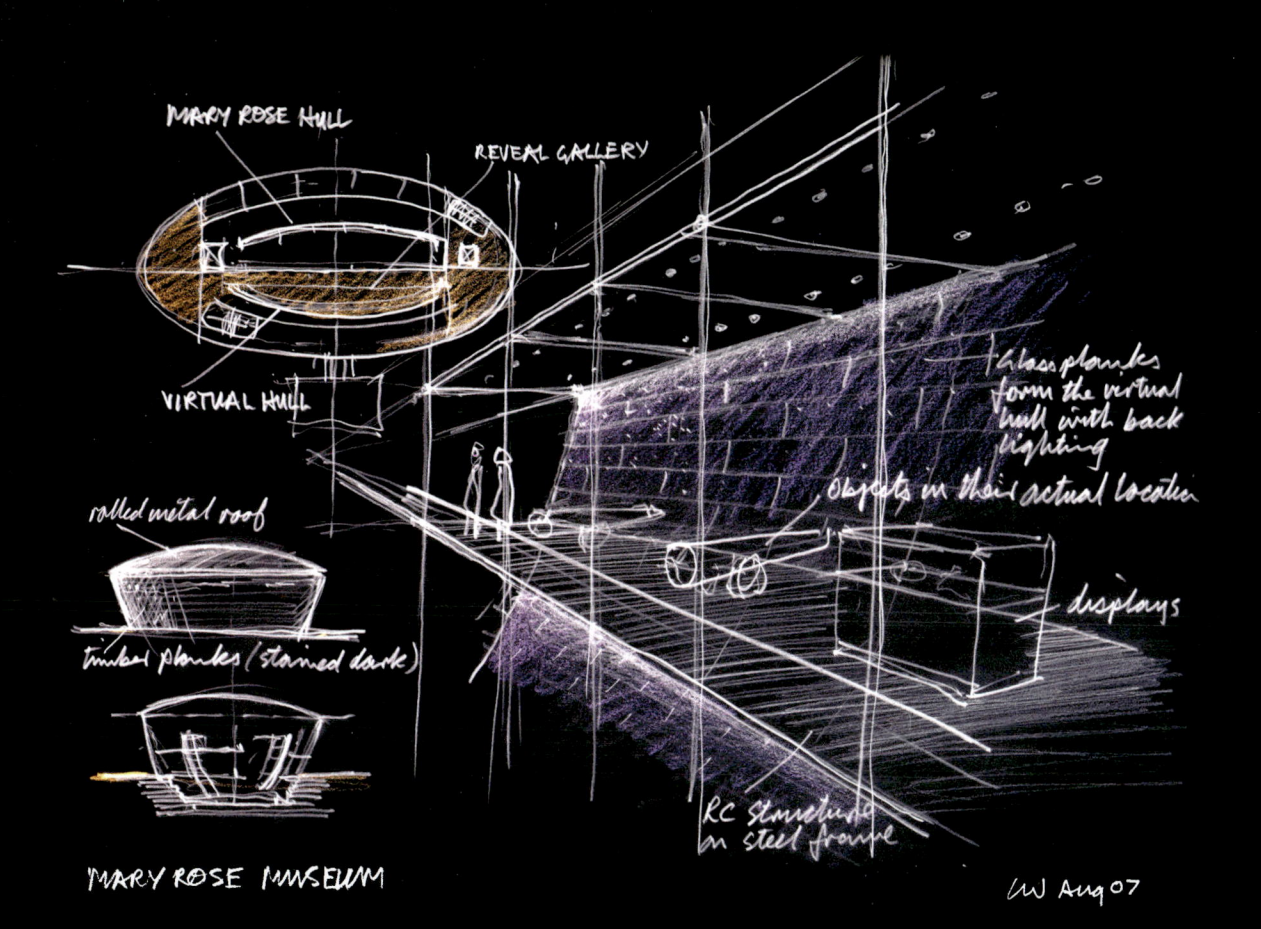

The context galleries are low lit to reflect the cramped conditions below deck on the Tudor warship. The colossal number of artefacts retrieved from the wreck is nowhere more evident than in the ranks of cannon and piles of shot laid out here in their original positions. A sequence of windows of varying sizes and height currently frame views into the ship hall, although this space will be opened up once the conservation of the ship is complete and the hot box removed.

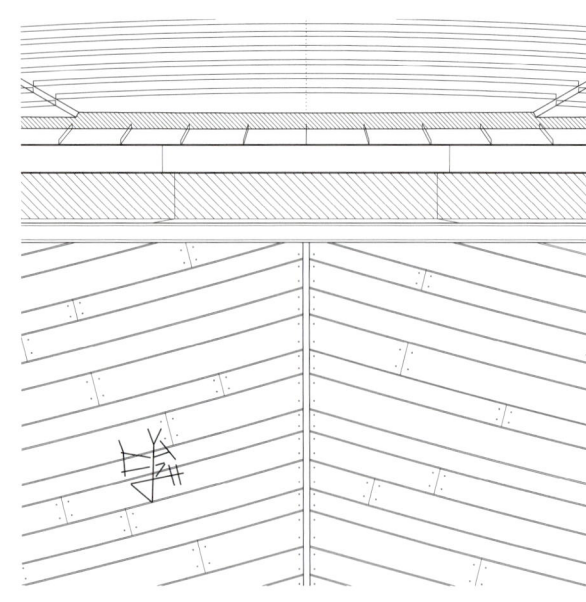

The main building is clad in timber planks of various lengths and widths, laid to mimic the *Mary Rose*'s carvel construction, where timbers were fixed with a minimal joint to allow expansion and avoid overlapping.

The walls are canted out in some places, the black timber cladding reflecting typical dock buildings and the seaside vernacular of England's south coast. Western red cedar was chosen, for its functionality and durability, and treated with Solignum, an architectural stain suitable for coastal environments.

Inscriptions based on the ciphers used by the crew of the *Mary Rose* to identify their personal belongings have been carved into the timber as a moving reminder of the lives lost in the wreck.

A balcony to the west of the building offers spectacular views of the harbour, the dockyard and its numerous listed buildings.

The roof is a pure ellipse, subtly articulated from the external walls, which become increasingly raked as they sweep around to the west end of the building. The shell-like roof form maintains a low profile to keep its proportions subservient to the adjacent listed buildings. It is clad with an aluminium standing seam system, the seams running across the width of the building.

Owing to the simplicity of the building's geometry, all the details are designed to be as clean as possible. At the transition between the roof and the external wall, a 'birdmouth' detail was introduced to emphasize the edge of the roof and reinforce the idea of the roof as the cap of a jewellery box holding the *Mary Rose* as a treasure inside.

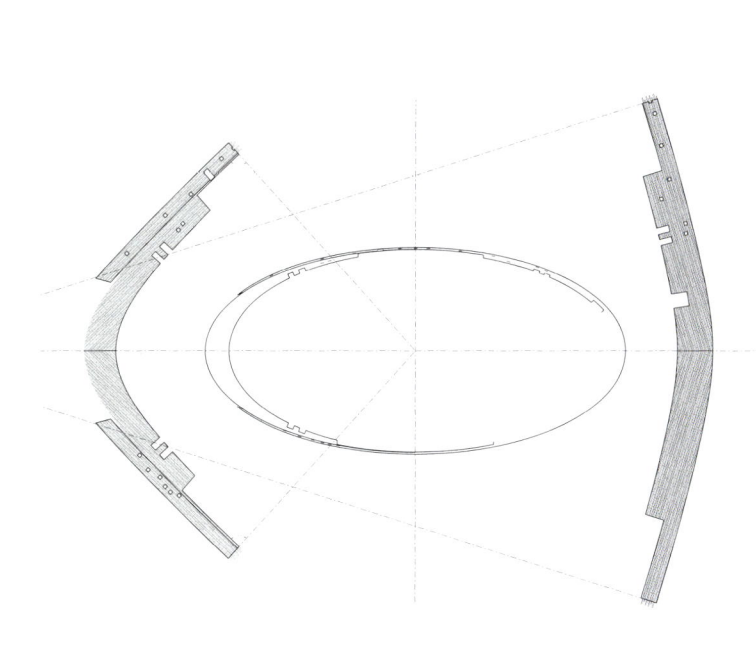

Water | Mary Rose Museum, Portsmouth, UK

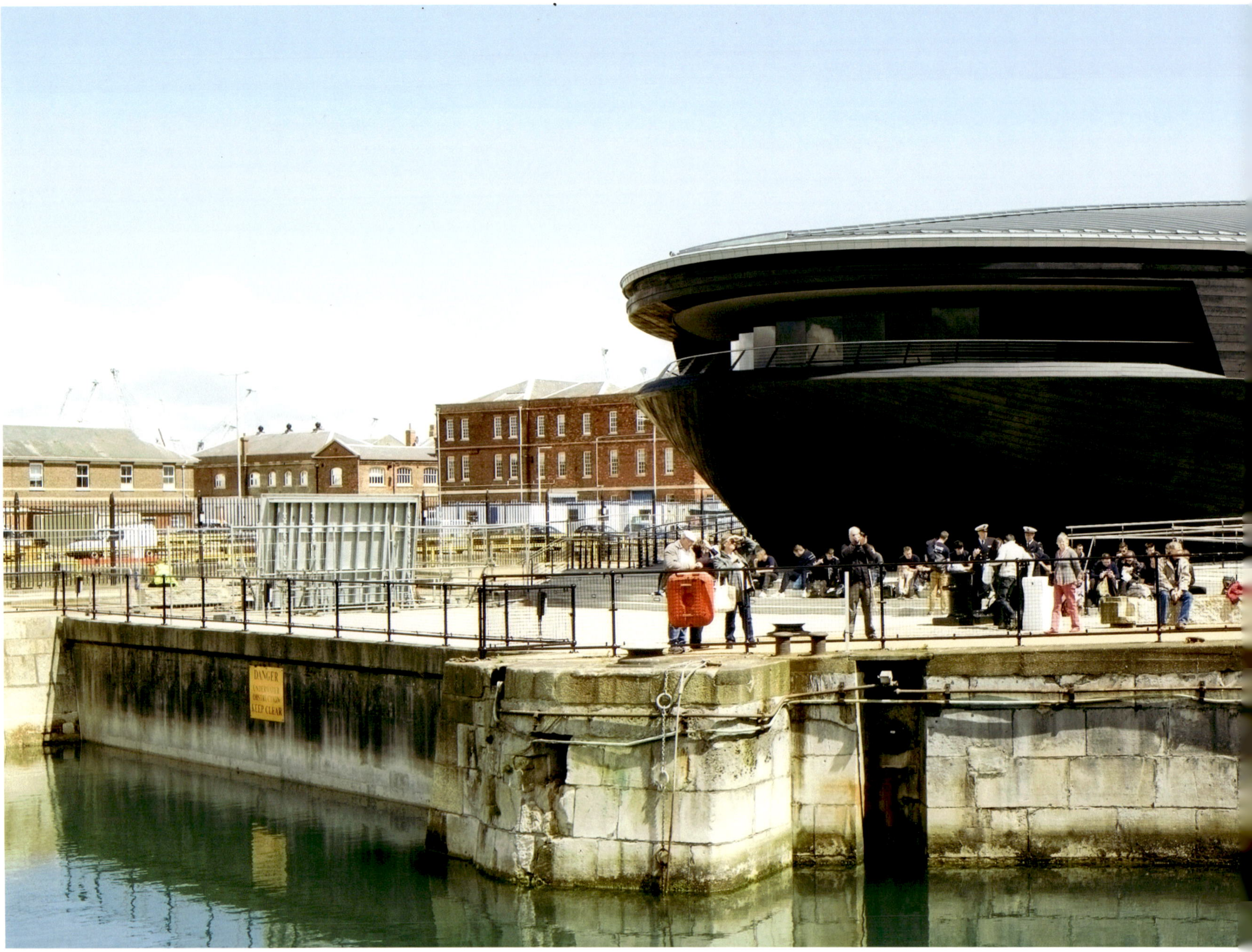
DANGER
KEEP CLEAR

Water | Mary Rose Museum, Portsmouth, UK

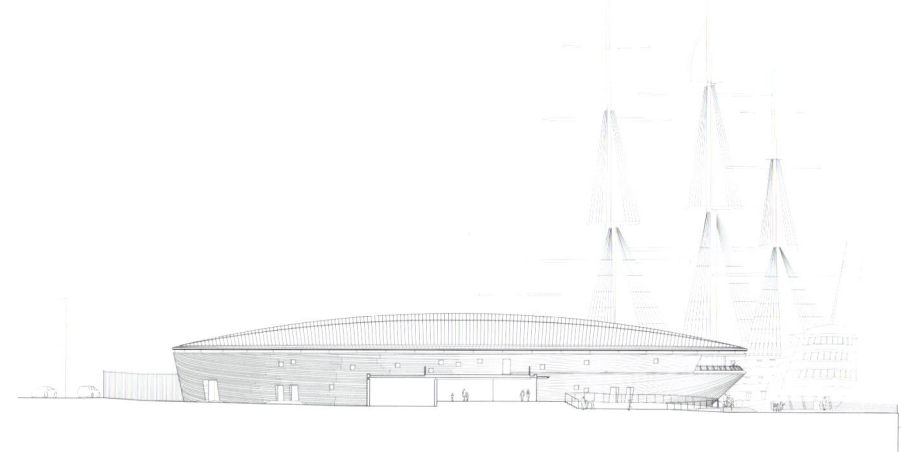

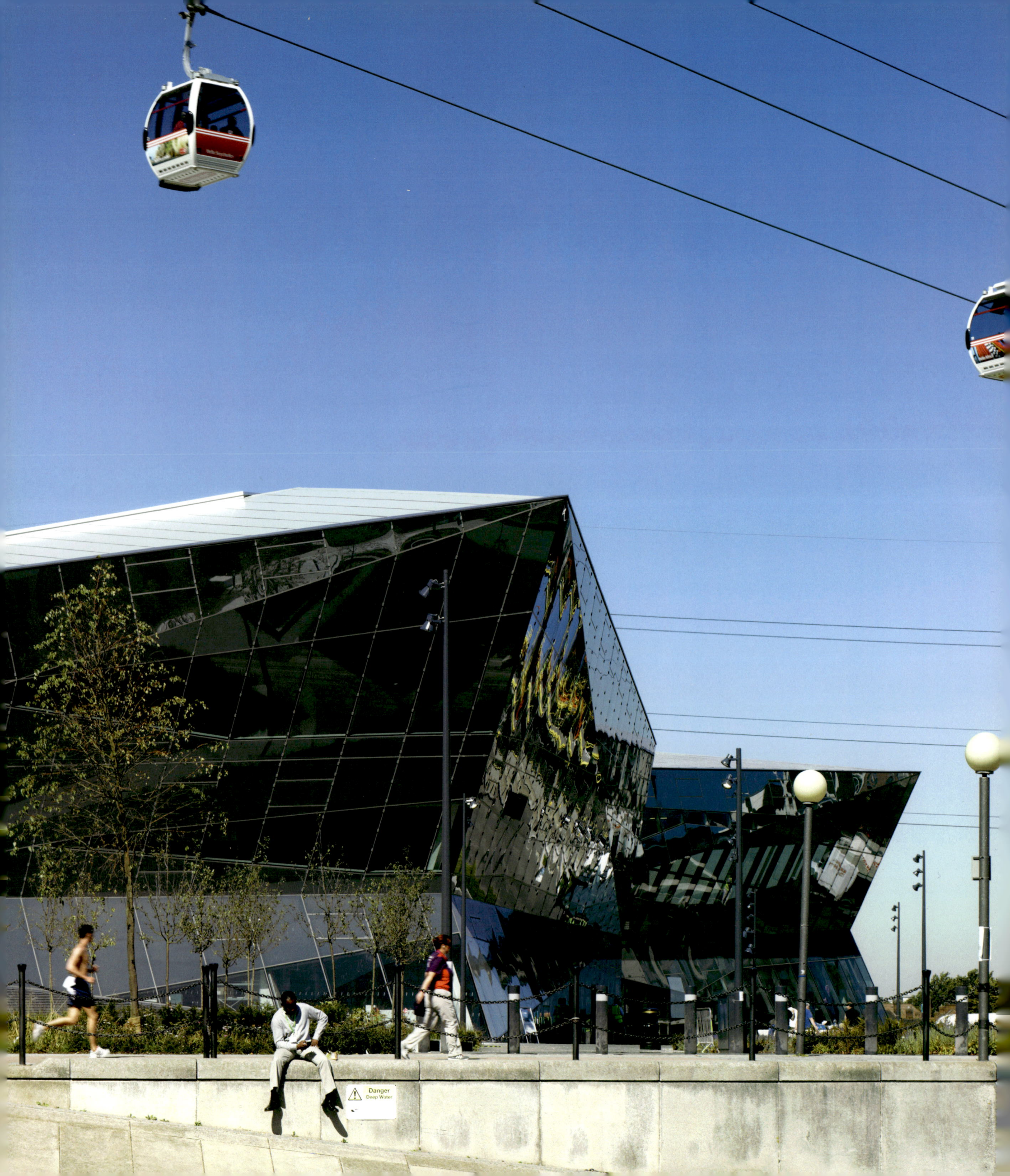
Danger
Deep Water

The Crystal
London, UK

East London's Green Enterprise District is anchored by the Crystal, a new forum for debate on sustainable urban living and development. The building was commissioned by engineering and electronics firm Siemens to galvanize regeneration in this part of the Royal Docks, and is both exhibition space and think tank, exemplifying sustainable design on a site with broad horizons and exposure to the waters of dock and river.

Sited next to Wilkinson Eyre's Emirates Air Line cable-car terminal at Royal Victoria Dock, the Crystal is designed to be a 'pavilion in the park', the many facets of its crystalline form providing interest as it is viewed in the round (and from the cable car above), and reflecting the strong light of its dockside location. The all-glass building challenges conventional ideas on sustainability, championing the use of advanced technology to minimize energy use. Six different types of highly insulated glass have been used in the cladding, each with varying levels of transparency to moderate solar gain and frame views into and out of the building. Reflective glass is used on the upwards-facing facets to repel the sun, while transparent glass is used on the inner faces angled towards the ground. This is combined with large areas of back-painted glass with insulation. Efficiencies have also been achieved by reducing the leakage of air through the glazing framework. This glazed envelope provides the wrapping for a sequence of internal spaces designed in collaboration with architects Pringle Brandon Perkins + Will. These spaces are divided into two distinct 'crystals', one containing office space and a conference centre with a 270-seat auditorium, and the other more public spaces – exhibition areas and a cafe.

The extensive display spaces are open to the public, and are located to the north of a central circulation space. The more private office and conference facilities – home to Siemens' Global Center of Competence Cities, a team of multidisciplinary experts devoted to the innovative growth of sustainable cities – are situated to the south, with the auditorium enclosed in a bright-red shell.

The building has exemplary environmental credentials, receiving BREEAM Outstanding and LEED Platinum ratings on completion. As a demonstration of sustainable design, it employs a number of new technologies to reduce energy use, rather than relying solely on passive systems. Much of its efficiency is due to a sophisticated management system, which allows every element in this all-electric building to be monitored, benchmarked and fine-tuned to minimize energy use. These controls respond not only to the needs of the building's users, but also to the requirements of the National Grid and the comparative performance of other buildings, so that the Crystal functions in synergy with them – envisioning a future city where buildings and spaces will work together symbiotically to save energy, rather than as separate entities.

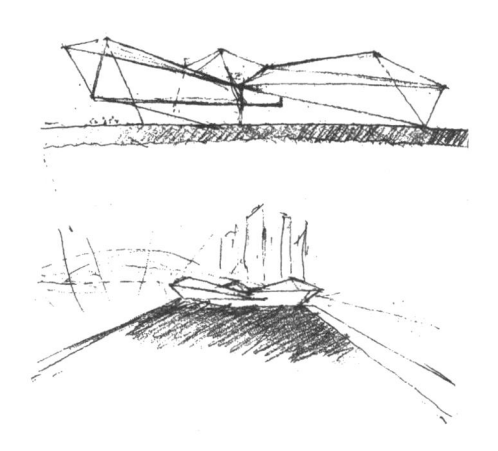

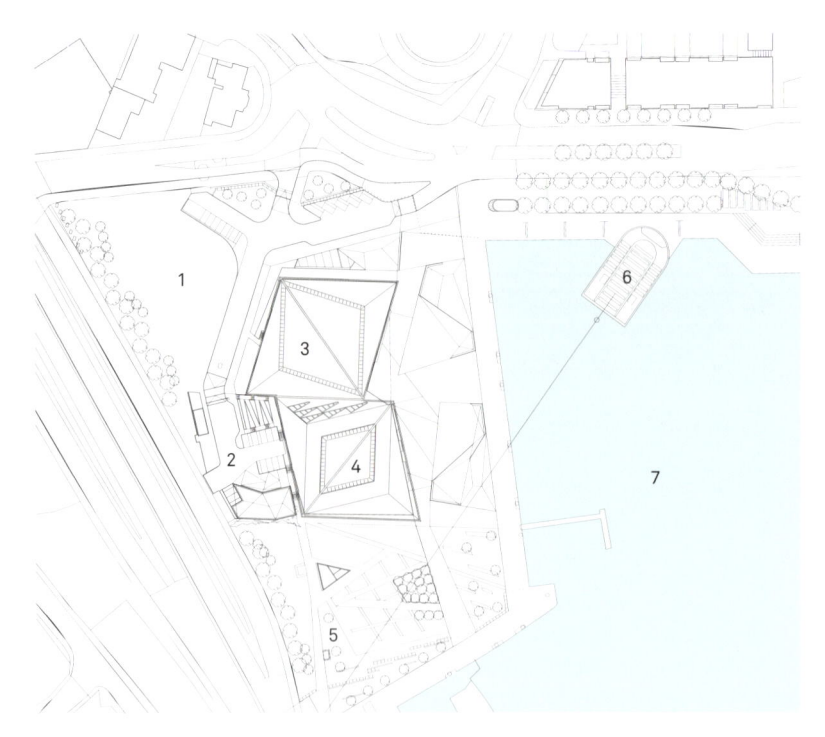

Site plan

1 Meadow
2 Energy centre
3 Office crystal
4 Exhibition crystal
5 Community gardens
6 Emirates Air Line (north terminal)
7 Royal Victoria Dock

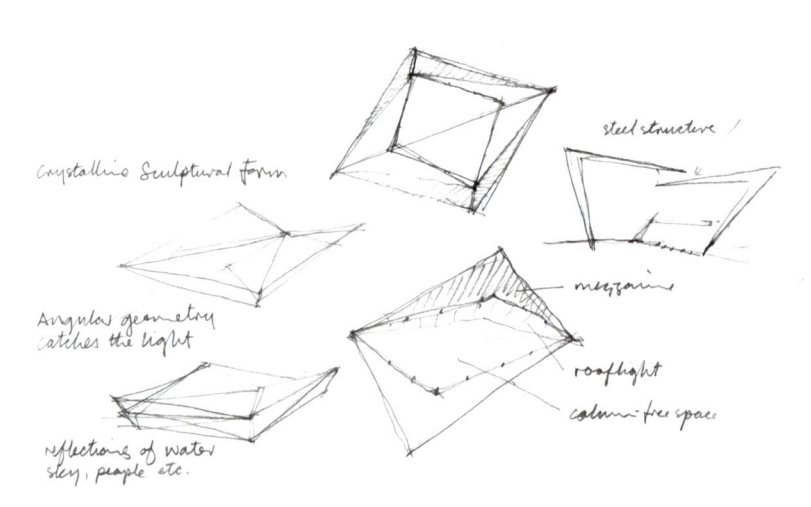

The Crystal is located in the north-west corner of the Royal Victoria Dock, adjacent to the northern terminal of the cross-river cable car. Its geometry forms a series of angular, crystalline shapes, which in turn inspired the building's name. It does not have front or back façades, or a traditionally defined roof, but instead is folded into a sequence of facets to provide interest from every viewpoint.

Cladding detail

1 Translucent stick glazing system
2 Opaque, insulated stick glazing system
3 Openable air vent
4 Openable vent for air exhaust
5 Clear-vision stick glazing system

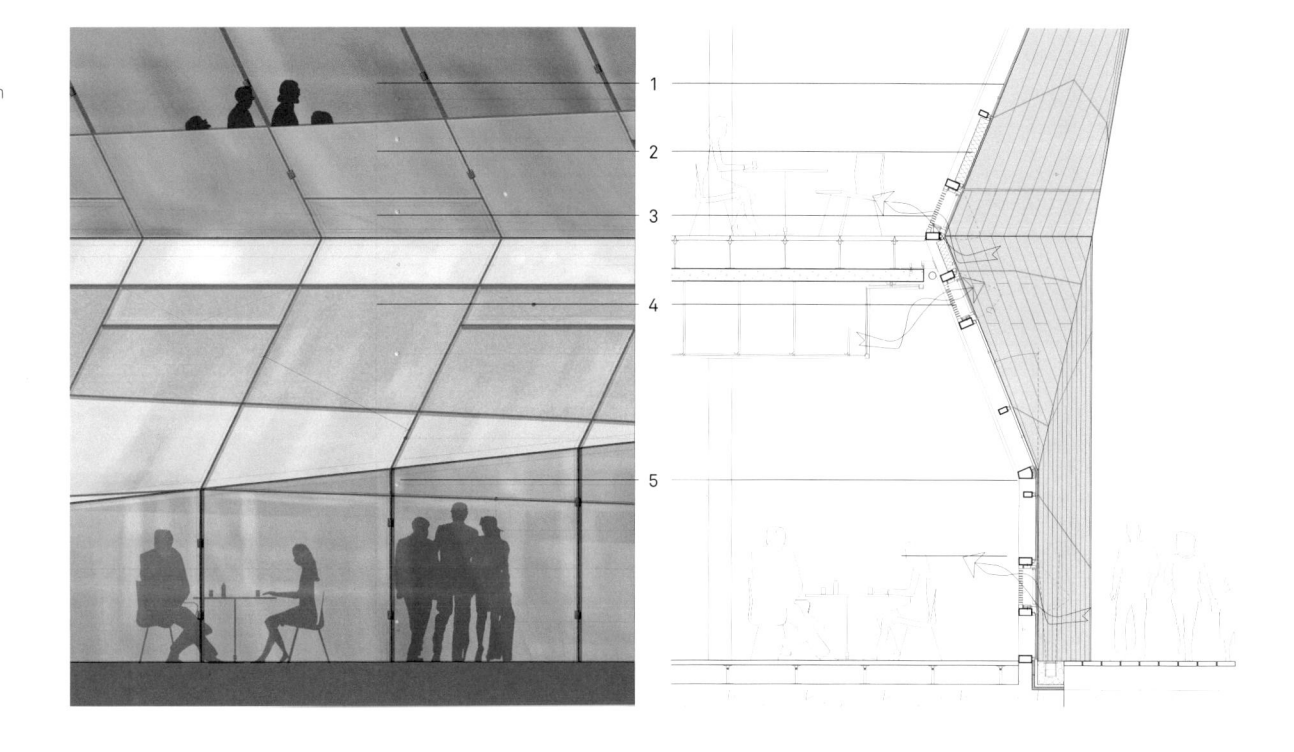

Cross and long sections

1 Internal street (beyond)
2 Exhibition space
3 Auditorium
4 Atrium
5 Internal street
6 Exhibition space

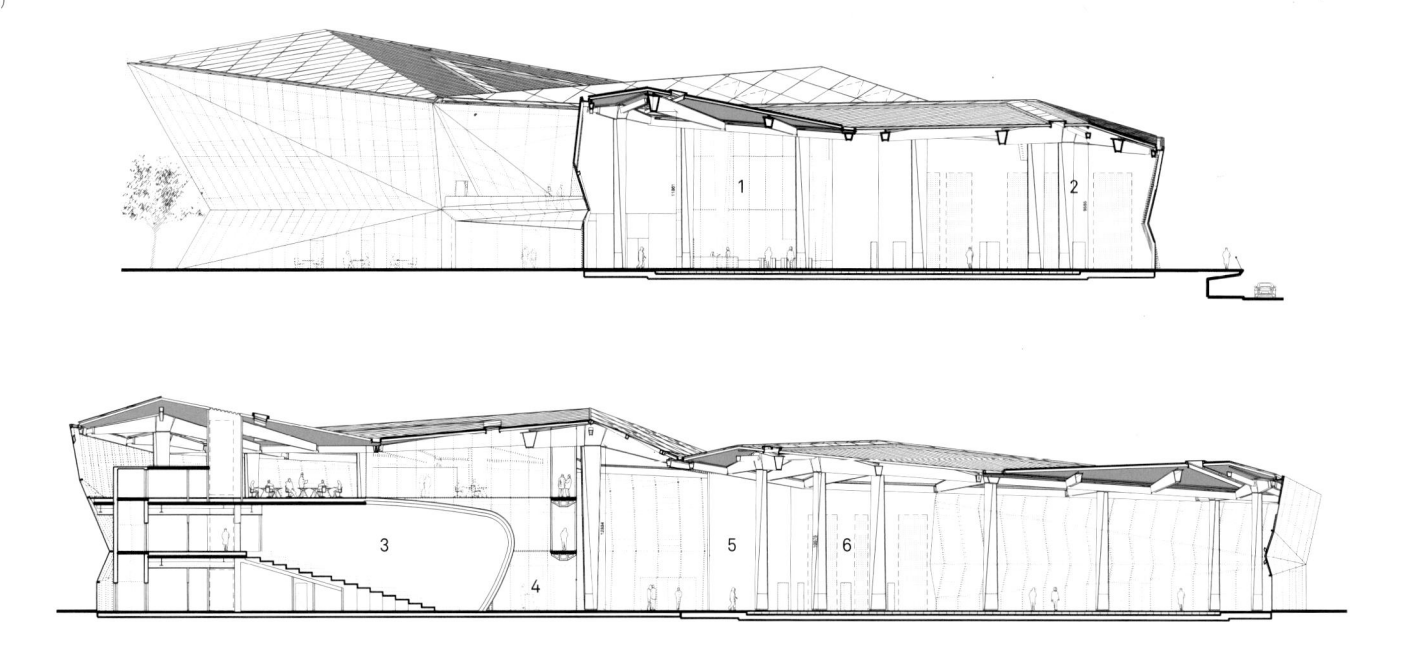

Water | The Crystal, London, UK

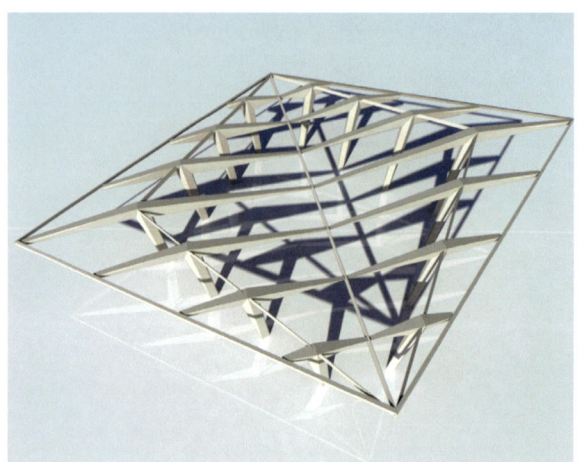

The Crystal's steel frame is parametrically designed, offering a set of varied spans and sections, each of which responds to the overall geometry. All beams and columns are tapered to create the lightest possible structure, while the cross sections of the columns are unusual in that they twist through 90 degrees to avoid the need for cross bracing. These twisting columns remain visible inside the completed building. There is no secondary steelwork, with the roof and façade structures directly supported by the frame.

First-floor plan

1 Office space
2 Auditorium
3 Meeting rooms
4 Void to internal street below
5 Internal balcony
6 External balcony
7 Plant
8 Void to exhibition space below

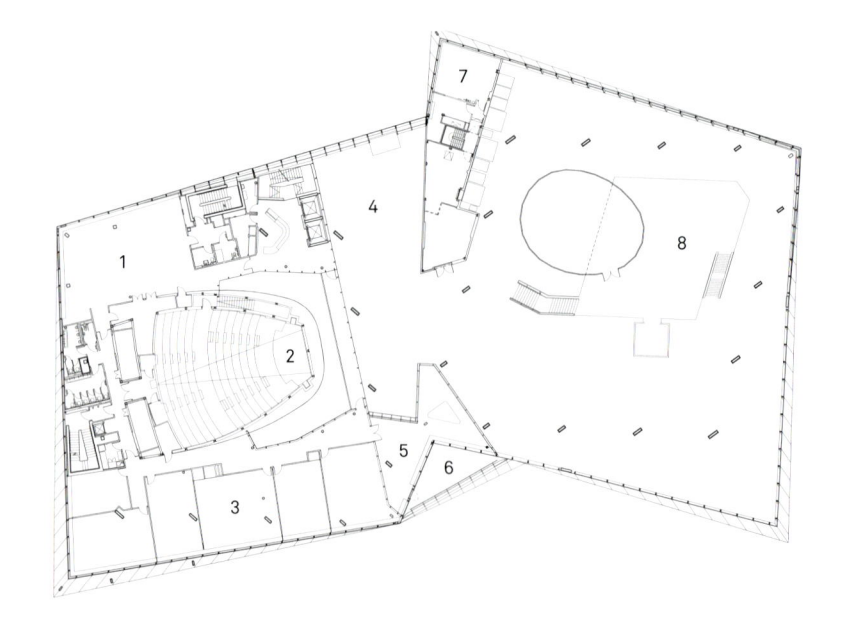

The building incorporates an intelligent, mixed-mode ventilation system. Where seasonally possible, it is naturally ventilated by motor-operated vents in the façades and roof planes. All the necessary additional air conditioning is provided by an array of geothermal piles, with warm air taken from the building and put back into the ground on hot days, and heat drawn from the ground to keep the building warm when the weather is cooler.

A significant part of the electrical power required by the building is generated by the photovoltaic roof panels, which collect the sun's energy and convert it via Siemens inverters to meet the building's needs. An intelligent energy centre manages heat recovery, monitoring it so extensively that every kilowatt of energy used for heat and cooling (and every litre of water consumed) can be measured from inside the building and benchmarked against the performance of other buildings.

The Crystal is the first commercial building in the UK to have a water-safety plan, guaranteeing that the water supplied on site is safe for human consumption. All rain water falling on to the site is harvested and cleaned to drinking quality; black water is also treated on site, making the building 90 per cent self-sufficient in terms of its water supply.

Environmental diagram

1. Building-management system
2. Natural daylight into building
3. Low-energy mixed-mode ventilation
4. Intelligent all-electric building
5. Rainwater harvesting and recycling
6. Black-water recycling
7. Efficient heating systems
8. Sustainable landscaping

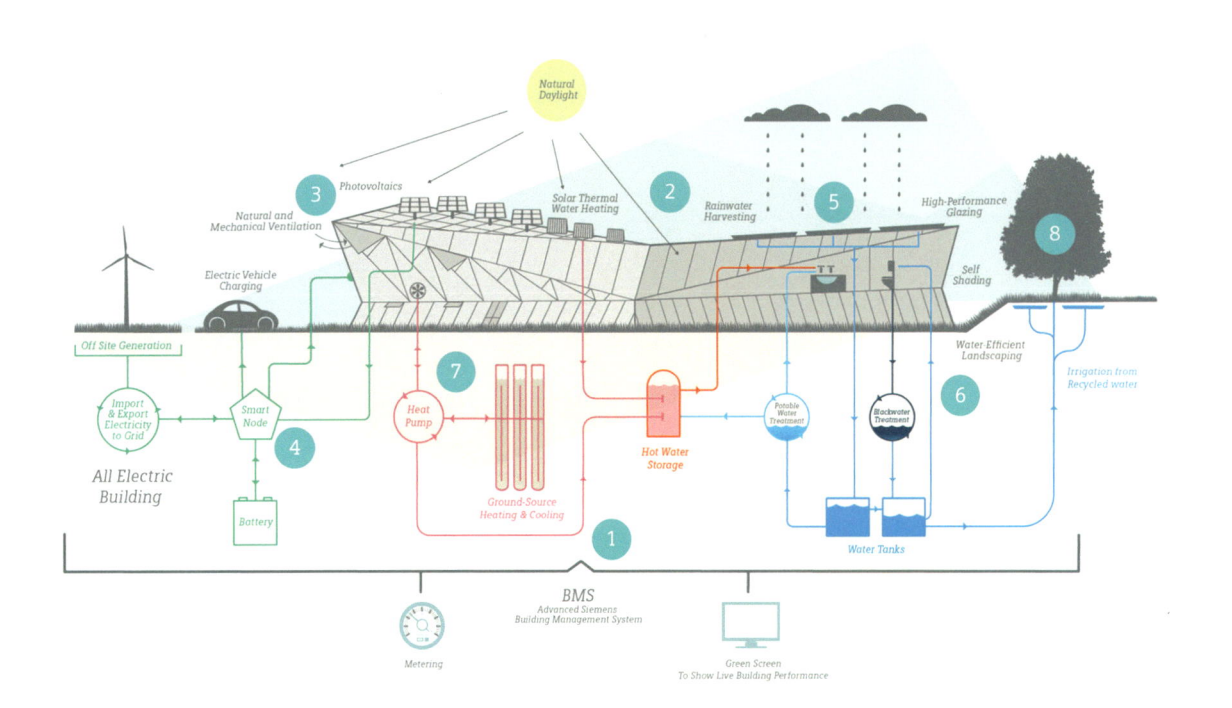

Water | The Crystal, London, UK

The Crystal serves as an anchor for East London's Green Enterprise District, which aims to regenerate the local economy through low-carbon development around the former docks.

Water | The Crystal, London, UK

Crown Hotel
Sydney, Australia

Instantly identifiable, the landscape of Sydney Harbour represents a dramatic dialogue between water, nature and architecture. Many of the city's well-known buildings – the most famous among them being Jørn Utzon's Sydney Opera House – are located on the waterfront, and the harbour is integral to city life. Within this context, Wilkinson Eyre's tower for Crown Hotels, the winner of an international design competition in 2013 and located on the Barangaroo waterfront in East Darling Harbour, constitutes a once-in-a-lifetime opportunity to add to this spectacular urban composition.

Central to the design of the hotel is the idea that it should be a sculptural, curvilinear form, an 'inhabited artwork', which will contrast with the more orthogonal geometry of the tall buildings in the central business district. Viewed from the opera house, its 275-metre-tall tower will mark the western edge of Sydney's high-rise skyline – the defining structure of a wider, 22-hectare regeneration site, which is being developed to a masterplan by Rogers Stirk Harbour + Partners. This masterplan is defined by a prominent cluster of towers on the waterfront, combining leisure and commercial space with residential apartments and retail outlets.

With the premise of creating something new and unique, the concept does not mimic any particular plant or flower, but instead is an abstract, sculptural shape derived from the specificities of site and brief, with three petal-like forms rising and twisting together to form a tower. One petal peels away from the central stem at a low level, spreading out to form the main hotel accommodation, with the whole composition visually grounded by a curvilinear four-storey podium.

The complex geometry of the tower was devised using parametric 3D modelling. It combines a 60-degree twist in the outer skin with helical columns on the perimeter and a vertical core structure. The challenges that this creates for the internal layout of the tower are addressed by the spiral-like arrangement of the residential villas and apartments, while the majority of the hotel rooms are stacked vertically in their own wing. The twisting form maximizes views of the opera house and Sydney Harbour Bridge, and is glazed with light-coloured reflective glass of varying transparency, with the curvature accommodated by stepped rectangular planar panels. By contrast, on the west elevation, which faces Darling Harbour, triangulation has been adopted to deal with the more pronounced curvature of the form. Roof terraces above the podium and hotel wing provide spaces for swimming pools and leisure areas, and the tower itself is topped out with a three-storey penthouse with stunning views across the city.

Most of the public spaces – cafes, bars, shops and restaurants – are contained in the podium, along with the hotel reception and gaming rooms. Many of these facilities take full advantage of the harbour views from terraces around the perimeter, which are overlaid by a veil of stone tracery that provides some shading and helps to unify the overall mass.

Water | Crown Hotel, Sydney, Australia

The harbour lies at the very heart of the city, and the wharves around its edge were pivotal to Sydney's growth as a port during the nineteenth century. Although the wharf infrastructure was continually re-thought to adapt to changes in the shipping industry, technological developments made East Darling Harbour impossible to sustain as a container terminal. As a consequence, in 2003 the government of New South Wales announced that the area would be transformed and given back to the city. The 22-hectare zone at Barangaroo will be developed in phases, the new Crown Hotel occupying one of the most prominent plots.

The site is bounded on two sides by water and on two others by park, and is skirted by an alley of trees at the harbour edge – part of a wider landscape concept developed by PWP Landscape Architecture. The active frontages of the hotel and podium will overlook a new urban theatre to the north, providing the backdrop to a large number of public concerts and events.

Site plan
1 Millers Point
2 Landscaped park and public-event space
3 Crown Hotel
4 Barangaroo South development

Water | Crown Hotel, Sydney, Australia   175

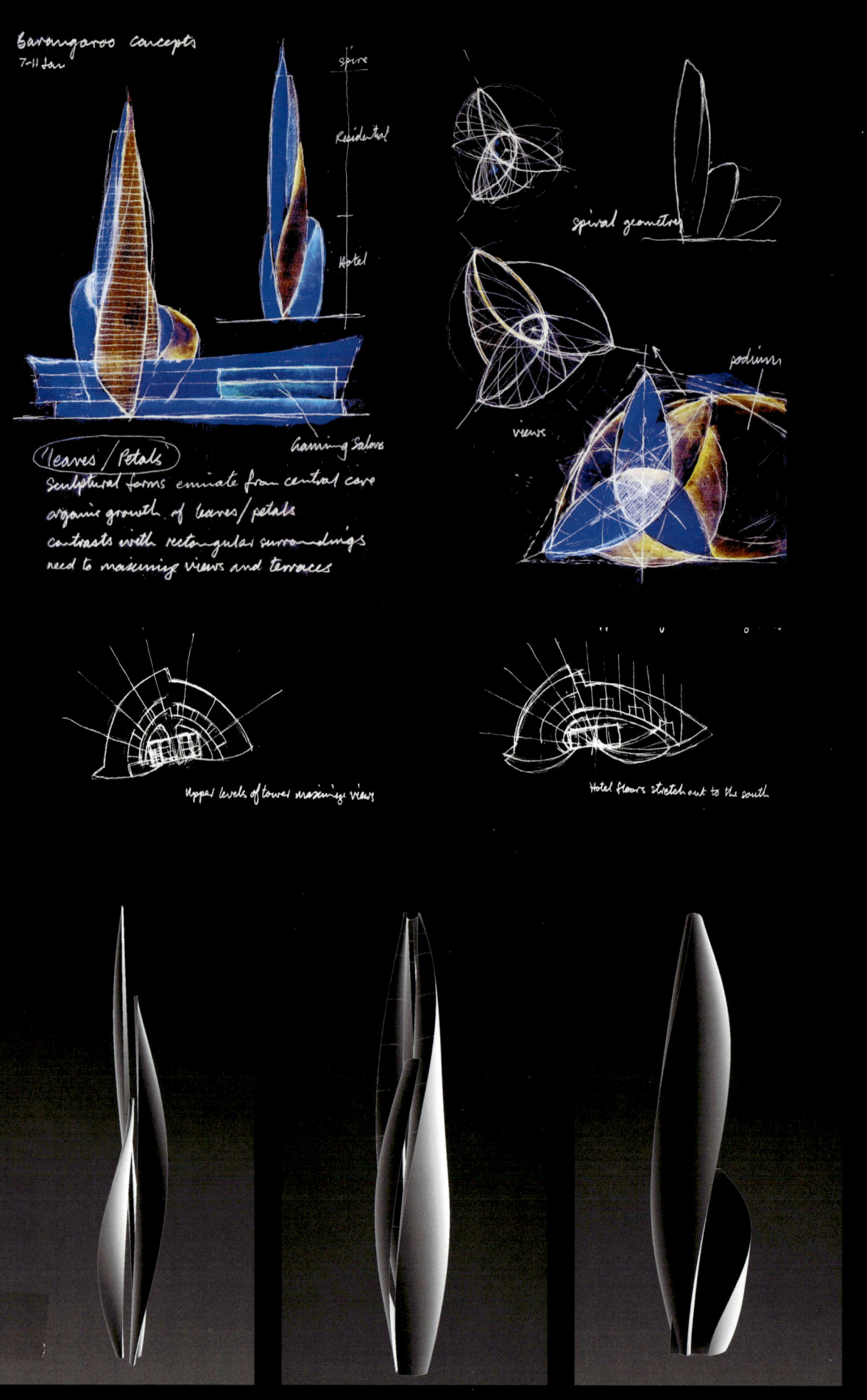

Diagrams and sketches show the evolution of a complex architectural form. Composed of three twisting petals that rise up into the air, the tower represents a distinctive new addition to the Sydney skyline.

Conceived using parametric modelling, the main elements of the hotel consist of irregular curved surfaces that are visually related to one another through their geometry and materiality. This approach has enabled a complex yet efficient sculptural form to be achieved, and has also ensured that the structural and environmental requirements of the building are met.

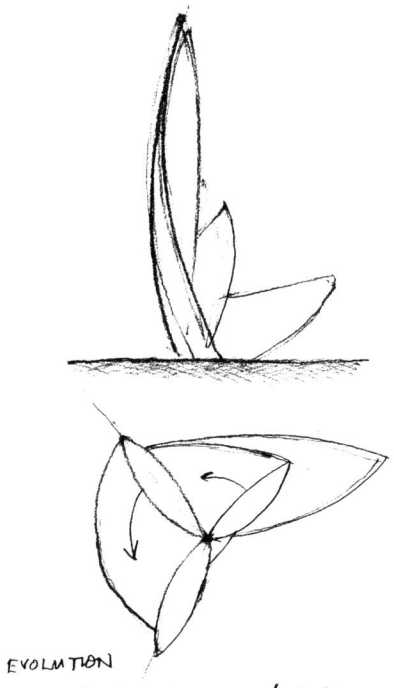

EVOLUTION

3 petals twist through 90°
2 reach up to form the tower and extends
1 tails off at mid level, creating the hotel

Water | Crown Hotel, Sydney, Australia

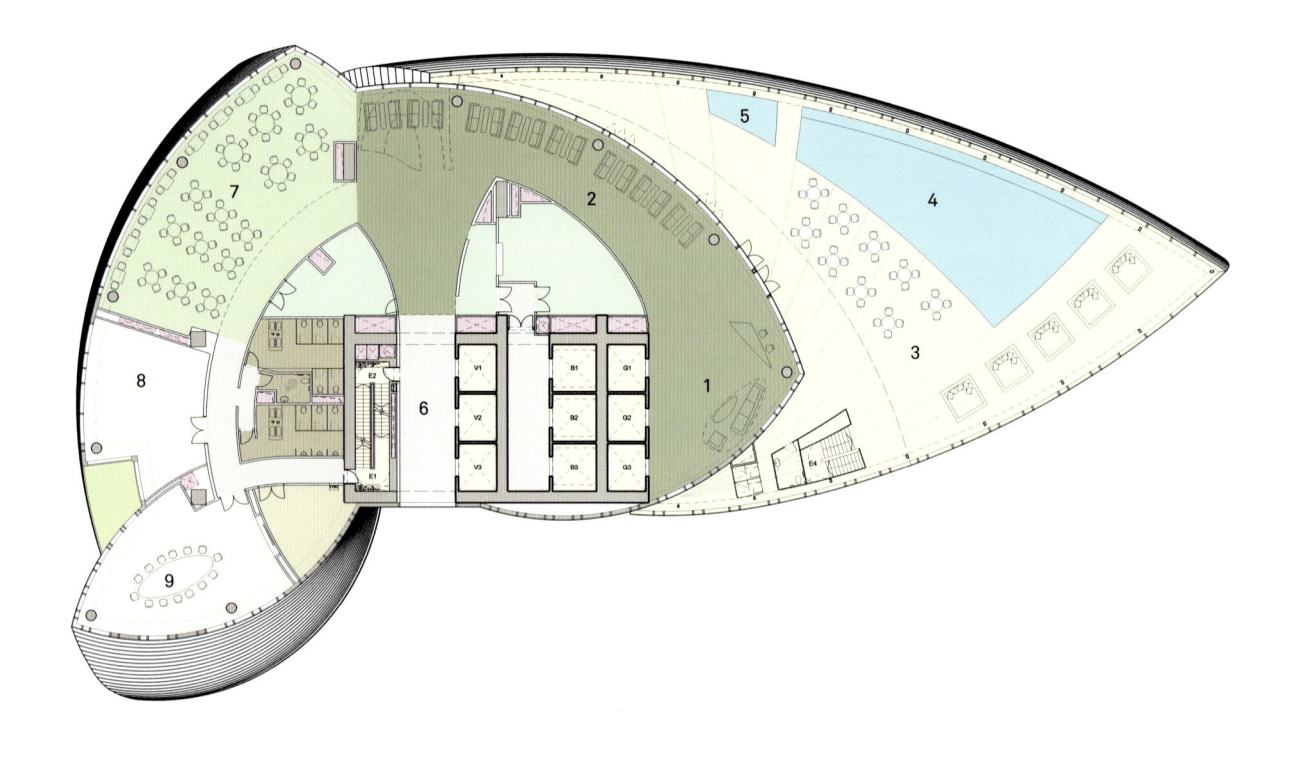

Crystal Club floor plan

1 Reception
2 Lounge
3 Terrace
4 Pool
5 Jacuzzi
6 VIP lobby
7 Restaurant
8 Function room
9 Boardroom

The terrace on level 24 of the hotel wing is home to the luxurious Crystal Club, and offers spectacular views of Sydney Harbour Bridge to the north-east, and across the harbour waters to the west.

The need to maximize these views of both opera house and harbour bridge was also central to the development of the residential apartments in the tower. An angle bisector was set between the two icons, and the building's tower oriented along that line. The central point of this angle bisector was then located, and the twist of the tower manipulated to ensure that as many rooms as possible have the best view at all floor levels.

Level 69 | Supervilla

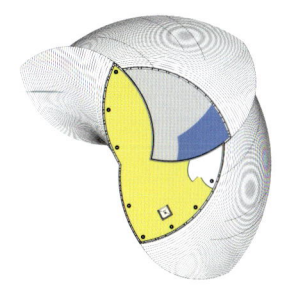

Level 68 | Supervilla

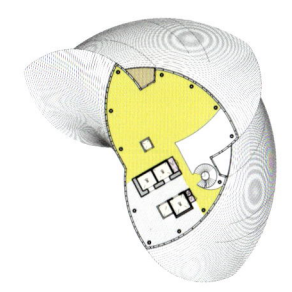

Level 67 | Supervilla

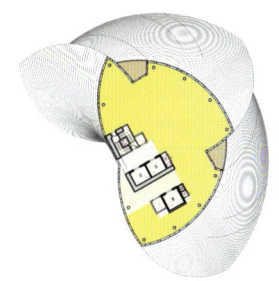

Level 66 | Supervilla

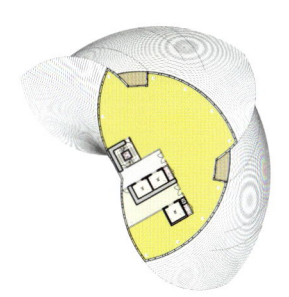

Level 65 | Plant

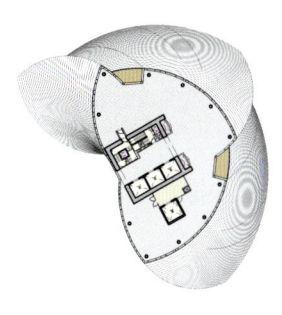

Level 64 | 1 apartment per floor

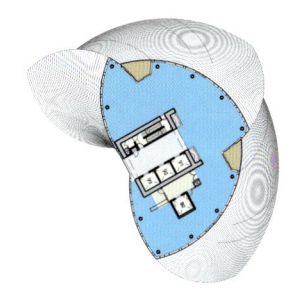

Level 57 | 1 apartment per floor

Level 56 | Residential/plant

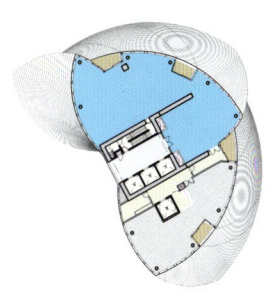

Level 55 | 2 apartments per floor

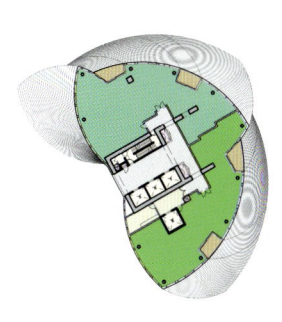

Level 51 | 2 apartments per floor

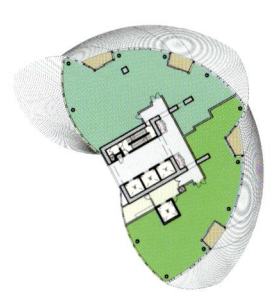

Level 50 | 3 apartments per floor

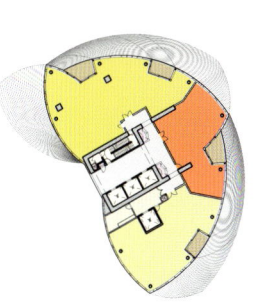

Level 47 | 2 apartments per floor

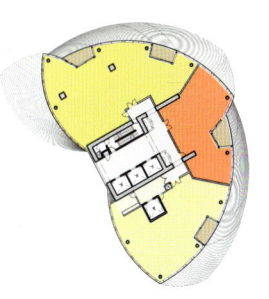

Water | Crown Hotel, Sydney, Australia

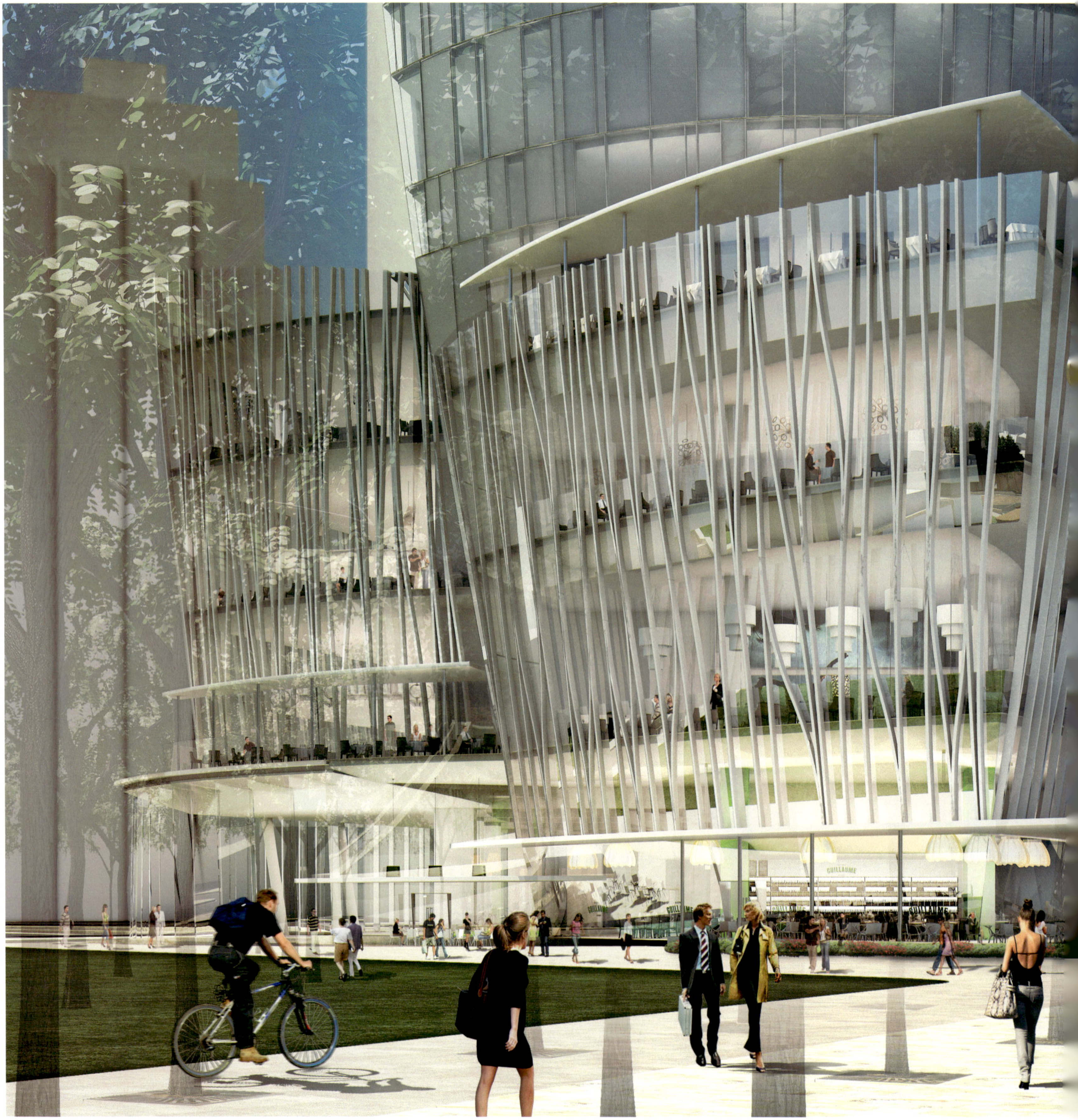
GUILLAUME

A veil of stone tracery, the design of which is based on an apparently random repeating pattern, provides the upper terraces of the podium with shading and unifies the podium's appearance. The almost Gothic aesthetic references the delicate structural stone vaulting of the Vladislav Hall at Prague Castle in the Czech Republic.

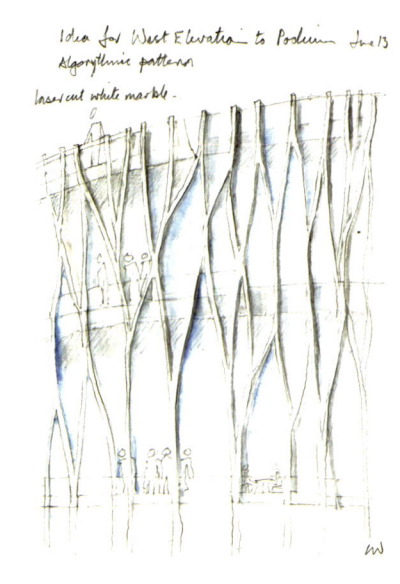

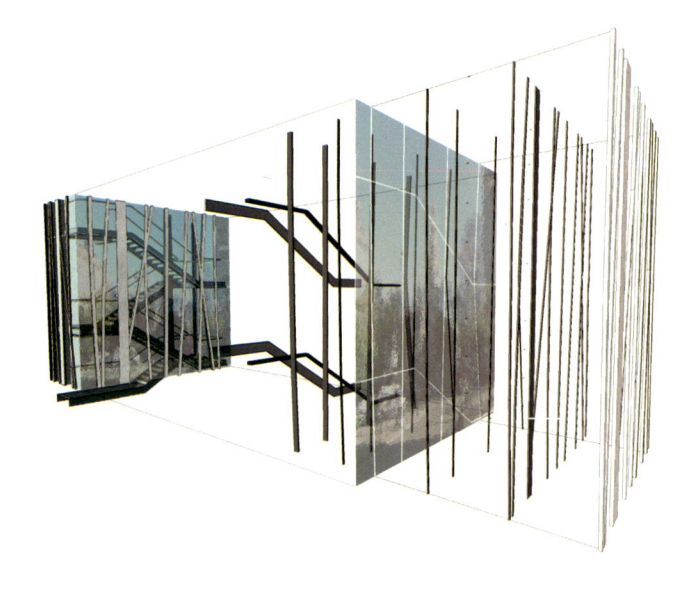

Water | Crown Hotel, Sydney, Australia

The smooth, curved form of the north façade defines the north-west boundary of the main Sydney Harbour skyline.

Water | Crown Hotel, Sydney, Australia

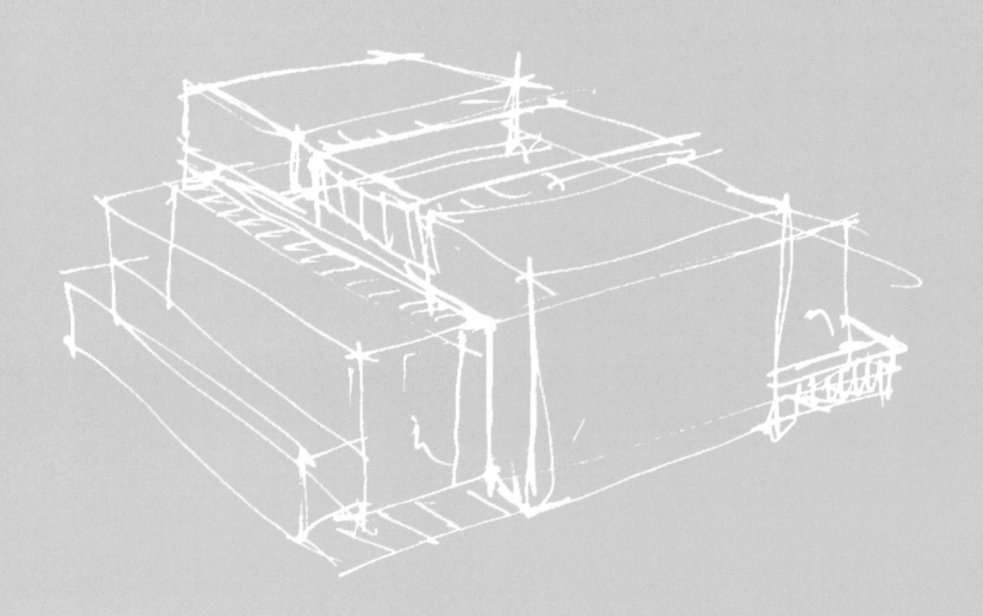

City

The city is a place of continual reinvention, a phenomenon that delivers both conundrum and wonder. Working in the city involves logistical ingenuity as well as imaginative design: here is history to be respected, communities to be developed and renewed, a sustainable future to be secured.

10 Brock Street, London, UK	186
Paradise Street Interchange, Liverpool, UK	194
Ceramics Galleries Bridge, London, UK	200
Museum of London, UK	203
Department of Earth Sciences, Oxford, UK	208
25 Great Pulteney Street, London, UK	218
Queen Mary, University of London, UK	223
New Bodleian (Weston) Library, Oxford, UK	231
Battersea Power Station, London, UK	241

10 Brock Street
London, UK

Regent's Place is a mixed-use estate, regenerated by British Land and located immediately to the north of the Euston Road in central London. The site has been incrementally developed over almost two decades, and is noteworthy for its ambition not only to create a new commercial and residential space within the site, but also to introduce, via such small interventions as public art, imaginative landscaping and pedestrian prioritization, wider urban renewal in the surrounding Euston Road corridor. Wilkinson Eyre's building at 10 Brock Street occupies the north-eastern quadrant of the site, and completes the estate. The design's evolution reflects changing commercial responses to the economic climate, as well as increasingly stringent requirements for energy efficiency in large urban developments.

Although envisioned in the original masterplan as a single-volume building on a square footprint, the building is articulated as three volumes of differing heights. This strategy is intended to break down the building's mass, and to minimize its impact both on strategic views into the site from both Parliament and Primrose hills, and on the more modestly scaled buildings on the residential streets nearby. The staggered sizes and angled planes of the volumes also help to mediate between the height of the adjacent Euston Tower and the adjoining buildings to the west, suggesting a spiralling movement in the composition.

The original plan for the building, developed soon after Wilkinson Eyre's initial appointment in 2003, showed the three volumes separated by narrow atria. Following a two-year interlude after the financial crisis of 2008, however, the needs of the market had changed, and it was felt that larger, uninterrupted floor plates were required. On revisiting the scheme, the design team refined the conceptual diagram, moving the main core to the north and introducing a new, lateral atrium. This enabled the floor plates facing south across the plaza to Euston Road to be opened up across the full width of the building; it also created a much larger space for the soaring entrance lobby, which acts as a continuation of the large public square in front of the building. A rich palette of traditional and contemporary materials has been chosen for the lobby, with each bespoke element – furniture, reception desk and so on – also designed by Wilkinson Eyre.

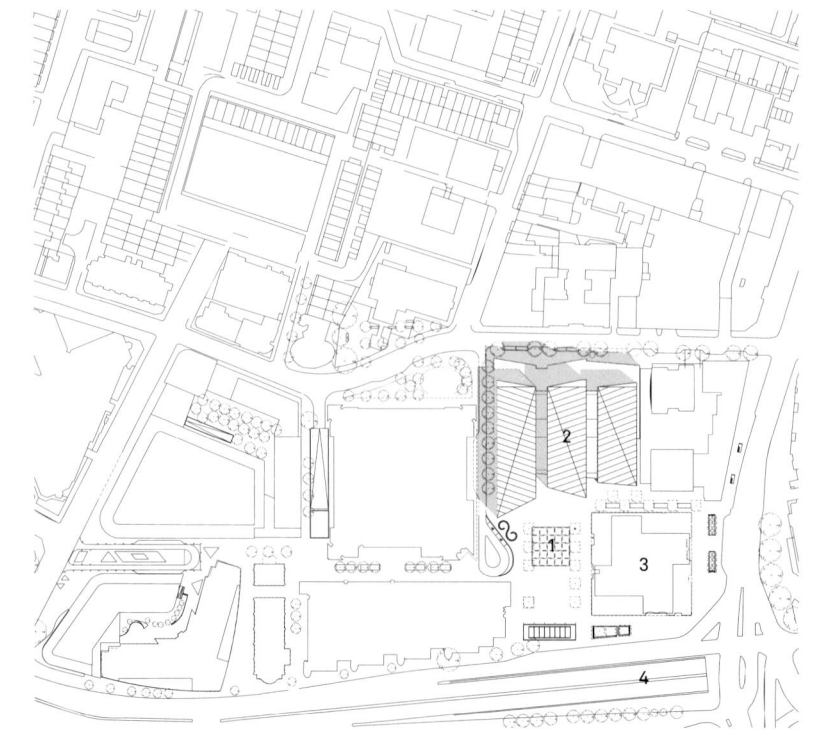

Site plan

1 Triton Square
2 10 Brock Street
3 Euston Tower
4 Euston Road

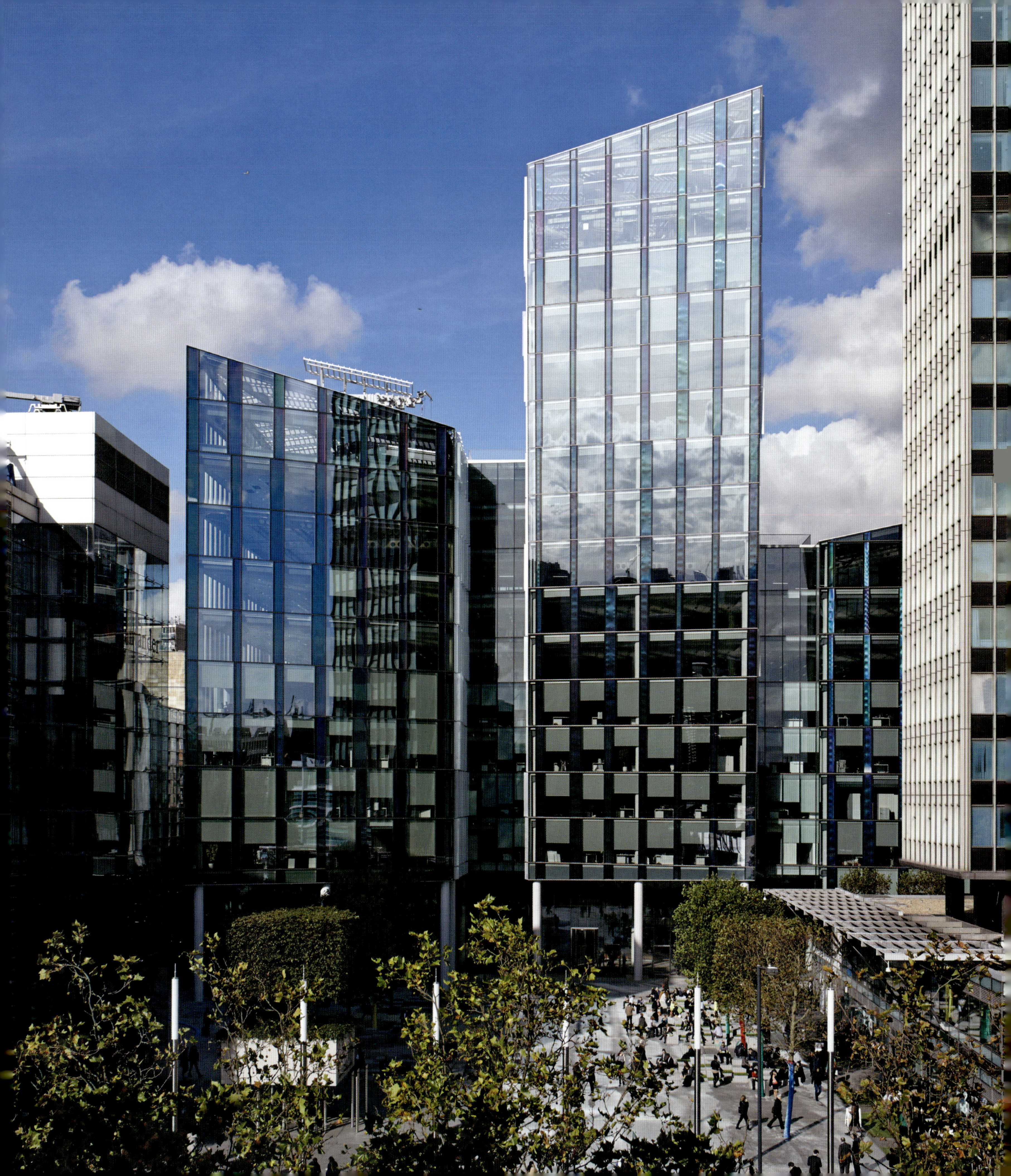

During the 1960s Regent's Place was developed as the 'Euston Centre' around the Euston Tower, one of the first high-rise office buildings in London's West End. Since British Land took stewardship of the estate in 1996, it has been developed in two phases to a masterplan by Farrells.

A lower, four-storey volume at the rear of the building follows the roof line of the smaller structures on Drummond Street to the north of the site, with the north-facing façades of the tower volumes – which reach up to fifteen storeys – leaning away from the street. On the south side, the façade planes lean forward to frame and shelter the plaza.

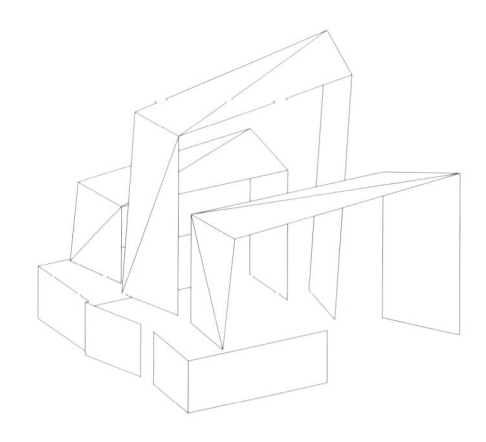

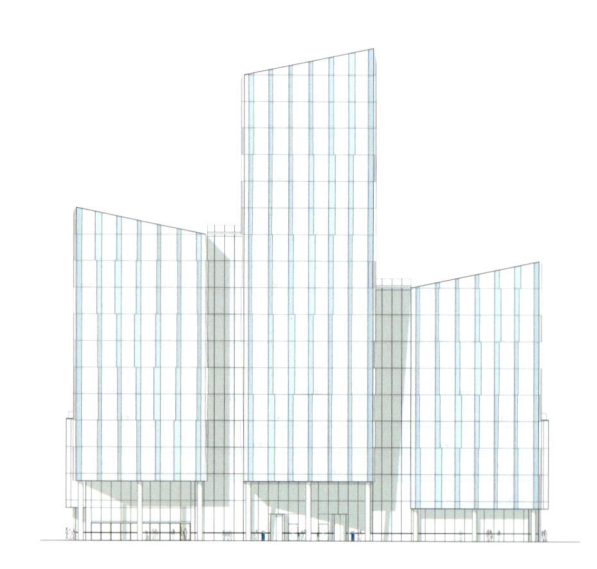

Typical office floor plan
and upper floor plan

1 Flexible open-plan office
2 Meeting rooms
3 WCs
4 Lift lobby

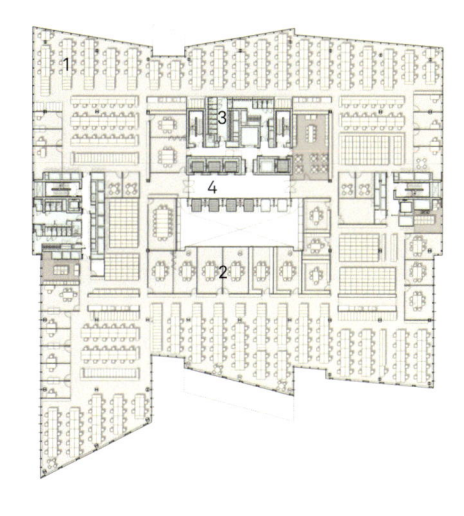

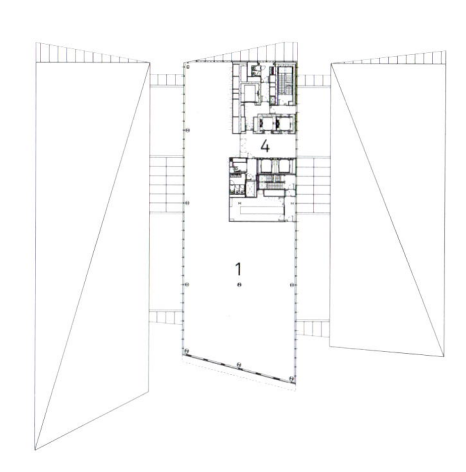

City | 10 Brock Street, London, UK

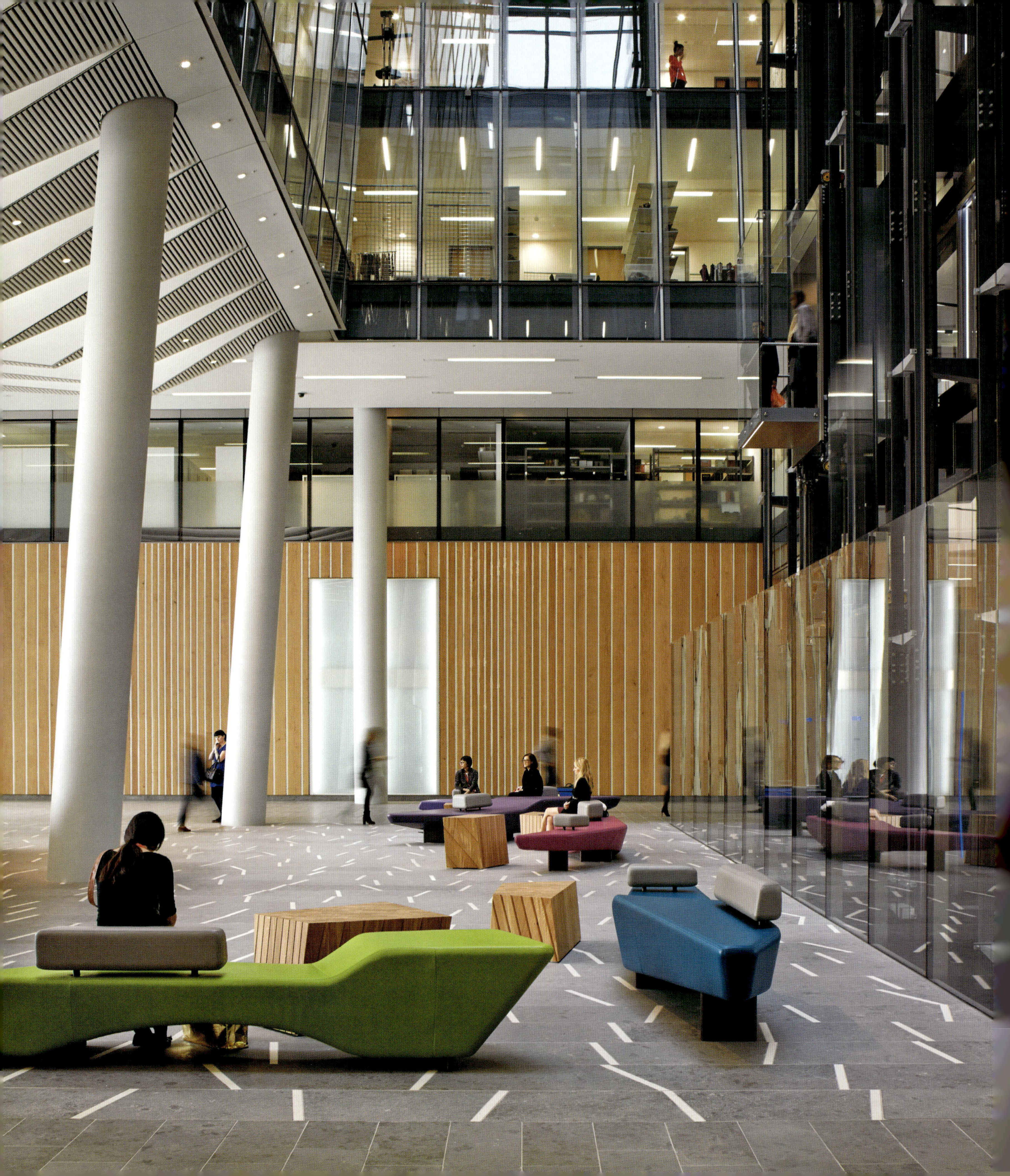

All furniture and signage in the reception lobby was designed by Wilkinson Eyre, including the island reception desk, which sits centre stage. The bronze desk takes its geometry from the theme of angled planes developed throughout the building. Lifting slightly at the edges, its spiralling form creates desktops of three different heights. Five individual free-form seats, each in its own coloured leather, occupy the floor space, interspersed with geometric tables made of solid oak.

Conceived as a series of irregular 'gills', the ceiling acts as a device to link the sloping façade of the central tower volume with the reciprocal sloping wall of the atrium. The gills themselves emit light through hidden light boxes, which form a concentration above the central reception desk.

The lobby floor is composed of grey Spanish limestone, with each slab separated by a strip of Asiago marble. The trapezoidal shapes of the slabs combine to mimic the floor plates of the building, with the marble forming highlights in the never-repeating pattern. The side walls are clad with Danish oak planks separated by strips of the same Asiago marble, the differing widths of the planks creating the sense of a compression wave along the 50-metre-long wall of the lobby.

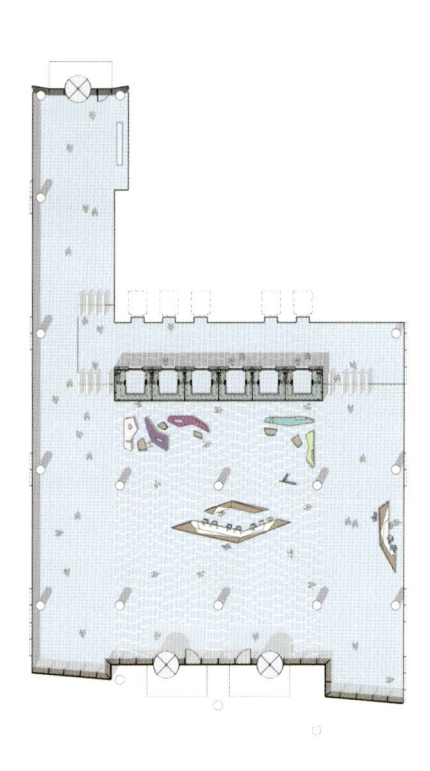

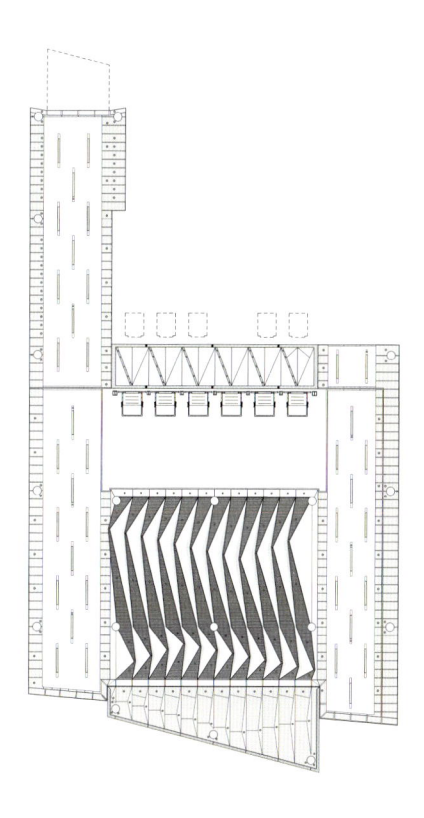

Entrance lobby plan

Entrance lobby ceiling plan

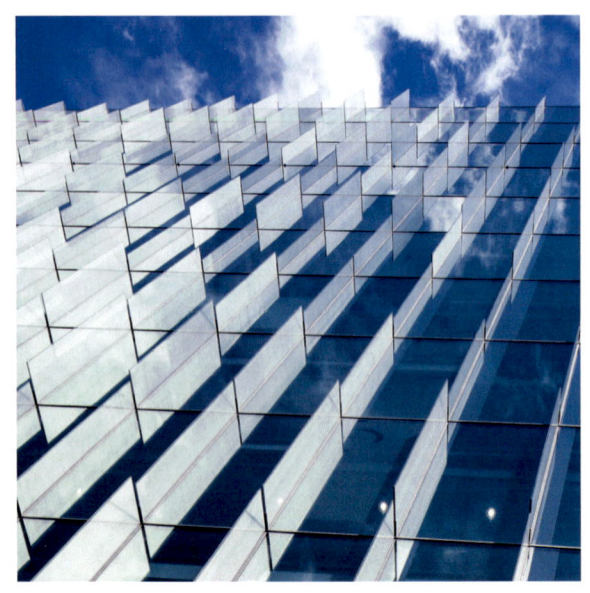

The design of the building's glass façades evolved significantly throughout the project to ensure energy efficiency, the renewed requirements of Part L of the UK Building Regulations representing an opportunity to experiment with some interesting materials and techniques. Solid panels of profiled dichroic-surfaced stainless steel, for example, provide insulated façade areas to the south. Depending on how these panels catch the light, their colour and luminosity varies.

Fritting was used on various surfaces of the double-glazed units, while the glass fins attached to the east and west façades have a translucent, aluminium-coated mesh embedded in the laminate.

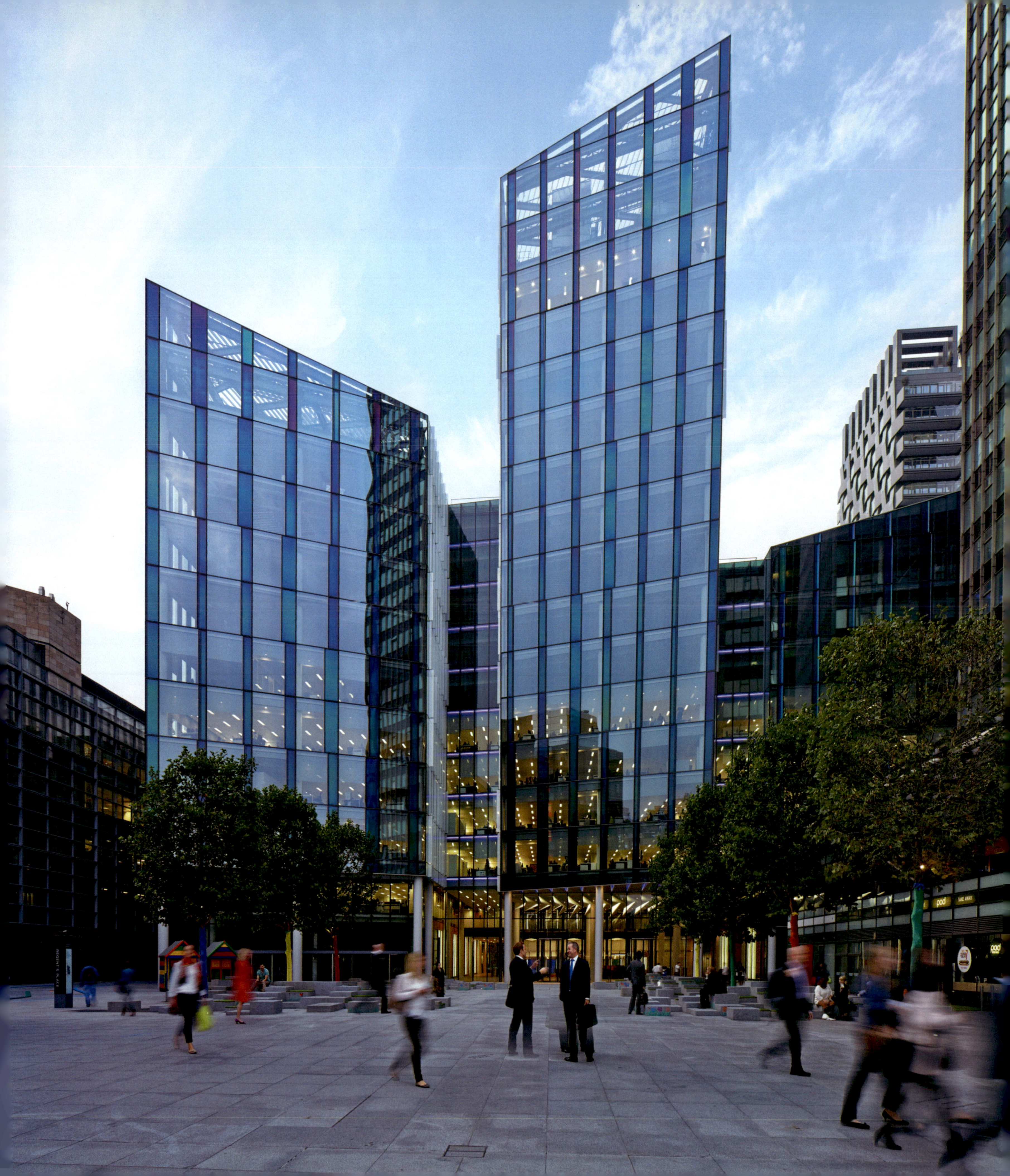

Paradise Street Interchange
Liverpool, UK

Liverpool One was one of the most significant – and successful – developments to accompany Liverpool's year as European Capital of Culture in 2008. It effectively regenerated 17 hectares of land around Paradise Street, sandwiched between the city centre and the docks of the Maritime Mercantile City, a UNESCO World Heritage Site. As commercial activity surrounding the docks gradually declined during the late nineteenth century, so did the urban fabric of this part of the city, with the riverfront slowly becoming cut off from the central business and shopping districts by a strip of industrial wasteland. Liverpool One which combines retail with residential and leisure uses – has introduced a new sense of cohesion, strengthening links between the city's commercial heart and new destinations in the reinvigorated docks, such as Tate Liverpool and the International Slavery Museum.

Among the first elements to be completed within the development were Wilkinson Eyre's transport interchange, car park and pedestrian link bridge at the southern end of the site. These provide the development with its logistical anchor, their design helping to reinforce new routes between the riverfront and the heart of Paradise Street, with the spaces between each building in the composition becoming almost as important as the volumes themselves.

The car park can be a cumbersome type of building to work with, but Wilkinson Eyre's design employs the simplest and most efficient of layouts: a stack of orthogonal parking floor plates, with a pedestrian bridge, ramps, lifts and other services plugged into the façades as discrete elements. A varied and innovative palette of robust materials lends character and interest. The movement of vehicles and pedestrians within, for example, is celebrated with the addition of a translucent fibreglass screen to the west elevation. This screen not only fulfils the pragmatic brief of blocking views into the adjacent police headquarters, but also, from the outside, is animated by activity on the parking floors behind – particularly at night, when headlights wind lazily through the space. It is cut away to reveal the bold, cantilevering concrete entrance/exit ramp at its base, painted bright red to highlight the diagram of disparate elements plugged into the orthogonal structure. Above, a small block of accommodation for the car-park operator is articulated as a zinc-clad box, and, again, is cantilevered out from the central volume. In contrast, the east elevation is clad in an anodized louvre screen, the shiny bronze colour of which provides a tonal counterpoint to the cantilevered, steel-clad access ramps, staggered across the elevation to add dynamism to this façade. The bus layover area to the east of the site is protected by a 5-metre-high brick-faced boundary wall, each panel of which is 'folded' in a modern interpretation of the sturdy Victorian dock walls found all over Liverpool.

Connected to the car park's northern façade is a sinuous pedestrian bridge, which provides shoppers with an enclosed link to Liverpool One's anchor department store. Located at the end of the east–west axis defined by the bus interchange, one of the main pedestrian routes to the docks, it has its own sculptural identity, appearing as a solid structure interlocking with a glazed enclosure. From certain angles the cranked external form of the bridge gives the illusion of impossible slenderness, although strong sight lines and legibility have been retained within. Faceted planes of sheet steel and transparent cladding wrap around the bridge deck, the steel lined on the inside with coloured translucent resin panels to give pedestrians using the bridge a point of visual interest.

Near by, the bus station is signalled by two elegantly twisting, timber-lined canopies, which geometrically reference the shape of a ship's hull in response to the location: the site of Liverpool's 'Old Dock' – the first commercial wet dock in the world, and the foundation of the city's mercantile power. The canopies, which are clad on the upper side with titanium, shelter twin public concourses, each with six in-line bus stands. Transparent waiting enclosures are positioned around the circular steel columns that support the roof.

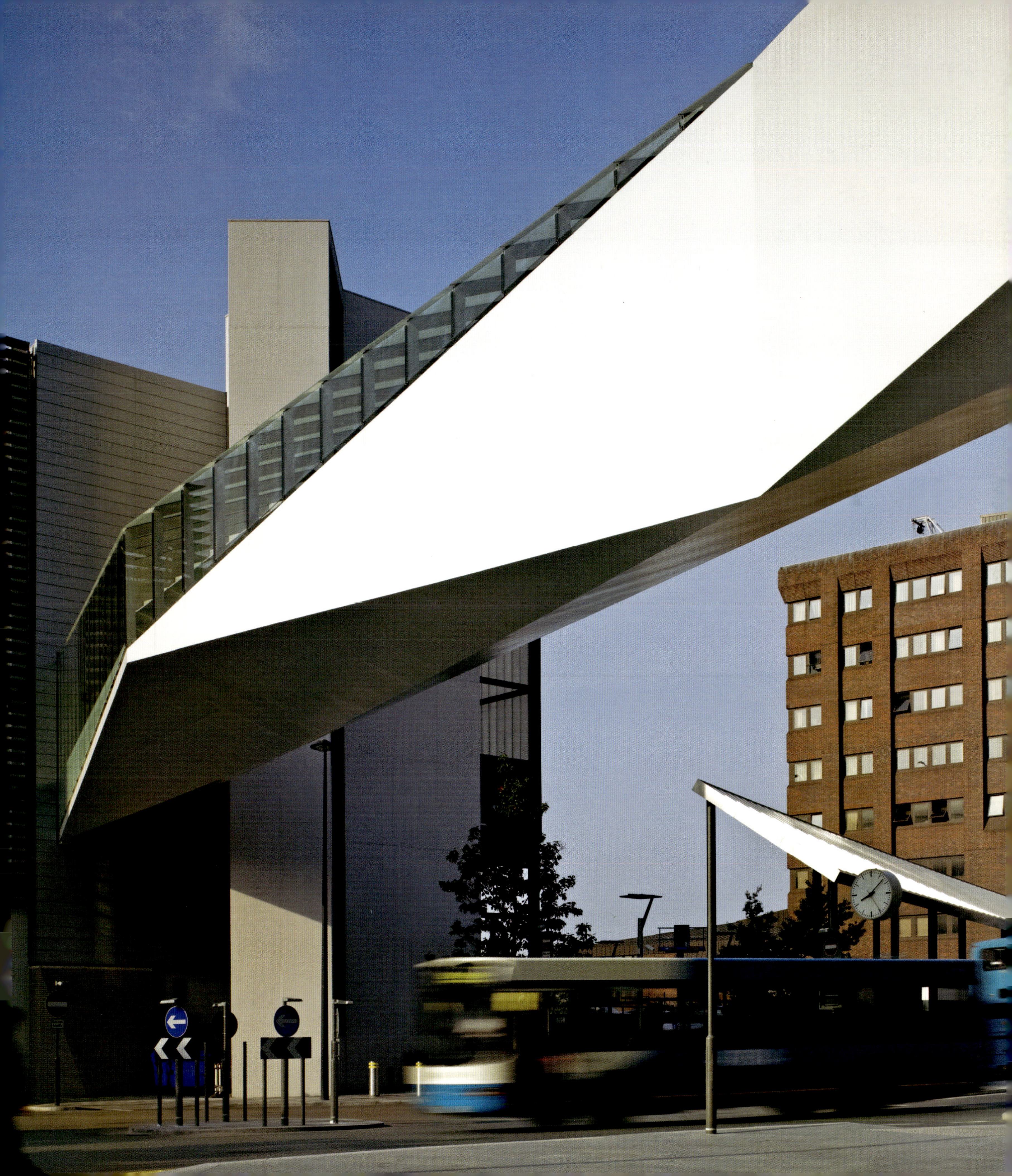

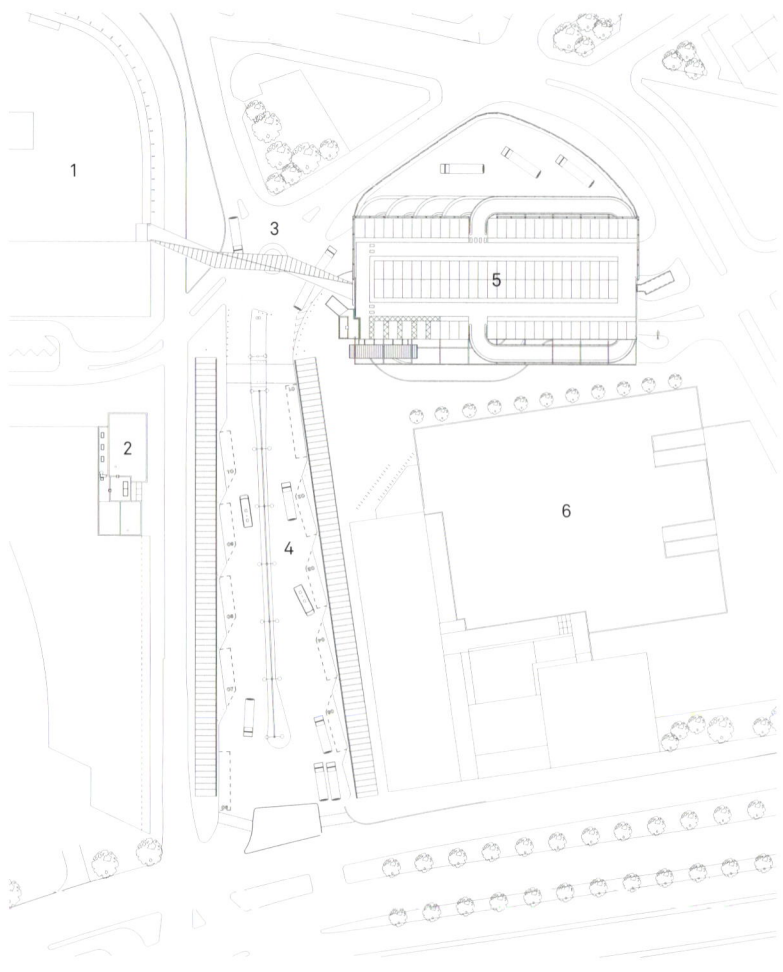

Site plan

1. Department store
2. Ticket office
3. Pedestrian bridge
4. Bus station
5. Liver Street car park and bus layover
6. Police headquarters

The car park was realigned from its masterplanned position to better define the north–south connection with Kings Waterfront. Pedestrian activity is concentrated at its north-west corner, closest to the bus interchange, the entrance to the car park and a taxi rank.

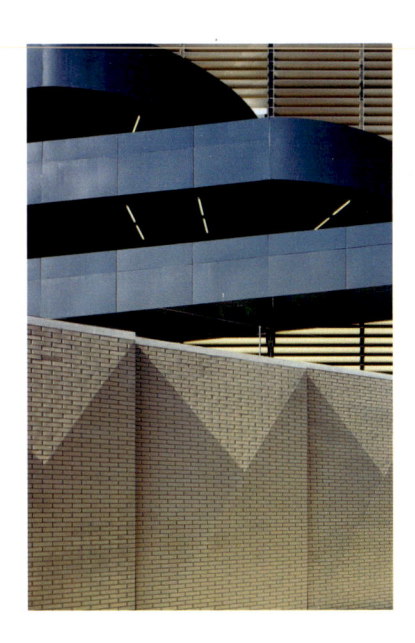

The car park uses a variety of façade materials. To the north, angled louvres conceal the parking floors, the angle of the blades varying across the height of the building to prevent views of the ceiling soffits from street level while maintaining the required amount of ventilation. To the south, the fibreglass screen – constructed by a boat builder on the Isle of Wight – features a wave form, which adds texture to the screen and breaks down its overall mass.

Each panel of the boundary wall is folded, allowing the modular vertical panels to be articulated and broken along their length, while also revealing a depth that is highlighted at night by the inclusion of linear light fittings. This sculptural origami gives the site an attractive and fluid perimeter.

City | Paradise Street Interchange, Liverpool, UK

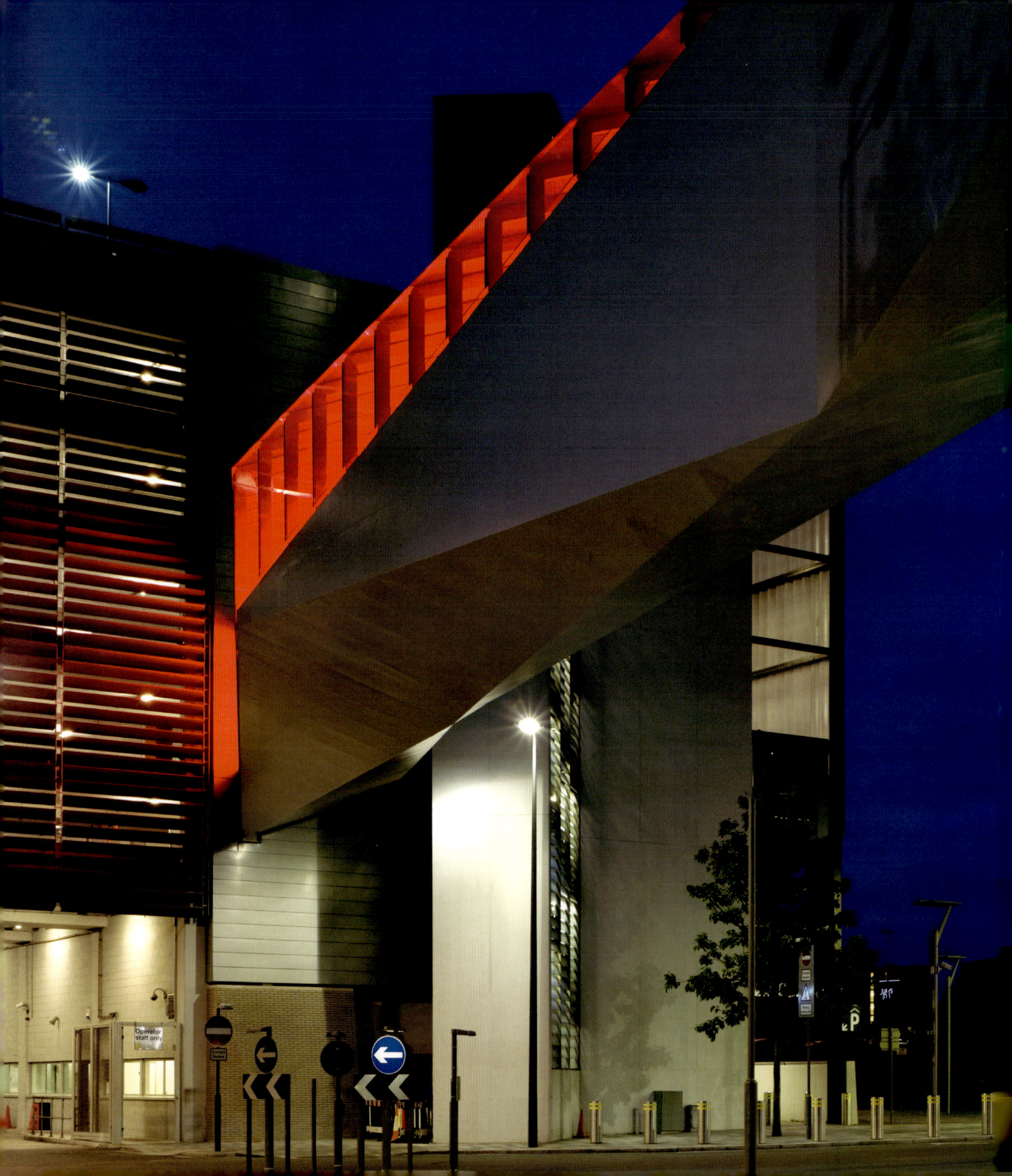
Operator
staff only

The geometry of the bridge was generated by the locations of its springing points, which are not aligned. This resulted in a cranked structure in three equal lengths, with the middle length perpendicular to the buildings the bridge connects. Despite the crank in the bridge's plan, a straight sight line has been maintained internally, which is visually reinforced by the apex of the roof.

Lighting provides a safe environment for pedestrians using the bridge at night. It also accentuates the geometry in order to dramatize the crossing without distracting drivers on the road below.

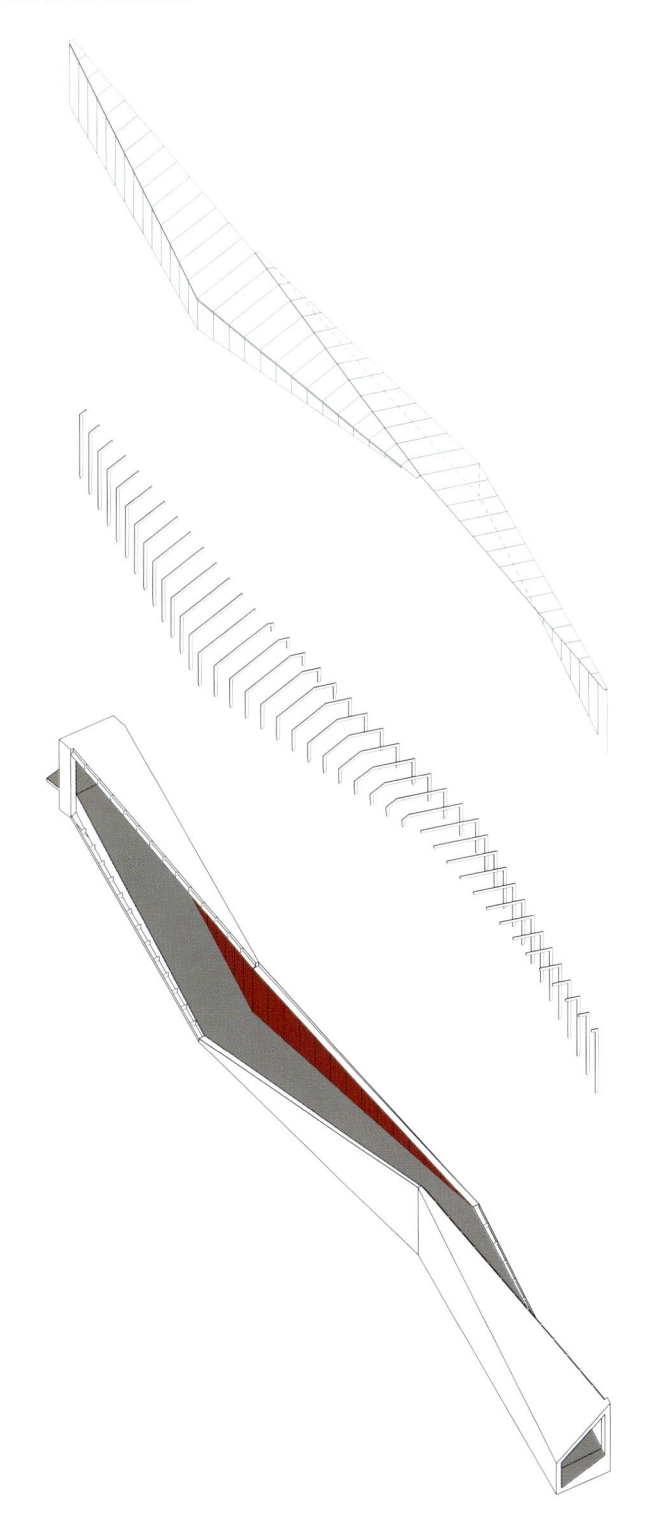

City | Paradise Street Interchange, Liverpool, UK

Ceramics Galleries Bridge
London, UK

The 4.5 million objects held by London's Victoria and Albert Museum make it the world's greatest collection of decorative arts and design. The refurbishment of the Ceramics galleries was central to the first phase of the museum's Future Plan, which will restore and reconfigure the vast complex over a twenty-year period. Opened in 1909, the galleries were purpose-built for the ceramics collection, and so, together with a curatorial need to refresh the display for new audiences, there were many practical considerations within the design brief. Among these was the very prosaic requirement for a new fire-escape stair: the introduction of the galleries had lengthened the existing escape path and inadvertently created an unacceptable dead end.

This small bridge provides the necessary escape route, connecting the top floor of the red-brick Aston Webb building on the Cromwell Road with the adjacent Secretariat Building across an external space that forms the latter's entrance. At just 7 metres long, infrequently used and barely visible to the general public, it is also something of a hidden jewel, its ownership residing firmly with the museum's staff and visitors. The starting point for the design was that the bridge should be a functional object, prefabricated to allow it to be craned into position with the minimum of disruption; in reality, however, it is a far more dynamic, sculptural intervention. The form appears to cascade, unsupported, from one building to the other like a shuffle of cards, linking the two springing points with a frozen ripple of glass and steel. The form is expressed by a series of vertical portals, aligned with each stair tread. To create a sense of movement, the portals gradually lean away from the vertical, reaching an angle of 15 degrees in the centre of the bridge, and recovering to a fully upright position at the lower end. An incremental curve to the inner edge of the portal frames creates a dishing effect along the length of the bridge's interior. To enhance the feeling that the bridge is jumping between the two buildings, the main structure – a torsion box beam – is hidden; the bridge frames cantilever out from this, as though suspended in mid-air.

The bridge performs in suspended animation against the stainless-steel backdrop of the new Medieval and Renaissance Galleries, and its materials complement this context. The portal frames are steel plate, while the stair of folded, galvanized steel is perforated to enhance the bridge's transparency and to provide a non-slip surface. Light floods in through each cantilevered glass portal; above, overlapping glass shingles protect bridge users from the elements. Emergency lighting has been integrated into a series of translucent acrylic light boxes on the western enclosure of the bridge, which enhance the reading of the geometry through light and shadow.

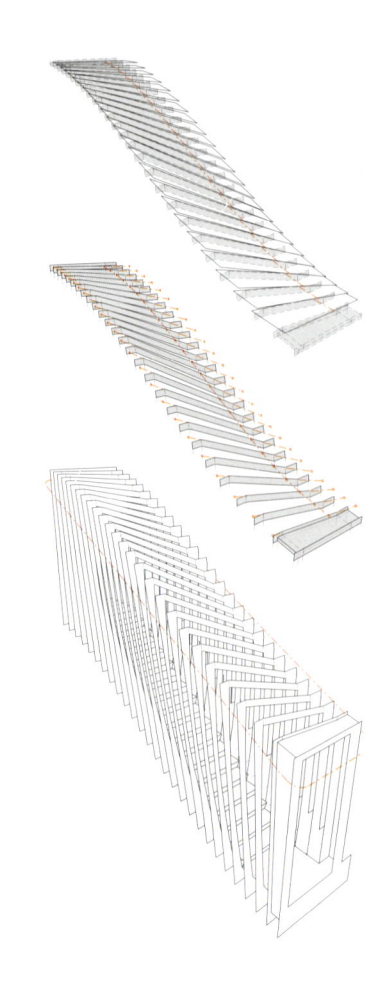

City | Ceramics Galleries Bridge, London, UK

MUSEUM O

Museum of London
UK

The Museum of London was opened in 1976, and, with more than a million objects in its archive, is the world's largest urban-history museum. It attracts in excess of 300,000 visitors a year to its permanent galleries and temporary special exhibitions, but these displays form just a small part of the museum's activities. It is the custodian of vast costume and working-history collections, hosts around 80,000 young people every year as part of its education and outreach programme, and created Europe's largest archaeological unit – MOLA (Museum of London Archeology) – which investigates almost every major building project within the City.

Wilkinson Eyre first became involved with the museum's development in 2002, with each small piece of work laying the ground for the long-term reconfiguration of the galleries. The original building was designed by Powell Moya & Partners in 1976, and is linked to the Highwalk, the complex system of raised walkways that has come to define the Barbican estate. Although innovative at the time, this re-routing of pedestrians meant that the museum had very little visibility at street level and a confusing internal diagram. A first phase of work, the Core Access Project, focused on improving public access. This involved reorganizing the museum's circulation by way of a new vertical core, but also by creating a new entrance canopy sheltering an extended reception, shop and orientation area. A new special-exhibitions gallery was also formed from a void between the museum and an access road below.

The second phase of work was concerned with the northern wing of the museum and the redevelopment of the Clore Learning Centre. This is composed of a series of flexible classroom spaces designed to support school trips focusing on specific areas of the National Curriculum. They are linked vertically by a hanging staircase, which signals the museum's presence on Aldersgate Street, as well as allowing this wing to function autonomously as a conference venue. Meanwhile, the Weston Theatre has been refurbished to provide a venue for films, performances and talks.

The subsequent Capital City Project, completed in 2010, involved making more dramatic changes to the original building, although Philip Powell and Hidalgo Moya's humane modernism continued to provide a stylistic starting point for the work. The curatorial strategy was to reconfigure the existing galleries, including the famous Fire of London experience, into a less prescriptive sequence, and to extend them beyond 1914 to create a new twentieth-century gallery. The introduction of more natural light was a common theme: a glass frontage was created for the London Wall façade, allowing visitors to see into the museum – and the ornate Lord Mayor's Coach – from street level for the first time, while a new, glazed elevation on to the central garden court introduced light into new galleries on the lower floor. These Galleries of Modern London, developed in collaboration with a specialist in-house team, dramatize the museum's collections through a series of immersive spaces and interactive exhibits. They continue a spiral of circulation through London's history, which begins on the upper floors with the Roman and medieval galleries.

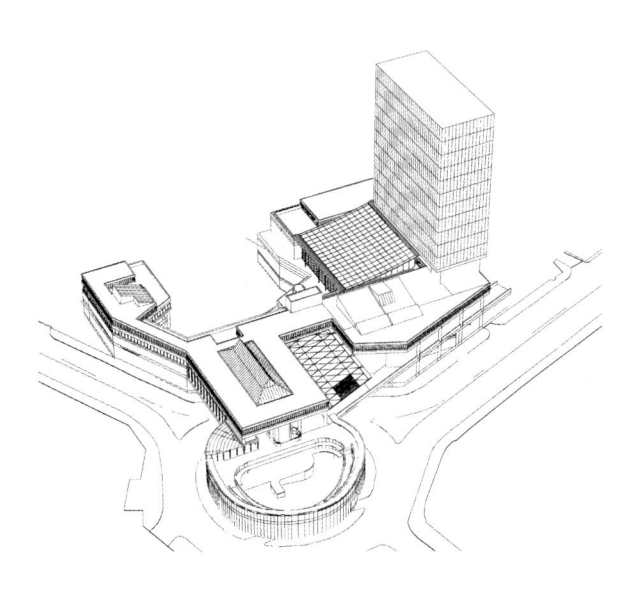

On its completion in 1976, the Museum of London was described by one architectural critic as the most retiring public building in the capital. The dense urban context has informed almost every aspect of Wilkinson Eyre's three phases of work at the museum – from a consideration of the proximity of the listed Ironmongers' Hall, and the necessity of minimizing disruption to the museum's corporate and residential neighbours, to the need to improve visibility and ease of access.

While the centrepiece of the Core Access Project provided the museum with a new orientation and entrance area, the Capital City Project increased gallery space by around 25 per cent. This includes the new glass frontage on to London Wall, which allows one of the largest objects in the museum's collection – the Lord Mayor's Coach – to be showcased to passers-by.

> Entrance
1 Twentieth-century galleries
2 Lord Mayor's Coach
3 Linbury Gallery
4 Ironmongers' Hall
5 New entrance and shop
6 Core access stair, lifts and WCs
7 Clore Learning Centre
8 London Wall
9 Aldersgate Street

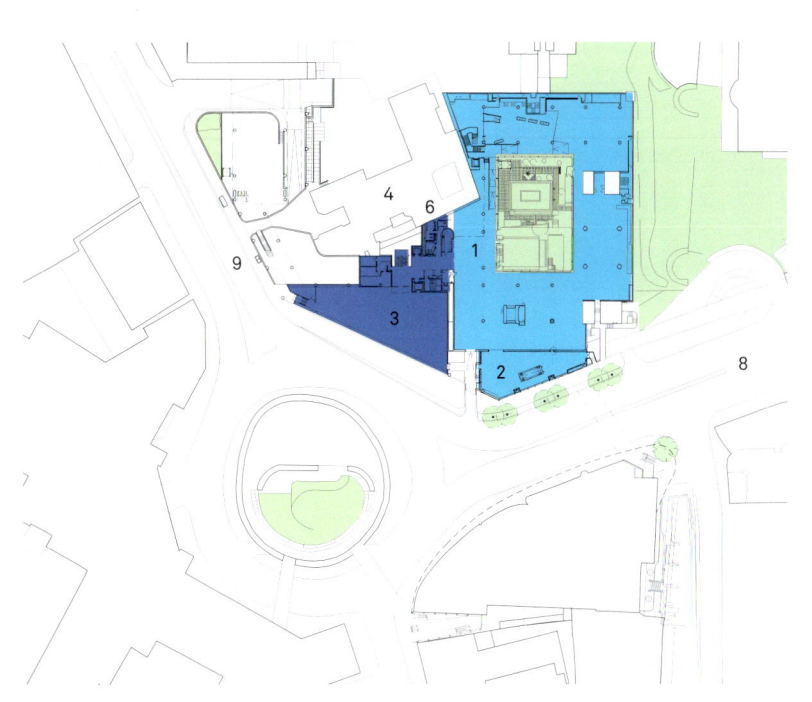

Highwalk level

○ Original galleries and schools' picnic area
● Phase 1 – Core Access Project
● Phase 2 – Clore Learning Centre
● Phase 3 – Capital City Project

Street level

City | Museum of London, UK

205

Learning is central to the work of the museum, and the new Clore Learning Centre provides a suite of classrooms and associated support spaces – display areas, cloakrooms and WCs – to facilitate a wide range of educational activities.

The spectacular hanging staircase not only allows the learning wing to function as a stand-alone venue for conferences, but also helps to raise the museum's profile on Aldersgate Street, a key route into the City. At night, the large areas of glazing turn the stair into a huge light box and reveal the fine craftsmanship of the timber stair within.

Department of Earth Sciences
University of Oxford, UK

Oxford is a city shaped by its university. The broad streets and marketplaces of the historic centre are interlinked by a complex network of lanes, passages and gateways that, once entered, reveal a secret world of colleges and quadrangles. The density of the city has led many academic departments and institutes to build outside the historic centre in recent years, or to redevelop existing sites in highly sensitive surroundings. The new Department of Earth Sciences occupies one such site, sitting on a tiny plot carved out of the Science Area. Although the area's original 1930s masterplan has been updated in recent years to provide an improved research infrastructure, its main attraction remains the incredible scope for the kind of interaction and cross-disciplinary initiatives that are inevitable when world-class scientists work closely together in the same community.

The brief for the new departmental building on this small site was ambitious. It needed to be a showcase for a department conducting research in some of the areas most critical to the earth's future sustainability, with a suite of specialist laboratories, including field- and metal-free environments; it also needed to be capable of housing huge pieces of kit, such as the department's expanding collection of mass spectrometers. The basic diagram places the accommodation in two separate zones: one wing for the laboratories, and one for office space. These are connected by an airy atrium intended to promote the chance encounters for which the department's old building was known; this same space is topped with a senior common room and roof terrace to provide plenty of opportunities for dialogue away from the work areas. In section, the building is also zoned according to the user brief, with the ground floor accommodating the main undergraduate teaching laboratories and an informal learning area open to the atrium. The departmental library occupies the ground-floor street frontage, while a flexible seminar room at the base of the office wing overlooks the newly landscaped Le Gros Clark Place. The lab wing has four floors of laboratory space, flexibly planned to allow research groups to expand and contract in response to changing research avenues and funding. The second floor was designed with removable windows, so that a particularly large mass spectrometer could be craned into position after the building's completion. In contrast, the office wing has five floors and a mixture of cellular offices for the senior lectureship and open-plan group offices of varying sizes for graduate students and postdoctoral researchers.

Overlying the written brief for the building was an unwritten one related to the department's character and personality, much of it developed while watching staff and students at work in the field. Their careful reading of the natural landscape reinforced the view that this building should speak clearly of the work taking place inside it. The resulting 'narrative wall' is an architectural device that reinforces the department's identity, as well as drawing visitors in to the building. The wall runs along the southern façade of the laboratory wing and on into the atrium of the building, its distinctive strata composed of fossil-rich rock types chosen in collaboration with the department.

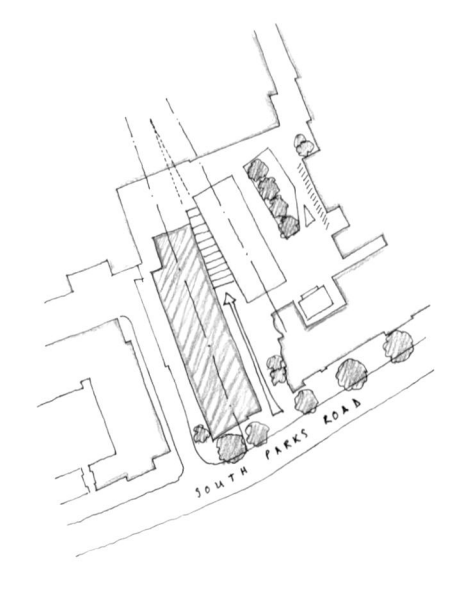

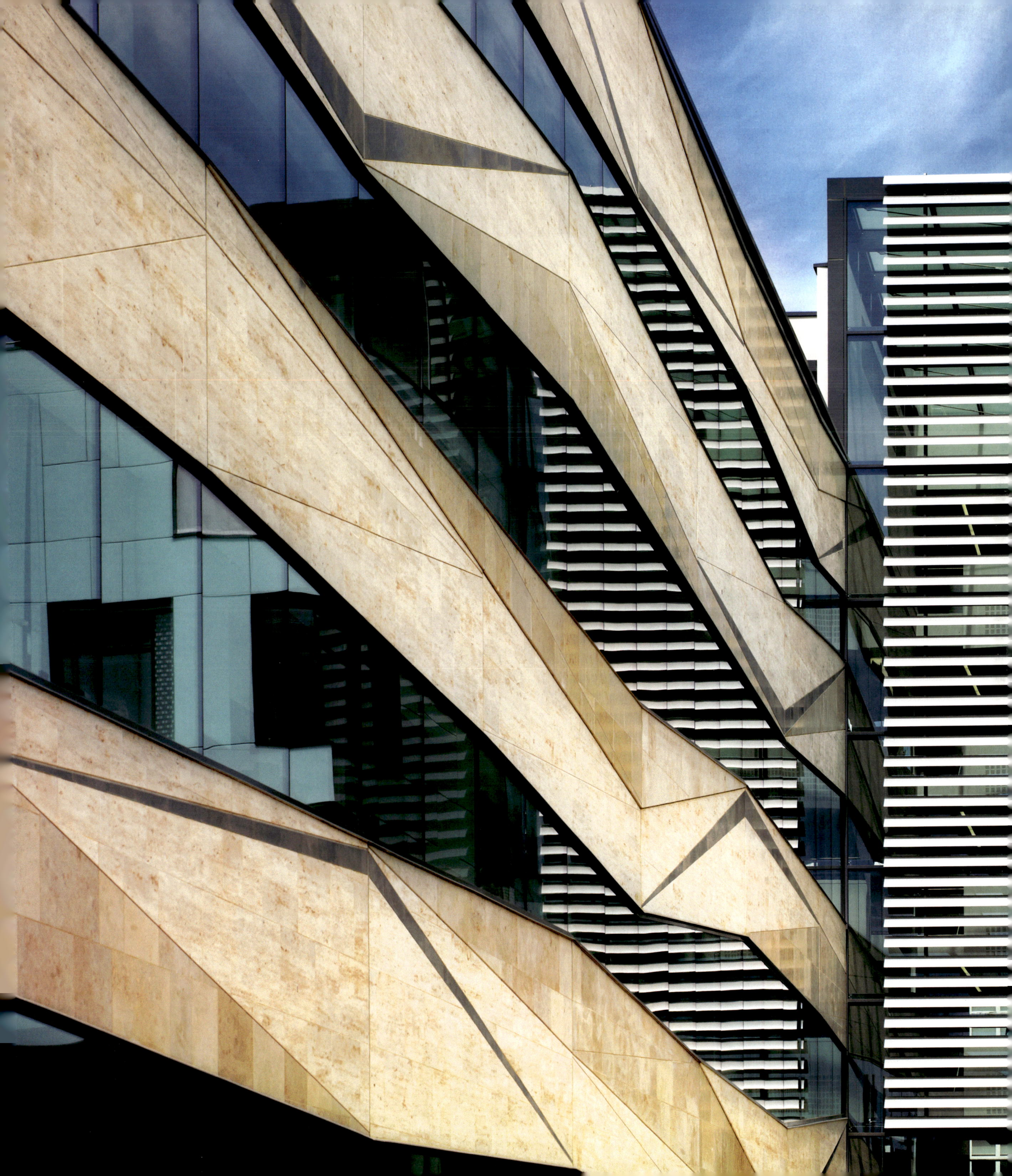

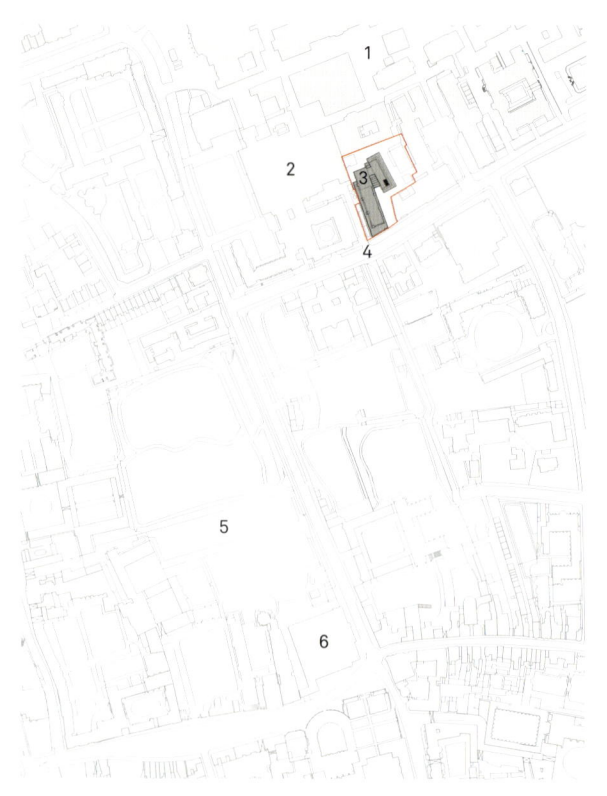

Location plan
1 Science Area
2 Museum of Natural History
3 Department of Earth Sciences
4 South Parks Road
5 Trinity College
6 New Bodleian (Weston) Library

The Science Area, located to the north-east of the city centre, was originally masterplanned in 1935 by Lanchester & Lodge, and proposed three strips of development – for medical and biological, museum, and chemistry subjects.

The Natural History and Pitt Rivers museums lie at the heart of the site. A masterplan by Farrells from 2007 set out the principles for the site's future, identifying buildings to be retained, new zones and individual plots for redevelopment, and improved landscaping and access/circulation. The Earth Sciences site is on the southern edge of the Science Area, with a narrow frontage on to South Parks Road.

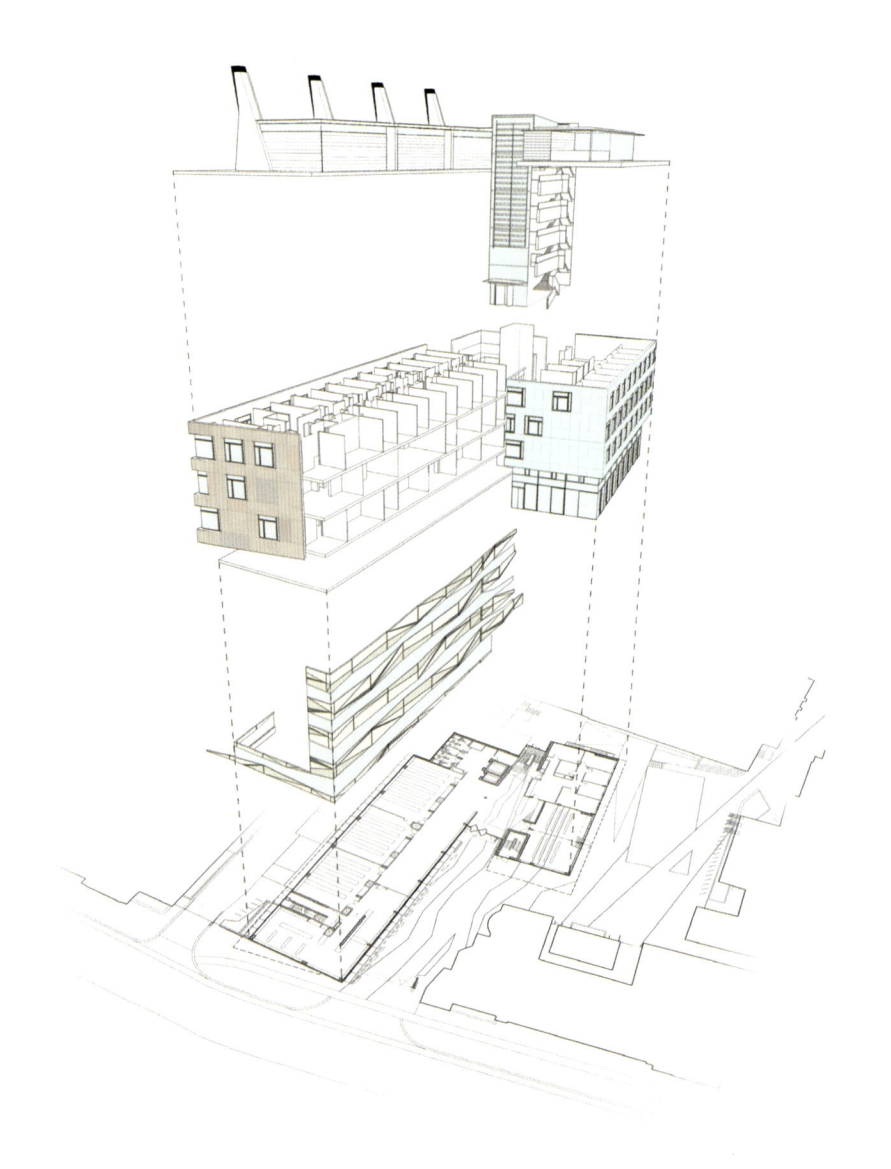

210

'Carfax height' is defined by the Carfax Tower on Oxford's High Street, and generally sets the maximum permissible height for new development in the city at 79.3 metres above sea level. This line is punctured by the strong verticals of the city's famous spires; on the Earth Sciences building, consent was given for the flues, plant room and top-floor senior common room, all set back from the façade, also to exceed Carfax height.

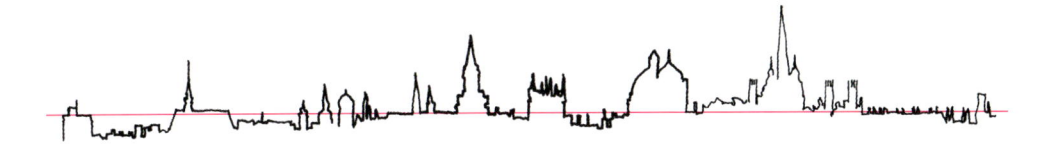

City | Department of Earth Sciences, Oxford, UK

The central environmental challenge on this project was to minimize energy use while providing the specialist environments required by advanced research. The strategy of separating the highly serviced laboratories from the primarily naturally ventilated office accommodation emerged early in the design process – not only because it supported the energy strategy, but also because it would facilitate interaction between building users moving from one zone to another. A closed-loop ground-source energy system consisting of 63 boreholes beneath the building is predicted to save 31 per cent of its delivered energy requirement and 17 per cent of its carbon emissions, as compared to more traditional sources of building energy.

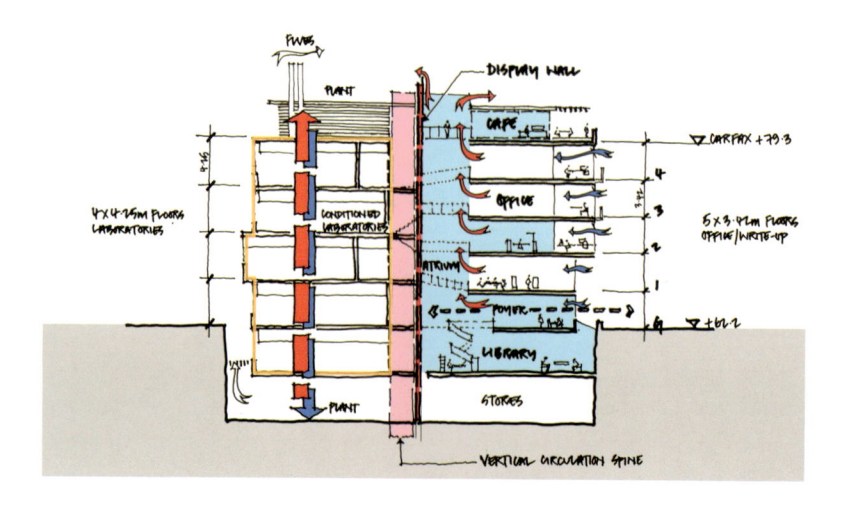

Ground plan
1 Reception
2 Seminar rooms
3 Administrative offices
4 Undergraduate common area
5 Teaching laboratories
6 Library

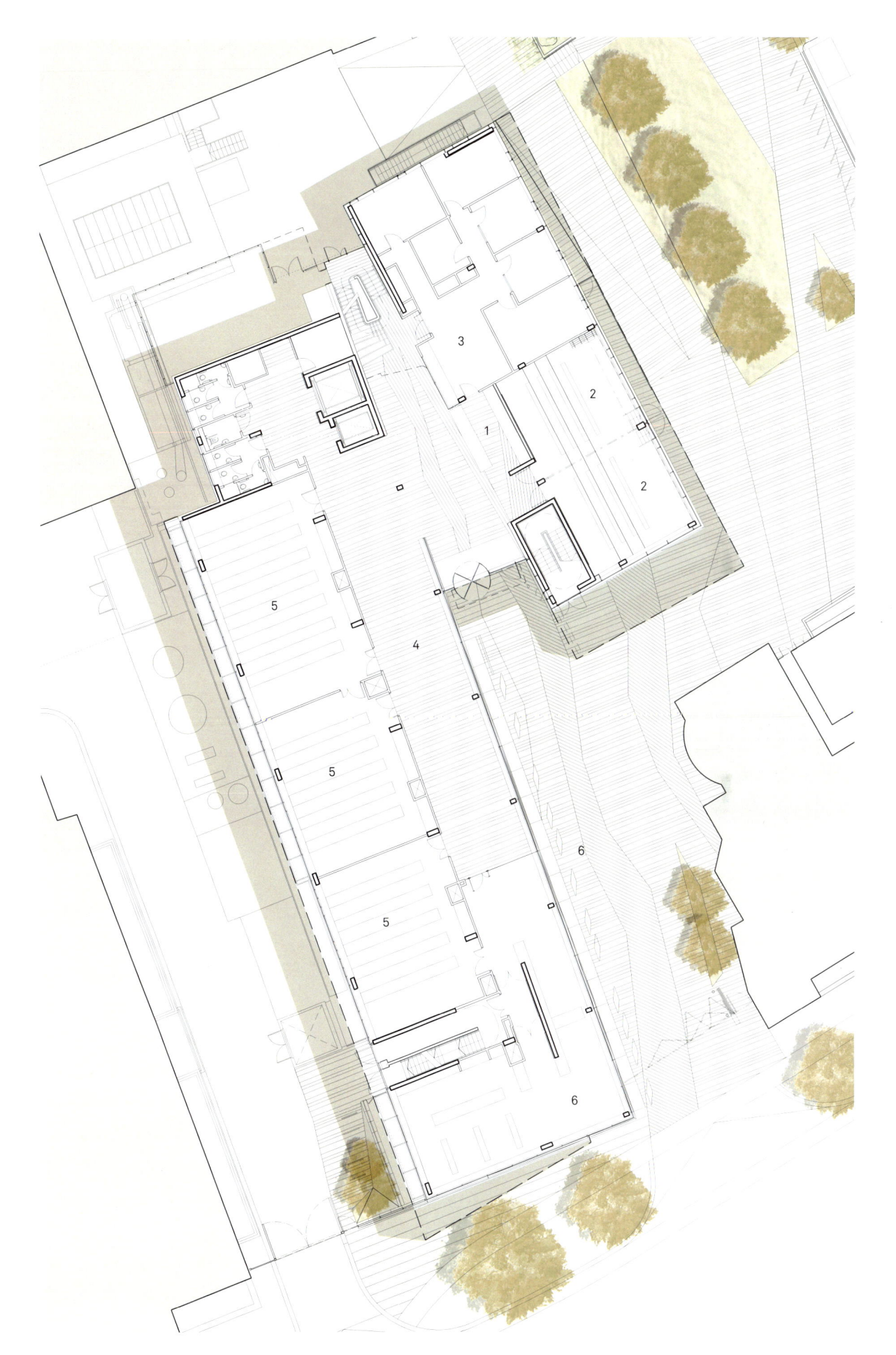

City | Department of Earth Sciences, Oxford, UK

Earth Sciences' first proper home was a purpose-built 1940s building adjacent to the Museum of Natural History, the collections of which provided much of the material required by the students for their studies. There, serendipitous encounters in the cramped warren of rooms and corridors created a strong sense of departmental belonging, as well as numerous chances for conversation. The new building is arranged around a soaring atrium to provide similar opportunities for interaction.

Level five plan
1 Senior common room
2 External terrace
3 Plant
4 Green roof

Level two plan
1 Academic offices
2 Postgraduate research group
3 Mass spectrometry suite

Above the library and undergraduate lecture spaces on the ground floor, the laboratories provide the many highly specialist environments necessary for the department's research, particularly in the field of geochemistry. These environments include a suite of metal-free labs, the need for which is determined by the corrosive properties of the acid-rich air in such environments, and a field-free lab, designed to channel the external magnetic field around the outside of the space so that researchers can measure the very weak magnetic properties of natural materials otherwise affected by external forces.

Communal coffee breaks were a feature of life in the department's old building, and continue to be so in the new rooftop senior common room. The faculty's interdisciplinary nature is one of its most striking characteristics, with many advances in scientific research triggered by informal discussion among academics.

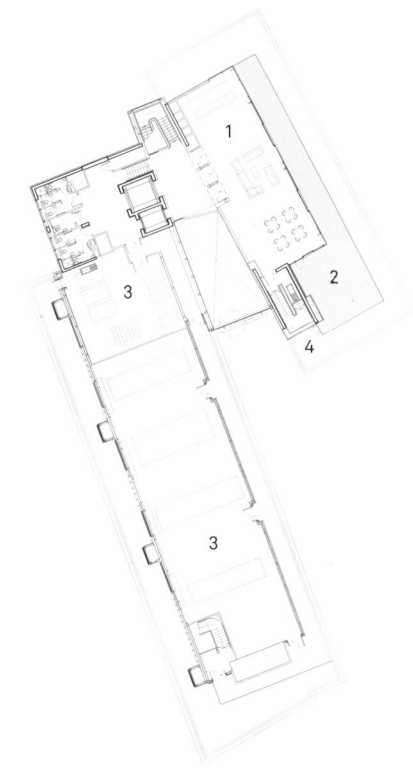

Level five plan

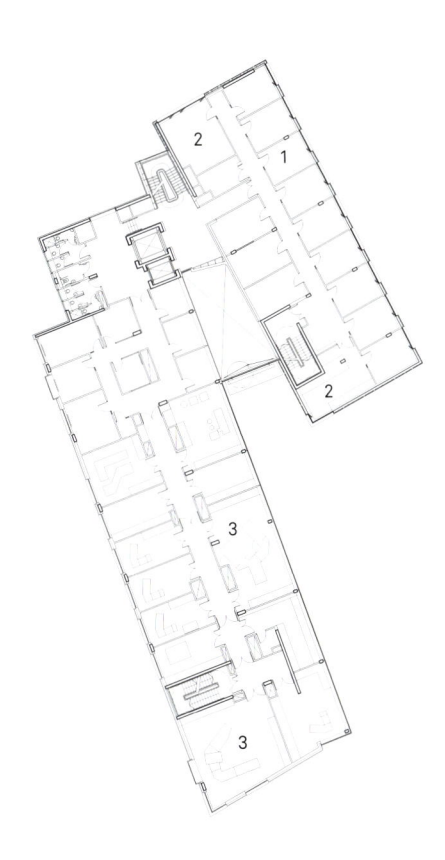

Level two plan

City | Department of Earth Sciences, Oxford, UK   215

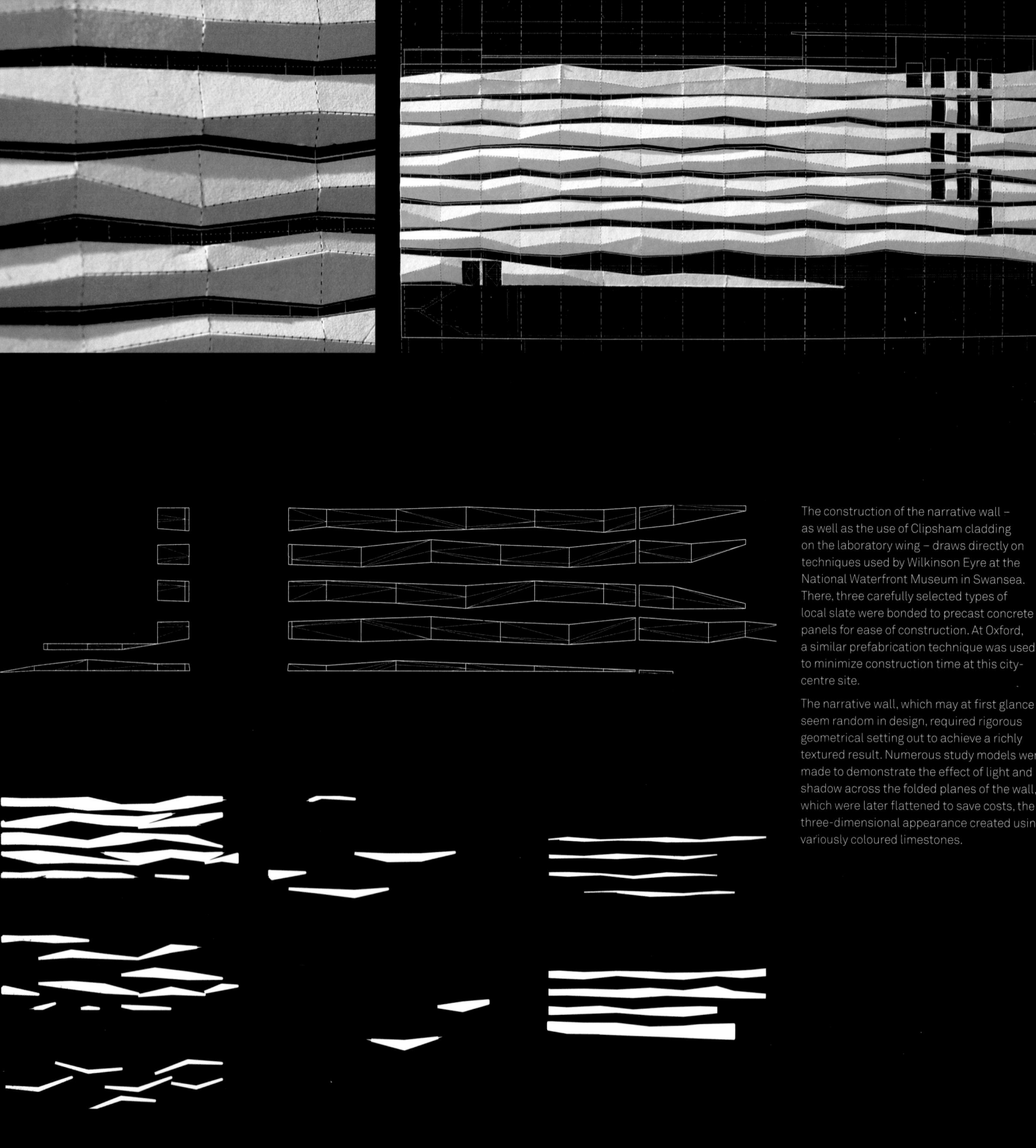

The construction of the narrative wall – as well as the use of Clipsham cladding on the laboratory wing – draws directly on techniques used by Wilkinson Eyre at the National Waterfront Museum in Swansea. There, three carefully selected types of local slate were bonded to precast concrete panels for ease of construction. At Oxford, a similar prefabrication technique was used to minimize construction time at this city-centre site.

The narrative wall, which may at first glance seem random in design, required rigorous geometrical setting out to achieve a richly textured result. Numerous study models were made to demonstrate the effect of light and shadow across the folded planes of the wall, which were later flattened to save costs, the three-dimensional appearance created using variously coloured limestones.

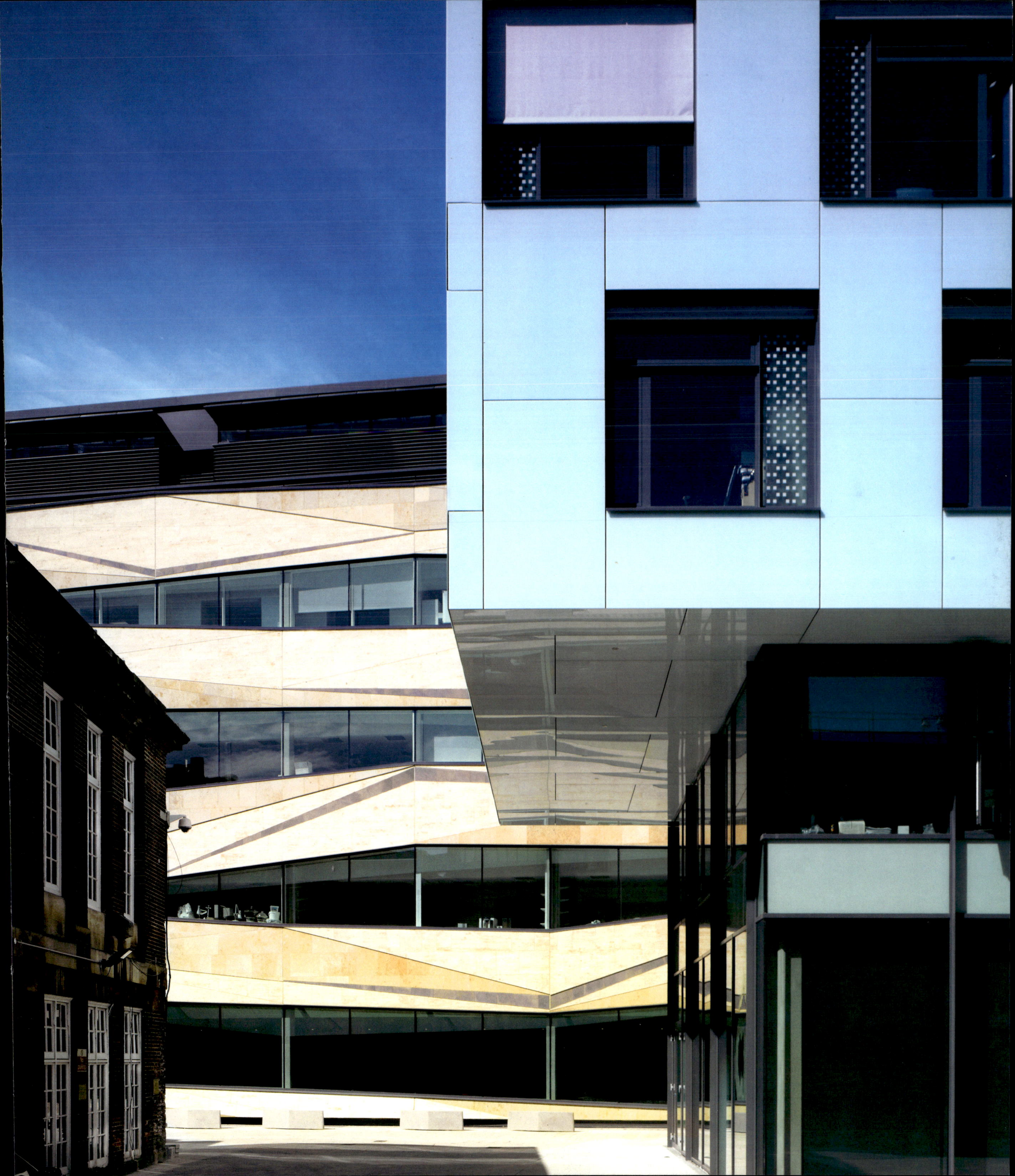

25 Great Pulteney Street
London, UK

Soho's dense grid of narrow streets and alleyways, much of it laid out during the seventeenth century, is intrinsic to the colourful character of this most central of London districts. Great Pulteney Street was developed as part of the Pulteney Estate during the early 1700s, and many of the original residences still survive as listed buildings amid a richly varied streetscape. Within this context, where space is limited and the urban fabric so sensitive, new-build offices are unusual, but attract high rents, demanding a considered architectural approach to balance the requirements of developers and conservationists.

The site at number 25 was bombed during the Second World War, and was subsequently occupied by a poor-quality 1960s building. This new office development therefore draws extensively on the proportion, rhythm and massing of the surrounding streetscape in order to form an appropriate bridge between the historic buildings of the street and more modern developments near by, although the building is uncompromisingly contemporary. The colour and materials palette is also inspired by the context. The green glass-accents on the front façade, for example, draw on the striking glazed-brick building on the corner of Beak Street, while the rear elevation is composed of an abstract arrangement of projecting window bays set within a white glazed-brick wall, a treatment used extensively on tiny Bridle Lane.

The organization of the seven-storey building is intended to avoid the sense of isolation created by typical sealed-box workplaces. The rear elevation features a series of stepped, curving terraces, which reduce the mass of the building and serve the floor spaces within. Increased glazing to the upper floors enables extensive views across the Soho roofscape. A delightful communal roof garden, mirroring the pockets of greenery found all over Soho, provides occupiers with a place to relax or work outdoors. Large windows punctuate the front façade, again creating a greater sense of connection with the life of the street. Although most of the building is intended for office use, an area suitable for B1C use (light industry) has been integrated into the ground and lower-ground floors. With a dedicated entrance and facilities, this space can work independently of the main building, and is intended to attract media occupiers, such as the many music- or film-production companies working within Soho's creative economy.

At pavement level, the building engages with the street through a public-art piece by Cinimod Studio. Titled *Finial Response*, the piece reinvents traditional street railings as an interactive installation. Covering 20 metres at street level, 109 black steel forms, echoing the ornamental finials found throughout the borough of Westminster, sandwich illuminated acrylic, the colour of which is modified by the interaction of passers-by. Anyone walking past the piece triggers a trail of white pools of light, which often results in a spontaneous response as the person realizes that their movement is the cause of this delicate rippling effect.

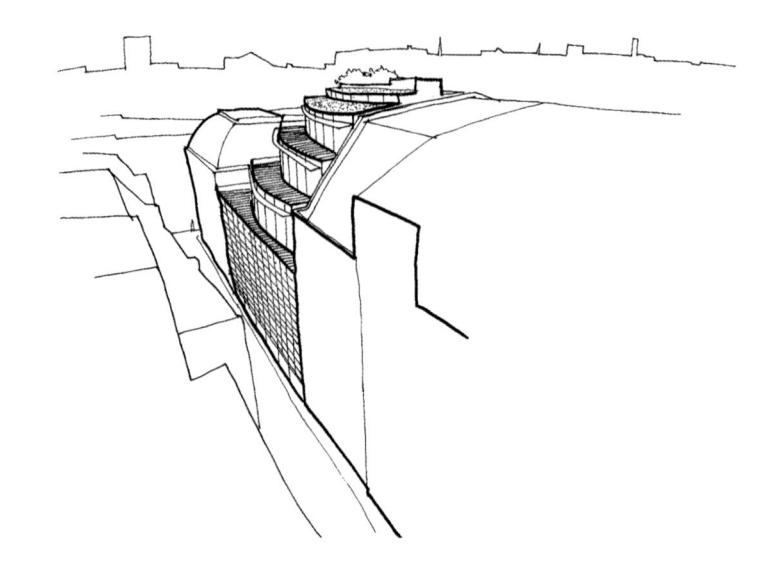

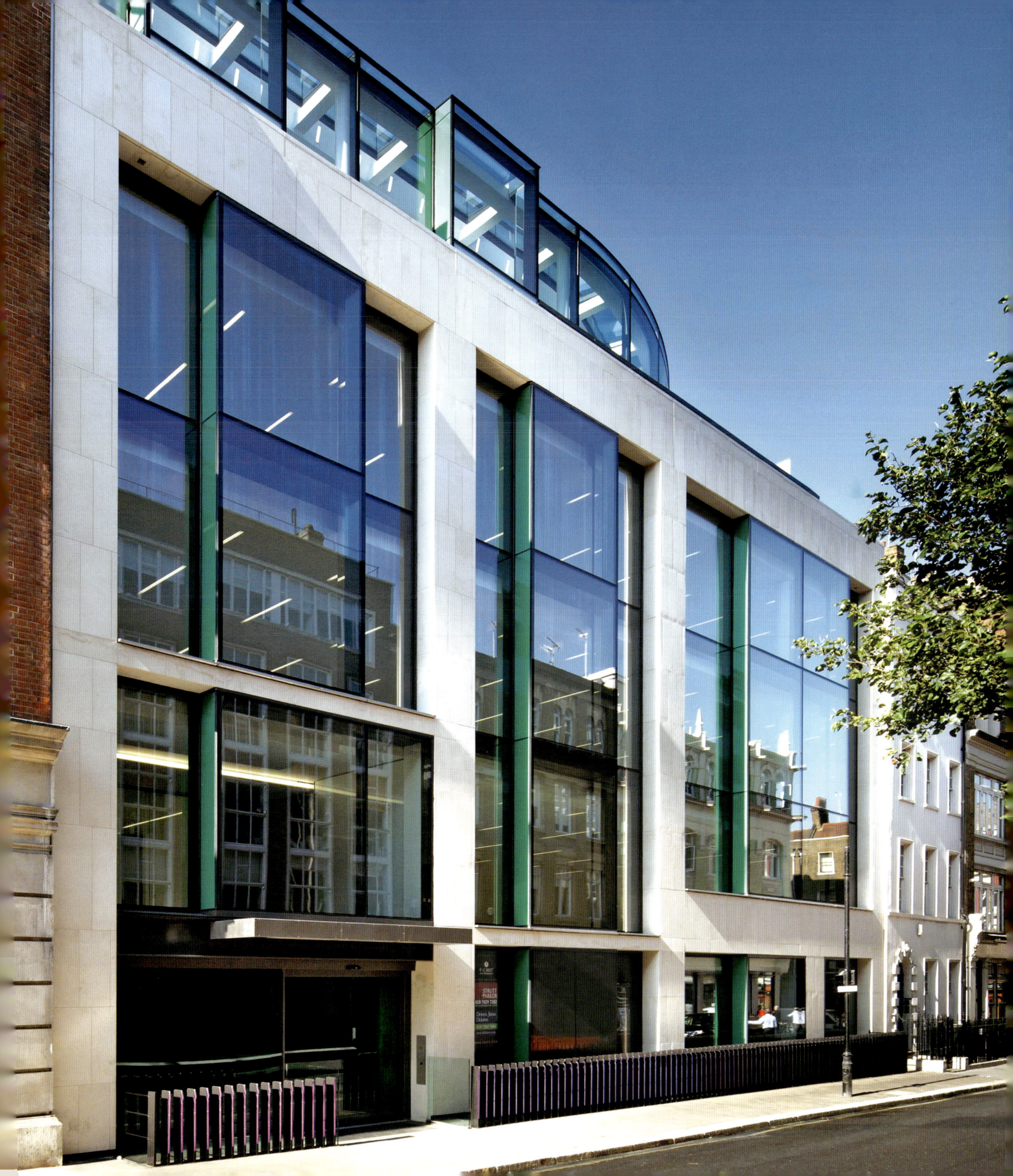

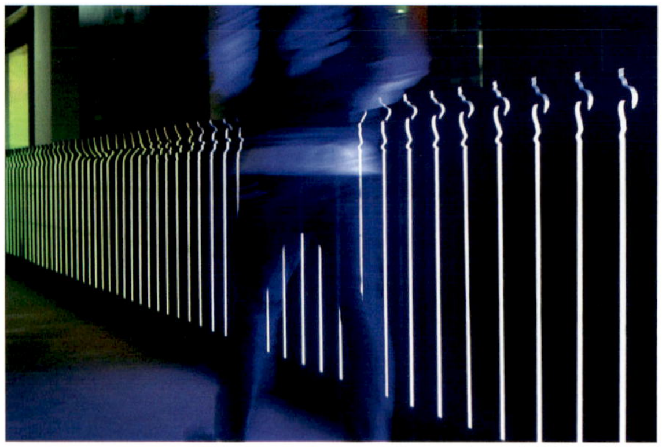

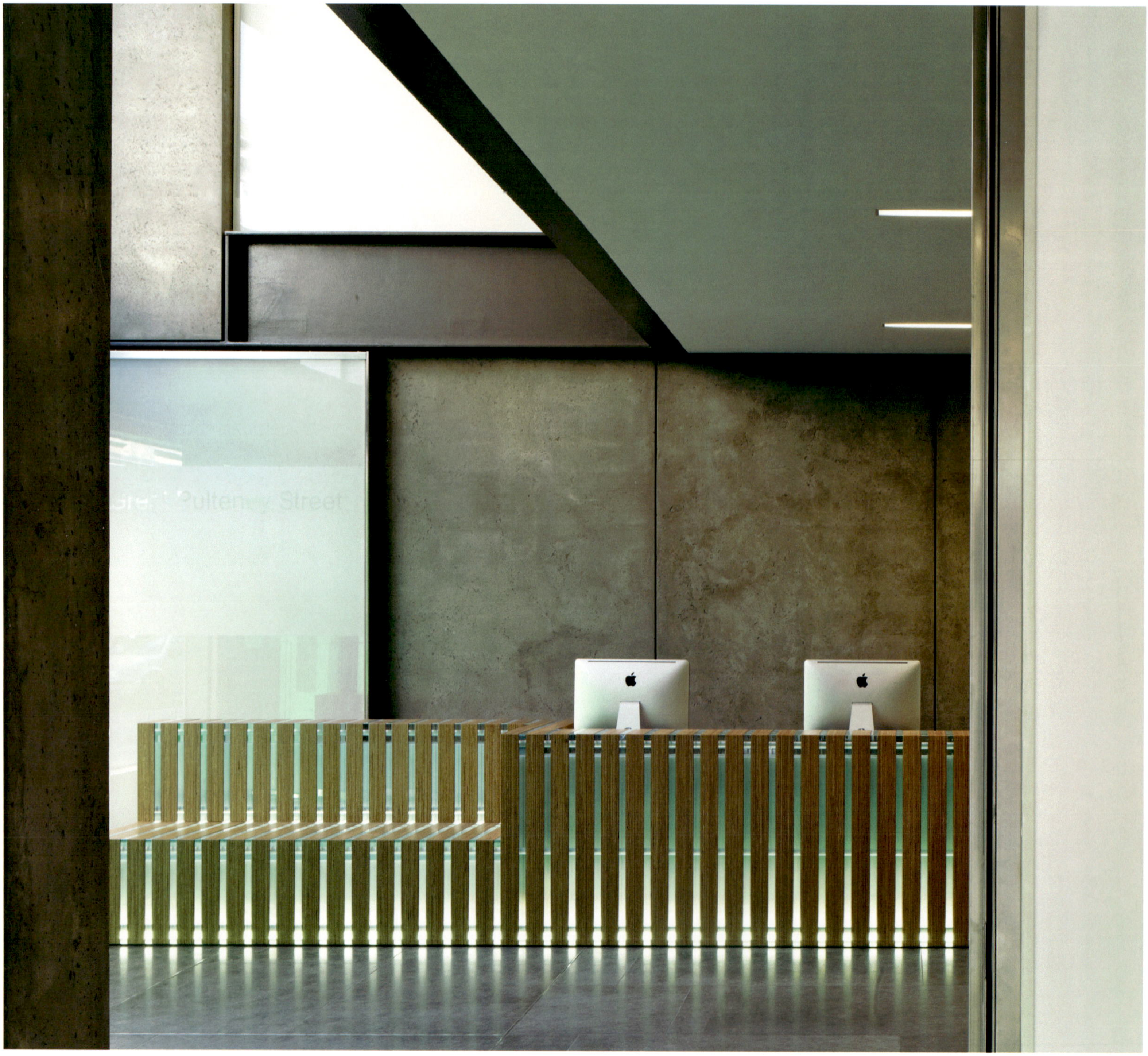

The varied materials palette selected for the building combines quality with an inherent durability. It includes white glazed brick, natural stone and highly finished concrete, as well as glass, stainless steel and bronze-coloured aluminium.

City | 25 Great Pulteney Street, London, UK

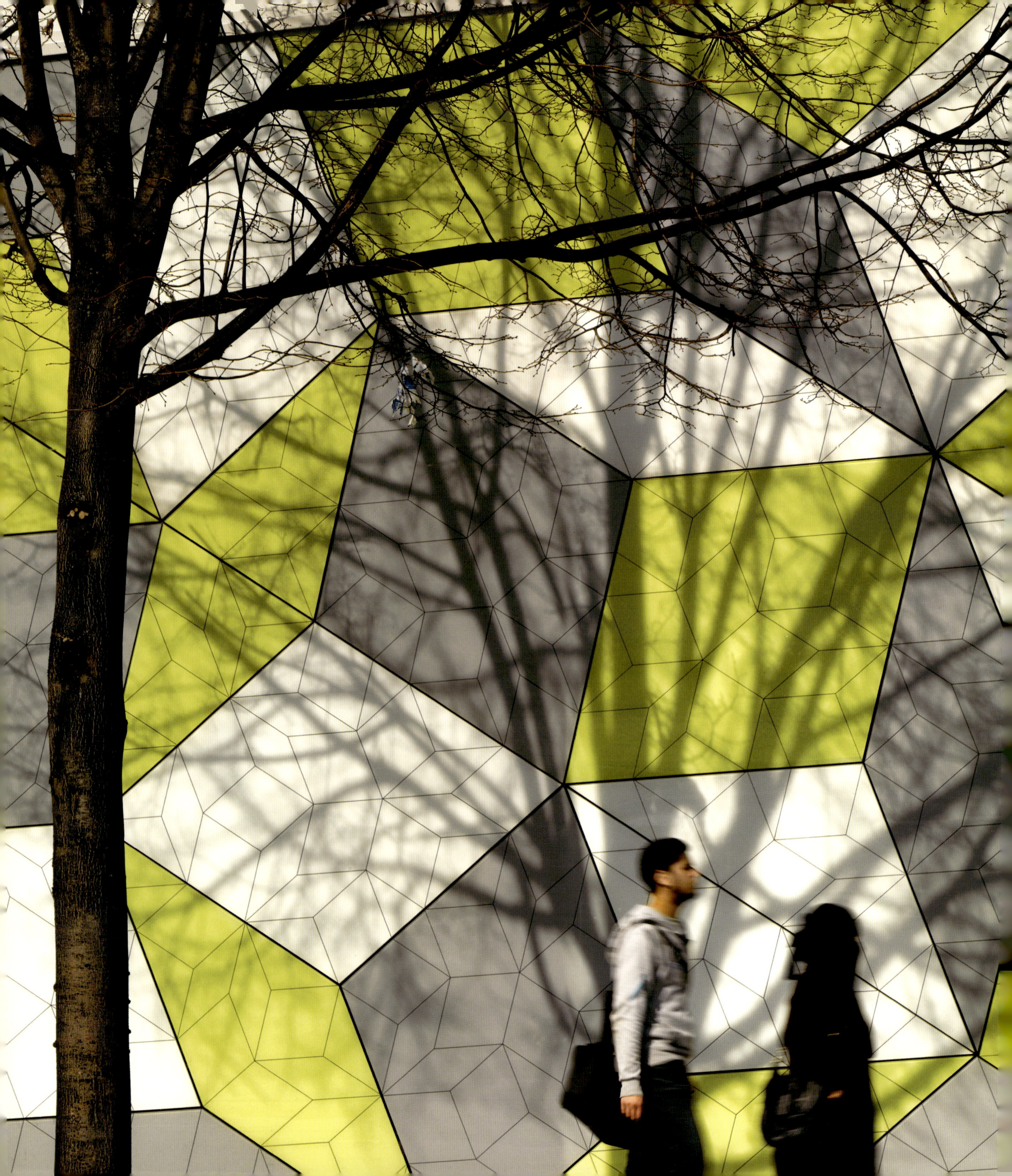

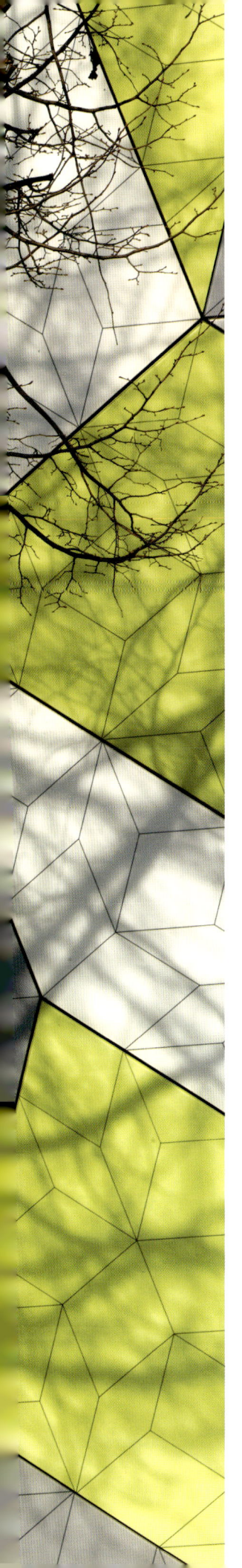

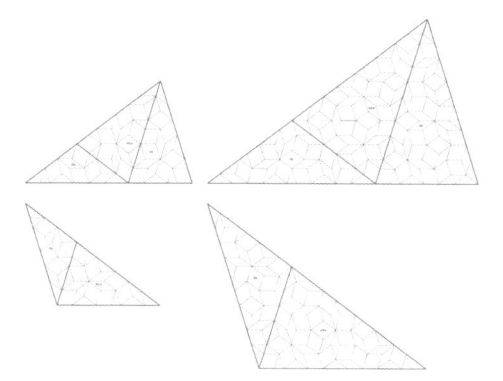

Queen Mary, University of London
UK

Queen Mary, University of London is a Russell Group university with a well-established research programme and many successful alumni. Although its principal campus has a formal presence on Mile End Road, and includes buildings from many different eras, it does not effectively signpost the university's identity on this otherwise rather dull arterial route into the City of London. As a consequence, fundamental to the brief for Wilkinson Eyre's recent buildings at Queen Mary was the need for greater expression within the wider cityscape, providing important visual markers for the aspirations of the university, as well as reinforcing the campus infrastructure.

Wilkinson Eyre has designed several buildings for the university – two of which are now complete – and these form part of an ongoing transformation of the campus intended to attract top students from the capital and further afield. The practice's first built commission is Arts Two, a 4,000-square-metre building that houses the highly regarded History Department, as well as mixed-use teaching areas for other humanities subjects and a 300-seat auditorium. The site was one of the few remaining development opportunities fronting on to Mile End Road, and the building plays with strong, distinctive colour, materials and transparency to catch the attention of passers-by and act as a shopfront for the university.

The different accommodation types are expressed as a series of interlocking elements within the enclosing rectangular form. The beech-clad drum of the auditorium – which is used for both public and university events – is visible through the glass windows that face on to the main road, while a double-height film and drama studio is articulated as a dramatic cantilevered glass box above. Featuring a graphic treatment by artist Jacqueline Poncelet, this volume has become an artwork in itself, with the glass cladding printed with piles of books to reflect the academic activity within.

The office and teaching accommodation is arranged according to a diagram that allows all the internal spaces to be naturally ventilated. The clever use of a glazed corridor adjacent to the busy street, protected by filigree shading, creates an environmental buffer zone to shield a bank of academic offices, which in turn face on to a tranquil internal courtyard. It is difficult to imagine the existence of this secret garden – which provides staff with a highly restful working environment – so close to the noise and pollution of the road outside. The main entrance is on the northern side of the building, facing into the main campus. Here, there is a Jewish cemetery dating from 1733, which is still consecrated. Sensitive landscaping by the architect Seth Stein helps to mediate between the two, with the listed perimeter wall of the cemetery continuing to run right through the new building.

A little further west along the Mile End Road, a new foyer and entrance building for the university's School of Mathematical Sciences makes a similarly strong impact on this undistinguished urban street with a distinctive piece of sculptural geometry, reflecting brief and subject matter through its architectural concept. Although small, the bold intervention gives the school a renewed visual profile and makes a strong statement about its relative importance within the wider campus. The single-storey structure wraps around the foot of a 1960s tower, the horizontality of its folded planes contrasting with the vertical emphasis and proportions of the existing building. It is clad in glass that has been screen-printed with a Penrose tiling pattern; Sir Roger Penrose is visiting professor to the school, and willingly gave permission for his innovative mathematical pattern to be used on the new building. The complex internal spaces created within the angular form have large areas of glazing and strong colour, which provide a fitting place for creative thought and the exchange of ideas between students and academic staff.

The collaboration between Wilkinson Eyre and the university has continued, and in 2012 work began on a new Graduate Centre.

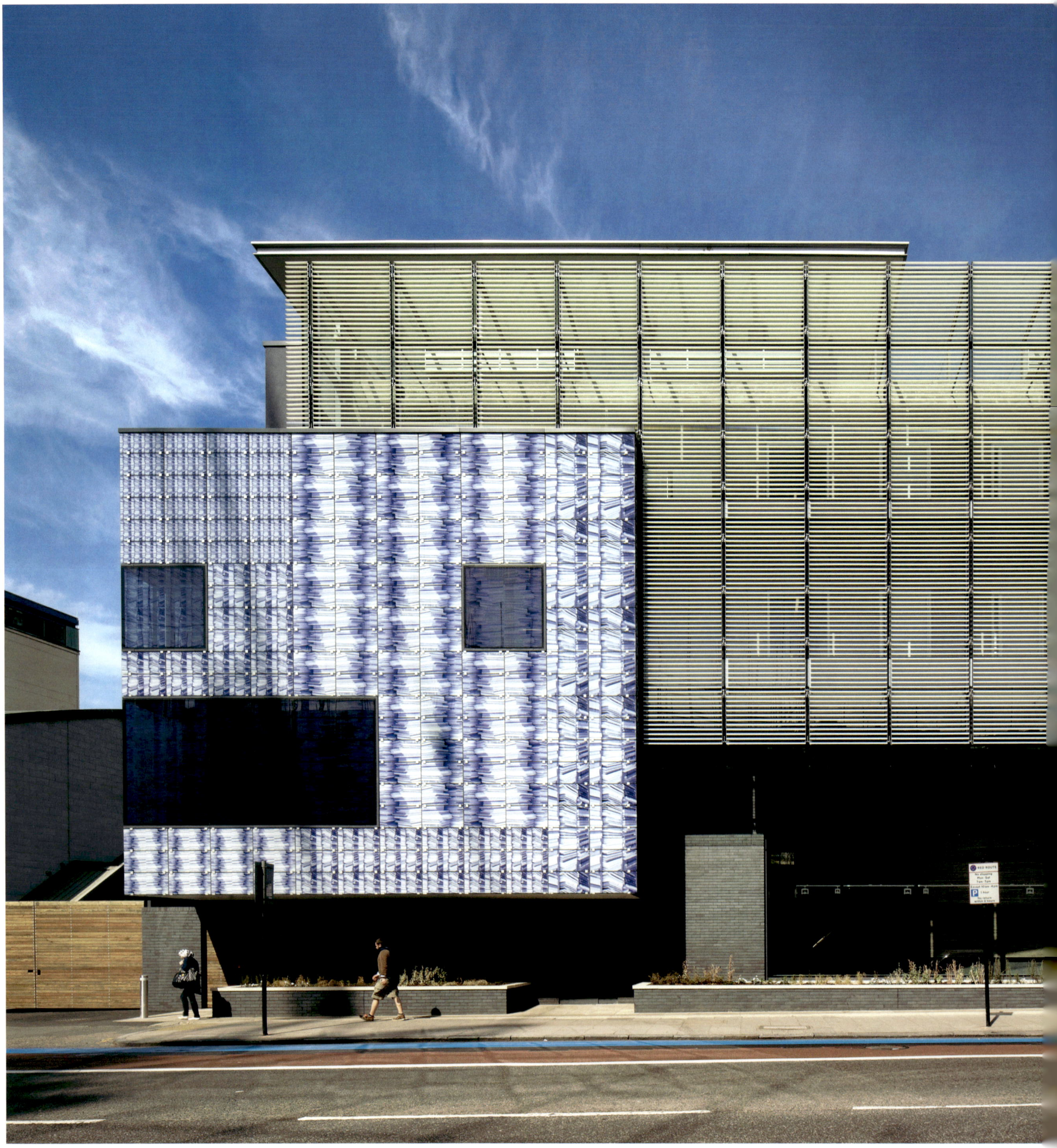
RED ROUTE

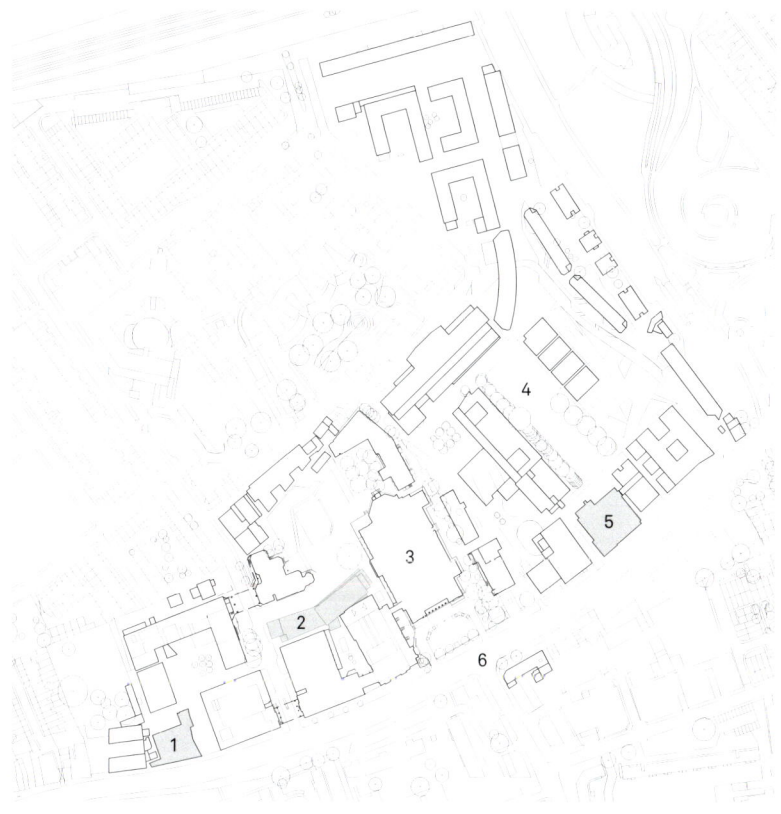

Campus plan

1   Mathematical Sciences
2   Graduate Centre
3   Queens' Building
4   Nuevo Jewish Cemetery
5   Arts Two
6   Mile End Road

Mile End Road forms the southern boundary to the Queen Mary campus. For security reasons, and to engender a sense of connectivity and enclosure within the site, most of the main departmental entrances are accessed from inside the campus, rather than directly from the street. Wilkinson Eyre's Arts Two building balances this need for a secure entrance with a requirement to raise the university's profile on the main street frontage.

This is achieved in part through a large-scale artwork by the artist Jacqueline Poncelet, who developed the graphic treatment for the projecting volume of the film and drama studio. Piles of books, repeated in tones of blue and multiplied to create textured patterns, have been digitally printed on to the glass tiles that clad the façade, symbolizing the gathering, storing and sharing of knowledge across the humanities.

It was something of a logistical challenge to maintain the effect of a shopfront on Mile End Road, given that the main entrance was located on the other, northern side of the building. The differing characters of each façade were addressed with a change of scale and materials. A carefully detailed timber staircase rises up the height of the building, and is showcased in a crisp glass enclosure. This identifies the main circulation, with the lifts behind. These open on to interconnecting layers of breakout areas, which serve the auditorium and act as a gathering space for students using both it and the seminar and teaching spaces above.

Ground-source energy loops beneath the building provide it with 10 per cent of its total energy requirements, in line with the Greater London Authority's guidelines regarding on-site renewable-energy generation. All south-facing accommodation is protected from solar gain by external sunshading. A double-height corridor around the academic offices acts as an environmental and acoustic buffer zone, as well as a solar chimney to draw heat up and out of the building via a stack effect. The offices face on to the internal courtyard, and are naturally ventilated.

The proximity of the Mile End Road was a critical factor in the development of the building's acoustic strategy too, with the structure built on anti-vibration pads to reduce rumble from the road and the Underground line beneath. Displacement ventilation was used in the lecture theatre, and chilled beams in the upper-floor teaching areas, which cannot be naturally ventilated because of the road noise.

Environmental section

1. Mile End Road
2. Corridor/environmental buffer zone
3. Naturally ventilated academic offices
4. Auditorium
5. Underground line
6. Anti-vibration mounts on pile caps
7. Ground-source energy loops

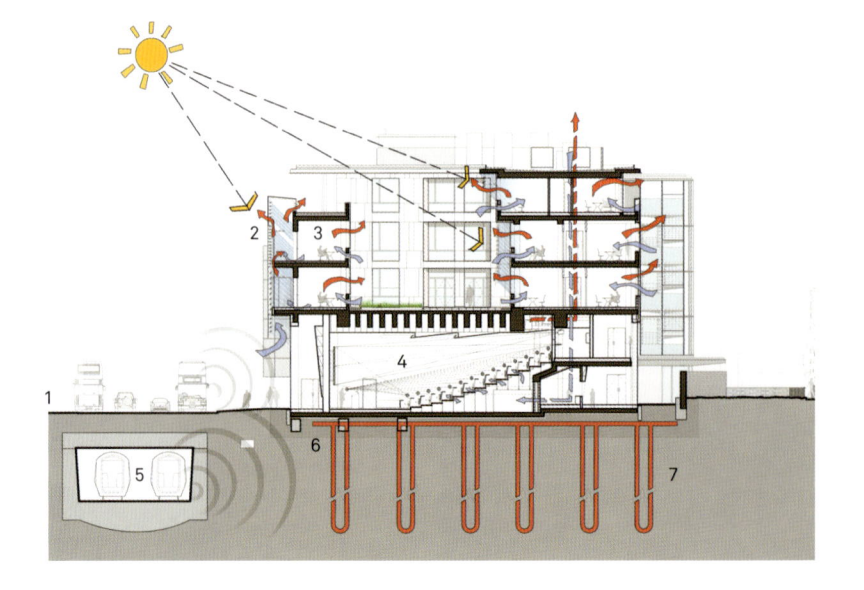

Second-floor plan

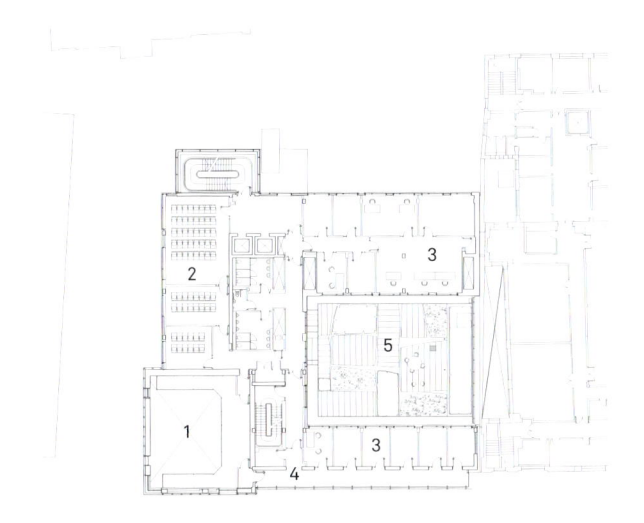

First-floor plan

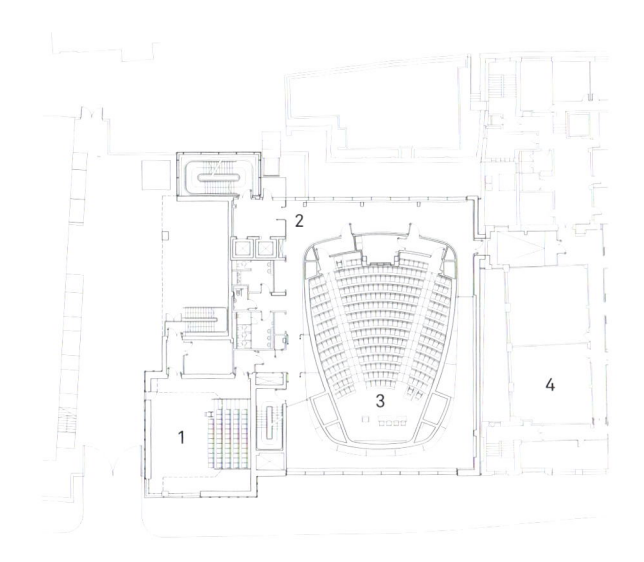

Second-floor plan

1 Film and drama studio
2 Small lecture and seminar rooms
3 Academic offices
4 Corridor/environmental buffer zone
5 Internal courtyard

First-floor plan

1 Film and drama studio
2 Breakout and circulation space
3 Auditorium
4 Laws Building

City | Queen Mary, University of London, UK

Ground floor

> Entrance
1 Lobby
2 New foyer, social study space and waiting area
3 Existing lecture centre
4 External covered platform lift

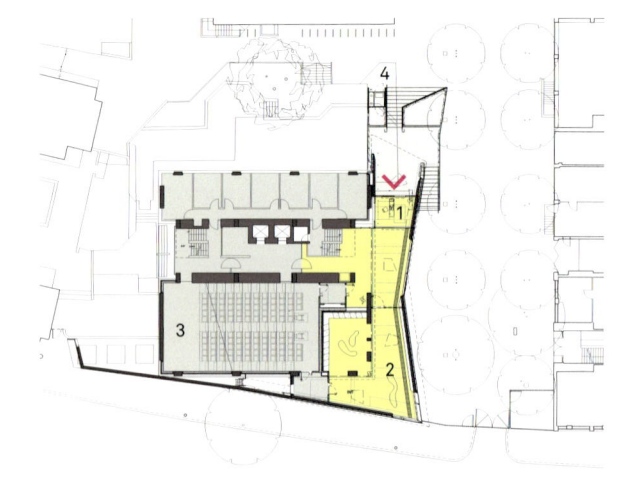

The cladding for the extension to the School of Mathematical Sciences was inspired by the work of the department, where Sir Roger Penrose is a visiting professor. The design is a Penrose tiling pattern, featuring a combination of repeated elements (for ease of manufacture) and a non-repeating, aperiodic pattern to add visual complexity.

City | Queen Mary, University of London, UK

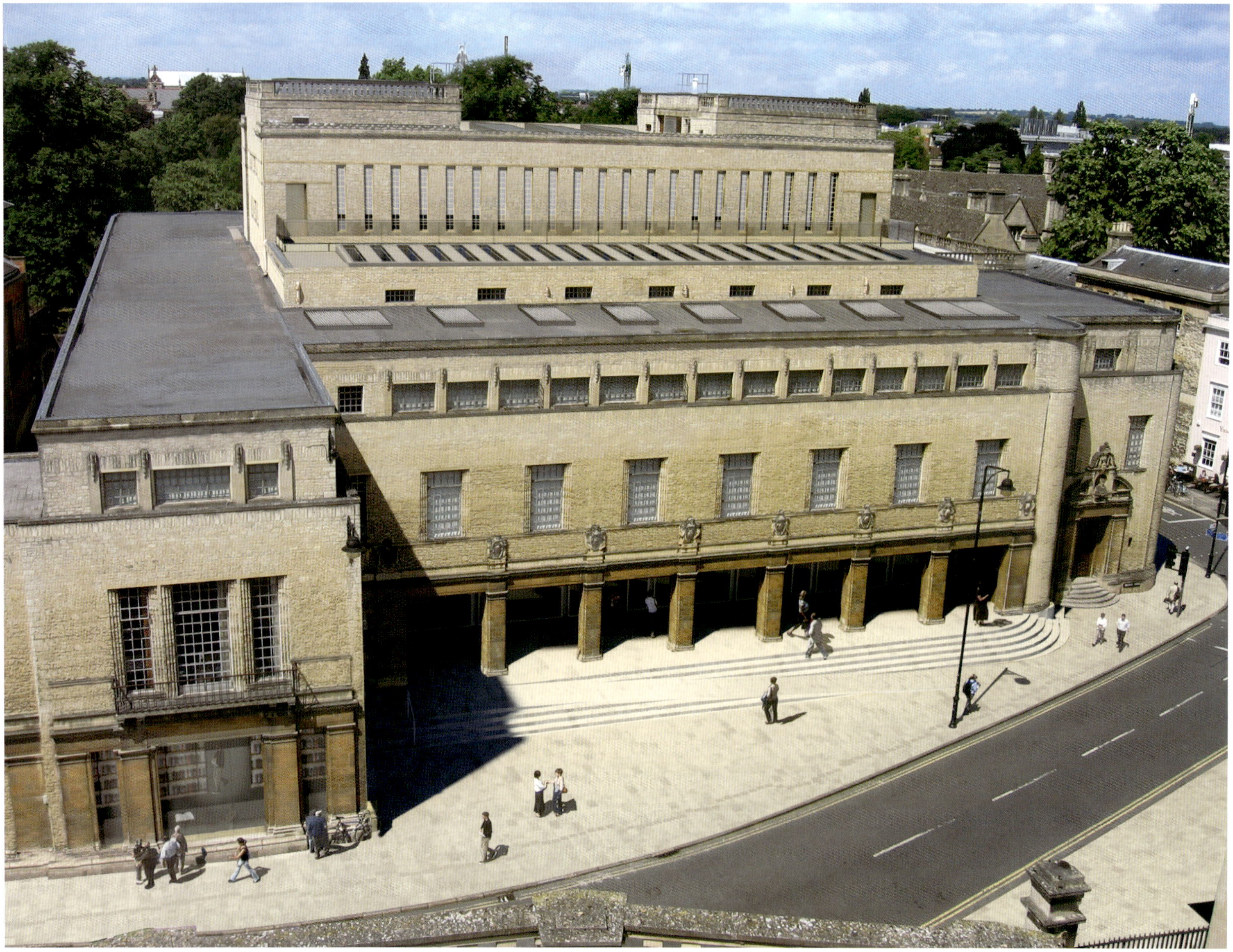

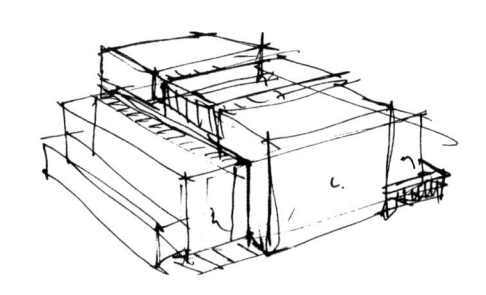

New Bodleian (Weston) Library
Oxford, UK

The Bodleian Library at the University of Oxford is among the oldest and most important research libraries in the world, and has custodianship of more than 11 million items. It occupies a series of buildings in the historic heart of the university, the most famous of which is the circular Radcliffe Camera, built in the nineteenth century and now used almost exclusively as a reading room. The dramatic urban set piece of Radcliffe Camera, Old Schools Quadrangle, Nicholas Hawksmoor's Clarendon Building and Sir Christopher Wren's Sheldonian Theatre establishes a sequence of spaces leading towards the newest of the library's central-Oxford locations: the Grade II-listed New Bodleian building, designed by Sir Giles Gilbert Scott in the 1930s and located on the north side of Broad Street.

Scott's New Bodleian was never intended as a public building; rather, it was essentially a storage facility, focused entirely on the bookstack and its contents, and linked by underground delivery passages to reading rooms elsewhere. The library's unrivalled collection of treasures – from Jane Austen manuscripts to a Gutenberg Bible, and from the first Penguin paperbacks to fragments of classical poetry on papyrus – outgrew the bookstack space, which itself no longer offered sufficient fire protection, environmental control or ease of access and distribution.

In 2010 the university opened a new storage facility at South Marston near Swindon. The high-density facility contains 8 million books, and functions rather like a delivery depot or dispatch house, able to process 2,500 volumes a day by delivering them either in physical form to researchers and readers, or in scanned format to their desktop. With some of the bookstack space at the New Bodleian freed up as a consequence, the project to transform the building – renamed the Weston Library for its donors in 2009 – has brought together the special collections remaining on site with conservation and research facilities, publicly accessible exhibition spaces and a new internal court. This has opened the building up, revealing more of its treasures and generating greater visibility and understanding among the public; it also represents a response to the changing role of the library against a background of increasing digitization.

The project has updated the building without compromising its historic, richly detailed character. Internally, Scott's original building followed the template of the Oxford quadrangle – albeit inverted so that the central 'quad' was fully occupied by the bookstack. This volume, the beating heart of the building, is now celebrated with a horizontal space at ground level: as visitors enter, the bookstack appears to float above them. The building's quadrangle character is vital to its architectural legibility, and this is maintained through the voids that have been opened up to frame the central bookstack volume. On the lower floors, the spaces around the perimeter of the stack have been refurbished – with special attention given to the many heritage features still intact – to provide special exhibition galleries, reading rooms, seminar and research facilities, and areas for conservation and curatorial activities. Above, there is an open-access book gallery in the upper stack, a visiting-scholars' centre and a new reading room with extraordinary views across the city.

Although individual reading chairs were not introduced until the eighteenth century, specialist furniture for reading and studying has long been an integral part of the design of the Bodleian libraries. Scott's New Bodleian, however, was the first to be created as a *Gesamtkunstwerk*, or 'total work of art', with the furniture forming part of his commission. Continuing this tradition, a competition was held in 2013 to design a new reader's chair. The competition was won by the design studio Barber Osgerby, which, in collaboration with the manufacturer Isokon, has developed a timber chair with a simple straight back and a continuously curving arm and bottom rail, which enclose and cradle the researcher at work.

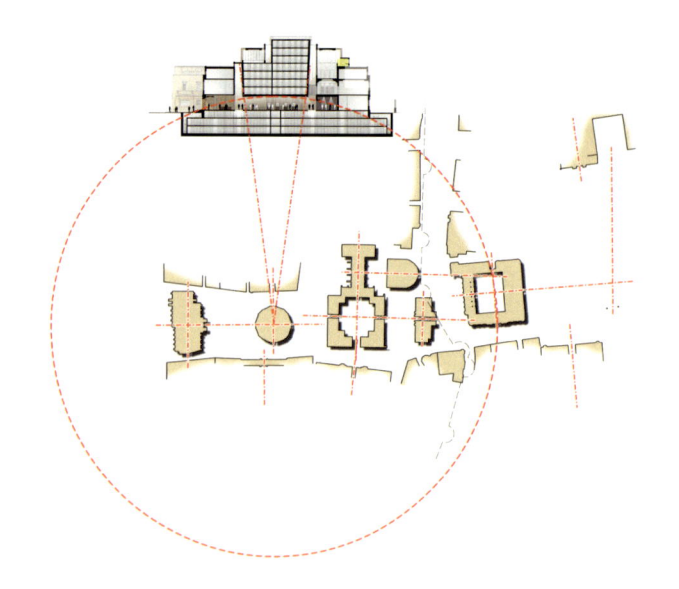

While the project was strongly focused on improving storage and research facilities inside the building, it also provided an opportunity to enhance the library's relationship with its urban setting by addressing Broad Street and the main Bodleian Library building opposite. The design knits the library more closely into its context by extending the axis created by Radcliffe Camera, Old Schools Quadrangle and the Clarendon Building, a logical move designed to encourage the public inside.

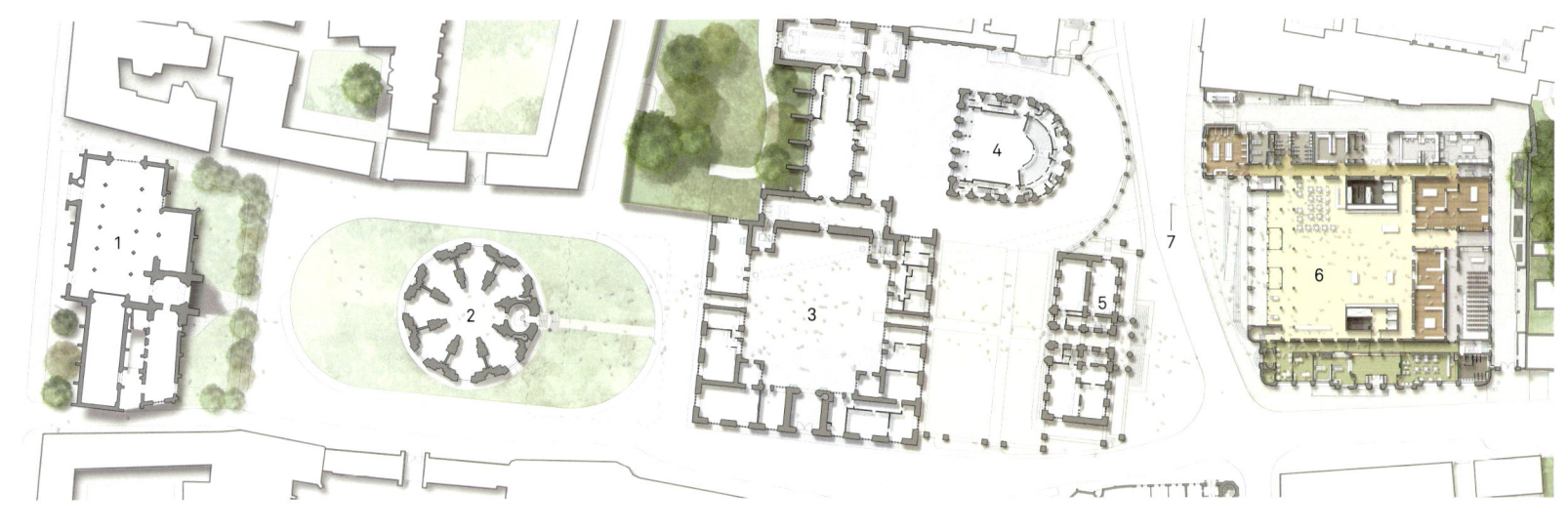

Site plan/site section
1. University Church of St Mary the Virgin
2. Radcliffe Camera
3. Old Schools Quadrangle
4. Sheldonian Theatre
5. Clarendon Building
6. New Bodleian (Weston) Library
7. Underground tunnel between New Bodleian and Gladstone Link

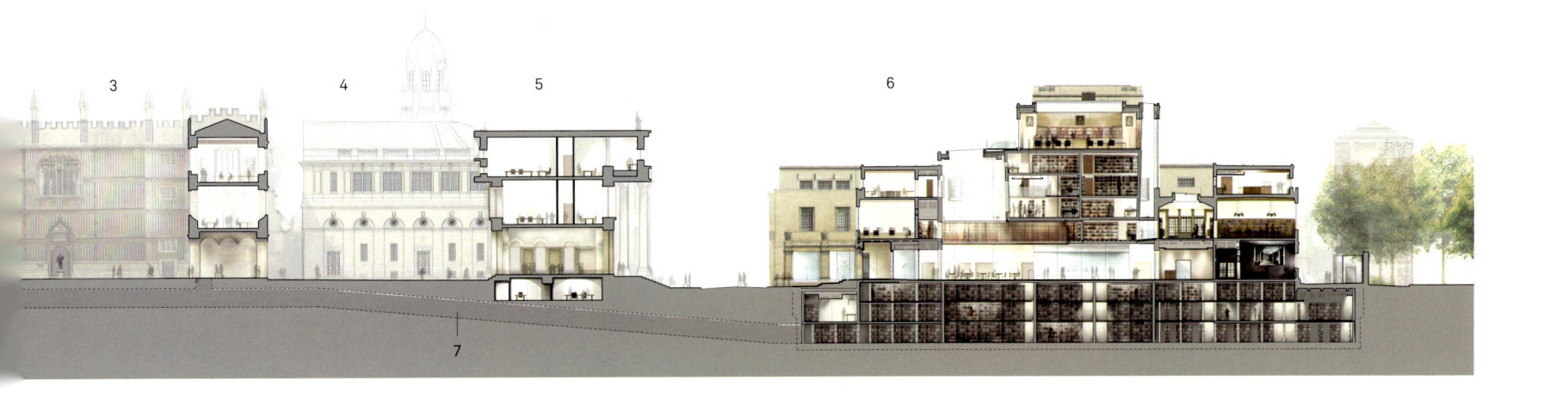

City | New Bodleian (Weston) Library, Oxford, UK

The existing windows and panels between the pilasters were removed to create a new entrance colonnade, while the plinth was taken away and replaced with steps and an integrated ramp. The colonnade leads directly into the new ground-floor entrance hall under the 'floating' bookstack.

The original eleven-storey central bookstack has been removed, and a new basement stack, entrance hall and high-level central stack constructed in its place. This continues the complex interplay of void and volume present in Scott's original building.

Section

1 Image studio
2 Reading room
3 Offices and seminar rooms
4 Public entrance from colonnade
5 Foyer (book gallery above)
6 Rooftop reading room
7 Special research suite
8 Bookstack
9 Exhibition space

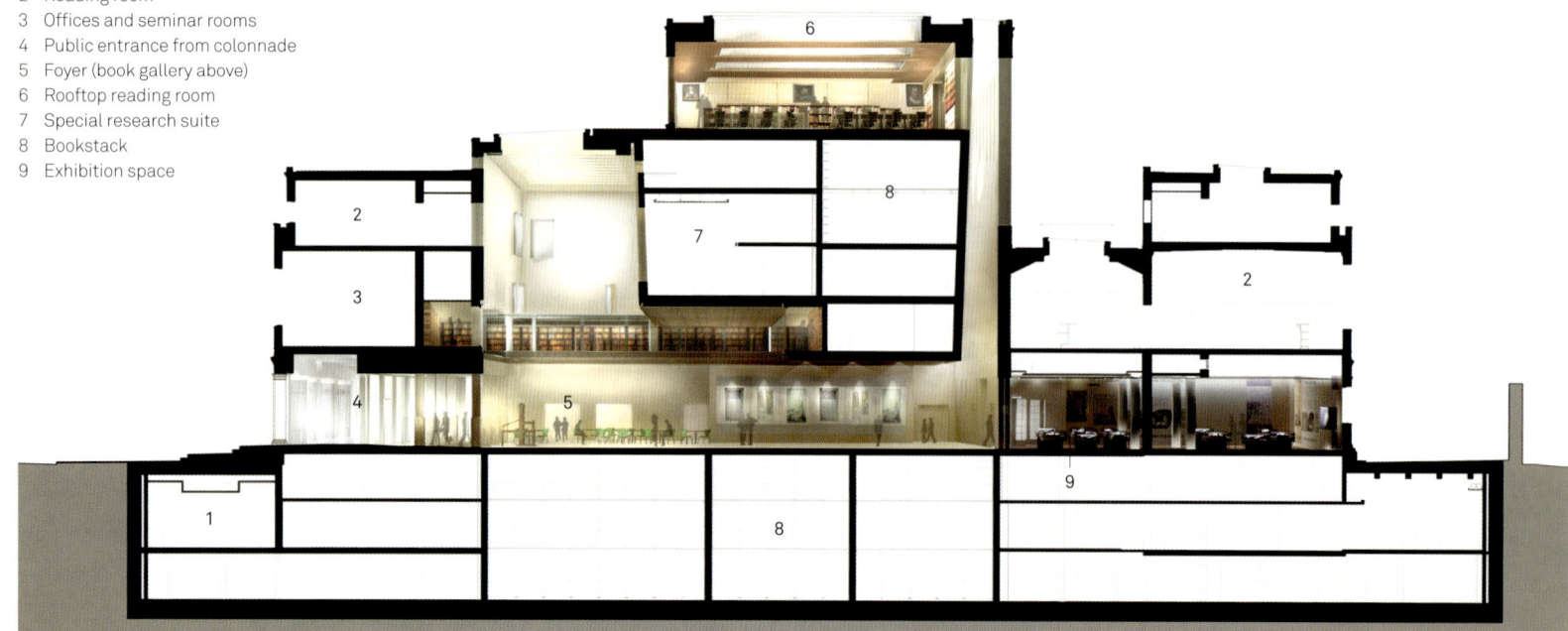

Inside the building, a careful hierarchy has been established to allow the public entrance and exhibition spaces to exist alongside more private areas for research and reading. Scott's original wall to the south bookstack, which was previously hidden from view, has been rebuilt to form the wall of a new rooftop reading room. This sits within the tower of the upper stack, and has views out across the city.

Ground-floor plan

1. Blackwell Hall
2. Shop
3. Temporary exhibitions
4. Treasures Gallery
5. Auditorium
6. Admissions and readers' access

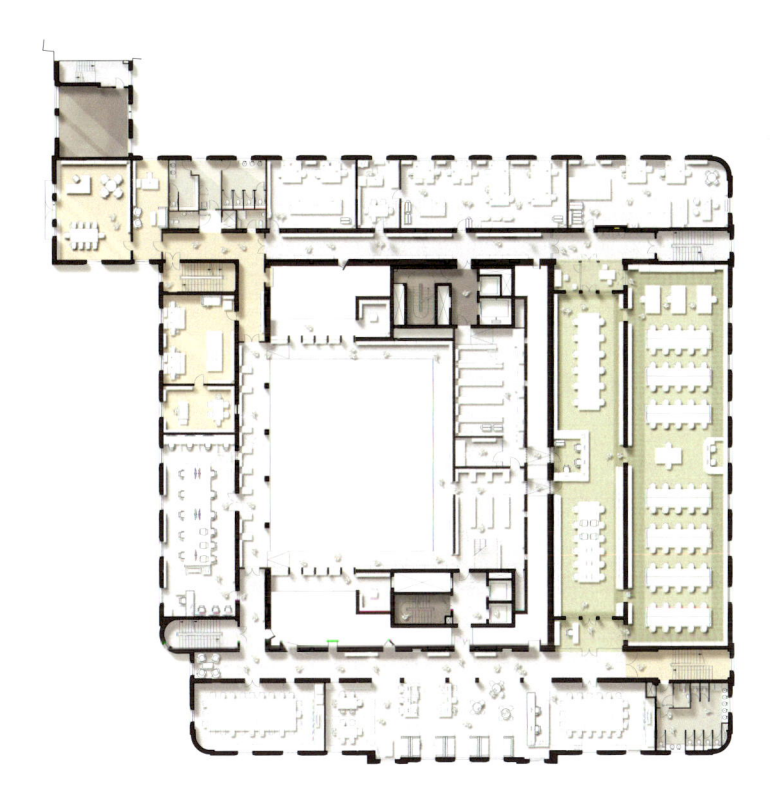

First-floor plan (Level F)

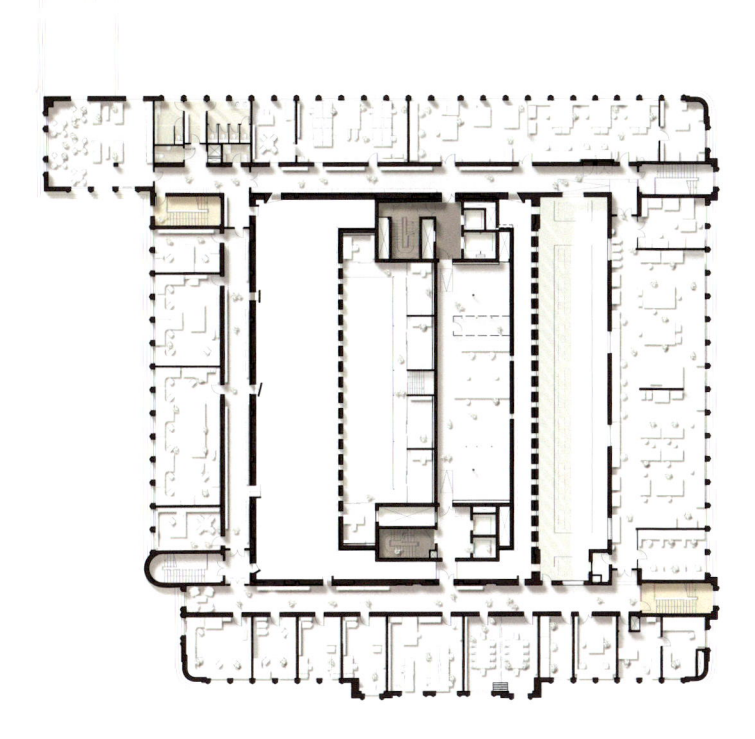

Second-floor plan (Level D)

City | New Bodleian (Weston) Library, Oxford, UK

The south façade of the building has been opened up to establish a new relationship with the Clarendon Building and Wren's Sheldonian Theatre on the far side of Broad Street.

City | New Bodleian (Weston) Library, Oxford, UK

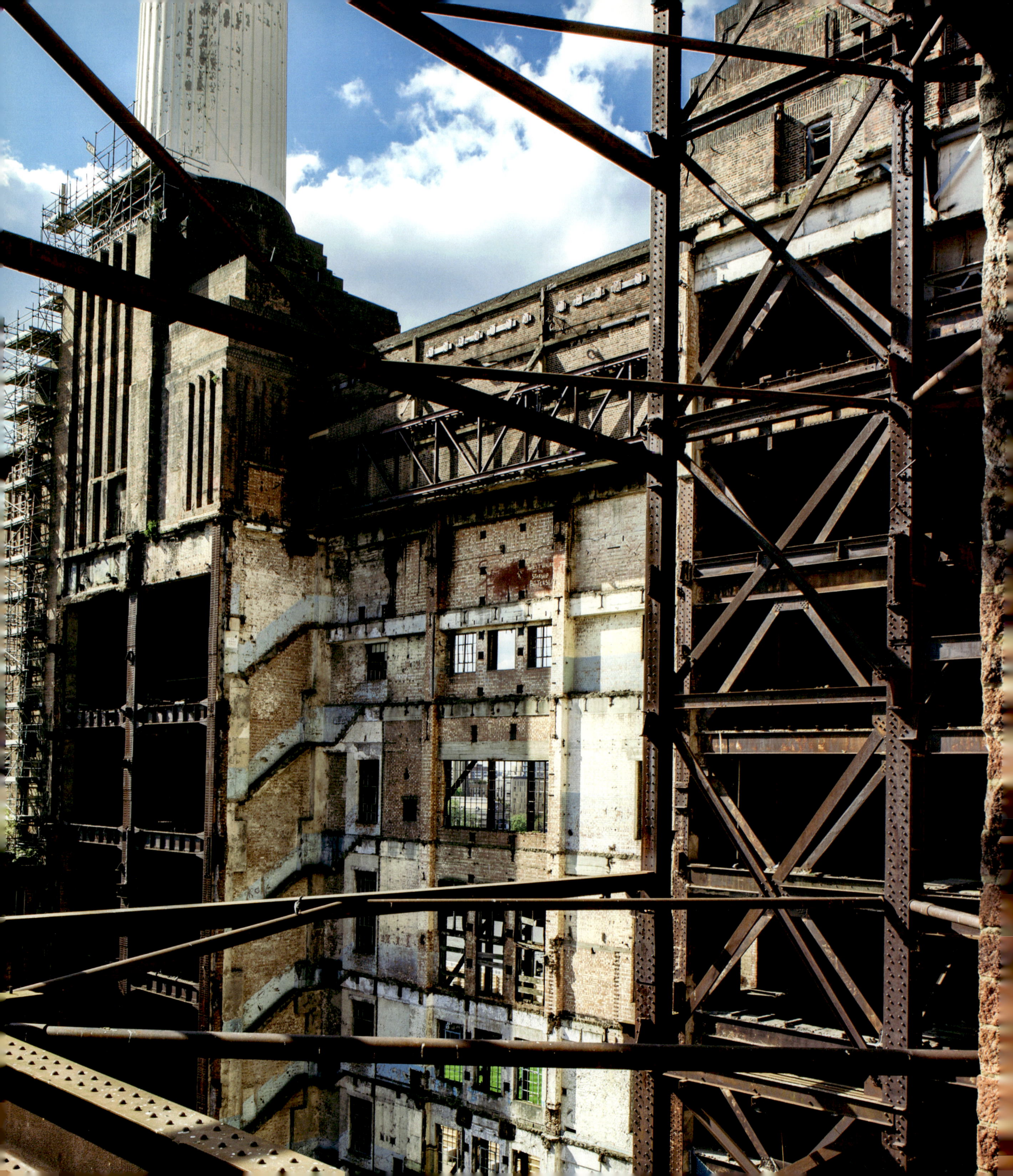

Battersea Power Station
London, UK

Sir Giles Gilbert Scott's Battersea Power Station predates his New Bodleian Library (page 231), but features the same dramatic brick mass and symmetry, finished with elegantly proportioned details. The power station was built in phases, first as one cathedral-like turbine hall running between a single pair of chimneys and their respective wash towers, with half of the final boiler house berthed alongside. A second, counterpart turbine hall was built later and linked to the original to give the distinctive four-stacked form immortalized on album covers and in feature films. Since it stopped generating electricity in 1983, the Grade II*-listed building has been subject to a series of stalled attempts at renewal; a new masterplan by Rafael Viñoly, however, has reframed it as part of a wider neighbourhood. The new neighbourhood will have improved infrastructure in the form of an extension to the Underground's Northern line, and will connect the Battersea site with nearby developments at Nine Elms, including a new US Embassy building and a revamped New Covent Garden Market. Within this masterplan context, Wilkinson Eyre is responsible for the reworking of the power station itself.

Underpinning the design is the need to preserve Scott's legacy and the unique architectural vocabulary of the site: cavernous turbine halls, soaring window lights, massive brick façades and some exquisite Art Deco interiors. The vast building – the largest brick structure in Europe – will accommodate a wide mixture of uses. Three levels of retail space will run between the two turbine halls and through the central boiler house. Over the retail space, the two existing lower-level annexes that sit to the east and west of the building will be refurbished and extended to provide residential accommodation; in between these annexes will be a triple-height leisure area with event space, cinema and hotel. Above this, six storeys of office space will be topped with a series of residential villas around a new high-level garden square, framed by the four iconic chimneys.

The new interventions respond to, and are inspired by, the rhythm, style and quality of the original power station. The spectacular voids formed by the two turbine halls will be retained as a constant reminder of the building's industrial heritage, with circulation and connections provided by means of lightweight bridge structures. New volumes, such as the floating 'folly' proposed for Turbine Hall A, will be created within the voids to emphasize the sheer scale of the space. As many of the original surface treatments – ceramic glazed tiles, brick and metal – will be kept as possible, their patina contrasting with the contemporary materials of the new interventions. Other areas, such as Control Room A – a rare example of a complete Art Deco interior – will be treated to a straightforward restoration to preserve their unique historic character for new uses.

The powerful near-symmetry of the building has informed the design of the main access route from the new Tube station, a curving high street that will culminate in a two-level public square in front of the south façade of the power station. A new 2.5-hectare riverside park to the north will open up 400 metres of hitherto unused Thames waterfront, creating a landscaped setting for the building when viewed from the river.

Site plan (ground floor)

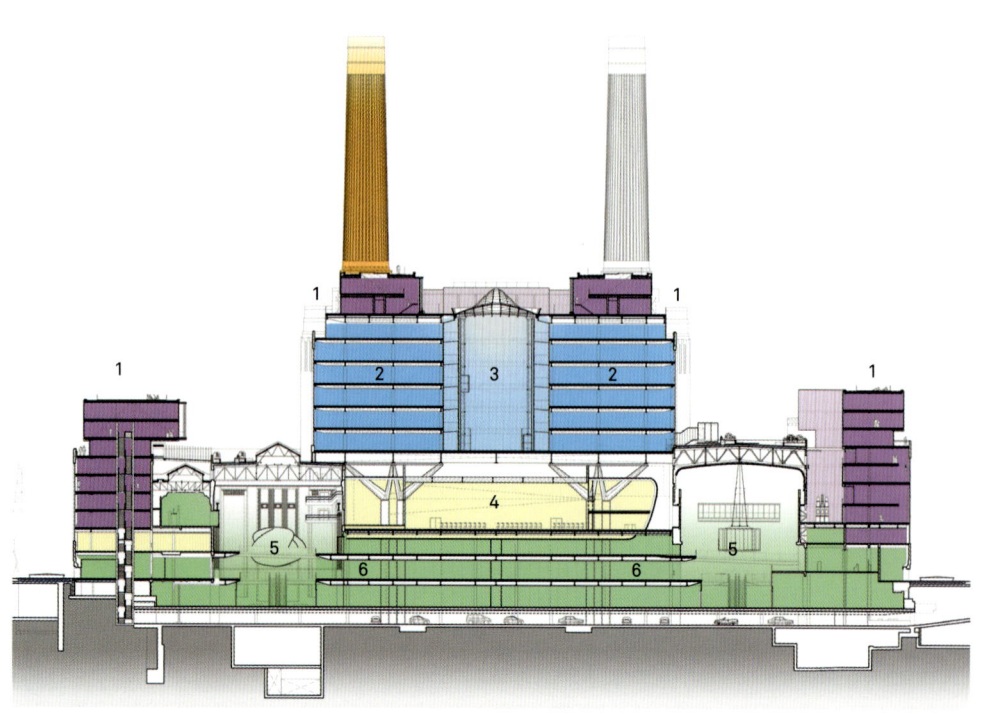

Cross section

1 Residential units
2 Office space
3 Atrium
4 Event space
5 Turbine halls
6 Retail

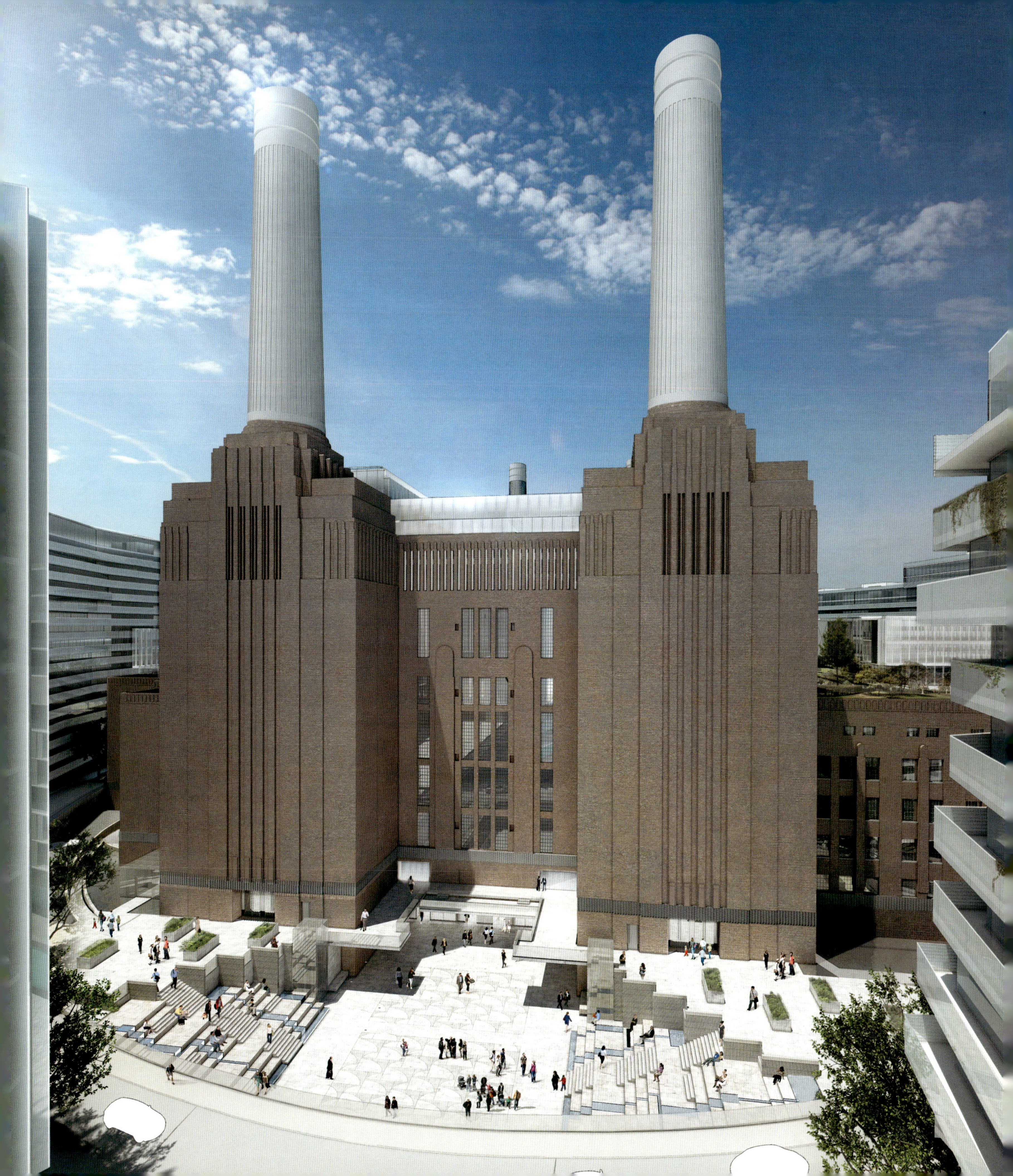

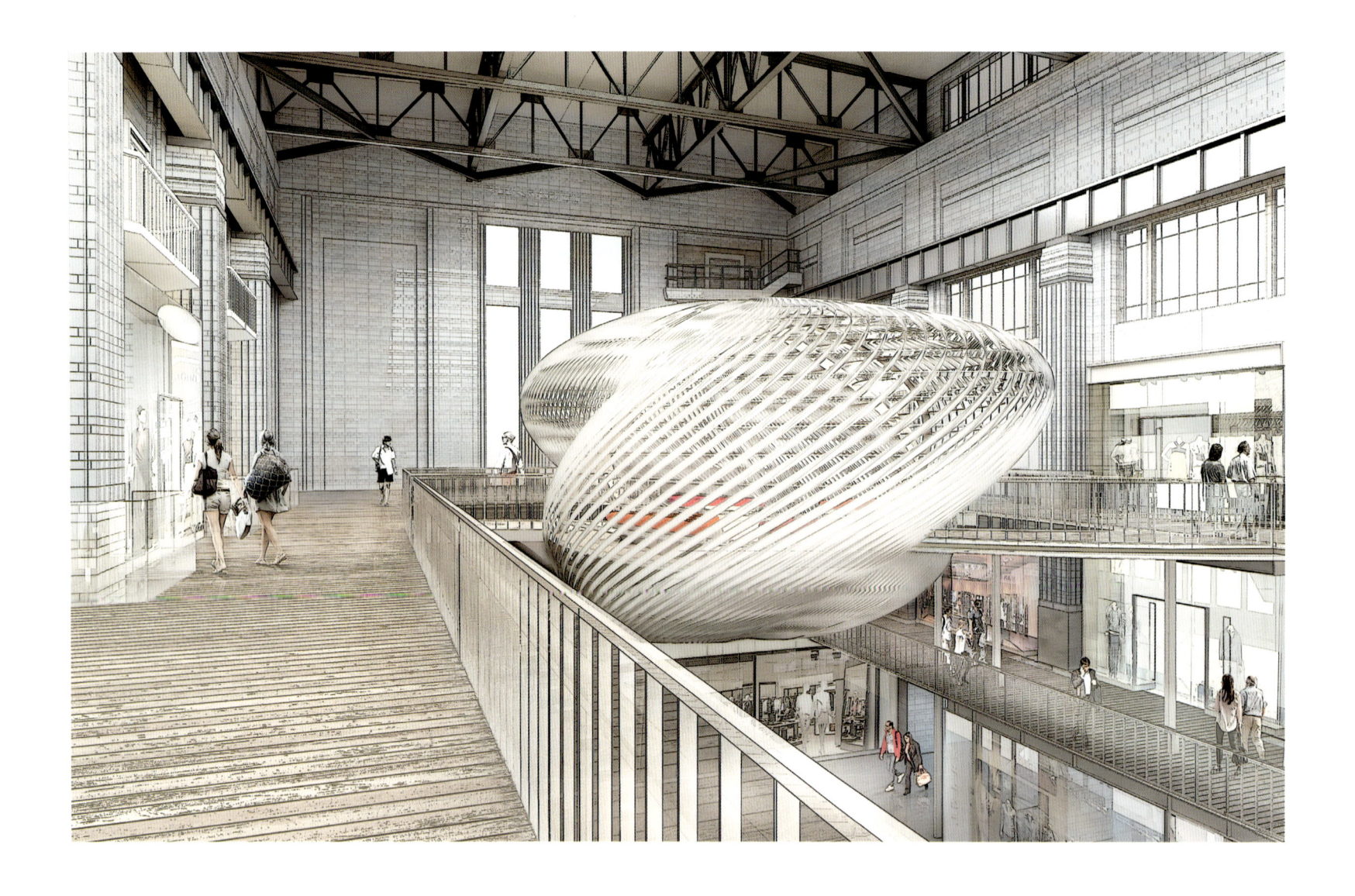

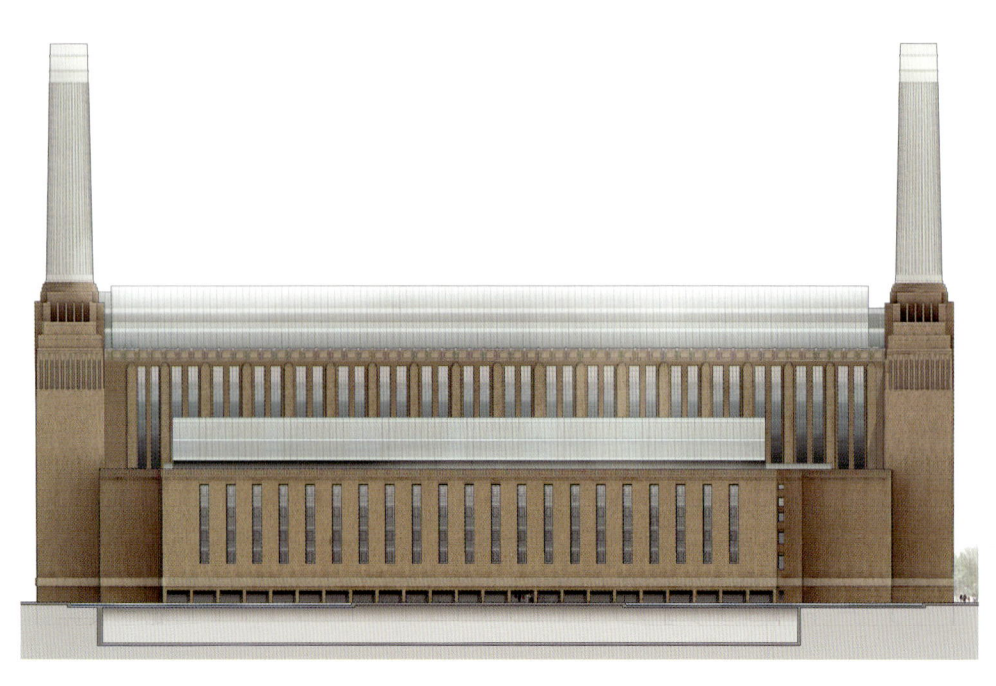

Even before the second phase of the power station was finished in 1953, completing the familiar four-chimneyed composition, the building was much admired. In a survey conducted by the *Architects' Journal* in 1939, a panel of celebrities voted it the second most popular modern building of the period.

244

The turbine halls are the heroic interior spaces of the power station; in fact, the vast walls of polished tiles in Turbine Hall A were once likened to a Greek temple to energy. The magnificent space is equal in size to the Turbine Hall at Tate Modern, London, and many of the original finishes and features survive. The cathedral-like windows at either end, infilled with brick during the Second World War, will be reopened to allow light to flood the space once more. A carefully crafted 'folly' – providing a venue for small events and pop-ups – will appear to float in the space, its mirrored surface reflecting the dramatic interior.

The retail space is set over three levels between the lower- and upper-ground floors, the main shopping zones in the turbine halls forming a circulation loop connected at north and south by dramatic entrance halls adjacent to the existing Boiler House façades.

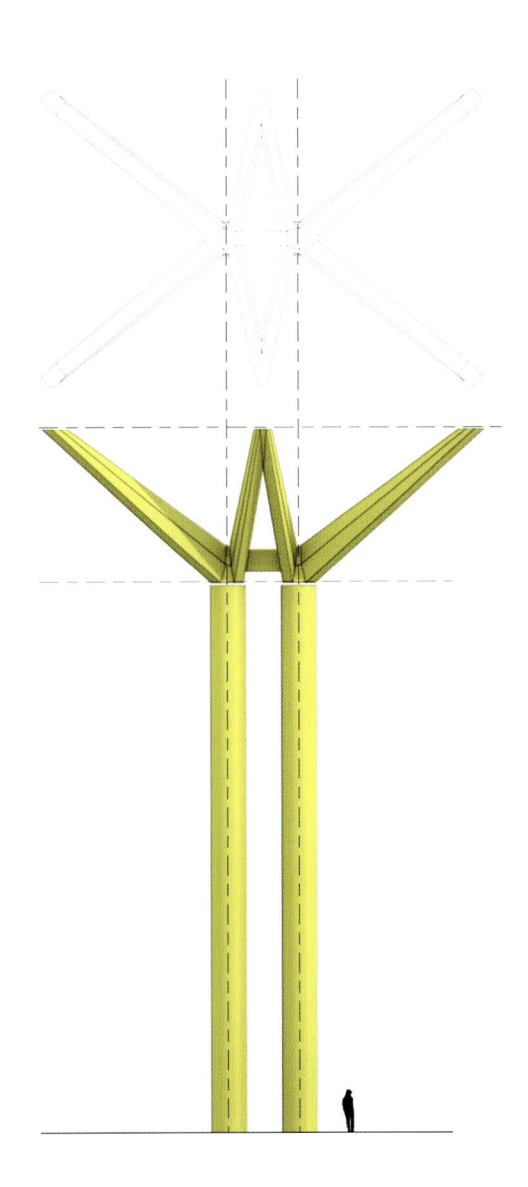

City | Battersea Power Station, London, UK

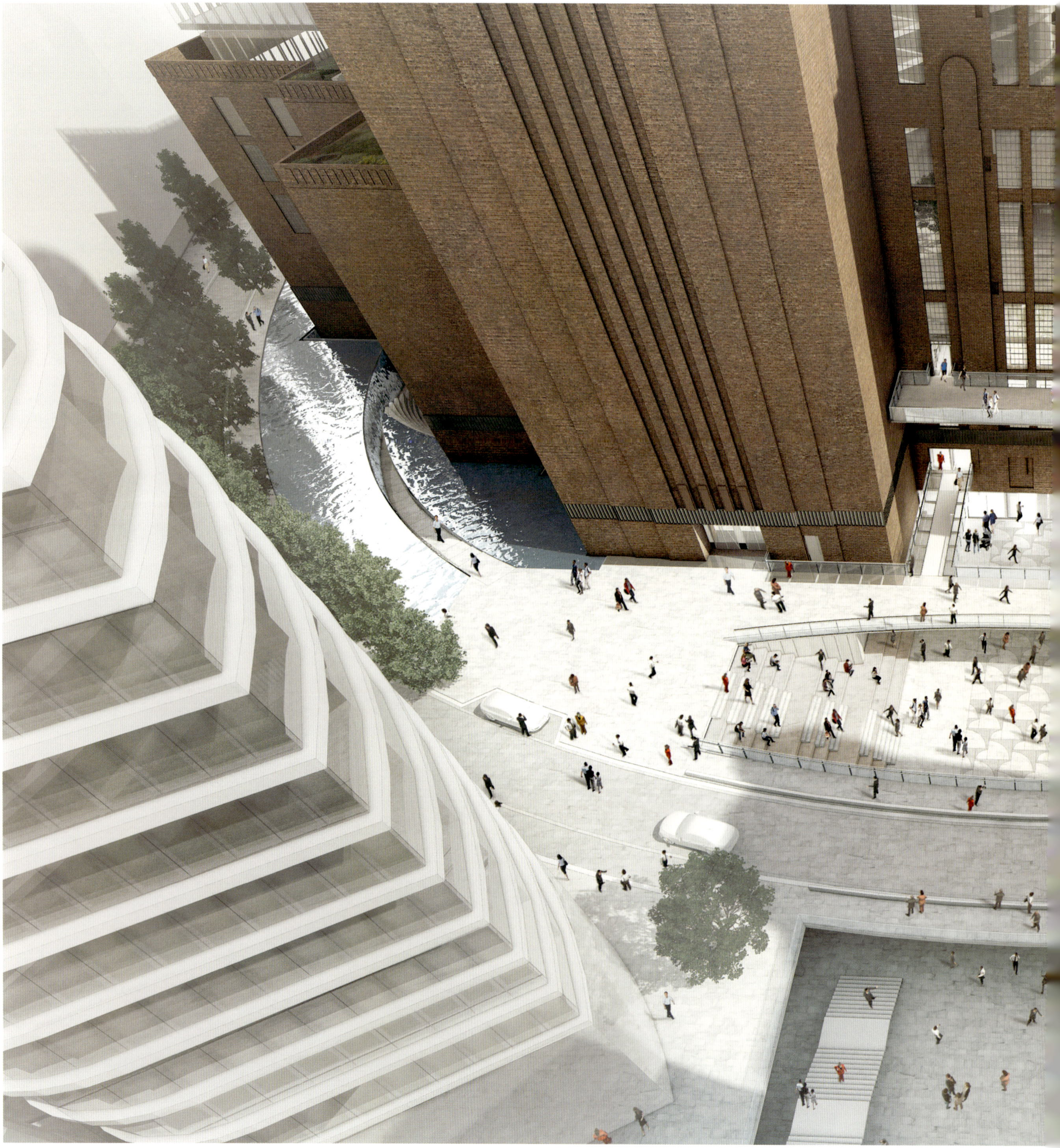

City | Battersea Power Station, London, UK

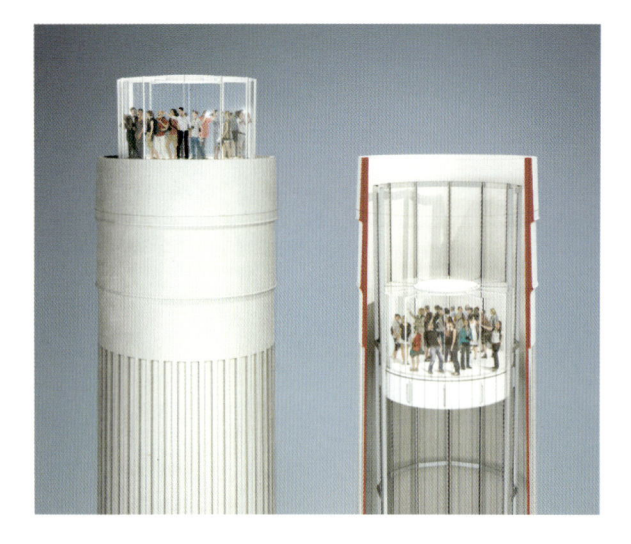

Together, the four chimneys of Battersea Power Station represent one of London's favourite landmarks, and a new lookout will enable visitors to experience them even more closely. A glass-clad platform lift will rise through the core of one of the chimneys, emerging into the daylight 100 metres above ground to provide a 360-degree view of the surrounding city.

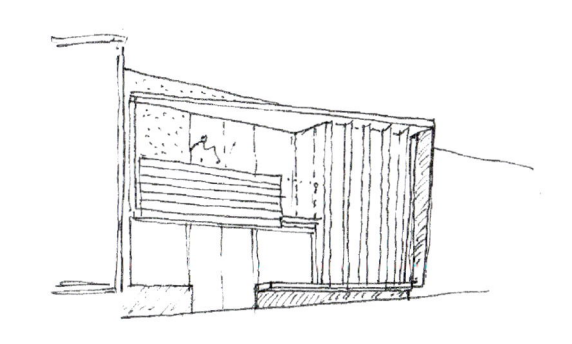

Residential accommodation will occupy the two annexes flanking the east and west sides of the power station, as well as the top of the Boiler House roof. Here, the villas will frame an open garden square, a chimney standing proud in each corner.

City | Battersea Power Station, London, UK

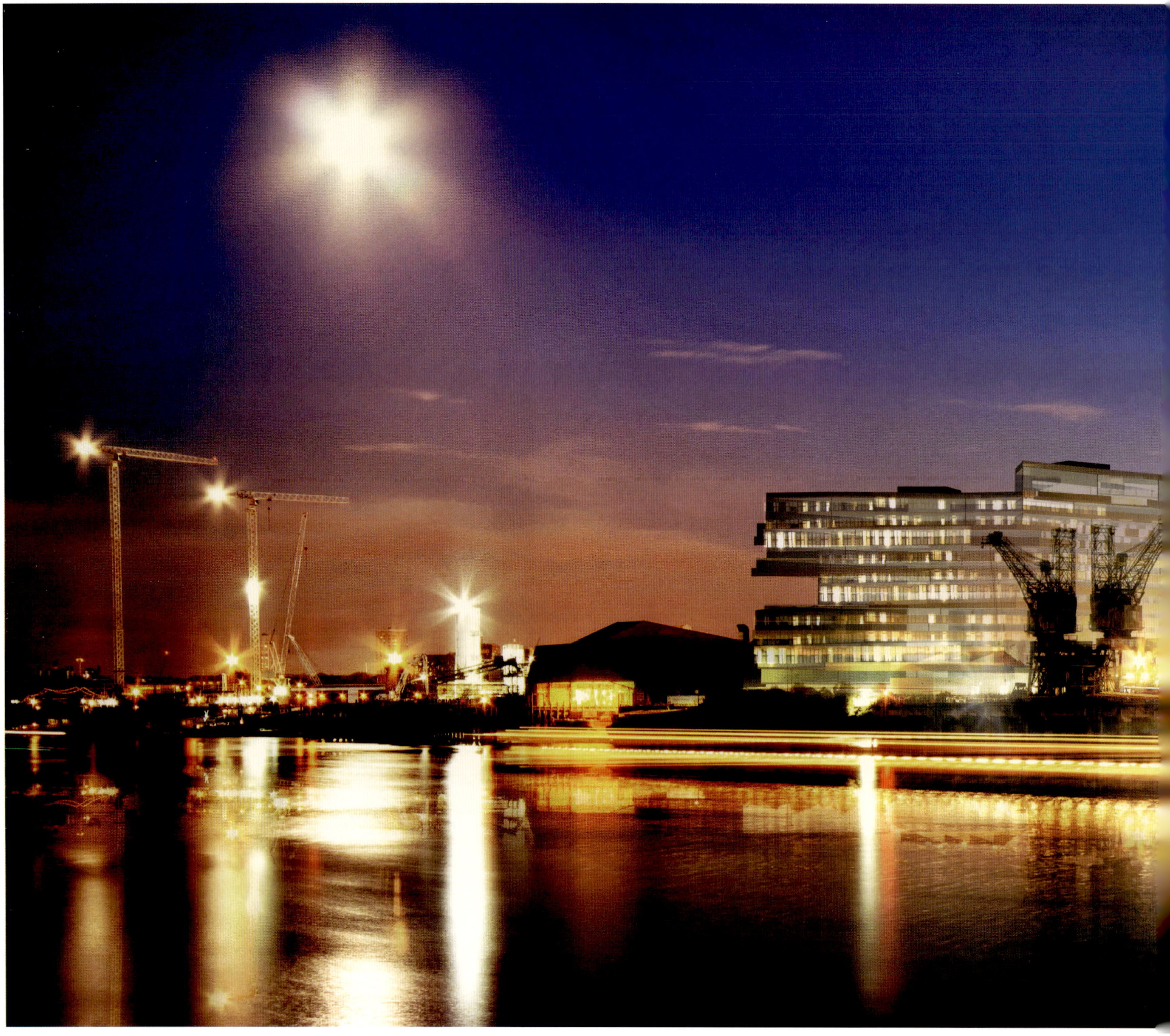

City | Battersea Power Station, London, UK

Portfolio and Practice

Selected projects 2005 onwards 254
In practice 266
Staff 2005–14 274
Selected awards 2005–14 276

2005 | 2006

National Waterfront Museum |
Swansea, UK
Client: National Museum Wales/City
& County of Swansea
Completed
Structural engineer: Arup
Mechanical & electrical engineer:
McCann & Partners
Exhibition design: Land Design Studio

**City and Islington College:
Centre for Business, Arts and Technology** |
London, UK
Client: City and Islington College
Completed
Structural/mechanical &
electrical engineer: Arup

Nescio brug | Amsterdam, The Netherlands
Client: Project Bureau IJburg
Completed
Structural engineer: Arup

20 Blackfriars Road (office scheme; p. 90) |
London, UK
Client: Land Securities
Proposals

Davies Alpine House (p. 51) | London, UK
Client: Royal Botanic Gardens, Kew
Completed
Structural engineer: Dewhurst Macfarlane
Environmental engineer: Atelier Ten

Jodrell Laboratory | London, UK
Client: Royal Botanic Gardens, Kew
Completed
Structural engineer:
Michael Barclay Partnership
Mechanical & electrical engineer: Atelier Ten

Mildmay Sports Centre | Chelmsford, UK
Client: Anglia Ruskin University
Completed
Structural engineer: WSP

Tindal Student Centre | Chelmsford, UK
Client: Anglia Ruskin University
Completed
Structural engineer: WSP

Oman Botanic Garden | Muscat, Oman
Client: Confidential
Competition
Structural engineer: Schlaich Bergermann
Landscape architect:
Charles Funke Associates
Lighting design: Speirs + Major

1 & 2 Aldgate Place | London, UK
Client: Tishman Speyer
Proposals
Structural engineer: Arup
Services engineer: DSA Engineering
Landscape architect: Edco Design

Brighton Marina | Brighton, UK
Client: Brunswick Developments
Planning permission granted
Consultant engineer: Mott MacDonald

Huang Gang Towers | Shenzhen, China
Client: Shenzhen Zuoyue Century Town
Real Estate
Proposals
Structural engineer: Arup

2007

Bristol Brunel Academy (p. 64) | Bristol, UK
Client: Skanska Construction
Completed
Structural engineer: Arup
Mechanical & electrical engineer: Buro Happold
Landscape architect: 4DLD

Cabot Circus | Bristol, UK
Client: Land Securities
Completed
Structural engineer: Waterman
Mechanical & electrical engineer: Hoare Lea

Euston Station | London, UK
Client: Network Rail
Competition
Civil/structural engineer: Halcrow Yolles
Transport engineer: Steer Davis Gleave
Landscape architect: Edco Design

John Madejski Academy (p. 64) | Reading, UK
Client: Department for Education and Skills
Completed
Structural/mechanical & electrical engineer: Arup
Landscape architect: Grant Associates

Living Bridge (p. 59) | Limerick, Ireland
Client: University of Limerick
Completed
Structural engineer: Arup

Victoria Transport Interchange | London, UK
Client: Land Securities
Proposals
Structural engineer: Whitbybird
Services engineer: Hoare Lea

William Harvey Building | Chelmsford, UK
Client: Anglia Ruskin University
Completed
Structural engineer: Alan Baxter & Associates
Mechanical & electrical engineer: Max Fordham

Jeddah Central District | Jeddah, Saudi Arabia
Client: Confidential
Redevelopment masterplan
Masterplanner: Arup

House of Human Rights | Milan, Italy
Client: Confidential
Concept
Engineer: Tekne

Olympic Velodrome | London, UK
Client: Olympic Delivery Authority
Competition
Structural engineer: Buro Happold
Services engineer: Faber Maunsell

Miami Science Museum | Miami, USA
Client: Miami Science Museum
Competition

Suzhou Supertower | Suzhou, China
Client: China-Singapore Industrial Park Real Estate
Competition
Structural engineer: Arup

Exeter Princesshay | Exeter, UK
Client: Land Securities
Completed
Structural engineer: Upton McGougan
Mechanical & electrical engineer: RW Gregory

Portfolio and Practice | Selected projects 2005 onwards

2008 | 2009

Guangzhou East Tower | Guangzhou, China
Client: Yuexiu Investment
Competition

Grosvenor Place | London, UK
Client: Grosvenor
Proposals
Structural engineer: Whitbybird

Guangzhou Velodrome | Guangzhou, China
Client: Confidential
Competition

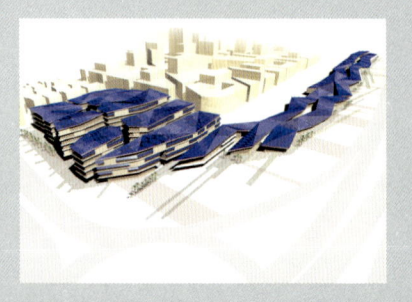

Cairo Westown Masterplan | Cairo, Egypt
Client: SODIC/Solidere International
Masterplan

Dyson School of Design Innovation | Bath, UK
Client: The Dyson Foundation
Proposals
Structural/mechanical & electrical engineer: Buro Happold

Westgate Bridge | Melbourne, Australia
Client: Flint & Neill/Westgate Bridge Strengthening Alliance
Proposals
Structural engineer: Flint & Neill

20 Blackfriars Road (p. 90) | London, UK
Client: Circleplane
Planning inquiry approved
Structural engineer: Whitbybird
Services engineer: Roger Preston & Partners
Façade engineer: Arup
Public realm: Space Syntax
Landscape architect: Grant Associates

Apraksin Dvor Masterplan | St Petersburg, Russia
Client: Glavstroy Spb
Masterplan

BaiYun Masterplan | Guangzhou, China
Client: City of Guangzhou
Masterplan

Bridge Learning Campus | Bristol, UK
Client: Skanska Construction
Completed
Structural engineer: Skanska Technology
Mechanical & electrical engineer: Buro Happold
Landscape architect: Grant Associates

Brislington Enterprise College (p. 64) | Bristol, UK
Client: Skanska Construction
Completed
Collaborating architect: FLACQ Architects
Landscape architect: Grant Associates

Bristol Metropolitan Academy (p. 64) | Bristol, UK
Client: Skanska Construction
Completed
Structural engineer: Arup
Mechanical & electrical engineer: Buro Happold
Landscape architect: Grant Associates

Ceramics Galleries Bridge (p. 200) | London, UK
Client: Victoria and Albert Museum
Completed
Structural engineer: Dewhurst MacFarlane

Guangzhou Exhibition Centre | Guangzhou, China
Client: Guangzhou East Jin Xin District Development Ltd
Competition

Humanities Building | Oxford, UK
Client: University of Oxford
Competition

Library of Birmingham | Birmingham, UK
Client: Birmingham City Council
Competition
Structural engineer: Alan Baxter & Associates
Environmental engineer: Hurley Palmer Flatt

Bath Southgate Transport Interchange | Bath, UK
Client: Multi Developments
Completed
Structural engineer: Beattie Watkinson
Mechanical & electrical engineer: Arup

Audi West London | London, UK
Client: Audi UK
Completed
Structural engineer: Expedition
Mechanical & electrical engineer: Atelier Ten

Forthside Footbridge | Stirling, UK
Client: Stirling Council
Completed
Structural engineer: Gifford
Lighting design: Speirs + Major

Arundel Great Court | London, UK
Client: Land Securities
Planning permission granted
Structural engineer: Clarke Nicholls Marcel
Services engineer: Grontmij

Liverpool Arena and Convention Centre
(p. 140) | Liverpool, UK
Client: Liverpool City Council
Completed
Structural engineer: Buro Happold
Mechanical & electrical engineer: Faber Maunsell
Acoustics: Sandy Brown Associates
Landscape architect: Gustafson Porter
Lighting design: Speirs + Major
Sport consultant: Sport Concepts
Theatre consultant: Theatre Projects

Mecca West Masterplan | Mecca, Saudi Arabia
Client: Sheikh Abdul Aziz Kamel Consultants
Masterplan

The National Archives | London, UK
Client: The National Archives
Completed
Mechanical & electrical engineer: Ian Mackay Associates

Nizhny Novgorod Winter Sports Complex |
Nizhny Novgorod, Russia
Client: SU153
Competition

Paradise Street Interchange & Bridge
(p. 140) | Liverpool, UK
Client: Grosvenor
Completed
Structural engineer: Waterman/WSP
(bus interchange only)

Quarantine House | London, UK
Client: Royal Botanic Gardens, Kew
Completed
Engineer: Skelly & Couch

School of Public Policy | Oxford, UK
Client: University of Oxford
Competition

Wuhan Tianhe Airport: Terminal Three |
Wuhan, China
Client: Hubei Airport Group
Competition
Engineer: WSP
Local architect: LDI

Museum of the Future | London, UK
Client: The Science Museum
Proposals

2010 | 2011

Viaduc de la Savoureuse | Savoureuse, France
Client: LGV Rhin-Rhône
Completed
Structural engineer: Jean Muller International
Landscape architect: Alfred Peter

Columbus Tower | London, UK
Client: Confidential
Competition

East London Line (Hoxton and Shoreditch stations) | London, UK
Client: East London Line Project
Completed
Structural engineer: Mott MacDonald

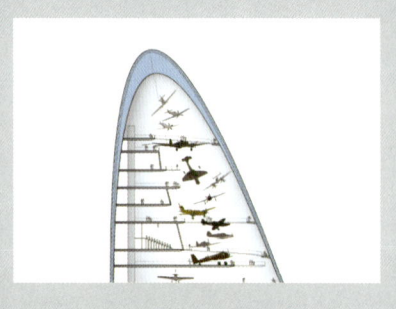

Battle of Britain Beacon | London, UK
Client: Royal Air Force Museum
Proposals

Beagle House | London, UK
Client: Molloy Properties
Planning permission granted
Structural engineer: Arup
Mechanical & electrical engineer: DSA Engineering

Shanghai Post-Expo Development | Shanghai, China
Client: Shanghai Expo Co. Ltd
Competition

25 Great Pulteney Street (p. 218) | London, UK
Client: F&C Property Asset Management
Completed
Structural engineer: Waterman
Mechanical & electrical engineer: Mott MacDonald Fulcrum

Arts Two (p. 223) | London, UK
Client: Queen Mary, University of London
Completed
Structural engineer: Arup
Mechanical & electrical engineer: DSSR

Beijing Lize Metro Station | Beijing, China
Client: MTR
Proposals
Local architect: BIAD

Brisbane Airport | Brisbane, Australia
Client: Brisbane Airport Corporation
Competition

Capital City Project (p. 203) | London, UK
Client: Museum of London
Completed
Structural engineer: Whitbybird
Mechanical & electrical engineer: SVM
Acoustics: Sandy Brown Associates

Department of Earth Sciences (p. 208) | Oxford, UK
Client: University of Oxford
Completed
Structural engineer: Pell Frischmann
Mechanical & electrical engineer: Hoare Lea

Guangzhou International Finance Centre (p. 94) | Guangzhou, China
Client: Guangzhou Construction Committee
Completed
Structural engineer: Arup

Hang Lung Plaza | Wuhan, China
Client: Hang Lung Properties
Proposals

Mathematics Building (p. 223) | London, UK
Client: Queen Mary, University of London
Completed
Structural engineer: Conisbee
Environmental engineer: Troup Bywaters + Anders

Media City Footbridge (p. 152) | Salford, UK
Client: Peel Holdings
Completed
Structural engineer: Ramboll
Mechanical engineer: Atkins Bennett

Peace Bridge (p. 151) | Derry, UK
Client: Graham Construction/Ilex URC
Completed
Structural engineer: Faber Maunsell (Aecom)

Student Centre | London, UK
Client: Queen Mary, University of London
Completed
Structural engineer: Chamberlain Consulting
Mechanical & electrical engineer: Hoare Lea

Hauser Forum | Cambridge, UK
Client: University of Cambridge
Completed
Structural engineer: Mott MacDonald
Mechanical & electrical engineer: White Young Green

Portfolio and Practice | Selected projects 2005 onwards

2012 | 2013

BBC North/Media City UK | Salford, UK
Client: Peel Holdings
Completed
Structural engineer: Jacobs
Mechanical & electrical engineer:
Faber Maunsell

North-West Cambridge | Cambridge, UK
Client: University of Cambridge
Completed
Masterplanner: Aecom

Deutsche Bank Bridge | London, UK
Client: Deutsche Bank
Planning permission granted
Structural engineer: Flint & Neill
Mechanical & electrical engineer: Hurley Palmer Flatt
Lighting design: Speirs + Major

Baakenhafen West Bridge | Hamburg, Germany Client: HafenCity
Completed
Engineer: Buro Happold

Bath Spa Railway Station | Bath, UK
Client: Multi Developments
Completed
Structural engineer: Beattie Watkinson
Mechanical & electrical engineer: Arup

10 Brock Street (p. 186) | London, UK
Client: British Land
Completed
Structural engineer: CH2M HILL
Mechanical & electrical engineer: WPP

The Crystal (p. 165) | London, UK
Client: Siemens
Completed
Interior architect: Pringle Brandon
Structural/mechanical & electrical engineer: Arup
Landscape architect: Townshend Landscape Architects
Exhibition design: Event Communications

Emirates Air Line (p. 84) | London, UK
Client: Transport for London
Completed
Engineer: Expedition

The Forum (p. 43) | Exeter, UK
Client: University of Exeter
Completed
Structural/services engineer: Buro Happold
Landscape architect: Hargreaves

From Landscape to Portrait (p. 110) | London, UK
Client: Royal Academy of Arts
Completed

Gardens by the Bay (p. 28) | Singapore
Client: National Parks Board
Completed
Masterplanner/landscape architect: Grant Associates
Structural engineer: Atelier One
Environmental engineer: Atelier Ten
Exhibition design: Land Design Studio

London 2012 Basketball Arena (p. 113) | London, UK
Client: Olympic Delivery Authority
Completed
Structural/environmental engineer: SKM
Sports architect: KSS

Mary Rose Museum (p. 155) | Portsmouth, UK
Client: The Mary Rose Trust
Completed
Interior architect: Pringle Brandon
Exhibition design: Land Design Studio
Structural/mechanical & electrical engineer: Ramboll

New Place | Stratford-upon-Avon, UK
Client: The Shakespeare Birthplace Trust
Competition
Structural engineer: Fluid Structures
Artists: *somewhere

Sebastian Street Graduate Centre | London, UK
Client: City University, London
Planning permission granted
Structural/mechanical & electrical engineer: Aecom

Splashpoint (p. 130) | Worthing, UK
Client: Worthing Borough Council
Completed
Engineer: Aecom

Toulouse Cable Car | Toulouse, France
Client: Tisseo-SMTC
Proposals
Engineer: Ingerop

Twin Sails Bridge (p. 107) | Poole, UK
Client: Borough of Poole
Completed
Structural engineer: Gifford & Partners
Mechanical engineer: Bennett Associates

Southampton SeaCity Museum
Southampton, UK
Client: Southampton City Council
Completed
Structural/environmental engineer: Ramboll
Exhibition design: Urban Salon

2014

Aldgate Tower | London, UK
Client: Aldgate Developments
Completion due
Structural engineer: Arup
Mechanical & electrical engineer: Aecom

Advanced Manufacturing Centre |
Melbourne, Australia
Client: Swinburne University of Technology
Completion due
Engineer: SKM

Beijing Beiyuan Mixed-Use Development |
Beijing, China
Client: Sino Railway Company
Completion (phase one) due
Engineer: Beijing Institute of Architecture
& Design

Cairo Westown: The Polygon | Cairo, Egypt
Client: SODIC/Solidere International
Completion (phase one) due
Local architect: EHAF
Structural engineer: Cosmos
Mechanical & electrical engineer: Shaker

Dyson Headquarters Remodelling |
Malmesbury, UK
Client: Dyson
Planning application submitted
Engineer: Buro Happold

Maggie's Centre (p. 77) | Oxford, UK
Client: Maggie's
Completion due
Structural engineer: Alan Baxter & Associates
Mechanical & electrical engineer: K J Tait
Landscape architect: Touchstone
Collaborations

New Bodleian (Weston) Library (p. 231) |
Oxford, UK
Client: University of Oxford
Completion due
Structural engineer: Pell Frischmann
Mechanical & electrical engineer: Hurley
Palmer Flatt

Wellcome Collection | London, UK
Client: The Wellcome Trust
Completion due
Structural engineer: AKT II
Mechanical & electrical engineer: Max Fordham

Portfolio and Practice | Selected projects 2005 onwards 263

2015 onwards

River Plate House | London, UK
Client: Mitsubishi/Stanhope
Completion due 2015
Structural engineer: Waterman
Mechanical & electrical engineer: WSP

St Lazare Bridge | Paris, France
Client: City of Paris
Completion due 2017
Structural engineer: Arcadis

Rio Olympics Masterplan & Handball Arena | Rio, Brazil
Client: City of Rio de Janeiro
Completion due 2015
Masterplanner/engineer: Aecom

Bath Rugby Club | Bath, UK
Client: Bath Rugby Club
Completion due 2015
Engineer: Buro Happold

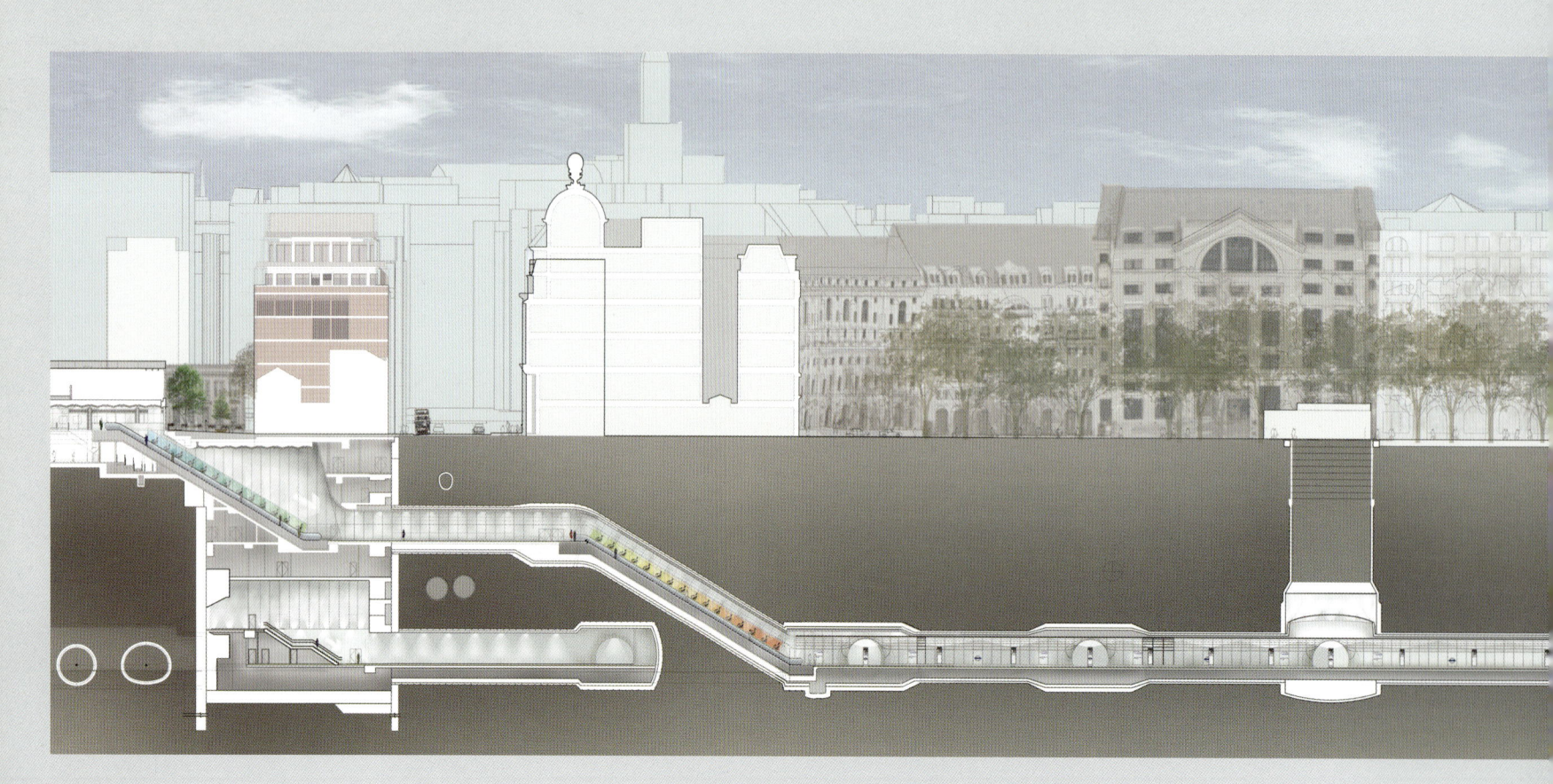

Carlsberg Visitor Centre |
Copenhagen, Denmark
Client: Carlsberg Breweries A/S
Completion due 2017
Structural/mechanical & electrical
engineer: NIRAS
Heritage consultant: Erik Miller Arkitekter

Bank Station | London, UK
Client: Transport for London
Completion due 2021
Engineer: URS
Tunnelling engineer: Dr Sauer Group

Battersea Power Station (p. 241) | London, UK
Client: Battersea Power Station Development Company
Completion due 2019
Structural engineer: Buro Happold
Mechanical & electrical engineer: Chapman BDSP

Calthorpe Street | London, UK
Client: Royal Mail Group
Completion due 2016
Structural engineer: CH2M HILL (Halcrow Yolles)
Mechanical & electrical engineer: Hoare Lea
Landscape architect: Camlins

Crown Hotel (p. 172) | Sydney, Australia
Client: Crown Hotels
Completion due 2019
Structural engineer: Robert Bird
Mechanical & electrical engineer: Aecom
Façade consultant: Arup

Fehmarnbelt Fixed Link | Germany/Denmark
Client: Ramboll Arup Tec (RAT) Consortium
Completion due 2020

Fry Building | Bristol, UK
Client: University of Bristol
Completion due 2016

Graduate Centre | London, UK
Client: Queen Mary, University of London
Completion due 2015
Structural/mechanical & electrical engineer: Buro Happold

King's Cross Gasholders (p. 122) | London, UK
Client: Argent St George
Completion due 2016

North-West Cambridge Graduate Housing, Foodstore & Energy Centre | Cambridge, UK
Client: University of Cambridge
Completion due 2016
Engineer: URS
Landscape architect: BBUK
Local architect: Mole

Wuhan Qiaoko Tower | Wuhan, China
Client: Yue Xiu Group
Completion due 2015
Structural engineer: Arup

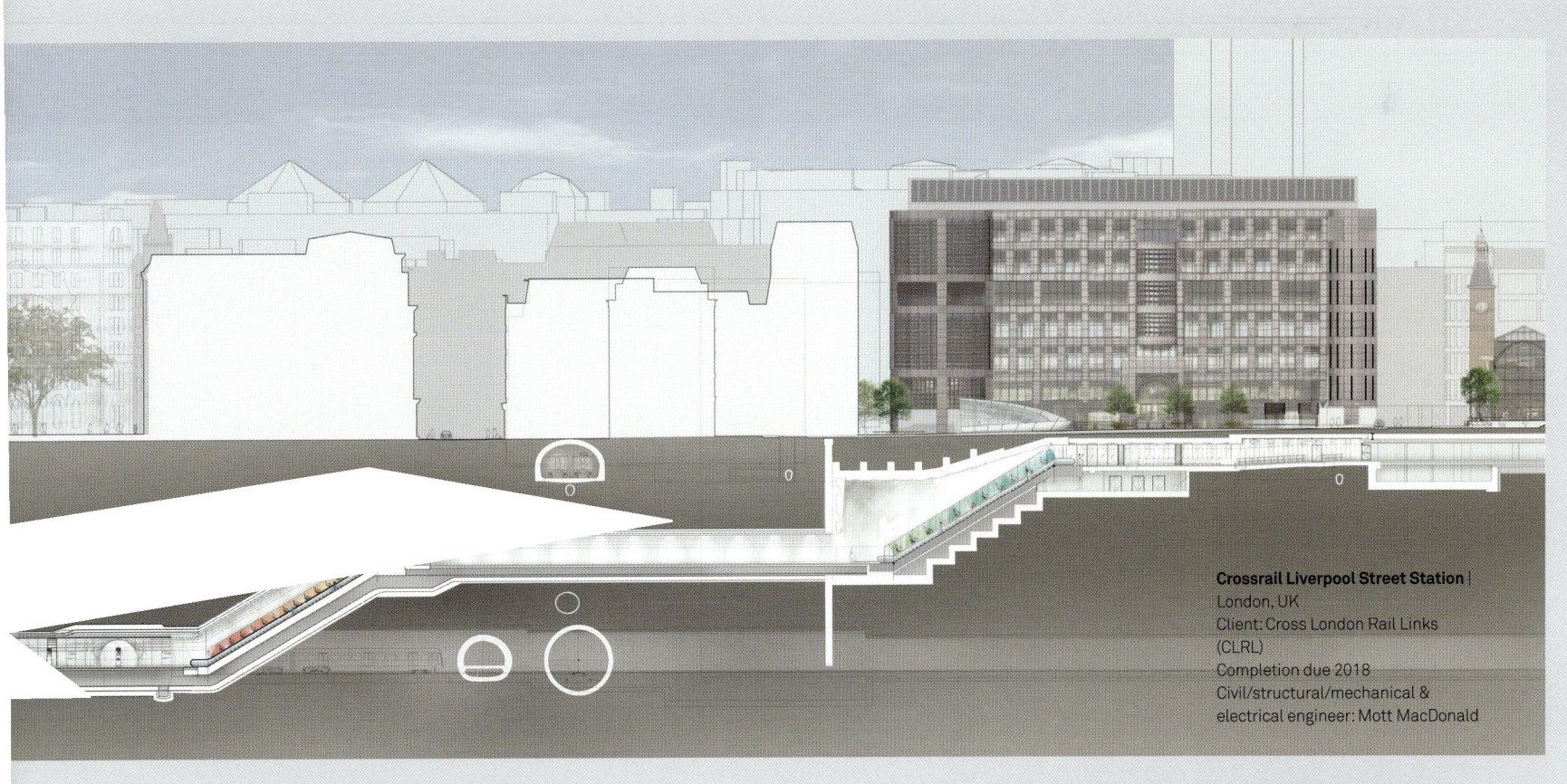

Crossrail Liverpool Street Station |
London, UK
Client: Cross London Rail Links (CLRL)
Completion due 2018
Civil/structural/mechanical & electrical engineer: Mott MacDonald

Portfolio and Practice | Selected projects 2005 onwards   265

Chris Wilkinson (right) and Jim Eyre

In practice

Chris Wilkinson, Founding Principal

I continue to be excited by the broad reach of architecture, as a pursuit that encompasses both the creative arts and technological innovation. It gives me the scope to fulfil my love of design, and feel I am making a worthwhile contribution to society. I see each project as an opportunity to explore new ideas, and to try and build good architecture.

I like to make use of the latest technology to create buildings that are both uplifting and responsive, drawing on a palette of natural and advanced materials. Engineering is always an integral part of the architectural design, and the structure is particularly important in giving meaning to forms that are derived from functional and aesthetic considerations.

Starting with a clear, rational diagram, geometry plays its part in determining the space and form of the architecture, and its subtleties and beauties of light and materiality. There can be no design formula: each project is designed to the specificity of its brief and context.

I see the history of architecture as an evolving continuum that closely follows technological progress – and I want to remain at the forefront of it.

Outside the office, I am just as committed to painting. I am fortunate, indeed, to be able to combine my love of art and architecture.

Jim Eyre, Founding Principal

It is thirty years since I qualified as an architect, and twenty-seven of those involve the growth of our practice and the evolution of my attitude to creating architecture. Through a series of explorations stirred by interaction with my fellow directors and the wider design team, a number of personal preoccupations have emerged.

Making architecture is not so much about problem-solving, but more about combining analysis and inspiration to arrive at preferred ways of expressing of ideas. It's a construct that should fulfil the many objectives of the participants, but arrive at something special. Irrepressibly inquisitive, I feel driven, each time, to find something new, to capture and refine the essence of the key architectural idea, which always stems from reading a site, and the purpose demanded of the building.

I am drawn to the rational and apparently effortless – that sense of a particular design being inevitable. But it is often moments of intuition that create the breakthroughs. Our earlier work on Stratford Market Depot was suitably industrial in character, with exposed structure. But a transition occurred in designing Stratford Regional Station, which explored expansive surfaces and light, juxtaposing geometric form with fine lines of structure, focusing on lightness and proportion in a space flooded by light.

A sense of arrival – of wonder, even – in the celebration of space, light and surface in a vocabulary of architectural volumes can be drawn out of typologies varying from spanning structures to the refinement of sculpting tall buildings, or even transforming old buildings with new interventions and uses.

Paul Baker, Director

I believe most great architecture comes from just a few good ideas, and then a tremendous amount of hard work by a great many people. It's essential to understand the brief and context, and, ideally, we should have a client that wants to explore the most interesting possibilities. Our aim is to create a built response that allows anyone who interacts with our architecture to function well, and to enrich their life by adding a little magic or humour or joy to it. I believe, absolutely, that the built form can influence people's behaviour, so if those who use and operate the building are involved in its design, both the process and the final outcomes are always better.

My fundamentals for good design begin with a simple, legible diagram that represents a clear concept. All design must explore and exploit space, light, colour and texture. Elegant form and proportion must be considered, and at all scales. Appropriate, high-quality materials should be used and expressed with clarity, ideally demonstrating skill and craft in their connections and details. All engineering, structural and environmental elements should be considered as part of a collaborative, fully integrated design process.

I like to blur the boundaries between inside and outside, playing with the spaces between and beyond the architecture. Opposites stimulate: heavy and light, old and new, lightness and darkness, order and disorder, straight and curved, rough and smooth, and so on. The practice's work balances science and art, intellect and emotion. We explore all options from many perspectives, so an important part of the process is trying out ideas, and testing them to see if they work by modelling them in 3D, either virtually or physically.

This creative dynamic allows the practice to develop ideas according to these fundamentals. We have gathered, and retained, some tremendous design talent over the years, and created some great architecture. And this has given us the confidence to cooperate and work with other talented people, across other disciplines, to create truly integrated design.

Stafford Critchlow, Director

I am interested in architecture as a vehicle for social change, be it an education building, museum or research facility. Interpreting and transforming a client's brief into a clear diagram for a building that can help improve lives or working practices through uplifting, well-defined spaces is, I believe, a key transformational skill for an architect.

The best new buildings marry the latest technology with high-quality materials, and subscribe to the 'long life, loose fit' notion that buildings sensibly planned around good daylight, ventilation and spatial organization can be adapted over time to suit changing needs.

At the same time, buildings should have personality. They should recognize and respond to their context, be of their time, and have an architectural legibility about what goes on in and around them. I enjoy the juxtaposition of new buildings, or new building elements, with old structures – and the human and contextual richness that this can provide. I see a clear lineage in Wilkinson Eyre projects that demonstrate these qualities, from Explore@Bristol and the Museum of London to the school projects, University of Exeter Forum and the University of Oxford Earth Sciences building.

Oliver Tyler, Director

My interest in architecture began at an early age with a keenness to construct things, and to see buildings being built. That interest developed with the recognition of a process that commenced with a drawing. When my parents rebuilt a large house, I was fascinated by the design drawings, and by the process of making them a reality. I wanted to be an architect from the age of nine, and that instinct never wavered.

I tend to be drawn to buildings that have a clarity and expression in how they are assembled, and particularly in their detailing. My practical interest in construction is increasingly influenced by an ever greater appreciation of architectural form, the nature of space in and around buildings, and light, texture and the treatment of surfaces.

I always seek to integrate closely the architecture and engineering, and, where appropriate, to express the engineering in the design. I really enjoy collaborating with engineers to resolve design challenges and develop solutions that satisfy the requirements of the different construction disciplines.

I believe that architecture should have order, rigour and rationality. I seek to develop designs that have a clear and legible diagram, that fit their context, and that aim to lift the spirit in some way. While aiming to address the numerous challenges of meeting the brief, budget and context requirements, I strive to create designs that have a quality of delight, and that will be thoroughly memorable in some way.

Dominic Bettison, Director

To me, the best buildings and masterplans frequently exhibit a strong conceptual diagram that reflects a thorough analysis and understanding of a client's brief, and of the proposed site. I strive to distil the major components of a brief into a strong, legible diagram, which concisely and elegantly informs a clear and logical approach to the building design.

We order the critical programmatic elements of the brief, establishing their relationship to one another, and their relationship to the site, the environment and the wider context. This process often produces a simple, apparently effortless solution in our architecture that is intuitively understood by its users, is enjoyable to use, but is not wilful or forced.

The notion of served and servant spaces is key to establishing a clear diagram and an appropriate hierarchy of spaces, with the served spaces often designed flexibly and loosely to ensure a building's usefulness and adaptability over a long period.

The clear integration of structure and built form is another crucial factor in achieving successful and delightful architecture. This may produce spaces apparently devoid of structure, or can be used expressively to reinforce the form of the building, or the sense of dynamic movement, or its solidity.

Architecture that stands the test of time is often characterized by a remarkably consistent approach to environmental design that minimizes the materials used, and the building's energy use. And this leads to better natural light and ventilation, outlooks, and screening from wind and rain. It's a sensitively integrated approach that produces elegant buildings that lift the spirits.

Giles Martin, Director

Like every architect, I want to make buildings that are beautiful and memorable. Everyone knows a beautiful building when they see one, but how do you create one? Very few of my favourite buildings are younger than fifty years old, and many date back 500 years or more. Clearly the answer isn't to recreate an architecture from the past; architecture must be of its age. Beautiful buildings have a timeless quality.

Architectural beauty is not something you can approach head-on. It needs to be coaxed out of a brief and a site. The process of dialogue, with a client, with a planning department (even if it's sometimes confrontational), leads to a building becoming better resolved, and richer in detail and presence.

The design process is about drawing out the strands that solve the particular design problem at hand: the piece of city it will occupy, the budget, the programme. Later, this problem-solving approach will involve the project's engineers, the contractors and, finally (probably my favourite part of the process), the specialists who work with the building materials that have been chosen.

I believe that the same detailed attention should be given to all aspects of design, and that a key question is, what should the chosen materials achieve, technically and architecturally? Only by following a linear progression of constant problem-solving – from a project's inception to its completion, and with understanding and integrity – does the architecture stand a chance of being beautiful.

Sebastien Ricard, Director

I studied architecture in Paris and at McGill University in Montreal, and then worked for Rice Francis Ritchie in Paris before joining Chris Wilkinson in 1997.

My design philosophy stems from a combination of academic ideas and a strong interest in how buildings and spaces can influence the sociocultural environment. I believe it's important to make the link between design and an understanding of human behaviour in a specific context: this ensures a much fuller response to an architectural brief.

As a student, I followed with great enthusiasm the lectures of Marc Mimram and Jean-François Blassel, key figures in French architectural debate. They argued that architectural beauty comes from an understanding of the various geometries found in our environment, and from a knowledge of the latest technologies available to us. In addition, there must be a detailed understanding of the key principles of structure and physics. I bring a structural logic to my work because I believe that the ideas expressed by architectural forms should be clearly and visibly justified.

I strive to create buildings where you can read that the architecture has gone beyond the brief. I see few boundaries between architecture and engineering, and I particularly enjoy the blurring between the disciplines. The close relationship between ideas, art, materials and techniques, and the team effort it takes to achieve a great design, is central to my approach. Buildings are at their most beautiful and effective when they represent the most obvious solution to the brief and context – and that's often the most difficult thing to achieve.

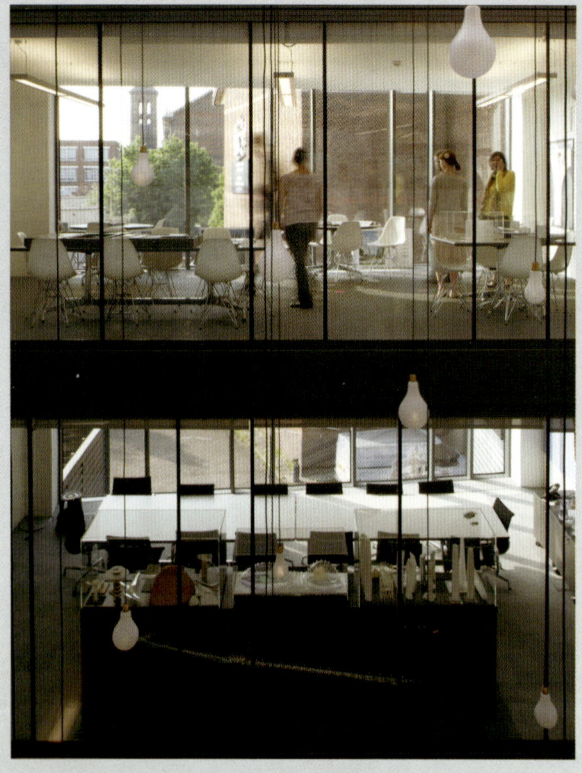
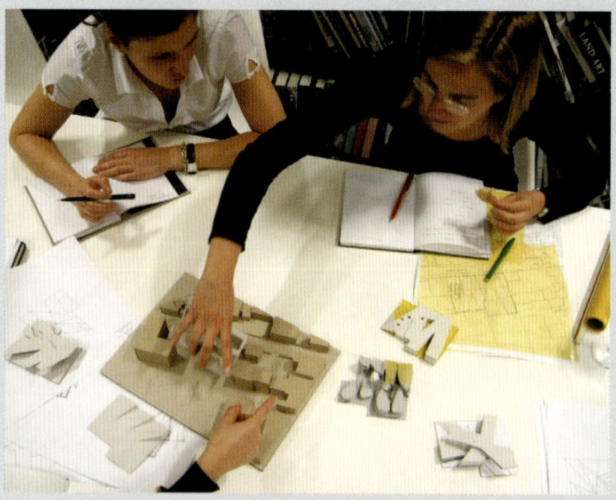
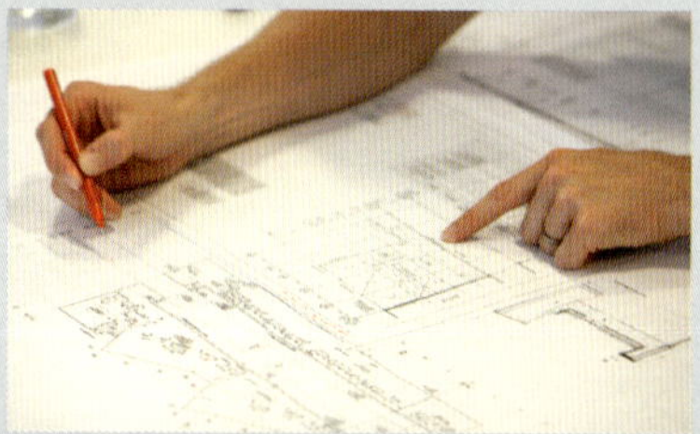
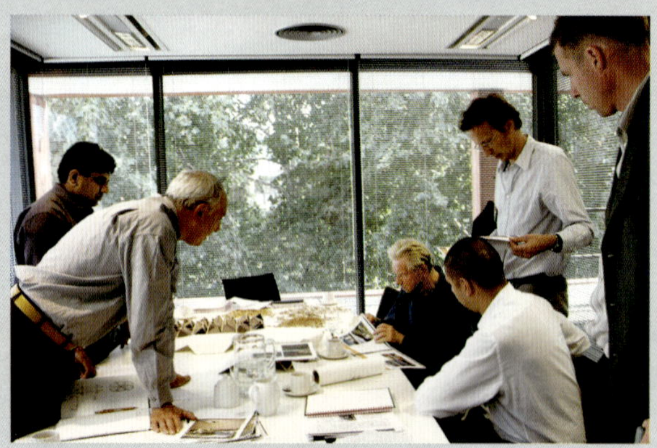
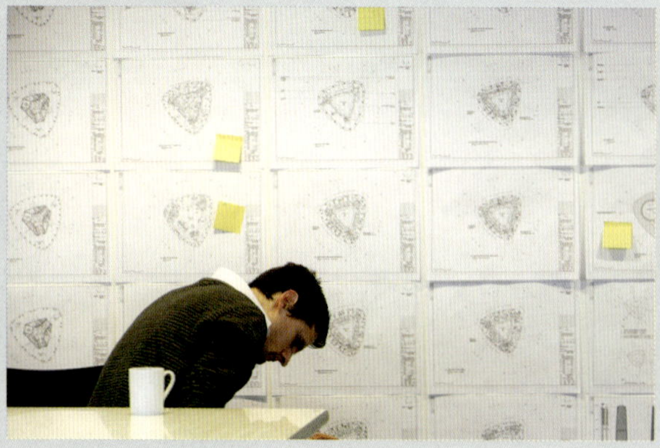
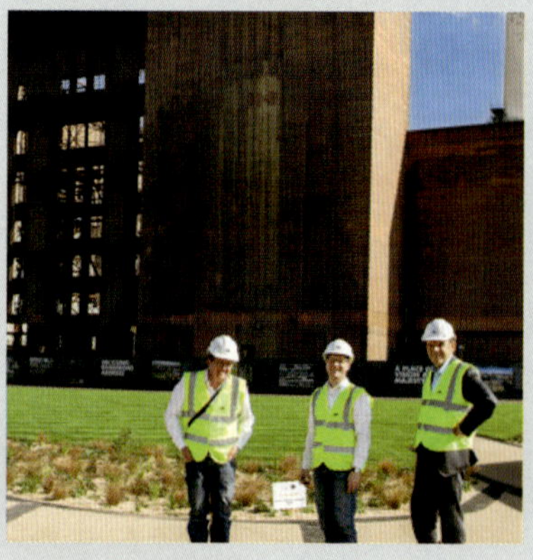
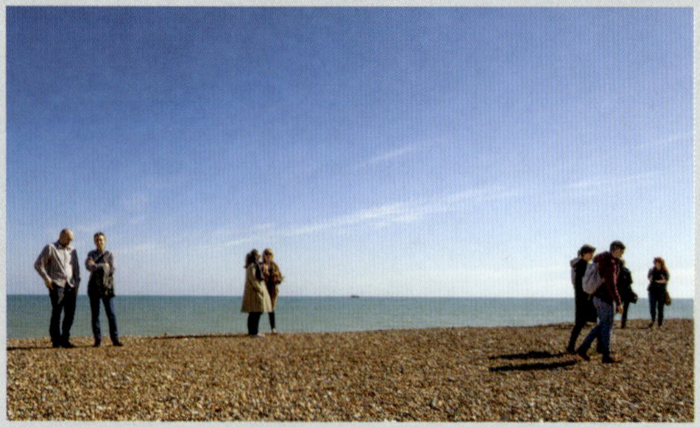
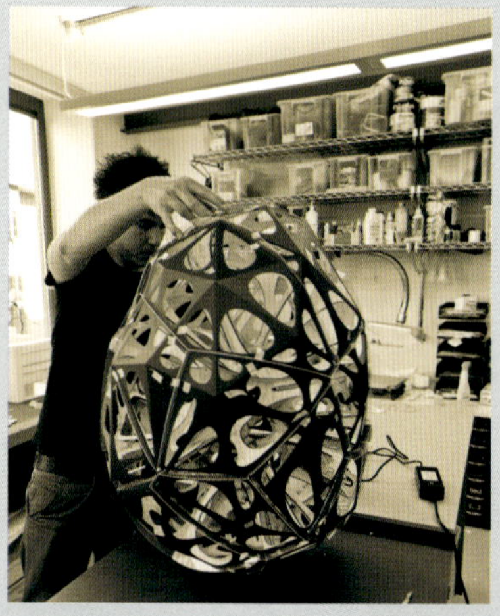
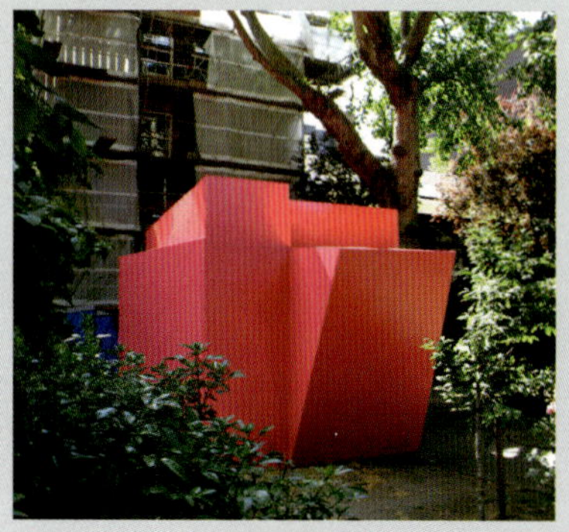

Portfolio and Practice | In practice 271

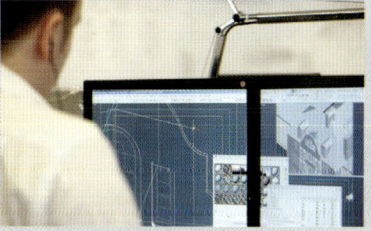

272

Wilkinson Eyre Architects, March 2014

Staff
2005–14

Valeria Abarca | Marwan Abdo | Shade Abdul | Michael Aling | Olga Alonso-Ferrer | Frederic Andre | Andres de Santiago Areizaga | Valentina Aurova | Alessandro Baccari | Berry Badas-Walker | Kevin Bai | Paul Baker | Florian Ballan | Joe Barbrooke-Morris | Julia Barker | Charlie Barnard | Rossana Barreto | James Barrington | Tim Barwell | Josie Barwick | Samiyah Bawamia | Anna Bazeley | Sophie Beard | Stuart Beattie | Stephanie Beck | Katarzyna Bedra | Tom Bell | Alice Beltrami | Sam Berrow | Dominic Bettison | Cely Bigando | Sascha Bischoff | Ben Bisek | Charlie Blanchard | Eleanor Boardman | Ivana Bocina | James Borley | Sarah Borowiecka | Yacine Bouzida | Hans Brasser | Andy Brisk | Sara Broadstock | Ingrid Brooke-Barnett | Richard Broom | Camilla Brown | Jack Brown | Keith Brownlie | Harry Bucknall | Amy Burgess | Janna Bystrykh | Xueting Cai | David Campos | Louise Cann | Thomas Carpentier | Carlo Castelli | Olivia Chaloner | Ivy Chan | Mark Chan | Gary Chapman | William Hailiang Chen | Milly Chiang | Joe Chilvers | Gladys Ching | Joseph Chisholm | Jake Choi | Yuni Choi | Sam Chong | James Christian | Raymond Chu | Gary Clark | Melissa Clinch | Charlie Coates | Gabi Code | Mark Coles | Paul Conibere | Grace Cooper | Joanne Cooper | Marco Corazza | Carin Crause | Stephen Crawford | Anthony Crescini | Stafford Critchlow | Alex Cruden | Ruth Cuenca | Joel Cullum | Lisa Cumming | Nichola Czyz | Ed Daines | Christopher Daniel | Chris Davies | Paul Davison | Benjamin Dawson | James Daykin | Mike Dean | Olivier Demangel | Andrew Demetrius | Lisa Dew | David Dickson | Ralph Dirkmann | Eva Diu | Deborah Dix | Charlotte Docherty | Eleanor Dodman | David Donaldson | Jennifer Donkor | Chris Donoghue | Shaun Donovan | Matthew Downey | Mark Dowsett | Thomas Dunn | Gary Dupont | Ayman El Hibri | Felicity English | Christian Ernst | Javier Esquembre | Stuart Evans | Mark Exon | Jim Eyre | Elvis Fan | Perrine Favier | Mike Fedak | Peter Feldman | Aimee Felton | Hugh Fernando | Etain Fitzpatrick | Clemence Fleytoux | Helen Floate | Daniela Fogasova | Dario Forte | Martin Fox | Rania Francis | Tim Francis | Paula Friar | Sabrina Friedl | Christian Froggatt | Matthias Fruntke | Jigna Gami | Clara Garcia Puig | Andrew Gardner | Piotr Garstecki | Joseph Gautrey | Jeremy Gay | Daniel Gebreiter | Pravin Ghosh | Nia Gibbons | Anneli Giencke | Julia Glynn-Smith | Alfonso Gonzalez-Ruiz | Tom Goodall | Romanos Gortsios | Matthew Gower | Anastasia Gravan | Vivienne Greenaway | Charlotte Griffiths | Ezra Groskin | Damian Groves | James Gunn | Lei Guo | Ramon Guthrie | Tong Mui Gwee | Max Hacke | Nick Hall | Jörg Hanson | Charlotte Harding | Ed Harris | Ben Hartwell | Robert Haworth | Alexandra Heffron | Christoph Helmdach | Andrew Hetherington | Molly Hiatt | Peter Hinchliffe | Eisuke Hiyama | Deborah Hobbs | Jordan Hodgson | Christian Höller | Courtenay Holden | Adam Holloway | Katie Hope | Oliver Houchell | Craig Hoverman | Katharine Hubbard | Elizabeth Hughes | Ruby Hutson-Gray | Thomas Ibbitson | Damian Iliev | Beata Jach | Nanette Jackowski | Michal Jagla | George Jamieson | Andrew Jewsbury | Leif Johannsen | Michelle Johnson | Calum Jones | Elin Jones | Jerry Joseph | Bernd Junker | Masaki Kakizoe | Chikako Kanamoto | Artemis Karaiskou | Gemma Kay | Nat Keast | Jing Zhi Kee | Priya Kerai | Alena Kereshun | Emma Keyte | Ben Kirk | Martin Knight | Fergus Knox | Zdenek Kolar | Fruzsina Korosy | Elliot Krause | Janice Kwok | Alex Kyriakides | John Lacey | Harsh Lad | Daniel Ladyman | Adrian Lai | Bosco Lam | Elisa Lam | Marios Lampouras | Anne Langer | Jeff Lee | Yan Lee | Tony Lees | Elisa Lei | Marcus Leinwand | Linda Lenthall | Felix Lewis | Michelle Lewis | Min Li |

Na Li | Angela Lim | Huai Lim | Meng Liu | Rui Liu | YiYi Liu | James Llewellyn | Elizabeth Loding | Andrew Logie | Janice Long | Cecilia Lubbock | Adam Lucette | Jason Luckett | Connie Luk | Jonas Luther | Oscar McDonald | Kirk MacDonnell | Angus McDougall | Lila MacFarlane | Mark McGough | Kay McLean | Max Malein | Cyril Manyara | Joel Rocky Marchant | Christos Markides | James Marks | Leszek Marszalek | Giles Martin | Anna Mason | Nicholas Masterton | Ami Matsumoto | Adam Matthews | Emma-Kate Matthews | Fei Meng | Heidi Mergl | Valentina Miceli | Paul Miles | Margit Millstein | Cordelia Mitchell | Philippe Monjaret | Emma Mooney | Oliver Moore | Catherine Moyes | Tim Murray | Tony Musson | Kathleen Nadeau | Massimo Napoleoni | Holly Neal | Katie Newall | Megan Ng | Janice Nhan | Alexander Nicholls | Leah Nicholls | Mia Nygren | Hannah Nyman | David Oakes | Gordon O'Connor Read | Aine O'Dwyer | Andrew O'Neill | Edward Osborne | David Ovalle-Costal | Vajini Pannila | Marco Pantaleoni | Georgina Panton | Jitka Panyrkova | Heonwoo Park | Jigna Patel | Rita Patel | Vinny Patel | Lee Paterson | Francesca Patterson | Eleni Pavlidou | Anthony Perera | Edward Perera | Callum Perry | James Perry | Christine Peters | Brenton Phillips | Robin Phillips | Claretta Pierantozzi | Tuomas Pirinen | Rodrigo Piwonka | Anja Poelk | Silvia Polito | Brian Poon | Suzaan Potgieter | Matthew Potter | Eugenie Poulet | Christian Poulton | Tobias Power | Gonzalo Prades | Danielle Purcell | Gideon Purser | Vidhya Pushpanathan | Paul Quang | Erik Ramelow | Rene Rammazzo | Helen Ramsden | Alexa Ratzlaff | Thomas Reeves | Mark Reimer | Luis Reis | Ciara Reynolds | Sebastien Ricard | Damon Richardson | Luke Richardson | Sam Rigby | Thomas Rigby | Laura Rigoni | Mark Rist | Esther Rivas Adrover | Stefan Robanus | Simon Roberts | Oscar Rodriguez | Alison Rolph | Lia Ronez | Owen Rutter | Ville Saarikoski | Catherine St Hill | Andrea Salvucci | Angela Santos | Priscila Santos | Melany Schaer | Fabian Schmid | Annika Schollin | Andrea Seegers | Eva Seo-Andersen | Hannah Sharkey | Jonathan Shaw | Nalika de Silva | Christine Skaar | Laura Smith | Thomas Smith | Timothy Smith | Claire Song | Rebecca Spencer | Madlen Staudt | Jasper Stevens | Ivan Subanovic | Mark Summerfield | Franc Sumner | Zorana Tang | Tim Tasker | Neil Taylor | Vahid Tehrani | Tim Thatcher | Richard Thebridge | Anne-Laure Thierry | Graham Thompson | Niels Thuesen | David Tigg | Glen Tomlin | Kim Towers | Van Tran | Chun Tai Tsai | Charis Tsang | Geoff Turner | Leon Turrell | Oliver Tyler | Miya Ushida | Filipa Valente | Juan Valeros | Naomi Vaughan | Karin Venter | Simon Vickers | Matthew Vieira | Marc Vinall | Friedrich Vitzthum | Jan Vogel | Jennifer Waggett | Nadine Wagner | Ewelina Wagner-Kuston | Andrew Walsh | Laurence Walter | Mu Wang | Yunlong Wang | Jan Warren | Annabelle Watson | Simon Watson | Camiel Weijenberg | Malcolm Welford | Craig West | Fiona Wheelwright | James White | Geoffrey Whittaker | Chris Wilkinson | Zoe Wilkinson | Becky Williams | Kimberleigh Williams | Cyan Wong | Lesta Woo | Lucy Wood | Anna Woodeson | Rebecca Woodhams | James Woodhouse | Conor Worth | Bethany Wren | Jacqueline Wright | Sam Wright | Bas van Wylick | Kenzo Yamashita | Szu Chin Yang | Tumpa Yasmin | Soo Yau | Yoana Yordanova | Wenlan Yuan | Maria Zunica

Selected awards
2005–14

10 Brock Street
BCO Awards 2014 (Shortlisted)

25 Great Pulteney Street
BCO Awards 2012 (Shortlisted)
LABC Building Excellence Awards 2012, Best Large Commercial Building (Finalist)

Arts Two, Queen Mary, University of London
New London Awards 2012 (Shortlisted)

Audi West London
Structural Steel Design Award 2010

Baakenhafen West Bridge
Beijing International Architecture Award 2011

Beijing Lize Masterplan
Beijing International Architecture Award 2011

Beijing Lize Shanluju MTR Station
Beijing Design Week Design Annual Award (Architecture) 2011

Bridge Learning Campus
Bristol Civic Society Award 2009

Brislington Enterprise College
Partnership for Schools BSF Awards 2008, Best New School Design (Highly Commended)
Partnership for Schools BSF Awards 2008, Best School Team

Bristol Brunel Academy
Public Private Finance Award 2008
RIBA Award 2008
RIBA Sorrell Foundation Award 2008 (Shortlisted)
RIBA Sustainability Award 2008 (Shortlisted)

Bristol BSF Schools
Constructing Excellence Awards 2008:
The Legacy Award

Bristol Metropolitan Academy
Prime Minister's Better Public Building Award 2009 (Shortlisted)

Cabot Circus Footbridge
BCSC Supreme Gold Award 2008
Structural Steel Design Awards 2009 (Commendation)

Ceramics Galleries Bridge, Victoria and Albert Museum
RIBA Awards 2010 (Shortlisted)

City & Islington College: Centre for Business, Arts and Technology
AIA/UK Excellence in Design Award 2006

Cooled Conservatories, Gardens by the Bay
MIPIM/Architectural Review Future Project Award 2009 (Commendation)
Condé Nast Traveller Innovation & Design Awards 2010, Sustainability Category (Shortlisted)
BCA Design and Engineering Excellence 2012
Design for Asia Grand Award 2012
Design for Asia Special Award for Technology 2012
Display Award, World Architecture Festival Awards 2012
SSSS Structural Steel Excellence Awards (Singapore) 2012, Trophy Award
World Building of the Year, World Architecture Festival Awards 2012
British Expertise Awards 2013, Best International Design Project
Chicago Athenaeum Architecture Awards 2013, International Architecture Award
IStructE [Structural] Awards 2013, Best Arts or Entertainment Structure
Landscape Institute Awards, Large Public Project 2013
Landscape Institute Fellows Award for Climate Change Adaption 2013
President's Design Awards 2013, Design of the Year
RIBA International Award 2013
RIBA Lubetkin Prize 2013
SIA Design Award 2013
Singapore Tourism Award for the Breakthrough Experience for a New Attraction 2013
Skyrise Greenery in a Garden Award 2013
Sustain Awards 2013, International Project of the Year
WAN Landscape Award 2013

The Crystal
BCO Innovation Award 2013
British Construction Industry Awards 2013, Building Project of the Year (Shortlisted)
Emirates Glass LEAF Awards 2013, Best Sustainable Development (Commendation)
ICE London Civil Engineering Awards 2013 (Shortlisted)
RIBA Awards 2013 (Shortlisted)
RICS Design and Innovation Award 2013 (Highly Commended)
Sustain Magazine Awards 2013, Architecture and Design Category (Finalist)

Davies Alpine House, Royal Botanic Gardens, Kew
Design Week Awards 2006 (Commendation)
IStructE [Structural] Awards 2006 (Shortlisted)
RIBA Award 2006
RIBA Stephen Lawrence Prize 2006 (Shortlisted)
Sustainability Awards 2006, Sustainable Building of the Year, Small Project (Finalist)
International Design Award 2007
Mies van der Rohe Prize 2007 (Longlisted)
Civic Trust Award 2008

Department of Earth Sciences, University of Oxford
ACE Engineering Excellence Award 2011, Large Structure
Oxford Preservation Trust Award 2011

Emirates Air Line
Civic Trust Award 2013 (Commendation)
ICE Evening Standard People's Choice Award 2013
IStructE [Structural] Awards 2013, Best Infrastructure or Transportation Structure
New London Award 2013, Transport and Infrastructure
RIBA Awards 2013 (Shortlisted)
Structural Steel Design Award 2013

Forthside Pedestrian Bridge
IStructE [Structural] Awards 2010, Pedestrian Bridges Category (Commendation)
Saltire Awards 2010, Award for Civil Engineering/Design Category (Commendation)
Footbridge Award 2011, Technical, Long Span Category (Highly Commended)

The Forum, University of Exeter
Wood Awards 2012, Structural Category (Highly Commended)
Hot Dip Galvanising Awards 2013 (Shortlisted)
IStructE [Structural] Awards 2013, Best Education or Healthcare Structure
Michelmores Western Morning News Property Awards Building of the Year 2013
RIBA Awards 2013, National Award
RIBA Awards 2013, South West and Wessex Award
World Architecture Festival Awards 2013, Higher Education & Research Building of the Year

Guangzhou International Finance Centre
MIPIM/AR Future Project Awards 2006, Tall Buildings (Commendation)
Council on Tall Buildings and Urban Habitat Best Building Award 2011, Asia and Australasia
RIBA International Award 2012
RIBA Lubetkin Prize 2012

Hauser Forum, University of Cambridge
Structural Steel Design Award 2011

Jodrell Laboratory, Royal Botanic Gardens, Kew
RIBA Award 2007
Civic Trust Award 2008

John Madejski Academy
World Architecture Festival Awards 2008, Learning Category (Shortlisted)

Liver Street Car Park
RIBA Award 2007

Liverpool Arena and Convention Centre
Regeneration & Renewal Awards 2008, Best Design-Led Regeneration Development (Commendation)
RIBA Award 2008
World Architecture Festival Awards 2008, Production Category (Highly Commended)
Civic Trust Award 2009
Civic Trust Night Vision Special Award 2009

Living Bridge, University of Limerick
Footbridge Awards 2008, Aesthetics, Medium Span Category (Finalist)
IStructE [Structural] Awards 2008, Pedestrian Bridges Category
RIBA European Award 2008
Syndicat de la Construction Metallique Awards 2008, Bridge Category
ACEI Award 2009, Bridge Category

London 2012 Basketball Arena
Westminster Society Biennial Award for a Contribution to Urban Vitality 2013

Mary Rose Museum
Wood Awards 2013 (Shortlisted)
World Architecture Festival Awards 2013, Cultural Building of the Year (Shortlisted)
Building Awards 2014, Project of the Year
Civic Trust Award 2014
Civic Trust Award 2014, Michael Middleton Special Award
RIBA Awards 2014, South Region

Media City Bridge
IStructE [Structural] Awards 2011, Pedestrian Bridges Category
ICE North West Awards 2012, Large Project of the Year
Structural Steel Design Awards 2012 (Shortlisted)

National Waterfront Museum Swansea
Civic Trust Award 2006
Design Week Awards 2006 (Shortlisted)
National Eisteddford/RSAW Awards 2006 (Exhibition)
Regeneration Awards 2006, Best Design-Led Regeneration Project
RIBA Award 2006
Structural Steel Design Awards 2006 (Commendation)

Nescio brug
BCI Awards 2006 (High Commendation)
International Bridge Conference Awards 2006, Arthur G. Hayden Medal
IStructE [Structural] Award 2007
ECCS Awards 2008 (Merit)

Paradise Street Footbridge
Liverpool Architectural Society Award 2008
Prix Acier 2009 (Commendation)
RIBA Award 2009
Civic Trust Award 2010
Civic Trust Award, National Panel Special Award 2010

Peace Bridge
Construction Employers Federation Award 2011
Tekla Global BIM Award 2011
AIA Awards 2012 (Civic Commendation)
British Construction Industry Awards 2012, Regeneration (Highly Commended)
ICE NE Robert Stephenson Award 2012, Small Project Category (Highly Commended)
International Bridge Conference Awards 2012, Arthur G. Hayden Medal
IStructE [Structural] Awards 2012, Pedestrian Bridges Category (Commendation)
Structural Steel Design Award 2012
The Waterways Renaissance Award 2012
Civic Trust Award 2013
Civic Trust Award, National Panel Special Award 2013

Southampton SeaCity Museum
Solent Design Awards, People's Choice Award 2012
Civic Trust Award 2013
RIBA Awards 2013 (Shortlisted)

Splashpoint
World Architecture Festival Awards 2013, Sports Building of the Year
Civic Trust Award 2014

Twin Sails Bridge
AL Light & Architecture Design Awards 2012, Outstanding Achievement
IStructE [Structural] Awards 2012, Highway Bridge Structures (Commendation)
ICE Awards 2013, Major Projects Award (Highly Commended)
RIBA Awards 2013 (Shortlisted)
RICS South West and Wales Award for Infrastructure 2013
Structural Steel Design Award 2013
Civic Trust Award 2014
RIBA Awards 2014, South West Region

Viaduc de la Savoureuse
ECCS Awards 2012 (Merit)

Westgate Bridge
National CCF Earth Award 2011
Victoria CCF Excellence Award 2011
IStructE [Structural] Heritage Award 2012
IStructE [Structural] Supreme Award 2012

Wilkinson Eyre Architects
BD Transport Architect of the Year 2009 (Finalist)
AJ100 Clients' Choice Award 2012
BD Education Architect of the Year 2012 (Shortlisted)
Designing for Champions 2012, Special Recognition for Contribution to the London 2012 Olympics
AJ100 Sustainable Practice of the Year 2013 (Highly Commended)

Index

Bold page numbers refer to major illustrated coverage of each project; other illustrations are indicated by *italic* page numbers.

10 Brock Street, London 4, 19, *19*, **188–93**, 260
20 Blackfriars Road, London **90–93**, 254, 256
25 Great Pulteney Street, London *10*, **218–21**, 258

abstract expressionism 20
Arachthos Viaduct, Greece 19
Arena and Convention Centre, Liverpool *3*, **140–49**, 257
awards 276–9

Baker, Paul 16, 23, 267, *267*
Battersea Power Station, London 16, *16*, *24*, 25, **240–51**, 265
Beleschenko, Alexander 43
Bettison, Dominic 16, 23, 268, *268*
Bowling Green Lane, London 16
Bridge of Aspiration, Royal Ballet School, London 22–3
bridges *see* Bridge of Aspiration, London; Ceramics Galleries Bridge, London; Gateshead Millennium Bridge; Living Bridge, University of Limerick; Media City Footbridge, Salford; Newcastle Botanic Bridge; Peace Bridge, Derry; South Quay footbridge, London; Twin Sails Bridge, Poole
Bristol:
    Explore@Bristol 19, 24
    schools 65, **70–75**, 255, 256

cable cars *see* Emirates Air Line; Toulouse Cable Car
Centre Pompidou, Paris 21, *21*
Ceramics Galleries Bridge, London *14*, **200–201**, 256
Craig, John 23
Critchlow, Stafford 16, 24, 267, *267*
Crown Hotel, Sydney 16, *16*, 17, 18, **172–83**, 265
The Crystal, London (Siemens Urban Sustainability Centre) 19–20, *19*, **165–71**, 260
Crystal Palace, London:
    Sir Joseph Paxton's construction 17, *17*
    Wilkinson Eyre proposed exhibition hall 20, *20*

Davey, Peter 18
Department of Earth Sciences, University of Oxford *9*, 24, *25*, **208–17**, 258
Derry: Peace Bridge **150–51**, 258
Dyson Headquarters, Malmesbury 23, 24, 262

Emirates Air Line, London (cable car) 22, **84–9**, *164*, 165, 260
Exeter *see* The Forum, University of Exeter
Explore@Bristol 19, 24
Eyre, Jim 16–18, 21, 25, 266, *266*
    'Movement and Geometry' (essay) 20

Forster, Kurt 20
The Forum, University of Exeter *7*, 24, **42–9**, 260
Foster, Norman, Lord 18, 20
    Foster Associates 21, 25
Four Seasons Hotel, Guangzhou 94, *101–3*
From Landscape to Portrait (installation) 110–11, 260

Gabo, Naum: *Linear Construction No. 2* 20, *20*
Galerie des Machines, Paris 17, *17*
Gardens by the Bay, Singapore 19, *22*, 23, **28–41**, 260, *284–5*
Gateshead Millennium Bridge *18*, 19
glasshouses *see* Gardens by the Bay, Singapore; Royal Botanic Gardens, Kew
Green, Katie 110
Guangzhou International Finance Centre 19, *19*, **94–105**, 258, *282*

Hadid, Zaha 16
High Tech 16, 20, 21, 23
Hopkins, Sir Michael 21
hotels *see* Crown Hotel, Sydney; Four Seasons Hotel, Guangzhou

IBM Travelling Technology Exhibition 16

Jiricna, Eva 110
John Madejski Academy, Reading 19, **64–9**, 255

Kew *see* Royal Botanic Gardens
King's Cross Gasholders, London **122–7**, 265

Lasdun, Sir Denys 20
Limerick *see* Living Bridge, University of Limerick
Liverpool *see* Arena and Convention Centre; Paradise Street Interchange
Living Bridge, University of Limerick **58–63**, 255
Lloyd's building, London 23, *23*
London 2012 Olympic Games 64, 113
    Basketball Arena **112–21**, 260

Maggie's Centre, Oxford **78–81**, 262
Magna Science Adventure Centre, Rotherham 24, *24*
Marks Barfield 51
Martin, Giles 16, 24, 269, *269*
Mary Rose Museum, Portsmouth 25, *25*, **154–63**, 260, *287*
Media City Footbridge, Salford **152–3**, 258
Meier, Richard 24
Mies van der Rohe, Ludwig 17
modernism 16, 17, 18, 20, 24, 25
Museum of London **202–7**

National Waterfront Museum, Swansea 216, *254*
New Bodleian (Weston) Library, Oxford 25, **230–39**, 241, 262
Newcastle Botanic Bridge 19
Norwich: Sainsbury Centre for the Visual Arts 21, 25, *25*
Notre Dame de Raincy, Paris 18, *18*

Oxford *see* Department of Earth Sciences, University of Oxford; Maggie's Centre; New Bodleian (Weston) Library

Paradise Street Interchange, Liverpool **194–9**, 257
    Liver Street Car Park *2*, 24–5, *24*, 194, *196–7*
Pawley, Martin 21
Pawson, John 51
Peace Bridge, Derry **150–51**, 258
Perry, Chris 16
Piano, Renzo 16, 21
Poncelet, Jacqueline 225
Poole: Twin Sails Bridge **106–9**, 260

Portsmouth *see* Mary Rose Museum
Priestman, Matthew 16

Queen Mary, University of London **223–9**
    Arts Two *6*, 223, *224–7*, 258
    Graduate Centre 223, 265
    School of Mathematical Sciences 223, *228–9*, 258

Reading *see* John Madejski Academy
Ricard, Sebastien 16, 24, 269, *269*
Rogers, Richard, Lord 20, 21, 23
Rotherham: Magna Science Adventure Centre 24, *24*
Royal Academy of Arts, London: *From Landscape to Portrait* (installation) **110–11**, 260
Royal Ballet School, London: Bridge of Aspiration 22–3
Royal Botanic Gardens, Kew **50–57**
    Davies Alpine House *1*, 24, *24*, 33, *33*, 51, *53*, *54–5*, 254
    Jodrell Laboratory 51, *53*, 254
    Quarantine House 51, 257
Royal Docks, London 16, 84, *86*, 165, *170–71*

Sainsbury Centre for the Visual Arts, Norwich 21, 25, *25*
St Pancras station, London 17, *17*
Salford: Media City Footbridge **152–3**, 258
Scarpa, Carlo 24
schools: Building Schools for the Future programme 19, **64–75**, 255, 256
Scott, Sir Giles Gilbert 16, 25, 231, 241
Siemens Urban Sustainability Centre, London *see* The Crystal

Singapore *see* Gardens by the Bay
skyscrapers *see* 20 Blackfriars Road, London; Crown Hotel, Sydney; Guangzhou International Finance Centre
South Quay footbridge, London 151
Splashpoint, Worthing 5, 8, **130–39**, 260
staff 266–75
Stratford Market Depot and Regional Station, London 16, *18*, 19, 21–2, *21*, *22*, 25
Sydney:
    harbour 172, *174–5*, *182–3*
    Opera House 19, 172
    see also Crown Hotel

Thorneycroft, Sir Hamo: *The Sower 50*, 53
Toulouse Cable Car 16, 24, 260
Turner, J. M. W.: *Rain, Steam, and Speed* ... 20, *20*
Twin Sails Bridge, Poole **106–9**, 260
Tyler, Oliver 16, 22, 268, *268*

Utzon, Jørn 19, 172

Victoria and Albert Museum, London: Ceramics Galleries Bridge *14*, **200–201**
Viñoly, Rafael 241

Wilkinson, Chris 16–18, 20, 23, 25, 110, 266, *266*
    Supersheds 21
Willis Faber & Dumas Headquarters, Ipswich 18, *18*
Worthing *see* Splashpoint

Yves Saint Laurent (shop), London 16

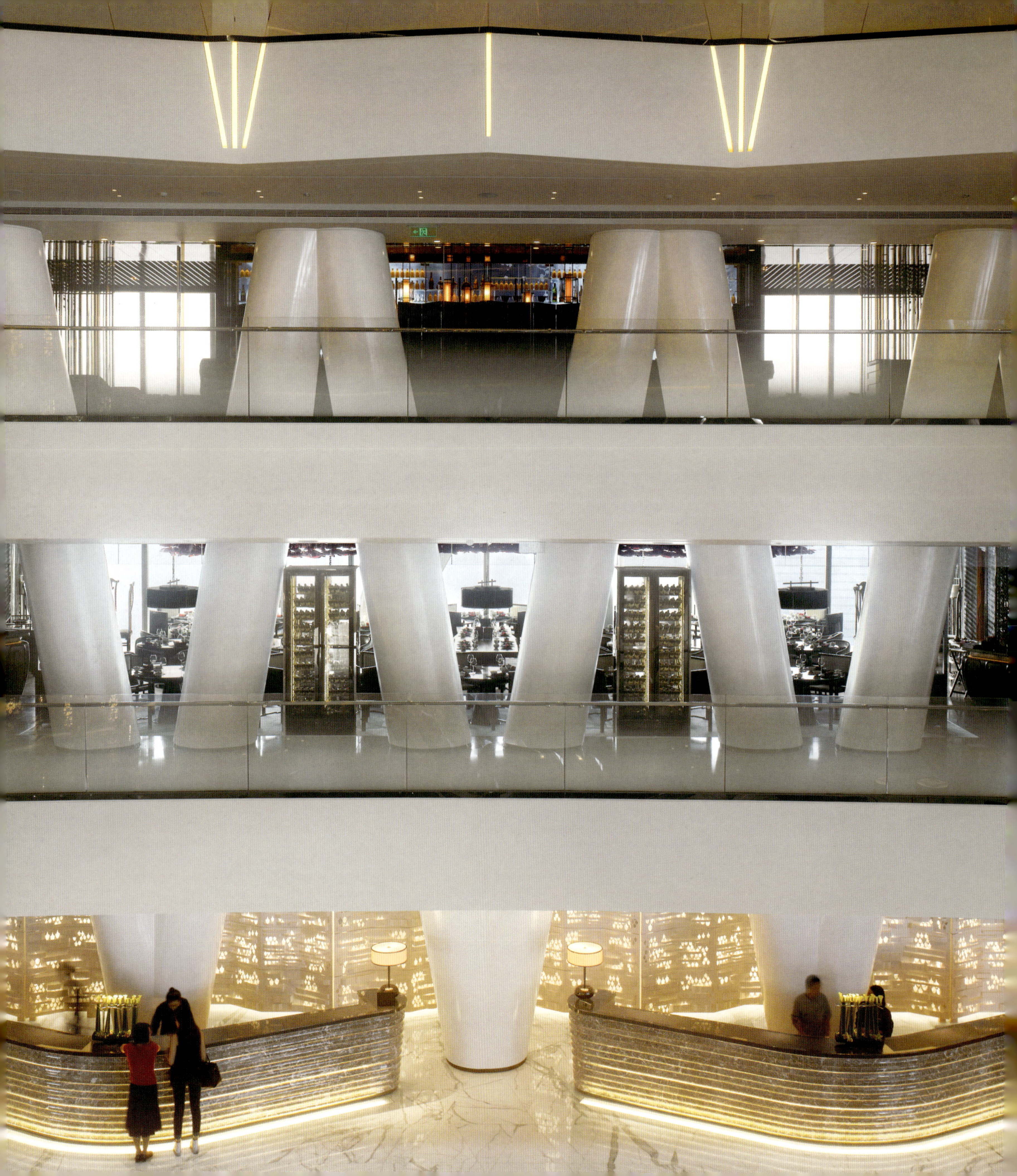

Picture credits

Julian Abrams: 5, 8, 131–9
ACC Liverpool: 146 (right), 147
Architectural Press Archive/RIBA Library Photographs Collection: 17 (top left and top right), 21 (top left)
Atelier Ten: 33 (centre), 54 (centre)
Hélène Binet: 1, 33 (bottom), 55, 141
James Brittain: 2, 53 (top), 56–7, 65, 67–73, 75 (right), 197–8 , 254 (top centre)
Graham Carlow: 201 (right and centre left)
Martin Charles/RIBA Library Photographs Collection: 21 (top right)
ORCH Chemollo/RIBA Library Photographs Collection: 23 (top)
Leon Chew: 257 (top, second from left)
Richard Chivers/VIEW: 162–3, 287
Corbis: 30 (top left), 156 (top)
Richard Davies: 23 (bottom right), 24 (top)
Chris Donaghue: 232
John Donat/RIBA Library Photographs Collection: 18 (bottom), 25 (centre)
English Partnerships/Mills Media/Ian Lawson: 143
F&C: 219, 221 (left)
Gareth Gardner: 25 (bottom)
Dennis Gilbert/VIEW: 18 (top left), 19 (bottom left), 21 (centre and bottom), 22 (top right), 187, 189–91, 192 (right), 193
Grant Associates: 30 (top right)
Nick Guttridge: 50, 53 (centre), 54 (top)
Rob't Hart: 254 (top right)
Luke Hayes: 86–8, 111, 154, 160, 161, 261
Daniel Hopkinson: 153
Hufton + Crow: 7, 42–9, 74, 157, 159
Alastair Hunter/RIBA Library Photographs Collection: 23 (centre)
iStock: 20 (bottom right), 125 (centre)
Ros Kavanagh: 58–63, 150
Jonathan Leijonhufvud: 95–6, 100
Ben Luxmoore: 85
Mott MacDonald: 259
Paul McMullin: 148–9, 257 (top, second from right)

Ioana Marinescu: 257 (top left)
Mary Evans Picture Library: 124
Mary Rose Trust: 156 (bottom)
Dave Morris/Speirs + Major: 106–9
Museum of London: 204 (bottom), 206 (top right)
The National Gallery: 20 (bottom left)
Olympic Delivery Authority: 113
Peel Media: 258 (top left)
David Pickersgill (Flickr: camperman64): 23 (bottom left)
Will Pryce: 102–3, 105, 282
RIBA Library Photographs Collection: 17 (centre), 18 (centre)
Christian Richters: 104
Scala Archives/The Museum of Modern Art (MoMA): 17 (bottom)
Craig Sheppard: 31, 33 (top), 35–7, 38 (bottom left), 284–5
Skanska: 75 (left)
Timothy Soar: 3, 10, 142, 145, 195, 199, 220, 221 (right)
Darren Soh: 29, 34, 38 (except bottom left), 39
Morley von Sternberg: 6, 25 (top), 146 (left), 196, 214 (right), 215, 224, 227 (bottom), 255 (bottom right)
John Sturrock: 258 (top, second from right)
Robert Such: 22 (centre)
Edmund Sumner: jacket, 9, 14, 24 (top), 118 (centre left), 119 (main image), 164, 168 (top left), 170–71, 202, 206 (top right and bottom), 207, 209, 211–12, 214 (top left), 217, 222, 226, 227 (top), 228–9 (main image), 254 (top left)
Max Tan: 40–41
Tate, London 2014: 20 (centre)
Transport for London: 89
Victoria and Albert Museum: 201 (top left)
Claude Weiss: 258 (top left)
Westgate Bridge Strengthening Alliance: 256 (bottom right)
Nick Wood: 22 (bottom)

All other drawings, images and visualizations by Wilkinson Eyre Architects

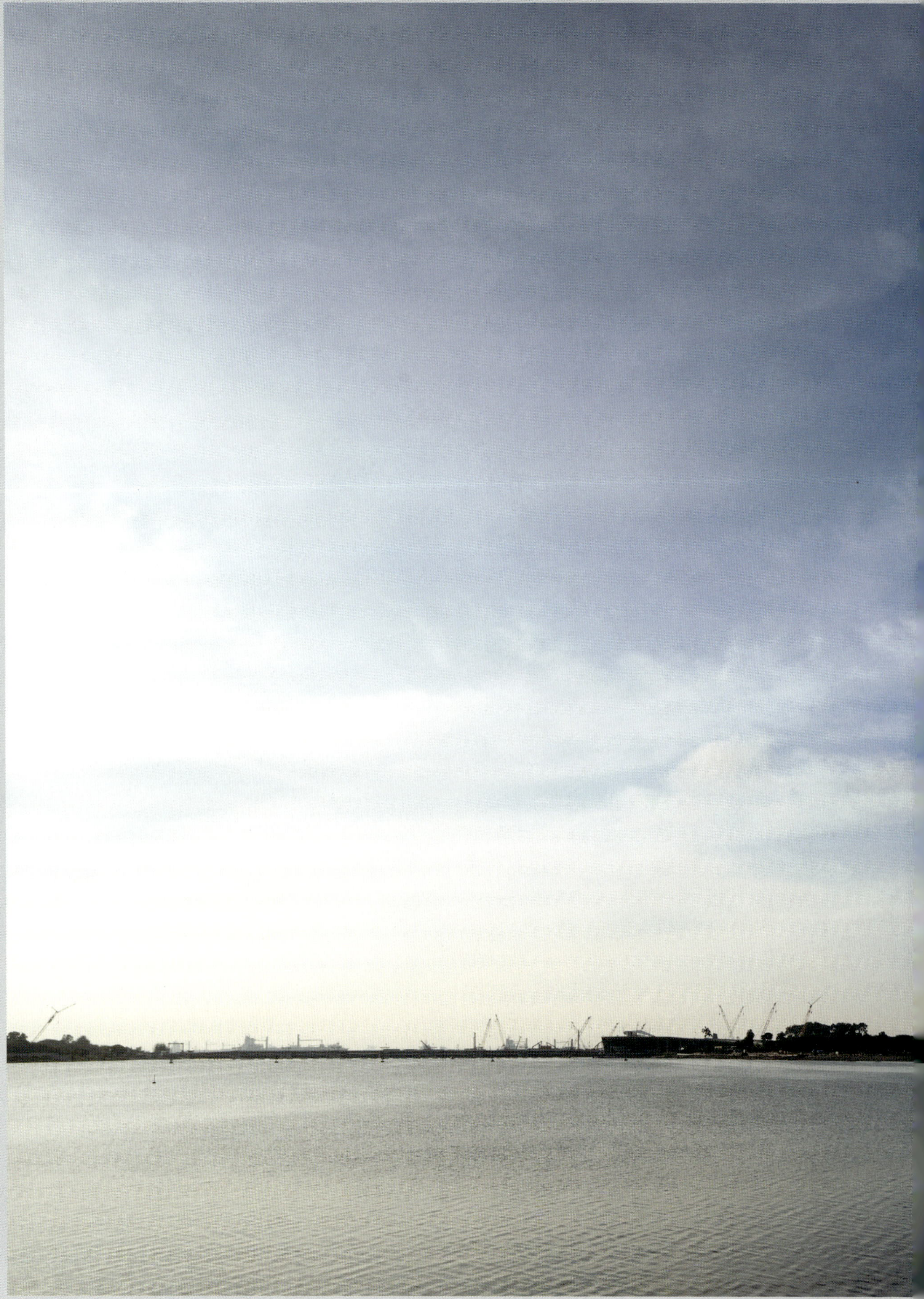

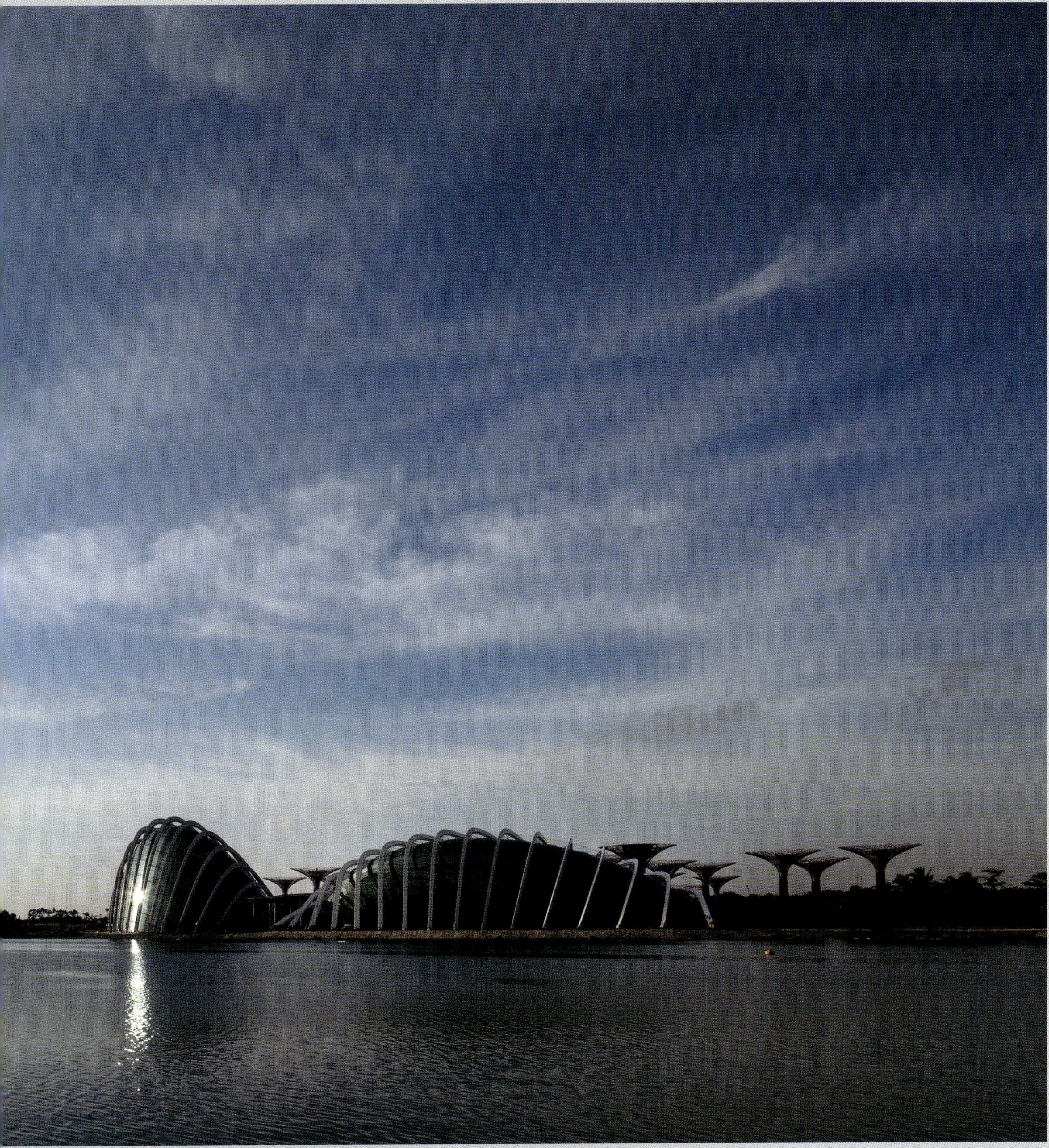

Acknowledgments

We owe a huge debt of gratitude to Jay Merrick for his introductory essay, and to Emma Keyte for writing and editing the main body of the project texts and for picture research: both have patiently listened to, analysed and interpreted what we have described to them, and have visited many of the buildings illustrated. It is always hard to find the time in a busy architectural practice to pause for breath and take stock; by asking the right questions and pursuing lines of enquiry, they have made the process of looking back over our work since 2005 to generate the material for this book both enjoyable and cathartic. Damon Richardson has delighted us with his design for the book. Many thanks to him for his good humour in always responding to the graphic challenges we have set, finding fresh ways to select and present drawings, sketches and photographs to interpret each project in an appropriate way.

We are enormously grateful to Julian Honer, Editorial Director at Thames & Hudson, for his advice on the shaping of the book, and to Mark Ralph, Aaron Hayden and Paul Hammond, also of Thames & Hudson, for their editorial, design and production expertise respectively.

A big thank you to everyone at Wilkinson Eyre who has helped compile material for this book, in particular George Jamieson, Elin Jones, Francesca Patterson and Anja Poelk for honing the line weights and tone of the drawings to make them fit for publication; and Andrew Hetherington, Katharine Hubbard, Liz Loding and Leah Nicholls for collating project data and information for the end matter.

Finally, none of the work illustrated would exist without the clients who commission us, the external engineering and other design consultants involved in our projects, and the energy and diligent efforts of the talented group of people with whom we work in the Wilkinson Eyre studio.

Thank you, all.

Sebastien Ricard, Stafford Critchlow, Chris Wilkinson, Oliver Tyler, Dominic Bettison, Paul Baker, Jim Eyre, Giles Martin